The Jains

Jainism – with Hinduism and Buddhism – is an integral part of Indian culture, and its adherents continue to make a vital contribution to the religious and economic life of the subcontinent. Furthermore, Jainism, with its distinctive views on matters such as non-violence and intellectual relativity, has clear relevance to life and thought in the twentieth century. In this up-to-date guide to one of the world's oldest religions, Paul Dundas goes beyond recent accounts of Jainism which have concentrated on doctrine, to give instead a strong sense of Jainism as a living and dynamic faith. He focuses on the Jains as agents within their own destinies and on the manner in which they have, over the centuries, structured and made sense of their lives as Jains.

Paul Dundas interprets the Jain religion as both a historical, evolving phenomenon and a mode of life which provides a coherent and satisfying world view for its followers. He demonstrates the complex and multi-dimensional nature of Jainism, traces its evolution, and assesses its principal doctrinal and sectarian characteristics, giving special attention to Jain attitudes towards scripture, and the role of ritual and sacred places. A particularly important section is devoted to recent attempts to reform or adapt Jainism, information which does not exist elsewhere in a western language.

The Jains will be of special interest to students and teachers of religion, and to members of the world-wide Jain community.

Paul Dundas is Lecturer in Sanskrit at the University of Edinburgh.

The Library of Religious Beliefs and Practices

Edited by John Hinnells
University of Manchester
and Ninian Smart,
University of California at Santa Barbara

This series provides pioneering and scholarly introductions to different religions in a readable form. It is concerned with the beliefs and practices of religions in their social, cultural and historical setting. Authors come from a variety of backgrounds and approach the study of religious beliefs and practices from their different points of view. Some focus mainly on questions of history, teachings, customs and ritual practices. Others consider, within the context of a specific region or geographical region, the inter-relationships between religions; the interaction of religion and the arts; religion and social organisation; the involvement of religion in political affairs; and, for ancient cultures, the interpretation of archaeological evidence. In this way the series brings out the multi-disciplinary nature of the study of religion. It is intended for students of religion, ideas, social sciences and history, and for the interested lay person.

Already published

The Ancient Egyptians
Their Religious Beliefs and Practices
A. Rosalie David

Jews
Their Religious Beliefs and Practices
Alan Unterman

The Sikhs
Their Religious Beliefs and Practices
W. Owen Cole and Piara Singh Sambhi

Zoroastrians
Their Religious Beliefs and Practices
Mary Boyce

Theravāda Buddhism
A Social History from Ancient Benares to Modern Colombo
Richard Gombrich

The British
Their Religious Beliefs and Practices
Terence Thomas

Mahāyāna Buddhism
Paul Williams

Muslims
Their Religious Beliefs and Practices
Andrew Rippin

Religions of South Africa
David Chidester

The Jains

Paul Dundas

London and New York

First published 1992
by Routledge
11 New Fetter Lane, London EC4P 4EE

Simultaneously published in the USA and Canada
by Routledge
a division of Routledge, Chapman and Hall, Inc.
29 West 35th Street, New York, NY 10001

Typeset in 10/12pt Times by Michael Mepham, Frome, Somerset
Printed and bound in Great Britain by
Biddles Ltd, Guildford and King's Lynn

British Library Cataloguing in Publication Data
A catalogue record for this book is available from the British Library.

Library of Congress Cataloging in Publication Data
Dundas, Paul, 1952–
The Jains/Paul Dundas.
p. cm. (The Library of religious beliefs and practices)
Includes bibliographical references and index.
1. Jainism. 2. Jains. I. Title. II. Series.
BL 1351.2.D86 1992
294.4–dc20 92—237
CIP

ISBN 0–415–05183–5
0–415–05184–3 (pbk)

To my parents

Contents

Acknowledgements

This book has been written for university students of Indian religions and members of the world-wide Jain community.

Two longstanding debts must be acknowledged at the outset: to John Brockington and K.R. Norman for much help and encouragement over the years.

Many other debts have also been incurred. John Cort has been a continual source of assistance and advice. Phyllis Granoff has inspired me with her enthusiasm and support. I have also been fortunate in having been able to discuss Jainism with Marcus Banks, Mike Carrithers, Lance Cousins, James Laidlaw, Tom McCormick, Jo Reynell and Bob Zydenbos.

Like all those working on the Jains during the last ten years or so, I owe much to the writings and counsel of Padmanabh Jaini. Unfortunately, his *Gender and Salvation* (Berkeley 1991) came to hand too late to be used in the writing of this book.

Thanks are also due to Nalini Balbir, Klaus Bruhn (for the single most useful piece of advice given me prior to starting writing), Eileen Dwyer, Tony Good, Savitri Holmstrom, Caroline Humphrey and Dave Jones.

It would have been impossible to have produced this book without the assistance of many Jains in India. In particular, I am grateful to: (in Gujarat) Muni Jambuvijaya, Kantibhai Vora and family, the directors and staff of the Lalbhai Dalphatbhai Institute of Indology, Ahmedabad, and Pavankumar Jain and other members of the Kanji Svami Panth at Songadh; (in Karnataka) Carukirti Svami Bhattarak of Shravana Belgola, Acarya Parshvasagar Muni, Professor M.D. Vasantharaj and Shubhacandra of the Department of Jainology and Prakrits, University of Mysore; and (in Rajasthan) Acarya Tulsi, Yuvacarya Mahaprajna, Muni Mahendrakumar and Mr R.L. Kothari.

I would like to express my gratitude to the British Academy for providing financial assistance on three occasions which enabled me to carry out research in India.

Finally, my thanks to John Hinnells for inviting me to write this book.

A note on transliteration and pronunciation

Owing to the exigencies brought about by typesetting costs, it has not proved possible to include diacritic marks in this book.

Sanskrit vocalic 'r' is represented by 'ri'. Palatal and retroflex 's' are represented by 'sh'.

Sanskrit 'e' is pronounced as the equivalent of the vowel in English 'hay'. The Sanskrit diphthong 'ai' is pronounced as the equivalent of the vowel in English 'tie'. However, in modern Indian languages, it is equivalent to the vowel in English 'hay' so that 'Jain' will normally rhyme with English 'drain'.

'C' is pronounced as in Italian 'ciao'. 'Th' is pronounced as in English 'pothole'.

Introduction

In the 'Deeds of the Ten Princes', a picaresque Sanskrit novel by Dandin dating from about the seventh century of the common era, one of its heroes encounters on his travels a naked Jain monk called Virupaka, 'Ugly'. The latter recounts how he was ruined by a courtesan to the extent of being left with only his loincloth, as a result of which he became disgusted with the world and, in misery and humiliation, converted to the Jain religion, abandoning clothes completely. He continues:

> However, covered with dirt and filth, in agony because of ripping out my hair, suffering greatly because of hunger and thirst and intensely distressed because of all the intense restraints imposed on me with regard to my standing, sitting, lying down and eating, as if I were an elephant in the course of being trained for the first time, I reflected: 'I am a member of the brahman caste. This descent into a heretical path cannot be my religion, for my forebears proceeded in a mode of life which was in accordance with the primordial Hindu scriptures. But now, wretch that I am, I have to assume the contemptible dress of nudity which is to all intents and purposes a fraud and will, through being obliged to listen to continual insults of the Hindu gods, end up in hell after I die, a rebirth which will not have any favourable result for me. I have to follow a totally irreligious path as if it were the true religion'. After thinking over this unhappy choice that I have made, I have come to this grove of trees and am now weeping my heart out.
>
> (DKC p. 47)

Dandin here provides the classical Hindu stereotype of Jainism as a religion practised by filthy and naked ascetics requiring pointless torture of the body, such as regular pulling out of the hair, and involving as part of its doctrine the subversion of basic Hindu values. Like all stereotypes, this contains a degree of truth. Jain ascetics are to this day enjoined not to wash themselves, both because personal cleanliness is regarded as being a feature of a world of social and sexual relations which they have abandoned, and also because bathing in water would destroy the minute organisms which Jain teachings are emphatic live there. Many Jain monks of the medieval period were given the admiring epithet 'Filthy' (*maladharin*) by their lay followers in acknowledgement that lack of concern for outward physical appearance was an index of their attainment of an inner spiritual purity. Thus, one medieval inscription admiringly describes how a monk was so covered in dirt that 'he looked as if he wore a closely fitting suit of black armour'.[1] Jainism has also throughout its history rejected traditional Hindu notions of the creation and dissolution of the world by all-powerful gods and has mocked the pretensions of Hindu theologians and the brahman caste which claimed ritual and social authority.

Yet, also like all stereotypes, Dandin's picture is inadequate and limited. Leaving aside the fact that Jain monks and nuns today are not covered with dirt, although there remains a proscription on their bathing in water, and that Jain doctrine taken on its own terms provides a powerful account of the workings of the universe, Dandin presents as paradigmatic for Jainism a member of only one sect, the Digambara, 'Sky-clad', whose male ascetics renounce the wearing of clothes. The major Jain sect, numerically at any rate, is the Shvetambara, 'White-clad', whose male and female ascetics wear white robes. This sect in turn became significantly differentiated in more recent times on the basis of adherence to or rejection of image worship. All Jain sects and their internal subdivisions have their own histories, traditions and ways of interpreting Jainism which often provoked intense disagreement amongst themselves. Furthermore, Jains, of whatever sect, are not exclusively ascetics but overwhelmingly lay people.

Dandin was not concerned to describe Jainism in strictly realistic or accurate terms but he provides an early example of a tendency which has persisted into this century and which would interpret one of the world's oldest religions in a manner so narrow as to be little better than caricature. As represented in many recent accounts, this view would see Jainism as unified in nearly all respects, essentially both ahistorical and eccentric, with its belief and practice revolving around extreme forms of ascetic behaviour, dietary restrictions and a near-pathological preoccupation with the minutiae of a doctrine of non-violence. This misconceived approach has been compounded by many contemporary Jain writers who, in an attempt to boost their religion's intellectual credibility, have often seemed principally concerned with presenting Jainism in purely metaphysical terms as little more than a gradualistic spiritual path in which the only truly significant historical event after the death of the founding teacher was a sectarian 'schism' and, typically, such writers make little or no reference to the main actors within the religion, the individuals, monks and nuns, laymen and laywomen, who would down through the centuries describe themselves and their mode of life as Jain. The appearance in the twentieth century of an autonomous academic discipline called 'Jainology', chairs of which exist in several Indian universities, certainly signifies an awareness of the importance and interest of Jainism but also suggests the manner in which a vital and living religion has all too often come to be reified by its students.

Classical Jainism came to see the universe and man's place within it as involving simultaneously the two polarities of permanence and change. Such an interpretation of reality can without too much damage be extended to the Jain religion itself for, although the basic concerns of Jainism became stable at a fairly early date, its history nonetheless evinces a rich and complex evolution over the centuries. It is the capacity of Jains to adapt themselves to changing circumstances while remaining true to certain principles viewed as eternally valid which is one of the clues to the tenacity of their religion and mode of life over two and a half millennia.

THE QUESTION OF JAIN IDENTITY

The Sanskrit word *Jaina* derives from *jina*, 'conqueror', an epithet given to a line of human teachers who, having overcome the passions and obtained enlightenment, teach the true doctrine of non-violence and subsequently attain the freedom from rebirth which constitutes spiritual deliverance. The Jains are at the most basic level those who credit these spiritual conquerors with total authority and act according to their teachings.

It is not clear when the term 'Jain' was first employed to designate an adherent of a specific religious path, although it was probably in use by the early centuries of the common era. The designation found in the ancient scriptures, *niggantha*, 'free from bonds' was employed to describe only members of the ascetic community and it was no doubt the gradual emergence of a self-aware laity supporting the bondless ascetics which led to 'Jain' eventually becoming current for both the teachings of the religion and those who followed them.

Demographically, the Jains form a tiny minority within India. The Census of India figures for 1981 show that, out of a total population of nearly 800 million, Jains constitute about 3.19 million, with the largest numbers being concentrated in the states of Gujarat (467,768), Karnataka (284,508), Madhya Pradesh (444,960), Maharashtra (939,392) and Rajasthan (624,317).[2] These figures relate to religious affiliation only and there is nothing as far as language or physical appearance are concerned which renders the Jains distinct from the broader Indian social world in which they live.

Simple as this might appear to be, a problem arises at this juncture, most clearly exemplified in article 25 of the Indian Constitution which states that when the terms 'Hindu' and 'Hinduism' are used within that Constitution, they are to be taken to include the Jains, along with the Sikhs and Buddhists (although in fact the Jains are elsewhere treated as exclusive for certain legal purposes). While this might be regarded as typical of Hinduism's inclusivistic perspective and a necessary expedient for a newly independent India, all the more so since in this century 'Hindu' has often come virtually to imply 'Indian', there is little doubt that over the last century and a half or so not just westerners but also some Jains and many Indian observers from outside the Jain community have been uncertain as to the nature of Jain identity.

The history of the Jains in the nineteenth century has hardly begun to be written but there are examples from this period which highlight a fluidity of attitude towards religious identity, the most striking perhaps being the return of the prominent Jain merchant house of Jagat Seth to Vaishnava Hinduism, a move which did not involve any form of formal reconversion but rather a simply effected reorientation of social and religious preference.[3] The type of world in which many Jains and Hindus lived in north India at the end of the nineteenth century is well evoked in the autobiography, first published in 1949, of Ganeshprasad Varni who was to become a *kshullaka*, a lower order Digambara monk, famous for his public speaking. Varni's family was Vaishnava Hindu but, as a large number of Jains lived in their village, his father seems as a matter of course to have adopted many of their customs. Varni describes his own desire to become a Jain as the result of a natural, spiritual urge brought about by observing the piety of the Jains who surrounded him.[4]

This fluidity of religious adherence is reflected in the questions raised in the course of the last century and a half by outside observers about Jain identity and the status of the Jain religion, most particularly in two contexts: legal judgements and the censuses organised under the British Raj. Many British judges in the nineteeenth century had no doubts about the independent nature and origin of Jainism. As early as 1847, it was stated by one that the Jains, along with other religious minorities such as the Sikhs and the Parsees, had 'nothing or next to nothing in common with brahmanical worship', while in 1874 another argued that Jains could not be subject to Hindu law since 'the term Hindoos means persons within the purview of the shastras, which shastras are at the bottom of Hindu law. If a person is out of that purview, Hindoo law cannot be applied to him'.[5]

However, the earliest censuses of India suggest that many Jains and members of other religious groups saw themselves as in fact constituting varieties of Hinduism and, according to the Census Report for the Punjab of 1921, 'in view of the unwillingness of large numbers of Jains and Sikhs to be classed separately from Hindus, permission was given to record such persons as Jain-Hindus and Sikh-Hindus'.[6] It is likely that the preconceptions of the census enumerators and their insistence on the necessity of a religious categorisation which was incapable of matching reality in part led to this confusing situation. But, if the term 'Jain-Hindu' was an unhappy and artificial compromise which did not long survive, twentieth century legal statements about the relationship of Jainism to Hinduism have hardly provided greater clarity, and judgements about whether Jains could come under the jurisdiction of Hindu law have often oscillated wildly, depending on differing interpretations about the origins of the religion. In 1921, for example, the Privy Council stated that the Jains were of Hindu origin and had to be judged as Hindus dissenters, whereas six years later the Chief Justice of the Madras High Court insisted that scholarly research had shown that the Jains were not in fact Hindu dissenters.[7]

Unquestionably, many prominent Jains exacerbated this situation by refusing to produce copies of their scriptural and legal texts in court for fear that they might be polluted by officials turning over pages with saliva on their fingers and thus the erroneous impression was created that Jain and Hindu custom were identical, as a consequence of which a great deal of dispute ensued in the courts over such matters as the legal validity of the specifically Jain practice of the wife, rather than the son, inheriting the deceased husband's estate. After independence, the Hindu Law Committee refused to accept the validity of any separate legal code and decreed that for the purposes of personal law the Jains should be subject to Hindu law, a decision confirmed by the High Court of India in 1971.[8]

Clearly, then, the question of whether the Jains are a Hindu sect has been in many eyes a controversial one and, indeed, differences in the articulation of their identity can be found amongst the Jains themselves throughout India today. Thus, a northern Digambara might be happy to describe himself as a Hindu in that he might accept that the term could have an encompassing sense,[9] whereas Shvetambaras in Gujarat and Digambaras in Karnataka would be unlikely to call themselves anything other than Jain and would be more insistent on the exclusivity of their religion. Again, in Rajasthan, while many Jain merchants might often subsume their identity as Jains within the broader and, depending on context, more meaningful category of *mahajan*, the name of the merchant caste to which both Jains and Hindus can belong, others might be more conscious of their exclusive identity as Jains.[10]

Certainly, it might be salutary for those who would compartmentalise Indian religions into discrete and mutually incompatible entities to reflect that, at various times and situations in India's past, what might be regarded as exclusive labels such as 'Hinduism' and 'Jainism' have not in fact always been sufficiently adequate indicators of the complex and often shifting nature of religious identity. Intermarriage between Jains and Hindus would naturally complicate this question but, broadly speaking, the types of conceptual boundaries which the west Asian monotheisms have tended to erect against each other have never functioned with the same degree of intensity in South Asia.

However, it would be misleading to pursue this too far. In common with many contemporary Jain writers, I would wish to see Jainism as representing the various levels of meaning embodied in the Sanskrit word *samskriti*, 'culture', 'civilisation', a specifically Jain mode of life which is independent, coherent and self-contained and yet at times can also intersect with the conceptual world which surrounds it, providing a distinctive moral universe within which individuals can function and develop, and which is to be located in diverse yet interlinked areas such as the teaching of sacred texts, the mendicant lives of the ascetic community, the sectarian traditions, the fasting of laywomen, the business activities of laymen, ritual and devotion, the celebration of festivals and so on. In the light of Jainism's manifest cultural distinctiveness, there seems to be little merit in puzzling over whether or not it can be regarded as Hindu.

WESTERN VIEWS OF THE JAINS

Europeans have been aware of the Jains since the beginning of the sixteenth century, albeit describing them as *bania*, 'merchant', a term which can be used of Hindu traders also. Predictably, western travellers and missionaries were more interested in the outward aspects of Jain life and the appearance of Jain ascetics and they are vague about the details of their doctrine and belief. References, by and large respectful, to non-violence, vegetarianism and ascetic practice are frequent, but since most of these observations took place in Gujarat, the Shvetambara stronghold, little mention is made of the Digambaras.[11]

The first serious attempt to get to grips with the Jains as a historical and social phenomenon took place with the advent of the British at the beginning of the nineteenth century, with some of their reports achieving a reasonable degree of accuracy, although not based on any knowledge of Jain literature.[12] Unfortunately, the likelihood of any genuinely informed judgement on the part of the early British observers was vitiated by their determination to view the Jains as a group almost entirely congruent with the Hindu caste system. While Jainism has rejected the traditional brahman idea of society being structured around purity and impurity, castes do nonetheless exist as a significant component within Jainism. However, an additional and equally important mode of social differentiation among the Shvetambaras (for it is they who in the main were being described) is sectarian division, a source of great confusion to the British who, in trying to impose an artificial model of unity and consistency upon Jainism, failed utterly, as have most other western commentators, to respond adequately to its complex and often idiosyncratic texture.[13]

German-speaking Indologists provided the first truly successful effort to reveal Jainism's past. It is indicative of the marginal position that Jain studies have always occupied that Albrecht Weber's 'Uber die Heiligen Schriften der Jainas' has never been acclaimed as one of the greatest feats not just of classical Indological scholarship but of nineteenth century scholarship in general. Working with manuscript material sent from India to the Preussiche Staatsbibliothek in Berlin, Weber (1825–1901), who himself never set foot in the country whose ancient literature he studied so assiduously, performed the prodigious task of sifting through and analysing the contents of the huge body of Shvetambara scriptures at a time when western knowledge of Jainism, its teachings and the dialect in which the scriptures were written was minimal.[14] Building on this groundbreaking work, scholars such as Buhler, Jacobi and Leumann started to produce editions of texts and studies of technical problems in Jain history and literature, the full implications of which in Leumann's case are only just now emerging. It was Jacobi who in a famous paper of 1874 authoritatively established that Jainism was not merely an offshoot of Buddhism, as some scholars had argued, but an independent religious and intellectual tradition.[15]

At the same time, a negative picture of Jainism was also emerging, no doubt in part because of the failure of its supposed founder, Mahavira, to conform to the stereotype of an Asian Socrates which had been so congenial to the first serious western interpreters of the life and teachings of the Buddha, and many European scholars came to express extreme discontent with the textual material with which they were working. Weber's comments about his weariness with the tedium and inelegance of the Shvetambara canon in time became received wisdom, although they are somewhat surprising in the light of the convoluted style in which he himself often wrote.[16] Barnett, one of the few British scholars to work on the Jain scriptures, clearly had an active dislike of the literature he translated which he extended into a denunciation of Jainism in general and what he described as its 'grim ideal' and 'morbid' view of life.[17] Certainly, the idiom of a great deal of Jain literature, its frequently repetitive subject matter and the complex classificatory systems employed in Jain teachings do indeed often make serious demands upon the student. However, there are specifically doctrinal and taxonomic reasons for such a style, in part deriving from the originally oral nature of early Jain literature, and it does not require much imagination to realise that ancient Jain teachers would have had more immediate concerns than the possible impact of their scriptures upon the aesthetic sensibilities of Victorian and Edwardian scholars.

Much of this unsympathetic approach to Jainism can be found embodied in the missionary Mrs Sinclair Stevenson's *The Heart of Jainism*, published for the first time in 1915 and still reprinted in India.[18] This book provides a mixture of accurate and inaccurate information, leavened with a lofty disdain for its subject matter. Jainism's 'heart', it would appear, is its heartlessness, the material wealth of its followers masking a spiritual impoverishment, a barrenness of belief far from the saving grace of Jesus. It has taken over sixty years for the English-speaking reader to gain an accurate sense of what Jainism involves with the publication of *The Jaina Path of Purification* by Professor P.S. Jaini, a Digambara from south India.[19]

I do not refer to western jibes and misunderstandings for their own sake but wish rather to suggest that their legacy is still very much in place today, with Jainism as a rule being interpreted as either colourless and austere or with reference to a few 'exotic' customs such as the wearing of the mouth-shield (*muhpatti*) to avoid violence to minute organisms living in the air, a practice hardly universal within the religion (see Chapter 9). More generally, there has been a failure to integrate Jainism adequately into the wider picture of Indian society and a concomitant lack of desire to allot it a recognisable place amongst the world's religions. This latter point can be seen most markedly in the recent multi-volume *Encyclopedia of Religions* edited by Mircea Eliade, which both sums up research over the last half-century and will to a large extent set the agenda for the study of religion in the immediate future.[20] Only three entries in this monumental work relate specifically to Jainism, and only one Jain individual, the last fordmaker Mahavira, is given a separate entry.

The largely textual orientation of nineteenth century and subsequent western scholarship has also been responsible for the creation of a distorted perspective on Jain society and its history. The excavation at the end of the last century of the great funerary monument (*stupa*) at the north-west Indian city of Mathura and the examination by the Austrian scholar Buhler of the inscriptional evidence there confirmed both that the information about ascetic lineages found in ancient scriptural texts had a genuine basis in reality and that the Jain ascetics formed a fully fledged religious community at a period prior to the common era. So mesmerised do Victorian scholars seem to have been by this corroboration, admittedly an important one, of the results of their textual researches that they failed to draw a more important conclusion. Jain ascetics are not allowed to erect buildings, religious or otherwise, and there is no evidence that the situation was any different in ancient Mathura. It is obvious that only a sizable and thriving lay community which must have been in existence for some time, in other words near to the very beginning of Jainism, could have been responsible for such an impressive undertaking.[21]

Unfortunately, the Jain lay community has never been adequately studied and the history of Jainism, inevitably based on literature emanating almost exclusively from the ascetic environment, has been presented solely in terms of the preoccupations of the ascetic community, with the laity emerging only intermittently and in largely idealised fashion. Yet, in purely numerical terms, to be a Jain today effectively means to be a layman or a laywoman since the ascetic community is now relatively very small: there are at this time, for example, little more than one hundred and twenty fully initiated monks and about half as many nuns out of a total Digambara population of around one million. Although statistics are nearly impossible to estimate for earlier periods of Jain history, there can be no doubt that lay people have throughout Jain history always constituted by far the more substantial proportion of the community, and the ascetic vocation, whatever its prestige and vital role in the construction and promulgation of Jain culture, has been adopted by only a few. However, virtually no ethnographic studies of the contemporary Jain lay community have been undertaken, with the only significant monograph to date dealing with the cooking and dietary customs of the Digambaras of Delhi, and the rituals and attitudes of lay people have been largely ignored, thus ensuring a distinctly lopsided view of Jainism.[22]

Western scholarship, then, has hardly begun to provide an adequate assessment of the Jain religion. Furthermore, despite the genuine achievement of figures such as Weber and, rather more recently in this century, Schubring, the west cannot be regarded as having in any serious manner retrieved Jainism for the Jain community or mediated the tradition to it.[23] The Jain situation is here different from that of Theravada Buddhism which was in the last century greatly influenced, at least in certain circles, by western scholarly interpretations of Buddhism as well as by the activities of Christian missionaries. While Jain ascetic culture, along with the learning and charismatic leadership associated with it, went into a decline in the eighteenth and nineteenth centuries, the impetus towards its regeneration and the reactivation of its scholarly tradition came very much from within the Jain community itself and, if it would be going too far to say that all ascetics this century have been uniformly learned, there have nonetheless emerged from within its ranks some major interpreters of Jainism's intellectual tradition. The great Shvetambara monk Muni Punyavijaya (1895–1971) is a striking example of a scholar whose mastery of a wide range of learning, cataloguing and editing of manuscripts and extensive publications in Hindi and Gujarati, all of which owe little or nothing to western prescriptions, set the highest possible standards. The Jain laity also, both Shvetambara and Digambara, has produced many remarkable scholars whose grasp of the technicalities of the Jain literary and philosophical tradition has remained largely unknown in the west, mainly because of the lack of interest of many of them in publishing in English.

It would be impertinent to pretend that any religious tradition can be encompassed in the short space available here. Nor does this book attempt to give an ethnographic account of Jainism. What I would wish to do is alert students of world religions to the richness of Jain history and to present it as far as possible in terms of the experience of those Jains, past and present, ascetic and lay, who have participated within it. Jains may be few today but they would not on that basis view their faith as a minority religion. As the renowned twelfth century Shvetambara teacher Jinadatta Suri stated, it is an upright community, not numbers, which is important (UR 55 with comm.).

1 The fordmakers

According to tradition, the great Shvetambara scholar-monk Haribhadra was in his early years a learned brahman who boasted that he would become the pupil of anyone whose teachings he could not controvert. One day he heard a Jain nun called Yakini reciting a verse which to his astonishment he could not understand. On being questioned she directed Haribhadra to her teacher who instructed him in the basics of Jain doctrine and converted him.[1]

Haribhadra's bemusement is understandable. The verse Yakini is supposed to have recited relates to a specifically Jain version of the legendary history of the world known as the 'Deeds of the Sixty-three Illustrious Men', or, as it is called by western scholars, the Universal History, which provides a description on a massive scale of the destinies, enacted over a vast period of time, of the twenty-four Jain teachers, the fordmakers, and their contemporaries.[2] Haribhadra would on studying the Universal History have found amongst other surprises that the supposedly eternal and authorless Hindu scripture, the Veda, had in fact been created by Bharata, the first Jain universal emperor of this world-era, and that two of the central focuses of Hindu religious devotion, Rama and Krishna, were themselves Jain laymen.

Jainism is believed by its followers to be everlasting, without beginning or end, the Universal History describing just one tiny portion of an eternal process. For those approaching Jainism from outside its tradition, there is of course another type of Jain history, reconstructed by scholars from the mass of literature, monastic chronicles and inscriptions, often full of gaps and vague in chronology. While a historian of the Jains will inevitably draw on such material, it must also be borne in mind that Jainism structures its own sense of history within a different temporal context. An early source records a prophecy that the *tirtha*, the community which puts the Jain doctrine into practice, will outlast Mahavira, the last of the omniscient fordmakers, by 21,000 years, during which time the religion will go into a decline, to be reawakened only during the course of the next world era (Bh 20.8).[3] The Jains share with the Hindus the notion of the *Kaliyuga*, the Corrupt Age, which for them involves a gradual diminishment of culture, religion and eventually even human stature. This age, in which we are living now, has been continually invoked by Jain writers from the early medieval period and provides an overarching principle with reference to which the tradition can explain the course of its own immediate fortunes after the death of Mahavira, that is, in the concluding part of the Universal History, as involving a continual tension between decline and attempted reform.

THE VEDIC BACKGROUND

Jainism emerged, along with Buddhism, towards the end of a time of great social transformation in north India which is usually called the Vedic period, after the Veda, the body of literature which in the absence of any large-scale archaeological evidence, forms our main source for this epoch. As Gombrich has provided in his volume on Theravada Buddhism in this series an authoritative account of Vedic India, it will not be necessary to repeat his conclusions in any detail.[4] I will, however, give a brief outline of those aspects of this period which have most bearing upon early Jainism.

It has become customary for scholars to interpret the Vedic period as developing in a simple linear fashion. Thus, an original nomadic or pastoral life followed from approximately the fifteenth to the tenth centuries BCE by the Aryans, the speakers of the earliest form of that language which was to be called Sanskrit, is usually stated to have been succeeded by the appearance of a more settled, agriculturally oriented mode of life from about the tenth to the sixth centuries BCE, this being followed in turn, through the generation of significant economic surpluses and the concomitant emergence of new forms of technology such as writing and iron, by urbanisation and the gradual appearance of state formations of varying size.

Conveniently enough for scholarship, the literature of this period has generally been interpreted as being composed in conformity to a similar chronologically linear model. This view would see the earliest texts, the *Rigveda*, hymns of praise and requests directed towards the gods of the Vedic pantheon, along with associated liturgical material, being followed by the *Brahmanas*, huge compilations concentrating in the main on the theory of the sacrifice as the main creative force in the universe. These were in turn succeeded by the *Aranyakas*, the esoteric 'Forest Books' and the famous *Upanishads* which attempted through mystical speculation to convey the relation between man's innermost spiritual being and the universe as a whole.

The reality was in fact much more complex than such simple linearity of interpretation would suggest. Pastoralism and settled agriculture, for example, must in actuality have functioned together in tandem for some considerable time, while the *Upanishads* do not simply represent a more spiritual advance on the *Brahmanas* but are permeated with the ideology and symbols of the sacrificial ritual. Moreover, the beginning of large-scale urbanisation was in the main located in the east of India, originally regarded by Vedic literature as a marginal and impure region, rather than the western areas which represented the heartland of Vedic culture. Nonetheless, it was both the change attendant upon the shift away from less organised forms of economic life and the influence of Vedic ideology which provided the social and intellectual backdrop against which the two great easterners, Mahavira and his contemporary, the Buddha, moved.

The dominant mode of conceptualising the world in north India by the sixth century BCE was the product of the elaborate speculation conducted by members of the learned brahman class into the nature and function of ritual. The Vedic sacrifice, which usually but by no means always involved the killing of animals, was composed of a variety of elements which might be expected to occur in any extended form of ritual activity: priestly specialists, praise of divinities, the making of offerings, requests for divine favours, sacred language, sanctified space in which the rites are conducted and so on. More uniquely, the sacrifice was also regarded as providing the context for consideration of the nature of man's position in the universe. In the *Brahmanas*, the theorists of the sacrifice present ritual as a means of perpetuating life, specifically that of the individual who sponsors the performance of the sacrifice, and as a profoundly creative force. The sacrifice came to be seen as implicated in the emergence of both the universe and the individual himself and the *Brahmanas* demonstrate at length the interrelatedness of the various parts of the ritual and the cosmos.

Two generalised ideas which were to be central for Indian religions resulted from these speculations. The first of these is the world of continuity and rebirth (*samsara*), an extension of the idea that the sacrifice could extend existence over more than one lifetime. The second idea is generally known as karma, a concept which developed from an original specifically ritual context in which a correctly performed sacrificial action (*karman*) resulted in birth and continued life in the next world to the generally held belief that any action of whatever quality generated rebirth as a consequence. In the *Upanishads*, there also occur the first statements of the view, dominant in Jain teachings and elsewhere, that rebirth is undesirable and that it is possible by controlling or stopping one's actions to put an end to it and attain a state of deliverance (*moksha*) which lies beyond action.[5]

The Jains, along with the Buddhists, accepted the ideas of karma and rebirth as representing basic facts of human experience, taken for granted in the earliest scriptures with no need being felt to justify their validity. That is not to say that the Jains subscribed to the cult of animal sacrifice itself, for they have always espoused as a central and necessary moral tenet the principle of *ahimsa*, 'non-violence' to all creatures and, indeed, they have contended that even the performance of a sacrifice with an inanimate surrogate is wrong, as in the famous story of Yashodhara who went to hell because of his innately violent mental disposition, despite having offered to a goddess merely a cockerel made of dough.[6]

Nonetheless, the Jains were also cognisant of the potency of sacrifice as a cultural symbol and sought to reinterpret both Vedic ritual and the brahman sacrificer who manipulated it in their own ethical terms. One of the most venerated Shvetambara scriptures describes how Harikesha, a Jain monk of untouchable origins, approached in silence some brahmans who were performing a sacrifice in order to get alms. On being violently attacked by them, he was saved by a tree-spirit who intervened on his behalf. The climax of the episode is Harikesha's explanation to the brahmans of the nature of the true, internal sacrifice of the Jain monk:

> Austerity is my sacrificial fire, my life is the place where the fire is kindled. Mental and physical efforts are my ladle for the oblation and my body is the dung fuel for the fire, my actions my firewood. I offer up an oblation praised by the wise seers consisting of my restraint, effort and calm.
> (UttS 12.44–5)

Harikesha's innate purity has nothing to do with birth or ritual purity but comes about through his celibacy and steadfastness in Jain principles. The heat (*tapas*) of the sacrificial fire is insignificant compared to the heat generated by the austerity (*tapas*) which remoulds life and destiny. Spiritual authority is in this context vested not in the ritual technician but in that individual who performs the morally correct action, the Jain monk.

GOING FORTH: THE INSTITUTION OF WORLD RENUNCIATION

If, as it came to be believed, freedom from action, initially taken as ritual performance and then extended to include social action, was the means of escaping from the continuity of rebirth, how was such an actionless state to be achieved? The answer was that the individual had to cast off the bonds of the householder's life, the world of the cooking and sacrificial fires, and enter the life of homelessness by becoming a renouncer, a wandering mendicant who could not grow, cook or buy his own food but instead subsisted on alms. The term *shramana*, 'striver', used of Mahavira and other renouncers to distinguish them from the brahmans, points to the physical and speculative exertion which was necessarily entailed in a life devoted to the minimising of the performance of external action and an accompanying control of inner activity.

It may well be that this 'going forth' (*pravrajya*) from home, an institution which was to be so productive for Indian religious life and thought, was given impetus by the changes which Indian society was undergoing from around the eighth century BCE and that the growth of communities of renouncers with their evolving doctrines and codes of conduct was a response to the breakdown of old social values in the face of aggressive new state formations and altered modes of social interaction and authority. However, while the Shvetambara scriptural text, the 'Exposition of Explanations', does preserve a memory of this period in a description couched in mythical terms of two conflicts called 'The War of the Big Stones' and 'The War of the Chariot and the Mace' in which the famous sixth century BCE king of Magadha, Kunika, (called by the Buddhists Ajatashatru) destroyed a confederation of smaller kingdoms and tribes (Bh 7.9),[7] early Jain literature shows very little interest in contemporary political circumstances and the question of some kind of psychological malaise or sense of anomie as constituting an influence on those who went forth to become mendicant renouncers can only remain hypothetical.

Nonetheless, there is no doubt that one of the most noteworthy features of world renunciation was its construction of alternative forms of social groupings akin to those of the world which had been left behind. Terms employed in Jainism and Buddhism to describe groups of ascetics such as *gana*, 'troop' and *sangha*, 'assembly' are used in early Vedic texts to refer to the warrior brotherhoods, the young men's bands which were a feature of Aryan nomadic life, and the stress found in the old codes of monastic law on requirements of youth, physical fitness and good birth for Jain and Buddhist monks, along with the frequent martial imagery of Jainism and its repeated stress on the crushing of spiritual enemies, may point to a degree of continuity with these earlier types of warrior. Certainly it is noteworthy that both Mahavira and the Buddha were members of the warrior caste.[8]

While the most ancient ideal of Jainism, as represented in Mahavira's early ascetic career, was isolation and solitude, going forth did not mean entry into an anarchic, unstructured world but rather entailed joining a new form of society with its own rules, internal relationships and groupings which in many respects replicated those of the social world which had been abandoned. The only major difference was the necessity for ascetic society to reproduce itself by means of recruitment and initiation since there was a necessary obligation for all renouncers to abandon sexual activity.[9] One of the most frequently used terms up to about the tenth century CE to describe a Shvetambara monastic group was *kula*, 'family'.

THE 'SAYINGS OF THE SEERS'

Jainism, then, was in origin merely one component of a north Indian ascetic culture which flourished in the Ganges basin around the sixth century BCE. Many individual participants within this culture had attained a marked degree of fame at this time, acknowledged by Jains and Buddhists alike, because of their supposed attainment of some form of knowledge or enlightenment,[10] and one early text provides particularly valuable evidence of how an attempt was made by the Jains to establish some sort of accommodation with non-Jain ascetics, both contemporary and ancient.

The 'Sayings of the Seers' (IBh) is seldom referred to in studies on Jainism not only because it is often difficult to understand but because its status and purpose are unclear. It contains a series of statements attributed to a variety of *rishis* or seers (the term in origin referred to a composer of a Vedic hymn), some familiar from other sources, others almost totally obscure, but all clearly regarded as in some way significant and authoritative in their own right. Unquestionably the 'Sayings' is one of the most ancient Jain texts available although, with a very provisional dating to the fourth BCE, it probably cannot be assigned to the very oldest stratum of the literature. Never completely forgotten, it seems nonetheless to have fallen at a fairly early date into a partial obscurity, with very few manuscripts of it being copied and no classical commentary on it being composed.

The subject matter of the 'Sayings' must have been the reason for this, for it juxtaposes Mahavira along with Parshva, regarded as the former's predecessor as fordmaker, on equal terms with figures from traditions which were to be regarded as Jainism's rivals, such as the Buddha's close disciples Shariputra and Mahakashyapa (the Buddha himself does not appear), various individuals from a brahmanical background such as Yajnavalkya, one of the preeminent teachers of the *Upanishads*, and even Makkhali Gosala whom later Jain writers were to see as the arch-enemy of Mahavira.

Mahavira's teachings are presented, under his given name of Vardhamana, at no great length and in no privileged manner. Suppression of the senses is given as the central tenet of his doctrine, sacrificial imagery being used to convey this: 'he who conquers the mind and the passions and performs austerity correctly, shines with pure soul like a fire in which the oblation has been poured' (IBh 29.17).

It is not Mahavira but the mysterious figure of Narada, who in classical Hinduism was to assume the role of a semi-divine intermediary between gods and men and whom the Jain Universal History linked with disproof of the efficacy of sacrifice, who is credited at the beginning of the 'Sayings' with enunciating the central teaching of the importance of non-violence in body, speech and mind (IBh 1). The 'Sayings' also contain what would have been to the Jains antipathetical cosmological views such as those of the wandering mendicant (*parivrajaka*) Giri who is associated with two claims, that the world and all life came about through a heated egg germinating in the cosmic waters and that the world was the product of the sacrifice, statements which are then followed somewhat uneasily with an enunciation of the standard Jain view of the eternality of the universe (IBh 37).

Particularly interesting is the section of the 'Sayings' which describes how the brahman mendicant Ambada is instructed that mere renunciation of the world is insufficient and that it requires to be put into the framework of correct Jain behaviour (IBh 25). In another later Shvetambara scriptural text, Ambada is described as the leader of a band of ascetics who resolve on suicide because they cannot find anybody to give them alms. Before dying the ascetics pay homage both to Ambada and Mahavira and are reborn as gods. Mahavira praises Ambada but emphasises that, despite his great qualities, it is impossible for him to become a Jain monk because his behaviour only approximates to the necessary requirements (Aup pp.230–50).

This Jainising of a variety of ascetic figures and their doctrines as evinced in the 'Sayings of the Seers' was an attempt by early Jainism to legitimise its own teachings by associating, without fully identifying, them with those whom the common tradition of the Ganges basin had come to regard as unquestionably great and enlightened men of the past.

THE FORDMAKERS AND THE FORD

In western-style histories of religions, Mahavira is generally treated as being the founder of Jainism in the same way as Jesus is regarded as the founder of Christianity. For the Jains, however, Mahavira is merely one of a chain of teachers who all communicate the same truth in broadly similar ways and his biography, rather than being discrete, has to be treated as part of the larger totality of the Universal History and as meshing, through the continuing dynamic of rebirth, with the lives of other participants within it. Not until the ninth century CE is there found a biography of Mahavira, written by the Sanskrit poet Asaga, which treats his career without reference to the other fordmakers. Nonetheless, since the historicity of Mahavira and his predecessor Parshva alone of all the fordmakers is not in question, and since it is the accounts of the life of Mahavira which are the most amenable to analysis, this chapter will focus upon the last fordmaker and associate the teachings of early Jainism with him. Firstly, though, I will contextualise Mahavira's life by giving a broad and brief account of the rhythm of the current movement of time as described in the Universal History.

Eras of time are conventionally represented in Jainism as being a continual series of downward and upward motions of a wheel, called respectively *avasarpini* and *utsarpini*. An *avasarpini* is divided into six spokes or ages, the first three representing a golden age which inaugurates a gradual process of degeneration leading to the fifth spoke, the *duhshama* or 'uneven' age, otherwise known as the *Kaliyuga* as we have already seen, followed by the sixth and final spoke when the Jain doctrine dies out, whereupon the *utsarpini* commences with the spokes in reverse order. While this process is beginningless and endless, the Universal History is in effect only concerned with this current *avasarpini* and that small area of the universe where human life is enacted.[11] No god is implicated in these spontaneous temporal movements, either in a creative or an overseeing role, and human beings and other creatures are repeatedly reborn under the impulse of their own actions.

During each motion of the wheel, twenty-four teachers, the fordmakers (*tirthankara*), appear in succession who activate the Three Jewels, the uncreated Jain teachings of right faith, right knowledge and right practice, and who found a community of ascetic and lay followers which serves as a spiritual ford (*tirtha*) for human beings over the ocean of rebirth. The pattern of the careers of these fordmakers is essentially identical. Always born into a family of the warrior class, they are generally awakened by the gods (in Jainism, beings who are subject like humans to the laws of rebirth but who cannot attain enlightenment in their divine state) to their destinies as great spiritual teachers and then renounce the world of the householder to become wandering mendicants. After an obligatory period in the practice of physical and mental austerities, facilitated by their uniquely powerful physical structure, to burn away the karma they have accumulated over innumerable existences, they attain the enlightenment which the Jains define as full omniscience. Finally, having engaged in a period of preaching and conversion, they die in meditation and their souls, freed from their bodies, travel to the top of the universe to abide in a state of bliss and pure consciousness along with the other liberated souls.

One important way in which the fordmakers are differentiated from each other is in their physical dimensions and length of life.[12] At the outset of the *avasarpini* they are massive in size and live for near incalculable periods of time. However, as the spokes of the wheel descend, the intervals between the fordmakers decrease, and their size and duration of life diminish until finally the twenty-third fordmaker Parshva (who traditionally lived for a hundred years) is separated from his successor Mahavira by only two hundred and fifty years and their size and duration of life are of near-normal human dimensions.

As the first fordmaker, Rishabha is inevitably allotted a great deal of space in the Universal History. He was born not as would be expected at the beginning of the *avasarpini* but near the end of the third spoke. Up to this point the needs of human beings had been satisfied by miraculous wishing trees but, as the efficacy of these decreased, society became unstructured and incapable of self-maintenance. One of Rishabha's roles prior to his renunciation of the world was the patriarchal one of inculcating social skills such as the preparation of food, the kindling of fire, agriculture, writing, marriage, an organised system of society and so on. The nature of the vital institution of giving (*dana*), whereby a layman gives alms to an ascetic and through that action gains merit, was articulated for the first time when a king, Shreyamsa, poured sugarcane juice into Rishabha's cupped hands to break the fordmaker's first fast as a renouncer. Rishabha can thus be viewed as unique among the fordmakers in that he is not just a spiritual teacher but a form of culture hero.

None of the other fordmakers have as highly developed biographies as the first and last, although the lives of two of them, Malli (for the Shvetambaras a woman) and Parshva, are distinctive and will be described later. Mahavira is linked by the Universal History to Rishabha through having been born as his heretical grandson Marici. After a succession of rebirths, including those of a hellbeing and a lion, Mahavira completed his penultimate birth in one of the heavens as a god prior to being born as the twenty-fourth fordmaker. He was then transported in embryo form by the general of the army of Indra, the king of the gods, initially to the womb of a brahman woman, a mistake explained by reference to some bad karma which Mahavira had acquired in his birth as Marici. He was then taken to the only womb appropriate for a fordmaker, that of a woman of the warrior caste whose name was Trishala, the wife of a king, Siddhartha.[13]

After his birth consecration, carried out by Indra on Mount Meru, the axis of the central cosmic continent of Jambudvipa, he was given the name Vardhamana, 'Increasing', because his family's prosperity increased after his birth. Having led a blameless youth during which he married a princess, Yashoda, who bore him a daughter, on his thirtieth birthday the gods performed the initiation ceremony for him and he renounced the world to become a mendicant ascetic. For twelve and a half years, Mahavira wandered in the region of the Ganges basin, part of which time he spent with another ascetic called Makkhali Gosala, often enduring physical abuse from men and attacks by animals, fasting and meditating all the while, as a result of which heroic mode of life he received the epithet 'Great Hero' (*mahavira*) and subsequently, in accordance with the destiny of all fordmakers, he attained enlightenment. He then converted eleven brahmans who were to become the 'leaders of the troop' (*ganadhara*), the heads of the ascetic order and the basis of the community as a whole. Mahavira died aged seventy-two at the town of Pava in what is now the state of Bihar. His body was cremated, with the gods taking his bones to heaven and his ashes being distributed throughout the Ganges region.

This story, drastically truncated here, would in essence be recognisable to all Jains, although the Digambaras reject certain elements of it such as the transfer of Mahavira's embryo and his marriage to Yashoda. In its broadest form, it is located in the versions of the Universal History produced by the Digambara poet Jinasena (ninth century CE) and his pupil Gunabhadra and the Shvetambaras Shilanka (ninth century CE) and Hemacandra (twelfth century CE) who drew upon themes scattered throughout the earlier scriptural tradition which had doubtless also been elaborated orally. When examined critically as a literary phenomenon, the Universal History in its widest extent gives the impression of being a massive introduction to the biography of Mahavira which itself expanded and evolved over a long period of time. We must now consider some of the features of that biography and the manner in which it presents a picture of Mahavira as exemplar of the Jain path.

THE SOURCES FOR MAHAVIRA'S BIOGRAPHY

An account of the nature and development of the Jain scriptures will be given in Chapter 3, but we may anticipate two points here. Firstly, the Shvetambara sources alone must be relied upon for an understanding of the earliest stages of Mahavira's biography, for the Digambara scriptures provide no significant early evidence. Secondly, the accounts of the Council of Valabhi, which took place in the first half of the fifth century CE and at which the Shvetambara scriptures were supposedly redacted for the final time, provide no help with regard to the dating of the actual sources involved. While we may be reasonably confident about the most important texts redacted at Valabhi, we can only establish a relative chronology for them on the basis of language, metre and the evidence of style. The datings which I adduce for the Shvetambara scriptures are therefore tentative, although deriving from what has become a scholarly consensus.

Generally accepted as being the oldest parts of the Shvetambara scriptures are the first books of the first and second 'limbs' (*anga*) of the canon, called the *Acaranga* (AS), because it relates to behaviour (*acara*), and the *Sutrakritanga* (SKS), probably so named because it describes the doctrines found in the writings (*sutra*) of those sects whom the Jains regarded as their opponents. Both of these books originated from about the fifth or fourth centuries BCE, although a slightly earlier dating cannot be ruled out, and they represent the most ancient stratum of Jain textual material.

The second book of the *Acaranga*, which is of particular importance since it presents (AS 2.15) Mahavira's life as a totality for the first time, is accepted by the commentators as being later than the first book. It can perhaps be assigned to the second or first centuries BCE and to a second stratum of biographical material, as can the *Kalpasutra* (KS), whose name relates to the monastic ritual (*kalpa*) which forms one of its main themes. It is the *Kalpasutra* which, as well as providing an extended biography of Mahavira, albeit one which concentrates on the events which led up to his birth, for the first time links the last fordmaker with a chain of twenty-three predecessors and gives very short accounts of the lives of three of them, Rishabha, Nemi and Parshva.

Still more difficult to date is the voluminous 'Exposition of Explanations' (*Vyakhyaprajnapti*), usually referred to by Jains as *Bhagavati*, 'Revered' (Bh). This contains a great deal of disparate material about Mahavira, his career and teachings, disciples and relations with other holy men, especially Makkhali Gosala who is not mentioned in the earlier scriptures. However, this is unquestionably a composite text and it is difficult to be confident about which portions of it are genuinely old and which originated nearer to the Council of Valabhi, although it can provisionally be taken as falling within the second stratum of the biography. The *Aupapatika* (Aup), which takes its name from the spontaneously born (*aupapatika*) gods and hellbeings described in the text, can probably, on the grounds of its often highly ornate prose style, be dated to the early centuries of the common era when such a mode of literary diction was emerging in Sanskrit and Prakrit belles-lettres and thus be provisionally located within a third biographical stratum.

Most important of all for the literary expansion of Mahavira's biography and for the development of the Universal History as a whole is the commentarial literature which came to cluster around the *Avashyakasutra*, the canonical text describing the six Obligatory Actions (*avashyaka*) incumbent upon every ascetic (see Chapter 6). The earliest portions of this material are the Prakrit mnemonic verses (*niryukti*) which perhaps date from about the second or third century CE, while the Prakrit prose commentary of Jinadasa was written in the seventh century CE. A further expansion of this exegetical literature was provided by Haribhadra. It was the commentators on the *Avashyakasutra* who organised the raw material for the Universal History, drawing together and expanding it to create an image of the promulgator of the true path with which they could confront the inadequate myths and hagiographies of their sectarian opponents.

MAHAVIRA'S DATE

It is fruitless to attempt to locate a historical Mahavira outwith the parameters of the texts which describe him. Even such a basic question as when he lived is not certain. So, while his traditional Shvetambara dating is 599 BCE to 527 BCE, the Digambaraṣ hold that he died in 510 BCE. There has been considerable scholarly debate about this matter since the nineteenth century and a variety of different datings have been proposed. The arguments are technical but it should be noted that Mahavira's dates depend in the last resort on synchronicity with those of the Buddha since the two were contemporaries and if, as is increasingly being suggested, a re-examination of early Buddhist historical material, nothing comparable to which exists in Jainism, necessitates a redating of the Buddha, then a shift in Mahavira's dating will also be entailed.[14]

Equally uncertain is the question of Mahavira's birthplace. The *Kalpasutra* states that he was born at Kundagrama, a site generally taken as having been in the vicinity of Vaishali, at that time one of the greatest towns of the Ganges basin. The exact location of Kundagrama has remained elusive, however, doubtless because the Jains began to migrate at a relatively early date from the east which subsequently went into economic and political decline for a considerable time so that accurate knowledge of the region where Mahavira had preached was soon at a premium, and there is still disagreement between the Shvetambaras and the Digambaras over this matter. This is in contrast to the general concord between the two sects with regard to the location of Mahavira's death, with the town of Pava mentioned in the *Kalpasutra* as the place where this event occurred being identified by about the thirteenth century with the village of Pavapur in the state of Bihar.

EPITHETS

There is no knowledge of Mahavira's given name Vardhamana in the earliest stratum of the biography and the use of the epithet Mahavira as a personal name, while occurring in the first book of the *Sutrakritanga*, is unknown in the first book of the *Acaranga*. Furthermore, the oldest texts never use the term 'fordmaker' and very seldom *jina*, the word which gives Jainism its name. Instead we find terms such as *Nayaputta*, 'son of the Nayas', an obscure expression which seems to refer to Mahavira's clan, called in Sanskrit *Jnatri*, and the name by which he is known in early Buddhist writings, 'ascetic' (*muni*, *samana*, *niggantha*), brahman, 'venerable' (*bhagavan*) and occasionally *araha*, 'worthy', a term found frequently in early Buddhism, and *veyavi*, 'knower of the Veda', which here may just signify 'wise'.

The *Acaranga* does not describe Mahavira as all-knowing but only as all-seeing.[15] However, a eulogy of Mahavira as ideal being, supposedly uttered by one of his disciples, occurs in the *Sutrakritanga* (SKS 1.6) and provides a remarkable picture of the qualities, principal among which was full omniscience, with which early Jain tradition credited him. Stress is laid on his humanity, freedom from the constraints of life and gaining of full physical and mental restraint. The limitless nature of his attainments, through which he sees and knows everything, 'this world and what lies beyond it'

(SKS 1.6.28), renders him the equal of the king of the gods and all the great mountains and oceans of the universe. The confidence which this ancient text expresses in the power of Mahavira's teachings to alter one's next birth for the better has characterised the attitude of Jains towards Mahavira and the other fordmakers to the present day.

THE TRANSFER OF THE EMBRYO

The first references to the transfer of Mahavira's embryo from the womb of a brahman woman called Devananda to that of Trishala, along with a reverse substitution of the embryo which was already in Trishala's womb, occur in the second chapter of the *Acaranga* and the *Kalpasutra*, that is to say, not in the oldest stratum of the biography. The reference in the 'Exposition of Explanations' to Mahavira's acknowledgement of Devananda as being his real mother clearly alludes to this aspect of the biography (Bh 9.33).[16]

It is possible to interpret this event in two ways. Firstly, the account in the *Kalpasutra* would appear to represent an attempt to devalorise the authority of the brahman caste which ranked itself hierarchically above the warrior caste into which all the fordmakers are born. Devananda's husband is depicted as somewhat vaingloriously rejoicing in the fact that his son, after being born, will master the Veda, a type of learning which Jainism rejected as being worthless. Indra, however, assumes control over the destination of the embryo since he knows that fordmakers can never be born into three types of low family, those of the poor, the insignificant or brahmans.[17]

Secondly, a comparison with the unusual births associated with hero figures of other religious traditions, such as the Buddha who was born from his mother's thigh or Jesus whose mother was a virgin, might suggest a desire to present Mahavira through his anomalous arrival in his final birth as both human and at the same time transcending the normal mortal state.

MAHAVIRA'S ASCETICISM

In the fully developed biography of Mahavira, much stress is placed on his pre-enlightenment career as a wandering ascetic, with relatively little being said about events between his enlightenment and his death. The core of this account, and the earliest version of any part of Mahavira's life, occurs in the eighth chapter of the first book of the *Acaranga* which is known as the 'Pillow Scripture' (*Uvahanasuya*) because Mahavira's various religious practices supported him as a pillow does the head. Up to this point the *Acaranga* had been giving a general description of monastic behaviour and then proceeds to particularise its injunctions with reference to the greatest ascetic of all. This must be taken as part of a larger oral account, for it commences with a reference to Mahavira's refusal to cover himself with 'that garment' (AS 1.8.1.1), an allusion understandable only in the light of the description in later strata of Indra's bestowing a divine robe upon him at the time of renunciation.

The 'Pillow Scripture' is concerned not so much with Mahavira's decision to reject the world as with the harshness and mortifying nature of the life which he led as a consequence of this. The violence shown to him by householders as he wandered, attacks by animals and insects, his nakedness and lack of concern about washing, his fasting, disregard for sleep, shelter or contact with other people, all are described as part of a long struggle to shake off the bondage brought about by body and mind and bring about a state of inner control: to abstain, in other words, from action (*karman*) and win through to spiritual freedom.

While it is likely that the 'Pillow Scripture' was composed retrospectively with full awareness of Mahavira's doctrine and the nature of his claim to enlightenment, it should be noted that he is portrayed prior to his enlightenment as being familiar with the fact that earth, water, air, fire and plants are full of life-forms and that true austerity involved causing them no injury (AS 1.8.1.11–12). Thus, knowledge of the underlying structure of life and a proper attitude towards it are presented in this early text as being the necessary preliminaries to enlightenment rather than its actual content.

The basic description of Mahavira's ascetic career was gradually expanded in later strata of the biography. The only specific region mentioned in the 'Pillow Scripture' as having been visited by the fordmaker was *Ladha*, now west Bengal, a dangerous and probably unaryan country where he was subjected to grievous treatment. An itinerary was subsequently provided for his travels by the *Kalpasutra* which gives a list of thirteen towns and cities in the Ganges basin where Mahavira passed various rainy seasons and the later strata connect these places with specific events in the biography.

At no point in the 'Pillow Scripture' and the second stratum of the biography is Mahavira described as being subjected in the course of his ascetic career to any sort of temptation or attack by supernatural forces. This is in contrast to the biography of the Buddha, a central motif of which, apparently deriving from a relatively early date, is his temptation by Mara, the god of death, who attempts to dissuade him forcibly from the attainment of enlightenment. While the Universal History was to introduce entirely new episodes into the biography of Mahavira in which he is attacked by inimical serpents and deities, the emphasis is firmly upon the great hero's forebearance and indifference in the face of difficulty; the issue of his ability to gain enlightenment is never called in question.[18]

A portion of the developed biography which may well be of Buddhist origin, or perhaps derives from some common fund of stories about the trials and tribulations of ascetics, is the episode in which a cowherd asked the meditating Mahavira, who in a previous life had mistreated him, whether he had seen his cows and on not receiving a reply drove blades of grass deep into the cavities of the ascetic's ears, the removal of which caused him great agony. The earliest reference to this occurs in the mnemonic verse commentary on the *Avashyakasutra* (AvNiry 525), that is, a text dating from the common era and representing approximately the third or perhaps fourth stratum of the biography, although the elliptical manner in which the theme is referred to implies its earlier existence. A similar incident is described as having befallen the Buddha in one of the oldest *sutras* of the Pali Canon and it was depicted on several occasions in Buddhist art and literature.[19]

The elaborate descriptions found in the Universal History of this particular period of Mahavira's life do not serve merely as a narrative preamble to the account of his enlightenment. There was at an early date abstracted from the textual delineation of his austerities what became a stereotyped list of twenty-two 'endurances' (*parishaha*), physical and mental afflictions which are regarded as encompassing all the difficulties to which Jain ascetics have always been subjected.[20] Every Jain monk and nun, through the hardships of fasting and mendicancy, partly replicates Mahavira's austerities.

MAHAVIRA'S RELATIONSHIP WITH MAKKHALI GOSALA

The most remarkable episode in the later descriptions of Mahavira's pre-enlightenment career is his period of fellow mendicancy with Makkhali Gosala who is generally regarded as having been the head of an ascetic order known as the Ajivikas, the 'Followers of the Way of Life'. Although there are references to Makkhali Gosala in the Buddhist Pali Canon, the fullest source which describes his life is the fifteenth chapter of the 'Exposition of Explanations' which is undoubtedly an interpolation into the larger text, showing a consistency and internal coherence unusual in that loosely structured work.[21]

According to this Jain story, Makkhali Gosala (the latter part of his name signifies that he was born in a *gosala* or stable) persuaded Mahavira in the second year after his renunciation to accept him as his disciple and the two then wandered together for a period of six years. Makkhali Gosala proved to be an unsatisfactory pupil, both headstrong and jealous of his teacher's ascetic attainments, trying fruitlessly to disprove Mahavira's powers of prescience and on one occasion having to be rescued by the fordmaker from a brahman ascetic whom he had antagonised. The expanded version in the Universal History describes other episodes of this sort.

Eventually, according to the 'Exposition of Explanations', Makkhali Gosala, after gaining a degree of magic power from his association with Mahavira, left his teacher and falsely proclaimed himself to be a spiritual conqueror. Furious at Mahavira's refusal to acknowledge his status, he attacked him with a blast of ascetic heat which he released from his body, but such was the adamantine nature of Mahavira's physique that it rebounded back upon Makkhali Gosala who eventually died after confessing that the fordmaker was a true spiritual teacher. Mahavira subsequently predicted that Gosala would eventually attain enlightenment and spiritual release.

The Ajivikas were undoubtedly a fully fledged ascetic corporation in their own right with a community of lay supporters and there is evidence that they were still in existence in south India as late as the thirteenth century. However, the precise nature of Makkhali Gosala's doctrine remains unclear. The account of it found in early Buddhist literature credits him with propounding an elaborate if obscure cosmology and of arguing that fate or destiny (*niyati*) was the central motive force in the universe against which no human effort could have any effect. All later accounts of Ajivika doctrine echo this description. In the absence of any Ajivika writings, any conclusions must remain speculative, but it seems doubtful whether a doctrine which genuinely advocated the lack of efficacy of individual effort could have formed the basis of a renunciatory path to spiritual liberation. An examination of the 'Sayings of the Seers', which counts Makkhali Gosala among the authoritative teachers, suggests that he was in fact simply arguing for the virtue of imperturbability in the face of the continued change and modification which were to be seen in the world (IBh 11).

The suspicion must be that the Jains and Buddhists deliberately distorted Ajivika doctrine for their own polemical purposes. Furthermore, it may well be that the developed biography of Mahavira could not easily dispense with Makkhali Gosala from its narrative structure because there was a persistent reminiscence of a genuine historical connection between the two, and there remains the possibility that Mahavira and early Jainism were influenced by the Ajivikas. There are, for example, inconsistencies in Jain karma theory which could be explained with reference to what little is known of Ajivika doctrine.[22]

MAHAVIRA'S RELATIONSHIP WITH PARSHVA

In the *Kalpasutra* there occurs the first description of the life of Parshva, the twenty-third fordmaker, extremely short in extent and probably modelled on that of Mahavira. Parshva is stated to have been born in Benares, to have renounced the world and founded a community of ascetics and lay people and, after a life of one hundred years, to have attained liberation on Mount Sammeta in the Ganges basin two hundred and fifty years prior to Mahavira. Circumstantial evidence, including a description of his teachings in the 'Sayings of the Seers' (IBh 31), dictates that he must be viewed as a historical figure. While the *Kalpasutra* does not formally link Parshva to Mahavira, placing his biography after that of the last fordmaker, a passing remark in the second chapter of the *Acaranga*, that is, not in the very earliest stratum of the biography, that Mahavira's parents were followers of Parshva and lay devotees of Jain ascetics (AS 2.15), has led to the general scholarly conclusion that Mahavira must have renounced within Parshva's ascetic lineage.

The question of the relationship between the two fordmakers hinges on the fact that Jain tradition holds that Parshva and his ascetic community followed a Fourfold Restraint (Prakrit *caujjama*). A definition of what this might be does not occur until about the second or third century CE when the *Sthananga*, one of the encyclopaedic texts of the Shvetambara canon, states that the fourfold vow involves abstention from violence, lying, taking what has not been given, and possession (Sth 266). Mahavira, on the other hand, according to tradition preached, or rather stipulated as a mode of ascetic initiation, five Great Vows (Prakrit *mahavvaya*), not seriously dealt with in the earliest stratum of the biography,[23] which consist of Parshva's Fourfold Restraint along with the avoidance of sexual relations. Yet the Buddhist Pali Canon, albeit not an infallible guide to early Jainism, consistently identifies Nigantha Nayaputta, that is Mahavira, with the preaching of a Fourfold Restraint alone.

A well-known passage in one of the older scriptures of the Shvetambara canon (UttS 23) attempts to explain why there should be a difference between the teachings of the two fordmakers. Keshin, a follower of Parshva, and Gautama, a disciple of Mahavira, are depicted as discussing whether the Fourfold Restraint or the five Great Vows represent the true doctrine. Gautama's explanation is that there is a discrepancy in the outward appearance of the doctrine, which is in reality unified, because the moral and intellectual capabilities of the followers of the fordmakers differed. In the time of the first fordmaker there was difficulty in understanding the doctrine which was being preached for the first time, while in the time of the last fordmaker, as the process of moral and spiritual decline began to take hold, people had difficulty in putting it into practice. In the time of the twenty-two intervening fordmakers, however, it was possible to both understand what was entailed by the doctrine and put it into practice. In other words, the first and last fordmakers formulated their teachings in the form of the five Great Vows in which prohibition of sexual relations is specifically prescribed as a result of the inadequacies of their followers, whereas such a ban would have been understood by the followers of the other fordmakers as being incorporated in the prohibition on possession. A further form of differentiation is said to be that the male ascetic followers of Rishabha and Mahavira were naked, while those of Parshva and the other fordmakers wore clothes.

In 1917, Jugalkishor Mukhtar wrote a paper in Hindi in which he argued, employing Digambara as well as Shvetambara sources, that the fordmakers had not all taught the doctrine in the same manner and that the second to the twenty-third had in fact taught one single restraint of 'equanimity' (*samayika*), whereas Rishabha and Mahavira had been obliged because of the defects of the times in which they lived to specify more precisely the five main areas of moral significance.[24] More recently, P.S. Jaini, drawing on research by P.K. Modi, although without any apparent reference to Mukhtar's work, has attempted to explain this problem in rather similar terms. Starting with the premise that Mahavira must have been initiated into the same ascetic vows as his predecessor Parshva, Jaini points to the common occurrence in both Shvetambara and Digambara literature of references to the *samayika* as representing the sole vow which Mahavira took at the time of renunciation and suggests that Parshva's Fourfold Restraint in fact related to the four modalities of the body (mind, body, speech and senses) while Mahavira's Great Vows were simply slightly different articulations of the same basic ethical and sensory equanimity.[25]

Leaving aside the difficulties that the modalities of the body are traditionally regarded as being three[26] and that none of the sources adduced concerning the single *samayika* can be located in the earliest stratum, this explanation has considerable merit. However, the criticism must remain that it derives from an insistence, difficult to sustain on a purely textual basis and deriving in the last resort from traditional Jain belief, that there was some kind of formal link between Parshva and Mahavira.

The 'Exposition of Explanations' is the best source for the relationship between Mahavira and contemporary followers of Parshva. Mahavira is portrayed in one passage as converting Parshvite monks by enunciating cosmological views which he describes as having already been taught by Parshva whom he refers to with respect. However, the conversion of these monks is effected by their abandoning the Fourfold Restraint and taking the five Great Vows: there is no suggestion that the two are parallel expressions of one single vow of renuciation (Bh 5.9).[27] Elsewhere, an elaborate description of the mechanism of rebirth is affirmed to be both based on Parshva's teachings and at the same time a truth which Mahavira had established for himself through his omniscience (Bh 9.3).[28]

It is impossible to be certain about the relationship between Mahavira and Parshva. What can be stressed is that all biographies of Mahavira portray him as, unlike all other fordmakers, renouncing the world alone (AvNiry 224–5) with only the gods in attendance, and there is never any suggestion that he entered an already existing ascetic corporation. A tentative explanation might therefore be that early Jainism coalesced out of an interaction between the cosmological ideas of Parshva and a more rigorous form of orthopraxy advocated by Mahavira, with the relationship between the two teachers eventually being formalised within the evolving fordmaker lineage.[29] It is noteworthy that later Jain writers did not see Parshva's monks as precursors of their own tradition. Starting with the *Sutrakritanga* where the Parshvites are associated with failure to think through the implications of a life based on non-violence (SKS 2.7), Shvetambaras came by medieval times to view them, long after they had disappeared, as pseudo-ascetics who gained their livelihood from the dubious practices of magic and astrology.[30]

Such speculations about the connections between the two fordmakers are a matter of irrelevance for the majority of Jains. For them, Parshva, as the fordmaker who removes obstacles and has the capacity to save, is the greatest focus of devotional activity within the religion and is indeed the most popular of all the fordmakers, as a census of images in Jain temples throughout India would clearly demonstrate. According to a famous story which does not appear in literary form until the eighth century, Parshva in his previous birth saved a snake which was being burnt in a brahman's sacrificial fire. Reborn as the twenty-third fordmaker, Parshva, sunk in meditation, was attacked by the brahman, now in demonic form, with fire and rocks, but the snake, also reborn, this time as a mighty cobra prince called Dharanendra, shielded Parshva by spreading his hoods over his head.[31]

A historian might point to the existence of images of Parshva with a canopy of cobra's hoods which date from just before and after the common era as evidence for Jainism's early assimilation of popular snake cults.[32] More significant is the way that various ethical themes in Jain teaching come together in the figure of this fordmaker: compassion, non-violence, fellowship with all living creatures, rejection of the Vedic sacrifice and awareness of the fact that actions have consequences which bind individuals together.

MAHAVIRA'S ENLIGHTENMENT

Until his enlightenment, Mahavira was imperfect and still subject to the occluding effects of karma. Finally, at the end of the thirteenth year after his renunciation, in a field belonging to a farmer called Samaga which was situated near a small village on a riverbank, he attained supreme and unique (*kevala*) knowledge, the omniscience which Jains regard as defining enlightenment. The earliest accounts of this event, precisely described as to date and location, occur in the second book of the *Acaranga* (AS 2.15.25–6) and, with near identical wording, in the *Kalpasutra*. No doubt partly retrospective and without any true awareness of what Mahavira really did experience in Samaga's field, it nonetheless gives a clear picture of what Jain tradition regards as defining each occurrence of the attainment of enlightenment.

Mahavira is described by the *Kalpasutra* as becoming enlightened after fasting for two and a half days without water, in the full glare of the sun, 'not far from' a tree, in the rigorously ascetic posture of squatting on his haunches. There may here be an implied contrast with the Buddha who is conventionally portrayed as having become enlightened while sitting under a tree in the lotus position, but there can be no question that Jainism regards bodily mortification as a necessary condition for that meditation which effects the achievement of the final goal.[33] Enlightenment in Jainism does not involve union with any sort of Absolute nor, as in Buddhism, is it described in a variety of differing ways in differing sources, but is instead clearly held to be a transcendent knowledge and vision which gives direct and simultaneous access to all forms of reality in the universe in every temporal and spatial dimension.

Mahavira's ability, and indeed willingness, as evinced by the 'Exposition of Explanations', to discuss matters beyond the limits of normal human experience, which contrasts markedly with the Buddha who refused to engage in metaphysical speculation not conducive to salvation, represents for Jains a guarantee of the truth of their religion's message, for it is only the omniscient person who can know and see what lies beneath reality and as a result teach the correct spiritual path.

THE PREACHING ASSEMBLY

With the exception of one or two sects, Jainism can today be said to be an actively proselytising religion only in that it advocates the universal practice of vegetarianism and non-violence. Mahavira, however, like all the fordmakers, was obliged to create a community and so the processes of preaching and conversion form an important part of his post-enlightenment biography.

No specific context for Mahavira's preaching is given in the earliest strata of his biography. It is in the *Aupapatika* (Aup) that there occurs an elaborate description which gives some sense of what early Jain tradition felt the experience of Mahavira's public teaching involved, the prelude to which, written in a form of highly poetical rhythmic prose (*vedha*), was to provide for other Shvetambara scriptures the standard textual example of such occasions. Significantly, the scene of this event is on the outskirts of the city of Campa at the shrine (*caitya*) of a tree-spirit (*yaksha*) called Purnabhadra which is suggestive of an early Jain strategy of incorporation of local cults, already alluded to in passing with reference to Parshva. The sermon itself was, according to this source, delivered in front of a vast throng of ascetics and lay people, including the king and queen of Campa, as well as the gods who descended from heaven to hear the fordmaker preach.

The details of this stylised account eventually became generalised into the literary and artistic idea of the *samavasarana*, a term which approximates to 'place of assembly'. As envisaged in the Universal History,[34] the *samavasarana* is a kind of circular open air preaching arena which the gods repeatedly reconstruct when each fordmaker is about to give his first sermon. It has a pavilion and a sacred tree at its centre which is surrounded by a series of concentric and richly caparisoned balustrades, linked by gateways, within which the audience can take their places. The fordmaker faces east and the gods magically create three replicas of him facing the other directions so that the assembly of humans, gods and animals can hear the sermon perfectly.[35]

Artistic representations of the *samavasarana* abound in Jainism, providing a focus for contemplation of the universality of Mahavira's message. Every Jain temple is regarded as being a replication of the fordmakers' preaching assembly and entry to this sacred space is thus envisioned as bringing about contact with what is implied in the true teachings. Certain stories (e.g. DhMV 84) describe how brahman sacred space was encompassed and surpassed by the discovery of images of fordmakers buried underneath Vedic sacrificial enclosures. While in the Vedic sacrifice the gods assemble to watch and approve human priests slaughtering animals, in the *samavasarana* the gods, humans and animals all gather together in harmony to listen to the preaching of non-violence (AvNiry 562).

MAHAVIRA AS GREAT MAN

Little interest is shown by the early texts in Mahavira's outward appearance. In the *Aupapatika*, however, there occurs an idealised picture, of the sort familiar from images and popular prints today, of a sleek and perfectly formed fordmaker whose body is in full conformity with classical Indian canons of male physique and whose internal organs are in a state of equilibrium. This description of Mahavira also delineates a variety of auspicious marks on his body and the royal paraphernalia which attended his progress (Aup pp.25–37).

The model on which this description is based, used also by the Buddhists, is that of the *cakravartin*, the universal emperor whose birth, like that of all the fordmakers and the Buddha, is presaged by fourteen dreams seen by his mother which indicate future greatness. For Mahavira to have a variety of emblematic marks on his body is a sign that he is a *cakravartin*, albeit not of the temporal world but rather of the spiritual realm, as a story in the Universal History makes clear. An astrologer skilled in interpreting bodily marks sees footprints marked with a wheel in the wet clay on the banks of the Ganges and follows them, thinking that a *cakravartin* has gone by who will reward him for service, and is astonished to come upon the ascetic Mahavira. The god Indra explains the situation to the astrologer:

> You know the outer signs only, but there are inner signs also. The Master's flesh and blood are as white as milk, free from odour. The breath of his lotus mouth resembles the fragrance of a lotus; the Lord's body is healthy, free from dirt and perspiration. For this man is the Lord of the Three Worlds of earth, heaven and the intermediate region, an emperor of religion, benefactor of the world, bestower of safety, Mahavira. The emperors from whom you expect a reward are of little importance.[36]

The wheel which the astrologer saw on Mahavira's footprint is perhaps the best known of all the auspicious marks, usually being taken as symbolic of the totality of a religious path or of temporal power. Its original significance may in fact lie in an old Vedic myth in which Indra rips off a wheel from the chariot of the sun and stamps it into the ground. By carrying a mark reminiscent of this cosmic event, Mahavira is shown to be a 'Great Man' (*mahapurusha*), assimilated to the ancient Vedic gods.[37]

It is likely that the development of the view of Mahavira as Great Man led to, or was accompanied by, a desire to furnish him with a royal genealogy, so that in the Universal History he is presented as related on his mother's side to king Shrenika and his son Kunika, two of the central figures in the rise of the dominance of the state of Magadha in sixth century BCE (the former being known to the Buddhists as Bimbisara) and both of whom Jain sources claim were devotees of the fordmaker. The attempt found in some texts to link Mahavira with the illustrious Ikshvaku dynasty can be regarded as part of the same process.[38]

THE CONVERSION OF THE *GANADHARAS*

According to the Universal History, a remarkable event, peculiar to this *avasarpini*, happened at Mahavira's first *samavasarana* which took place after his attainment of enlightenment. Only the gods assembled to hear him and so, as they cannot enter the spiritual path, the fordmaker chose not to preach and thus, initially, nobody was converted (AvNiry 564). The Digambaras explain Mahavira's unwillingness to preach at this event not as the result of the absence of human beings but, more specifically, because of the lack of disciples (*ganadharas*), whose function is to interpret and mediate to other people the divine sound (*divyadhvani*) which the Digambaras claim emanates from Mahavira's body when he preaches and which would otherwise be unintelligible.[39]

There are no significant references to the *ganadharas* in the early biographical literature. However, the most important of them, Indrabhuti

Gautama, usually called Gautama, occurs frequently in the 'Exposition of Explanations', as an interlocutor with Mahavira and occasionally as a converter of heretics. It is in this text that the fordmaker tells Gautama that the two of them have been bound together in friendship through a series of rebirths and they are now living in their final existence after which they will both be equal in the state of spiritual deliverance (Bh 14.7).[40] Two factors unite Gautama and the other ten *ganadharas*: they were all in origin brahmans, and they were all enlightened by Mahavira and became omniscient *kevalins* (literally 'possessing unique knowledge'), the difference between a fordmaker and a *kevalin* being that the former requires no teacher (AvNiry 657).

It is the Universal History which puts the conversion of the *ganadharas* into a narrative context, starting with a section of the mnemonic verses on *Avashyakasutra* (AvNiry 592–659) which provides the core of the story which was then elaborated by Jinabhadra (sixth century CE) in the 'Debate with the Ganadharas' (GV), a work associated with the literature on the *Avashyakasutra* but which has achieved quasi-autonomous status. According to this text, the learned brahman Gautama summoned the gods to a great sacrifice but instead they flew off to hear Mahavira preaching at his second *samavasarana* nearby. In fury, Gautama confronted Mahavira in debate, as did ten other brahmans in succession, with the fordmaker converting them all by a demonstration, underpinned by his claim to omniscience, that they had failed to understand the true purport of the Veda which in reality accorded with a variety of Jain doctrinal principles, such as the eternal and unique nature of every soul and the physicality of both the human body and karma.

In effect, only three of the *ganadharas* have any real significance: Sudharman, from whom Shvetambara ascetic lineages trace their descent,[41] Jambu, the last individual of this *avasarpini* to achieve enlightenment and Gautama, by far the most important. The biography of Gautama only starts to emerge as an independent entity by the common era and its most famous theme for Jains, his initial failure to win through to enlightenment, is a later episode, found for the first time in the developed Universal History. According to this story, Gautama, wishing to improve his chances of gaining enlightenment, went on pilgrimage to Mount Ashtapada, the site of the final deliverance of the first fordmaker, Rishabha, but although he had the magic power to scale the mountain effortlessly and was also the first person to have been converted by Mahavira, his efforts were to no avail. Mahavira told the disappointed Gautama on his return that it was his affection for his teacher that was holding him back, for any sort of emotion is a hindrance to the attainment of enlightenment. After the death of Mahavira, Gautama was distraught with grief both because of separation from his master and his continuing failure to achieve the goal but, on realising that the person for whom he was mourning was in reality liberated, he shook off the passions and at last became enlightened.

Gautama seems to have become an object of devotion in his own right among the Shvetambaras by the medieval period (he does not appear to be so popular amongst the Digambaras), with the earliest recorded image of him dating from 1277 CE.[42] There is a great deal of ritual literature which invokes Gautama's name in asking for help in the removal of obstacles or the gaining of magic power. Part of his attractiveness lies in the human qualities which he exemplifies. Gautama's portrayal in popular representations today as being chubby and jolly stems from an episode in the Universal History in which, preaching to some gods about the emaciation which fasting brings to monks, he is mocked by his audience because of his corpulence. Gautama's reply that inner qualities are what is significant is a warning to lay people that outer, physical appearance is not necessarily a guide to sanctity.

Another episode in the Universal History in which Gautama through his magic power feeds a group of monks with a tiny amount of food exemplifies his connection with prosperity in the Jain mind, and Jain business houses on the first day of the Jain new year, which occurs in November and coincides with Gautama's enlightenment, will write the name of Mahavira's chief disciple on the opening page of their fresh account books to ensure continuing auspiciousness.

THE EXPANSION OF THE FORDMAKER LINEAGE

The most ancient Jain texts are interested only in Mahavira, although there are sporadic references to ancient ascetics and teachers familiar with the continuity of the doctrine which the commentators regarded as referring to earlier fordmakers (AS 1.4.1.1 and 1.6.3.2). However, the Universal History pivots around the two cardinal figures of Mahavira and the first fordmaker Rishabha (also known as *Adinatha*, 'Lord of the Beginning'), the latter of whom in his role as progenitor of culture simultaneously embodies the realms of ascetic and lay values. Jain scholars today claim that Rishabha's historicity is guaranteed by the fact that his name, which means 'bull', is mentioned frequently in the Rigveda, and they also argue that a well-known Vedic hymn (Rigveda 10.136) which describes a long-haired sage (*keshin muni*) in fact refers to Rishabha who is frequently depicted iconographically with long hair down his back.

It is possible to interpret this differently. The word 'bull' does appear frequently in the Veda but as an epithet of the god Indra, while Rishabha's name and hair suggest a comparison with the Hindu high god Shiva who rides the bull Nandin, has a topknot or mass of matted hair on his head, is both householder and ascetic and whose mythology was taking shape at the same time as the first, skeletal biography of Rishabha was being written in the *Kalpasutra*.[43] Little more can be said about this matter and, instead of speculating about the existence of a teacher for whom no convincing historical evidence can be produced elsewhere, it seems better to view the story of Rishabha as structurally necessary for the Universal History and to conclude that his reality within the framework of Jain mythology and in the minds of his devotees is the more important factor.

The biographies of Rishabha and Parshva, along with that of the twenty-second fordmaker Nemi, given in the *Kalpasutra* are modelled on the life of Mahavira and lack any clear sense of individuality, although that is not to say that more distinctive biographies were not evolving elsewhere (cf. UttS 22 for Nemi). Whenever the full list of twenty-four fordmakers gained currency, the images discovered at Mathura, which are roughly contemporary with this textual material and are the earliest significant artistic evidence available, not unsurprisingly show that the four fordmakers given extended biographies in the *Kalpasutra* were by far the most prominent at the beginning of the common era. Moreover, there is no evidence at this early period, either textual or artistic, for the distinguishing emblems (e.g. Mahavira with lion) with which the fordmakers came to be associated and, with the exception of Parshva and his canopy of cobra hoods, the images can only be identified by their names engraved beneath them.[44]

The genuine existence of a chain of twenty-four teachers is not in itself implausible, but it should be recognised that the first reference, occurring in the *Kalpasutra*, to the twenty intermediate fordmakers, that is those between Rishabha and Nemi, does no more than name them and fit them into a vast timescale, and it may be suggested that this list of teachers was concocted about the second or first centuries BCE, in partial imitation of the lists of Vedic seers found in the Upanishads, as a means of validating the Jain community as a self-aware religious group through extending the origins of the propounders of the doctrine back into the past.[45] By the early common era, the fordmakers as a group had assumed their role as guides through the forest of existence and captains of the ship sailing over the ocean of rebirth (AvNiry 904–17), and the particular emblems by which Jain iconography signals awareness of their separate identities were gradually introduced from the late fourth century CE onwards.[46]

While there is no doubt that Jains have from a devotional point of view been preoccupied through the centuries largely with Mahavira, Parshva, Rishabha and Nemi, it should not be concluded that other fordmakers are mere ciphers. Omitting an account of Malli until the next chapter, one should single out as particularly important Shanti who is regarded as being the personification of peace while there also seem to be some regional and sectarian preferences, as in the case of Ananta who is popular today with southern Digambaras.

EARLY TEACHINGS

No religious tradition should be reduced to a simple set of basic principles nor, however congenial it might be to philological research, should an attempt be made to situate the complete essence of a religion in the words of some putative founder, both because it is usually extremely problematic to make objective decisions about what a founder actually said and because religions are obviously highly complex interlocking patterns of practice and belief which ultimately elude fixed categorisation. So, while we may be confident that the Jain scriptures preserve some reasonably accurate account of the content and style of Mahavira's teachings, the literal words of the fordmaker cannot be retrieved, a fact that is of no concern to Jains since, to them, Mahavira's teachings and the way Jainism, of whatever sect, manifests itself today are one and the same. Nonetheless, Jainism does have a history, even though its doctrinal component became stabilised at a relatively early date, and it is necessary to inspect the ancient texts to see what light they throw on the earliest phase of Jain teachings.

The extensive 'Enunciation of Explanations' provides the fullest textual account of Mahavira's teachings but because of the stereotyped manner in which they are presented, generally taking the form of a response to a question posed by Gautama, this particular scripture is perhaps more significant as an indication of the vast range of metaphysical interests of early Jainism as personified in the figure of the twenty-fourth fordmaker. It is impossible to demonstrate the existence of some original, pristine form of Jainism but the oldest sources available, the first books of the *Acaranga* and *Sutrakritanga*, do suggest what was most significant in Mahavira's teachings and how, as a path to deliverance, they linked up with the broader Indian thought world.

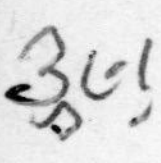

The *Acaranga* makes a firm statement about the central concern of the doctrine: 'All breathing, existing, living, sentient creatures should not be slain, nor treated with violence, nor abused, nor tormented, nor driven away. This is the pure, unchangeable, eternal law which the clever ones, who understand the world, have proclaimed' (AS 1.4.1.1–2; trans. Jacobi).

The world is characterised by ignorance, suffering and pain caused by action (AS 1.1.2.1). True understanding embodies itself in non-violence through an awareness that all living creatures, including oneself, do not wish to suffer in any way (SKS 2.11.9–10). As a broad ethical principle, this is fairly unexceptional and has to be fitted into a further series of conceptions: action, whether done, caused or condoned by oneself, brings about rebirth

(AS 1.1), and the world is in a state of suffering caused by the actions of ignorant people (AS 1.2.1) who do not know that they are surrounded by life-forms which exist in earth, water, air and fire, a true understanding of which can be gained from the teaching of Mahavira. Denial of the nature and reality of this world is tantamount to the denial of the experience of one's own inner self (AS 1.1.3.2).

Jainism, then, appears at the outset as a form of knowledge grounded on the authoritative insights of a teacher which enables a reorientation of one's attitude towards the world of living creatures and, consequently, towards oneself. It is not, however, envisaged as a path which can be followed by householders who of necessity perform all sorts of violent actions and are in thrall to the whirlpool of the senses (AS 1.1.5.1–3), for freedom from action can only arise from the mendicant and ascetic state of homelessness, which engenders the right mental stance with regard to the world and also requires fortitude in the face of difficulties (SKS 1.14).

The Jain monk is portrayed in the earliest texts as being fully responsible for his destiny and in control of his life, and his isolation and independence, which mirror the state of the soul as conceived by Jainism, are conveyed in stark terms:

> Man, it is you who are your only friend. Why do you want a friend other than yourself?
>
> (AS 1.3.3.4)

> When the monk realises that he is alone, that he has no connection with anyone and that no one has any connection with him, in the same way he should realise that his self is also alone.
>
> (AS 1.8.6.1)

The way to deliverance is abstention from action and the overcoming of the passions:

> The person who does not act gets no new karma and so knows what karma is. Through his knowledge, he is a great hero (*mahavira*) so that there is no further birth for him nor does he die.
>
> (SKS 1.15.7)

Deliverance is designated both as non-violence itself (SKS 1.3.4.20 and 1.11.11) and as a state free from corporeality from which 'words return in vain, about which no statements of mundane logic can be made and which the mind cannot fathom' (AS 1.5.6.3). The soul which has attained this state is totally unconditioned:

> It is not long nor small nor round nor triangular nor quadrangular nor circular; it is not black nor blue nor red nor green nor white; neither of

> good nor bad smell; not bitter nor pungent nor astringent nor sweet; neither rough nor soft; neither heavy nor light; neither cold nor hot; neither harsh nor smooth. It does not have a body, is not born again, has no attachment and is without sexual gender. While having knowledge and sentience, there is nonetheless nothing with which it can be compared. Its being is without form, there is no condition of the unconditioned. It is not sound nor form nor smell nor flavour nor touch or anything like that. This is what I say.
>
> (AS 1.5.6.4; trans. by Jacobi, emended)

The early Jain texts describe in nascent form concepts which were to be discussed in greater depth at a later period. They make no attempt to give an account of the process by which the soul is reborn nor the precise nature of its relationship with karma. The cosmography which later Jainism was to elaborate at such length is unknown, although there is acceptance of the existence of hells (SKS 1.5), and the basic ontological categories of classical Jain metaphysics are not found in systematic form at this stage. The householder's life is stigmatised as worthless and dangerous and the stress is very much on the difficult but noble life of the ascetic which, if performed correctly, is regarded as leading automatically to deliverance. However, there is only very sporadic reference to the Great Vows and there is found no attempt to adumbrate a formal code of ethics and monastic practice, beyond the stipulation that the passions must be conquered through withdrawal from the world of the senses and that any sort of violence or possession is bad.[47]

One of the old Jain names for the *Acaranga* is the Veda and indeed many similarities to the early Jain world view can be found both in the brahmanical literature of ritual theory and in the Upanishads. The *Chandogya Upanishad* (3.17.4), for example, describes the appropriate gifts to priests as being austerity, generosity (*dana*), uprightness, non-violence and truthfulness, qualities which, with the exception of generosity which is not discussed seriously in the early Jain texts, are not at variance with Mahavira's ethical prescriptions. The statement of the *Acaranga*,'that which is the soul is that which knows, that which is the knower is the soul, that by which one knows is the soul' (AS 1.5.5.5), is very much redolent of Upanishadic modes of expression, as can also be seen by the Jain source's use of *aya*, the Prakrit equivalent of Sanskrit *atman*, the usual word for self or soul in the Upanishads, rather than *jiva* which was to become the Jain technical term for a life-monad.[48]

What appears as new, however, and what must have served at the outset to distinguish the Jains from other groups of world renouncers, is the integration of previously established categories such as karma, rebirth and deliverance into a particularly rigorous mode of life based on a uniquely sensitive analysis of the nature of the external world and the various types of living creature which surrounded the individual. It is both the self-control and the compassion generated by this understanding, the awareness that all living creatures to a greater or lesser extent experience the same sort of feelings as humans, and the resultant desire for, as the Jains put it, friendship with all creatures, which mark out Jainism as a religion with universal concerns at its very beginning.

2 The Digambaras and the Shvetambaras

It has frequently been observed that the use of the term 'sect', although ubiquitous in the description of religions, is not without problems, for it implies the existence, often awkward to substantiate, of a mainstream, 'official' brand of a religion, from which a group emerges with a claim to purvey a purer variety of the faith. However, the Sanskrit word *sampradaya*, often translated as 'sect', suggests not so much a breaking away as a 'handing down' or 'transmission' of a particular set of doctrines, along with a lineage of teachers associated with this process.

I do not intend to discard the designation 'sect', but it should be borne in mind that Jainism, in common with other Indian religious traditions, places a high value upon correct pupillary descent which provides a channel of communication with ancient truths, manifesting itself most tangibly in correct forms of practice. However, an original, quintessential form of Jainism never really existed, or at least cannot be clearly identified, as an examination of the emergence of the Digambara and Shvetambara sects will show.

To clarify what follows, I will define the main characteristics of the Shvetambara and Digambara sects which served to differentiate them from each other and around which disputes developed, and merely point here to the existence of a large number of other areas of disagreement relating to details of the Universal History, cosmography, iconography and so on.

Shvetambara monks and nuns wear robes (an upper and a lower garment) and they use a bowl into which alms are deposited and from which they eat. They believe that women can attain spiritual deliverance and that the *kevalin*, the fully omniscient being, needs to take food. Digambara monks, on the other hand, wear no clothes at all (this does not apply to Digambara nuns) and do not use an alms bowl, eating their food from their cupped hands. They reject the authority of the Shvetambara scriptures, as well as the possibility of deliverance for women and the omniscient being's need for food.

See p49 2nd pp. "1400 women achieved salvation."! 'Deliverance' = Salvation! How do they (Realists) explain this!

SECTARIAN ORIGINS

According to Shvetambara tradition, eight 'concealments' (*nihnava*) of the doctrine, or heresies, occurred in the six centuries after Mahavira's attainment of enlightenment. The first of these which took place during Mahavira's lifetime supposedly originated with his son-in-law Jamali who rejected a tenet important for an understanding of the functioning of karma and attempted to found his own rival ascetic order. Jamali's heresy, like the six which came after him, stemmed from a clear misinterpretation of a point of doctrine and was easily controverted by the simple expedient of demonstrating its incoherence within the overall context of Jain metaphysics.

However, the eighth heresy, which in textual terms is probably a later addition to what was originally a list of seven, was much more significant in that it turned around a point of correct practice rather than belief, and the scurrilous career of its supposed perpetrator was to be referred to by Shvetambara polemicists for centuries. This story locates the rise of the Digambara sect 609 years after the death of Mahavira in the antics of an apostate Shvetambara called Shivabhuti who is described as having become a monk through self-initiation in a fit of pique after being locked out one night by his mother-in-law. Joining a group of Shvetambara monks, he heard his preceptor preaching about those who had followed the *jinakalpa*, the 'way of the conquerors' practised during Mahavira's lifetime, which involved the abandonment of clothes and had died out with Mahavira's disciple Jambu. Shivabhuti in arrogance thought that he was sufficiently advanced to imitate the fordmakers and so threw off his monastic robes. Expelled by the other monks, he prevailed upon his sister, a nun, to adopt nudity and follow him, with the hapless girl finally being persuaded of her error by a prostitute worried about her effect on trade. It is the self-initiated Shivabhuti and his immediate, illegitimate followers who are, according to the Shvetambaras, the founders of the heretical Digambara sect.

The equivalent Digambara story also highlights the supposed inadequacies of their sectarian rivals' origins, although without singling out any particular individual as a putative founder. In this account, the Shvetambaras are portrayed as the descendants of a backsliding section of what was an originally undifferentiated Jain community which remained in the north of India during a famine (the word *durbhiksha* means literally 'a time when it is difficult to gain alms' and can imply a state of political anarchy), while the rest of their co-religionists migrated to the south under the leadership of the teacher Bhadrabahu, the northern monks subsequently out of weakness taking to the heretical practice of wearing clothes.[1]

Neither of these stories, both of which purport to explain how deviant tendencies arose within Jainism, is genuinely ancient, with the Shvetambara account dating from about the fifth century CE, while the oldest literary version of the Digambara story is as late as the tenth century CE. They are in themselves of little historical worth, merely serving as indices of sectarian bitterness, although it should be noted in passing, as the Digambara story of the migration might suggest, that the Shvetambaras have had no significant long-term presence in the south. The situation as seen from the earliest evidence available is rather more complex.

An examination of early Shvetambara literature would seem to leave little room for doubt that Mahavira and his male followers were naked monks. The *Uttaradhyayana* points to the fact that nudity distinguished Mahavira's monks from those of Parshva (UttS 23) while the *Acaranga* describes lack of clothes as being in full conformity with Jain doctrine (AS 1.6.2.3). Another passage in the *Acaranga* refers to the sufferings of the naked monk and also to the fact that he does not need to beg for and repair clothes (AS 1.6.3.1–2).

Yet elsewhere in the *Acaranga* the monk is advised only to restrict himself in the wearing of clothes through not possessing too many garments and to be either very lightly clad or competely naked during summer as a form of penance (AS 1.8.4–5). Confirmation that there gradually arose options about the wearing of clothes by monks is provided by the *Sthananga*, an encyclopaedic text important for its delineation of the parameters of Jain teachings in the early common era, which states that it may be permissible for a monk to wear clothes for reasons of embarrassment, the disgust he might cause to others or his inability to endure the afflictions which occur in the course of the monastic life (Sth 171).[2] A growing sense of the pervasive influence of decline setting in at the beginning of the common era as the distance from the time of the last fordmaker grew ever longer no doubt suggested to those ascetics who had chosen to wear robes that there was no need to purge their scriptures of any references to naked monks and instead they devised two textual categories of asceticism, ubiquitous in the scriptural commentaries, to allow for the differences in early descriptions of monastic dress: the *jinakalpa*, the 'way of the *jinas*', the radical path of nakedness and often solitary asceticism which died out soon after Mahavira and which the legendary Shivabhuti mistakenly tried to revive, and the *sthavirakalpa*, the 'way of the elders', more suited to a period of decline, which allowed for the wearing of robes by monks and did not stress the deliberate seeking of difficulties and physical mortification through nakedness.

The archaeological and inscriptional evidence suggests that there was a gradual movement among Jain monks towards a differentiation based on apparel, or the lack of it, rather than any abrupt doctrinal split. All the earliest fordmaker images from Mathura are naked and it is not until the fifth century CE that there is found an image of Rishabha wearing a lower garment, with the practice of images being portrayed as clothed only becoming prevalent among Shvetambaras several centuries later. Moreover, an inscription commemorating a land grant to Jain sects by a late fifth century king from south India refers to the Shvetambaras but uses the old expression 'bondless' (*nirgrantha*) to refer to naked monks, evidence that even the name Digambara took some time to gain currency.[3]

An indication of what must have been an original fluidity with regard to sectarian affiliation can be seen in the existence of a sect known as the Yapaniyas, a name which may possibly mean 'following a life of restraint'. The tenth century Digambara Harishena traced their origin to those monks who had stayed in the north during the supposed famine referred to above and had been prevailed upon by their lay followers to cover their private parts with a strip of cloth (*ardhaphalaka*) while begging for alms (BKK 131 vv.54–8). That this so-called *ardhaphalaka* sect did genuinely exist can be seen from Mathura where images of monks with strips of cloth in their hands have been found.[4] The Yapaniyas, the descendants of the *ardhaphalakas* and inscriptional references to whom start to appear from the early medieval period, occupied an interstitial position between the Shvetambaras and Digambaras, with the latter viewing them as heretics. Digambara in outward appearance, the Yapaniyas seem to have compromised over the wearing of clothes when in contact with their lay supporters. Moreover, they also accepted the authority of the Shvetambara scriptures and the only full length writings by a Yapaniya writer which have survived defend the Shvetambara views about deliverance for women and the eating of food by the *kevalin*.[5] No trace of them is found after the fourteenth century.

The catalyst for the final hardening of boundaries between the Shvetambaras and the Digambaras was most likely the Council of Valabhi which took place in either 453 or 466 CE, depending on the reckoning. This was not a council in the Christian sense in which matters of doctrine were debated but rather an attempt to codify a scriptural tradition which Jainism had always seen as imperilled since Mahavira's day. The important point about this event is that it was exclusively Shvetambara, with no naked monks in attendance and indeed no record of it in any Digambara source. The Council of Valabhi bears witness to what had become a broad geographical distribution in the Jain community, with naked ascetics predominating in the south and the main sphere of influence of the white-robed Shvetambaras being in the west. As Jainism moved out of its original heartland in the east and spread throughout India, lines of communication between groups of ascetics could only have been stretched enormously, with a concomitant lack of any central authority about matters of monastic practice which in certain respects, such as the question of dress, must have originally been comparatively flexible. It was the stabilisation of an old scriptural tradition by one section of the community which finally confirmed the existence of fully self-conscious Shvetambara and Digambara sects, the latter rejecting the authority of the editorial process which had given rise to a Shvetambara canon (see Chapter 3).

SECTARIAN ATTITUDES

Doctrinally, there were no great differences between the two sects with, to a large extent, the Digambaras, in the form of figures such as Akalanka (eighth century), taking the lead in sharpening Jainism's logical and epistemological tools with a view to controverting its Buddhist and Hindu intellectual opponents. However, the fact that outward appearance was regarded as an index of proper understanding of the doctrine caused continuing controversy between the Shvetambaras and the Digambaras.

Aparajita's (eighth century) defence of ascetic nakedness gives the standard Digambara view which would relegate Shvetambara monks and nuns to the status of lay people (comm. on BhA 423). Nudity, claims Aparajita, is not just a matter of giving up wearing clothes: in actuality it must entail the abandonment of all possessions and the overcoming of the passions which are brought about by the desire to possess or, alternatively, by the fear that what one does possess might be taken away. Furthermore, the naked monk is no longer subject to pride or shame which are appropriate only to the social world and in his independence, which is like that of a bird, he manifests an inner, spiritual purity. Nudity also means that the monk does not infringe the cardinal vow of non-violence because dirty clothes would inevitably have attracted insects and microscopic creatures who might be crushed. In short, the naked monk imitates the fordmaker.

The Shvetambaras, having established to their satisfaction the impossibility in the age of decline of leading the identical mode of life followed by Mahavira, were unimpressed with such arguments. For the eleventh century canonical commentator Abhayadeva Suri, all monks are metaphorically naked if they are pure in spirit, while to be lacking clothes and other possessions is pointless if one is still afflicted by delusion. Clothes enhance the religious life, just as food keeps the body going. They protect from cold which might otherwise lead to the lighting of a fire, forbidden to Jain ascetics, and prevent coming into contact with life-forms in grass and the branches of trees (comm. on Sth 694).[6]

Another later Shvetambara writer, Yashovijaya (seventeenth century) attempted to refute the Digambara insistence that the true ascetic should not use an alms bowl. If owning a bowl implied being in thrall to material possessions, then by the same token the human body might be considered an alms bowl and a possession also. In reality, Yashovijaya claims, it is only infatuation which turns something into a spiritual tie, for nothing is in itself either a bond or a non-bond. Indeed, not to use an alms bowl could lead to the worst possible eventuality, destruction of life-forms, for if the monk were to eat using only his hands as a receptacle, then particles of food would drop down between the gaps in his fingers and attract insects which would then be trodden upon.[7]

Such arguments might strike us now as trivial, but that would be to underrate the importance to sects which claimed to be following a true spiritual path of correct behaviour as a badge of allegiance. In the hagiography of the legendary Shvetambara teacher Jiva found in Prabhacandra's (thirteenth century) 'Deeds of the Exalters of the Doctrine', there is a good example of what is involved in correct behaviour in a Jain context (PC 7). Jiva was originally a Shvetambara who had converted to Digambara Jainism and had become an illustrious teacher with great magic powers. His mother, upset at his leaving the Shvetambara fold, realised that as far as the fordmakers, the ethical and metaphysical prescriptions of the religion were concerned, there were no disagreements between the two sects but that, nonetheless, there was a substantial difference with regard to behaviour (PC 7.27). She compelled her son to convert back to Shvetambara monasticism by catching him out in an *adhakarmika* fault, that is, one of a category of offences relating to the consumption of food, for Jiva erroneously ate alms which had been specially prepared for him rather than offered at random.[8]

This story would seem to involve a simple matter of behaviour but the significant point about orthopraxy for Jainism is that to act improperly, whether in regard to food or, in sectarian terms, ascetic dress, betrays ignorance about the true workings of the world and inability to exercise appropriate caution in one's attitude towards it. Orthopraxy is grounded upon correct understanding, and knowledge and practice are regarded as closely interlinked.

SOCIAL INTERACTION

The initial evidence for interaction between the two sects, generally medieval Shvetambara in origin, gives evidence of real bitterness between their respective members, a good example of which can be seen in the accounts of the famous debate between the Shvetambara Vadideva and the Digambara Kumudacandra which took place in Patan in 1125 at the court of the Caulukya ruler of Gujarat, Jayasimha Siddharaja. This was an event which clearly caught the imagination of the Shvetambara community, judging by the frequency of its depiction on manuscript covers, and there exist two extended accounts of it, as well as a dramatised version.[9]

There can be little doubt that Kumudacandra's personality and behaviour, such as his supposed attempt to cheat in the debate and ignorance of Jain doctrine and even Sanskrit grammar, were viciously travestied by the

Shvetambara writers in the name of sectarian polemic but, in the absence of any Digambara account of the debate, it must be accepted that he succumbed to the greater cogency of Vadideva's argument. Kumudacandra was a southerner from Karnataka and, as Siddharaja's wife also came from this region, it is more than likely that there was also some sort of political issue involving royal sponsorship of sects at stake. Certainly, the aim of the hagiographical accounts of Vadideva's victory was to confirm the establishment of Shvetambara doctrine and practice as the 'official' Jainism of Gujarat, and in numerical terms this very much remains the situation today, apart from the recent attempted revival of a brand of Digambara Jainism by the Kanji Svami Panth (see Chapter 9).

The relationship between the Digambaras and the Shvetambaras should not always be viewed in purely adversarial terms. There are, for example, interesting medieval references to members of both sects going on large-scale pilgrimages together, and in areas where both Jain groups are found in number, each community can generally live comfortably enough together, although perhaps without engaging in any serious social or religious interaction.[10] However, if one longstanding source of sectarian animosity were to be singled out, it would be disputes over the ownership of shrines and holy places. The prototype of this type of conflict was the attempt by the Shvetambaras to dislodge the Digambaras from Mount Girnar in Gujarat, a site sacred to the fordmaker Nemi, the main events of whose life supposedly took place there, and also the legendary scene of the redaction of one of the most revered Digambara scriptures. Medieval Shvetambara sources describe the victory in debate over the Digambaras by the teacher Bappabhatti (*c.* eighth century CE) which led to the final establishment of Girnar as a Shvetambara holy spot, ritually signalled by 'clothing' the images of the naked fordmakers with jewellery and auspicious marks signifying robes, thus rendering them unsuitable to be worshipped by Digambaras.

The historicity of Bappabhatti's involvement and of the debate itself is doubtful and, as there is no significant inscriptional evidence to link him to Girnar,[11] it is most likely that the medieval hagiographies which describe this event reflect a period when the Shvetambaras were starting to establish themselves definitively as the dominant sect in Gujarat. The Digambaras for their part still regard Mount Girnar as one of their major holy places on the basis of long association and they point to their own tradition of a fourteenth century teacher defeating the Shvetambaras at the site by persuading an image of the goddess Sarasvati to speak out in favour of Digambara ownership. However, the paucity of Digambaras in Gujarat and the de facto association of Mount Girnar with the Shvetambara community ensures that it is no longer a focus of serious sectarian conflict.[12]

In the last two hundred years or so, the shifting demography of the Jain population for reasons of economic opportunity has seen the migration of Shvetambara traders and businessmen from Gujarat and the Marwar region of Rajasthan to other parts of India and this has often brought about disputes over holy places and the modes of worship to be followed there, particularly in areas such as the boundary of the states of Maharashtra and Karnataka where the indigenous Digambara community is largely rural and less well off. Sometimes the passions engendered spill over and have ramifications beyond purely Jain concerns, as in the well-publicised case of Bahubali Hill, a pilgrimage spot of local significance near the town of Kolhapur in south Maharashtra. There, what seems to have been the original permission granted in 1869 by the Digambaras, the owners of the hill, to the Shvetambaras to erect a temple of their own at Bahubali gradually developed through friendly competition between the two sects in the building and renovating of temples to a situation in the early 1980s where the quarrel over ownership of the site involved politicians of all hues, both regional and national, and was articulated in terms of patriotism and communalism against a background of violence, peace marches and fasts conducted by Digambara monks.[13]

Less well publicised, although in its own way equally intense, is a dispute in another part of Maharashtra over the ownership of the shrine at Sirpur whose image is known as 'Floating Parshva' (*Antariksha Parshva*) because it is supposed to have appeared in the air to its legendary discoverer when he was wandering in a forest unable to find a Jain temple.[14] Its fame was great in the middle ages and the Shvetambara Jinaprabha Suri (1261–1333) refers to it in his guide to pilgrimage places (VTK 58), while another source of about the same time claims that the image was consecrated by the Shvetambara teacher Abhayadeva the Filthy, which suggests some sort of early Shvetambara connection with the site, even if the influence of the sect in that region was to wane until this century.[15]

An undated but recent publication, emanating from the Digambara community at Sirpur and called 'A Look at the Truth' (*Satyadarshan*), describes in loving detail the litigation relating to the shrine which has taken place over the last seventy-five years and also contains photographs of some of the Digambara worshippers who, it is claimed, have been physically assaulted there. In addition, it gives some account of the history behind the dispute. Of great importance for the Digambaras is the testimony of a Shvetambara monk called Shilavijaya who toured south India in the seventeenth century (nothing is said of earlier Shvetambaras such as Jinaprabha). In his description of the various holy spots he visited, Shilavijaya refers to the shrine and the two main temples at Sirpur as at that time being Digambara and, for good measure, he represents the whole of that region up to the sea as also being Digambara.[16]

After describing the Digambara teachers responsible for various renovations of the shrine, 'A Look at the Truth' gives an interpretation of why the dispute came about:

> when the Shvetambaras first came to Maharashtra, they had no holy place of their own, so they had to adopt Floating Parshva. The Digambara community had the graciousness to allow their Shvetambara brothers to perform worship there. However, this graciousness has had a bitter result in the form of a breach of faith.[17]

Of the entire Shvetambara community in the vicinity of Sirpur, we are told, not one originated from Maharashtra, all having come from Gujarat and Marwar about a century and a half ago but, despite a great deal of provocation by the Shvetambaras, the Digambaras refrained from retaliating because that was not the Digambara nature. 'A Look at the Truth' shows how the dispute has been used by the Digambaras of Sirpur not just to establish the legitimacy of their claim to the site but also to present themselves both as patriotic Maharashtrians who are victims of 'foreign' aggressors and as followers of a purer Jainism through their refusal to be drawn into violence. The whole question can thus be viewed in both regional and sectarian terms.

It has been estimated that there are at present in India some 134 disputes over the ownership of Jain holy places,[18] and there can be no doubt that many Digambaras in the south are alarmed by what they perceive as their inferiority, both in numbers and financial resources, in the face of Shvetambara encroachment. Many prominent Jains of both sects, while often involved personally in these disputes, are embarrassed by them, particularly when they lead to violence, and would wish to underplay their significance. Certainly, all Jains have in common certain basic traditions and ideals which override sectarian differences and bind them together as a distinctive community within Indian society, and there has recently been a move in certain prominent Jain circles to create an ecumenical atmosphere among the various sects. Yet Shvetambara and Digambara ascetics, with a few exceptions, remain ignorant of or uninterested in each other and the general good will which exists between lay members of each sect can all too easily be dissipated by emotions such as fear and envy and the pull of regional loyalties from which the Jains are no more immune than any other section of Indian society. Nonetheless, there can also be no doubt that the existence of sects with their own traditions and interests lends a colour and complexity to any overall view of Jain culture.

CAN WOMEN ATTAIN DELIVERANCE?

Amongst the various areas of dispute between the Shvetambaras and Digambaras, two were treated at some length over the centuries. The debate

over whether the *kevalin*, the enlightened and omniscient person, needed to take food produced two different and incontrovertible pictures of this figure. For the Digambaras, he is more than merely human and in his lack of need for nourishment is perhaps a reflex of the naked ascetic who through restricted intake of food by means of his cupped hands alone represents an 'otherness' which sets him apart from the rest of the world. For the Shvetambaras, however, the *kevalin* is unquestionably a human of a highly developed type, but also one who has many of the characteristics, such as intake of food, of spiritually undeveloped people, just as the Shvetambara ascetic with his alms bowl approximates to worldly habits of eating.[19]

It is, however, the Jain sectarian dispute over the spiritual status of women which will strike a contemporary audience as being of particular interest. Female religiosity in south Asian religions is a subject which up to comparatively recently has been inadequately treated. However, Jainism is unusual in this respect in that a study of the religion has been written from the perspective of nuns [20] and, as further ethnographic data about the role of women, both lay and ascetic, starts to appear, there should be a partial readjustment away from the standard exclusively male-oriented perception of Jain society. It is, after all, obvious enough that women are profoundly implicated in the reproduction figure of the Jain community at all levels through the maintenance of forms of religious practice and through the socialisation of children into Jain civilisation.

The *Kalpasutra* is quite clear that on Mahavira's death the *tirtha* which he had founded contained a body of female ascetics two and a half times as large as the number of male ascetics (36,000/14,000) and a lay community containing twice as many laywomen as laymen (318,000/159,000), while it is also stated that during the fordmaker's lifetime 1,400 women as opposed to 700 men achieved salvation.[21] The dynamic involved in the formation of this community, with its suspiciously symmetrical numbers, is unclear and no conclusions can be drawn as to why there should have been a preponderance of women at the outset. However, spiritually heroic Jain women are a frequent theme in the Universal History and in the literature of pious exemplification, and it is particularly noteworthy that according to the Shvetambaras it is a woman, Marudevi, the mother of Rishabha, who has the distinction of being the first person of this world age to achieve liberation.

More strikingly still, the Shvetambaras claim that the nineteenth fordmaker, Malli, was a woman who, in a previous birth as a king, had in an excess of spiritual zeal reneged on an agreement about the practice of austerities made with some fellow kings. Having secretly exceeded the limit set and thus generated a degree of negative karma by this act of 'deception', he was reborn as a fordmaker with a woman's body. However, only one image of Malli with breasts and a long braid of hair, dating from about the ninth century CE, has so far been found and no Shvetambara temple depicts this fordmaker as a woman. The Digambaras reject the possibility of a female fordmaker and worship Malli as the male Mallinatha.[22]

The early Shvetambara literature shows no sign that the possibility of female liberation was in any way controversial and the question must have arisen as a consequence of the Digambara insistence, confirmed from about the fifth century CE or so as a result of the final hardening of sectarian boundaries, that ascetic nudity was an essential component of the path to liberation. There can be some confidence about this since important early Digambara texts, which can be located in about the third or fourth centuries CE, state that both monks and nuns can achieve deliverance.[23]

The appearance of a fully worked out defence of this position in the eighth century suggests that female religiosity had been a topic of debate for some time previously. The basic premise for Digambaras and Shvetambaras alike is that female nudity is impossible for social reasons and, if one Shvetambara writer does refer to the existence of naked female ascetics (*yogini*) amongst Hindus to suggest that this is not necessarily a cultural universal,[24] all the sectarian polemicists accept that clothes are essential to enable women to function in any type of life, ascetic or otherwise.

Prabhacandra, who gives the fullest Digambara discussion available (NKC pp.865–70), clearly regards this as the cornerstone of the rejection of female enlightenment. If, he says, it is a fact that a woman wandering around naked would inevitably be raped, then that must surely prove the point about the unsuitability of women for the ascetic life, while conversely, and somewhat disingenuously, he argues that naked Digambara monks are never the object of lascivious propositions by women. There cannot possibly be two different ascetic paths, nakedness and the wearing of clothes, which would bring about one result, enlightenment. Women, in other words, cannot be Jains in the same way as men.

I will not rehearse Prabhacandra's argument in full but two further points from it will indicate the tenor of the general Digambara attitude. Firstly, Prabhacandra denies the possibility of any genuine intensity of action, whether for good or bad, on the part of women. This does imply a partially positive view of women in that, owing to their inability to perform evil to the same extent as men, they can never be reborn in the seventh and bottommost hell of the Jain universe. However, the obvious corollary of this is that women can never follow the prescriptions of the Jain religion with the requisite degree of seriousness to bring about enlightenment. To reach the goal, they have to be reborn as males. Indeed, for a soul to be reborn in female form in the first place suggests some evil performed in the past.

Secondly, Prabhacandra regards the values of the transient, social world, in which women are deemed to be inferior to men through their innate propensity to delusion and immorality, as persisting in the world of ascetic renunciation and women's inability to exercise any authority in the former situation must therefore preclude their ability to do so in the latter. Thus, for the Digambaras, the realities of Indian society are transposed to a realm which has supposedly transcended them. The argument of a later Digambara that women by their very physiology generate and destroy life-forms within their sexual organs and other orifices of their body, thus repeatedly infringing non-violence, was not a significant component of the debate, although the statement of Todarmal (eighteenth century) that neither people of low social status nor women can attain enlightenment suggests that Indian notions of physical impurity, whether through caste or menstruation, served to inform Digambara ideas on this subject.[25]

A wide range of Shvetambara writers attacked this position and we may refer to Shakatayana as representative of the general Yapaniya-Shvetambara approach (SNP). Shakatayana places inevitable weight on the fact that the scriptures say nothing against the possibility of female enlightenment and that there are in fact frequent references both in the scriptures and in the Universal History to women renouncing and advancing to the end of the spiritual path. Furthermore, there can be no logical reason to deny the possibility of this. Shakatayana accepts that women cannot fall to the lowest hell but argues that this need have no bearing on their ability to rise to the pure, exalted state at the top of the universe where Jainism locates the world of liberated souls. Gender has no relevance for the religious life, just as it has none for liberated souls, and the only females who are specifically forbidden from becoming nuns are those who are pregnant (SNP 9). As for nudity, that cannot play any serious role in the development of the religious life, for otherwise deliverance could be attained simply by removing one's clothes. Wearing robes is merely an adjunct to spirituality like other types of ascetic behaviour such as inspecting the alms bowl or place where one is about to sit. Shakatayana argues that there are many ways to spiritual deliverance, just as there are many cures for a disease, and the Digambara argument that nudity must be the only way to gain it is invalid. As Jain legend which has many references to pious women of high morals demonstrates, females are no more prone to delusion and immorality than men so that, in short, women can be stated to be equal members of humanity (*manushyagati*) with men and thus capable of enlightenment.

This generous judgement about female spiritual potential has to be seen against the background of misogyny which runs through Jain literature, both Shvetambara and Digambara. Amidst the welter of denunciation of women and their evil desire to lure men away from the path, there seems to be only one significant scriptural warning to women of the dangers of male sexuality, the admittedly famous story of the nun Rajimati, previously the wife-to-be of the fordmaker Nemi, who dissuaded his brother, a monk, from his attempted seduction of her and compelled him to return to his vows (UttS 22). Much more indicative of what has remained a patriarchal attitude within the religion are the standard regulation in Shvetambara monastic law that a nun, no matter how long she has been in the order, must pay homage to even a newly initiated monk[26] and the attempt by the great medieval Shvetambara teacher Jinadatta Suri to ban women from worshipping the main fordmaker image in temples on the grounds of their possible polluting influence.[27]

Although Digambara texts say little about nuns, there exist today some sixty to seventy, sometimes of great learning and occasionally charged with the teaching of monks, but who accept that because of their female bodies and wearing of clothes their ability to advance seriously towards enlightenment is contingent on being reborn as a man.[28] Similarly, while there are Shvetambara nuns of some charisma whose preaching can attract large audiences, there is nonetheless a general feeling among the laity that interaction with a monk is more meritorious than with a nun.[29] Observation suggests that the life of nuns is for practical reasons often more difficult than that of monks and, if their lot has undoubtedly changed since the nineteenth century when their role was often little more than that of performers of menial tasks, it is significant that, of a recent survey of one hundred nuns of the Shvetambara Terapanthi sect, over seventy wanted some sort of change in their circumstances.[30]

3 Scriptures

In recent years there has been a welcome attempt on the part of historians of religion to dissociate sacred texts from the concept of 'scripture' in its literal sense, so common in conventional accounts of the great west Asian monotheistic traditions, of 'written word' enshrined in some kind of totally fixed canon and, instead, attention is increasingly being drawn to the way scripture can derive its meaning for believers from an oral or ritual context.[1] Indianists have long been familiar with the fact that the Veda, which is on one obvious level a body of textual material whose literal meaning can after philological labour be largely understood, takes its significance for Hindus through being viewed as something akin to a concept embodying the totality of Hindu values and that it communicates its real efficacy as scripture in the form of sound through being recited in ritual circumstances, instead of simply being read and understood in terms of specific meaning. Jain scripture is similar in certain respects and, rather than regarding it as little more than a repository of information from which can be built up a scholarly picture of early Jain teachings, we should bear in mind that the sacred writings of their religion have an importance for Jains which far outweighs the fact that the majority of them neither wish nor, as far as the original language is concerned, have the ability to read them.

The nearest equivalent to 'scripture' in Jainism is the Sanskrit word *agama*, a pan-Indián designation which signifies the 'coming' of a body of doctrine by means of transmission through a lineage of authoritative teachers. When each fordmaker preaches for the first time, every one of his disciples interprets his utterances, which for the Shvetambaras are enunciated in the sacred language Ardhamagadhi and for the Digambaras sound like a great echoing drum, and structures them, still orally, into his own recension of the 'twelve-limbed basket of the disciples' (*duvalasangaganipidaga*).[2] As a well-known statement has it, 'the Worthy One (*araha*) enunciates the meaning, then the disciples form the sacred text (*sutta*), and then the sacred text proceeds for the good of the doctrine' (AvNiry 92). Other sources state that Mahavira merely uttered the basic metaphysical truths of origin, continuity and disappearance as lying at the root of experience which the disciples then expanded into the *agama*.[3] For Jains, their scriptures represent the literal words of Mahavira and the other fordmakers only to the extent that the *agama* is a series of beginningless, endless and fixed truths, a tradition without any origin, human or divine, which in this world age has been channelled through Sudharman, the last of Mahavira's disciples to survive.

While this alone might be sufficient to demonstrate that there is no immediate overlap between the Jain *agama* and western ideas of a written scriptural corpus, the question is further complicated by the fact that the Digambaras claim, as part of their strategy of differentiation from the Shvetambaras, that the Jain scriptural tradition has been lost and so *agama* has become for them at best a metaphorical designation.[4] Moreover, though the main function of *agama* is to help the unenlightened along the path to spiritual deliverance through the access it gives to the inner workings of reality which can be known directly only by the omniscient ones, there exists a degree of uncertainty about the situation of scripture within this same spiritual path. So, for the early Digambara teacher Kundakunda, in words which must date from before the final acceptance by the Digambaras of the loss of the scriptural tradition, *agama* and the knowledge it contains are regarded as providing the impetus to the change of behaviour which leads to entry onto the path:

> The ascetic monk who is deficient in *agama* does not know his self. How can the monk who does not understand metaphysical entities destroy karma?
>
> Sacred texts (*sutta*) state that the person whose faith is not accompanied by *agama* has no restraint. How can the person without restraint be an ascetic?
>
> (PS 3.33 and 36)

However, an influential Shvetambara text also asserts that the knowledge derived from the scriptures will count for nothing if it is not accompanied by the practice of austerities, just as a boat will not cross the ocean without wind (AvNiry 95–6): in other words, study of the scriptures is not recommended to those who have not already entered the path.

As these two examples suggest, there is no truly unitary attitude towards scriptural texts within Jainism. However, there has been a general tendency throughout the religion's history to regard the study of them by the unqualified, whether lay or ascetic, as a dangerous and unwarranted activity. Some Shvetambara sects have placed specific restrictions upon the reading of sacred texts by lay people, either banning it completely or requiring the overseeing presence of a monk while, in the sixteenth century, the Shvetambara polemicist Dharmasagara identified the main cause of the emergence of heretical Jain sects as being the appeal on the part of their founding teachers to the evidence of scriptural texts alone as opposed to reliance upon the validation provided by a fully authenticated teacher lineage.[5]

In fact, the Jain view of what constitutes *agama* is at the same time precise and vague in that the term can be taken as denoting not just a canonical corpus of scriptural texts, along with the authority perceived as emanating from it and governing the totality of traditional Jain religious practice but, in addition, any text of a degree of antiquity which is accepted as having being written by an illustrious teacher. The following recent example is indicative of this latter point.

Shortly after Indian independence, the Committee into Religious and Charitable Endowments in the Province of Bombay initiated an inquiry into the use of property held by religious groups with a view to altering legislation so that trust funds and properties, such as hospitals, belonging to the members of one community could be made accessible to the members of another. This proposal, along with the Bombay State Temple Entry Bill which provided for the entry of untouchables into both Jain and Hindu temples, was historically significant in that it led to a mobilisation of Jain opinion and brought to the fore the Jain community's sense of its own identity. For our purposes, what is interesting about this controversy is that the textual references produced by the Shvetambara community in response to the Committee's request for scriptural evidence as to the inalienability of Jain temple funds are not taken from the early sacred writings, which do not concern themselves with such matters anyway, but in the main from commentaries and treatises dating from well into the medieval period, with one source stemming from as recently as the eighteenth century. Scripture here is perceived as being any text of reasonable or indeterminate age which is located within the tradition and supports the view of the person citing it.[6]

Scripture, then, is a concept which has to be treated carefully when studying Jainism and moreover, as I will show later in this chapter, the notion of a totally fixed canon of sacred writings is not so compelling as it might be in other traditions. However, before considering the nature and scope of Jain scriptures, I will give two examples of how sacred texts mediate themselves to a Jain audience.

SCRIPTURE AS SACRED OBJECT: THE MANUSCRIPTS AT MUDBIDRI

The 'Scripture of Six Parts' (*Shatkhandagama*) is the oldest Digambara sacred text. According to tradition, it is based on the oral teaching of a monk called Dharasena (approximately mid-second century CE) who, in alarm at the gradual dwindling away of scriptural knowledge, summoned two other monks, Pushpadanta and Bhutabali, to the Cave of the Moon, his retreat on Mount Girnar in Gujarat, and communicated what he remembered out of the originally vast extent of the sacred writings which they were afterwards to turn into the 'Scripture of Six Parts'.

Palm leaf manuscript copies of this long work, including an important eighth century commentary by Virasena, along with another old text, the 'Treatise on the Passions' (*Kasayapahuda*), supposedly composed not long after the 'Scripture in Six Parts' and also accompanied by a commentary, were at some time deposited in the Digambara holy place of Mudbidri, a small town in the south of Karnataka, where a temple was built to house them. Although the traditional source of Mudbidri's fame originally lay in the miraculous discovery there of an image of Parshva, its rise to prominence as a Digambara pilgrimage place and the lavish building projects undertaken there by south Indian kings from the thirteenth century were in part the result of possession of these manuscripts.

The great Digambara scholar Todarmal, writing in the eighteenth century far away to the north in Jaipur, was aware of the existence of the manuscripts, stating that they were purely for looking at reverentially (*darshan*) since owing to the effects of the corrupt world age nobody was capable of understanding them.[7] Towards the end of the nineteenth century, the manuscripts had become very worn and fragile, but when a merchant on pilgrimage to Mudbidri pointed this out to the clerical authorities there, he was told that the function of the manuscripts was to serve solely as objects of worship. However, it transpired that there was a local scholar who was capable of reading the old script in which the manuscripts had been written and the merchant decided to perform the meritorious action of getting the manuscripts transcribed with a view to their publication and wider dissemination. Money was raised from interested members of the Digambara community to pay for the copying into modern Kannada script and the *nagari* script of north India, the whole process being carried out between 1896 and 1922.

Despite this, the clerical authorities at Mudbidri stubbornly refused to allow publication, claiming, no doubt in full awareness that the tradition of Digambara monastic learning had died out some considerable time in the past, that such scriptures should be studied by monks alone, and it was only after the smuggling out of a copy and the fait accompli of the appearance in print of the early portions of the text under the editorship of the prominent Digambara academics, Hiralal Jain and A.N. Upadhye, that they relented and finally granted permission both for publication of the remainder of the text and for direct consultation of the original manuscripts by scholars.

There is no mystery about the contents of the Mudbidri manuscripts, although before their decipherment there was no clear idea about what they might represent. The 'Scripture of Six Parts' and the 'Treatise on the Passions' proved to be lengthy and highly technical accounts in Prakrit of the nature of the soul and its connection with karma which, while undoubtedly containing old material dating from about the beginning of the common era, are nonetheless hardly of immemorial antiquity as had been thought. But for Digambara Jains in general, who have little interest in philological enquiry, what the manuscripts represent is of more importance than what they actually say. As tangible evidence of an ancient and glorious past, they are regarded as constituting a direct link with the scholar-monks who created the Digambara tradition.

If the principle of lay people and others being able to study these scriptures, initially challenged out of fear of possible pollution, was to win the day since the published edition was provided with a Hindi translation, the Mudbidri manuscripts have retained their sanctity as sacred objects, and scripture in this particular Jain context gains a dimension of meaning from the associations and attitudes of reverence which it evokes in the minds of the Digambara Jain community. This is most clearly recognisable in the Digambara festival of *Shruta Pancami*, 'Scripture Fifth' (referring to the day of the month on which it is celebrated) celebrated in May and commemorating Pushpadanta and Bhutabali, in the course of which manuscripts and books containing scriptures are taken out of libraries, dusted down and, if necessary, recopied, as well as being worshipped.[8]

SCRIPTURE AS SPECTACLE: THE RECITATION OF THE *KALPASUTRA*

We have already encountered the *Kalpasutra* as one of the earlier texts associated with the development of the biography of Mahavira and, while it also contains important material relating to monastic regulations and history, it was doubtless this which led Jacobi to enshrine it as one of the four key texts which he translated in his *Jaina Sutras*, published in the 'Sacred Books of the East' series and a landmark in the presentation of Jainism to westerners.[9] Jacobi must also have been influenced in ascribing such importance to the *Kalpasutra* by the extraordinary proliferation of manuscripts of the text, far more than for any other Jain work, usually containing fine illuminations, which could only have suggested to him that it held a central place in the Shvetambara scriptural canon.[10]

It is certainly true that the *Kalpasutra* is a text of genuine significance for the historian of Jainism, but to the Shvetambara its particular importance derives from its connection with the festival of *Paryushan*, 'Abiding', the most important event in the Shvetambara ritual calendar. *Paryushan* is celebrated over a period of eight days in September and is the climax of *caturmas*, the 'four month' period when ascetics temporarily abandon the wandering life and settle down amidst the laity to see out the monsoon period. Originally, one of the customs associated with this period was the recitation of the *Kalpasutra*, the hearing of which, with its accounts of the ideal which the ascetics were striving to attain and specific injunctions about behaviour, functioned as an act of solidarity to bind the ascetic community together. The specific date on which *Paryushan* now takes place is connected with an ancient teacher called Kalaka, although there is no unanimity about who was responsible for extending the application of this ritual so that the *Kalpasutra* could be read out in front of local lay congregations from the fourth to the eighth day of the festival.

An important element of *Paryushan* in Gujarat today is the use by the monks on every day of the recitation, apart from the eighth, of a vernacular commentary which explains the basic text. When this custom started is unclear but it seems likely that it is connected with the temporary breakdown in the eighteenth and nineteenth centuries of Shvetambara monastic initiation with a concomitant decline in learning and the assumption of a form of religious leadership, which included the reading out of the *Kalpasutra*, by non-initiated clerics called *yati*, many of whom lacked even a minimal ability to interpret the text from the original Prakrit or from a Sanskrit commentary.[11]

On the final day of *Paryushan* which, unlike earlier days when the recitation is usually thinly attended, attracts the lay community en masse, the Gujarati commentary is discarded and the monks, usually two taking turns, proceed to recite the basic Prakrit text of the *Kalpasutra*. Anybody who witnesses this ceremony will be struck by two things: firstly, the breakneck gabble in which the text is enunciated, rendering it completely incomprehensible even to those who know Prakrit, who would be minimally represented in the audience anyway, and secondly, the leavening of the recitation by the display to the audience, carried out by a young layman prompted by signals from one of the monks, of illuminated pages from a copy of the *Kalpasutra* illustrating not just events from the life of Mahavira being described in the text but also stories in the medieval commentaries attached to it.

While the literal meaning of the *Kalpasutra* is not a completely marginal issue during *Paryushan*, as can be seen from the use of the Gujarati commentary by the monks on days four to seven, although this is also generally read in a helter-skelter manner, and the fact that a general explication is also sometimes given, the scripture fits into a much broader context of devotion and ritual. It is an object of worship in its own right and, to a limited extent, a focus of a degree of communal identity when on days three and four the copy of it is paraded through the streets. On the fifth day, the recitation of the passage which culminates in Mahavira's birth is the signal for an extremely important ceremony in which silver images of the fourteen dreams of Mahavira's mother are lowered from the ceiling of the monastic lodging house (*upashraya*) where the recitation takes place and members of the laity bid against each other in auction for the rights to touch and garland them (see Chapter 7). On the eighth and most important day of *Paryushan*, it is very much the element of spectacle, with the displayed pictures recapitulating a story with which the audience is already familiar and the monks sitting on a dais rushing through the recitation, which defines the status of the *Kalpasutra* as a central scripture, and the sound and sight of it during this festival confer a particular merit. Like the Mudbidri manuscripts for the Digambaras, the *Kalpasutra*, and every copy of it within a library, is an evocative symbol of the tradition to which the Shvetambaras belong.[12]

LOST SCRIPTURES: THE PURVAS

A point about which the Digambaras and the Shvetambaras are unanimous is the disappearance of a large body of scriptural material known as the 'previous' or 'ancient' (*purva*) texts. Each fordmaker is supposed to have first preached fourteen of these Purvas before going on to communicate the rest of the scriptures. Gautama's scriptural knowledge is always said to be with reference to the Purvas, as is that of the disciples of all the fordmakers prior to Mahavira.[13] The Shvetambaras claim that the Purvas, in fact regarded as the basis of the scriptural literature, were originally deposited in the third section of the *Drishtivada*, the 'Disputation about Views', the twelfth section or 'limb' (*anga*) of the canon. Knowledge of this text supposedly became vulnerable fairly soon after the death of the last of Mahavira's disciples owing to the effects of famine, with eventually only the teacher Bhadrabahu having command of it. Tradition has it that a monk called Sthulabhadra was sent to Bhadrabahu's retreat in Nepal to learn the texts from him but, according to one version, after mastering ten of the Purvas, he used his knowledge for magical purposes and Bhadrabahu refused to teach him the full import of the last four. In accordance with a prophecy of Mahavira, knowledge of the Purvas died out one thousand years after his death (Bh 20.8) and the whole *Drishtivada* eventually disappeared as well. The Digambaras, who reject the Shvetambara scriptures, further claim that the massive 'Scripture of Six Parts' was in part based on what little Dharasena remembered of just one of these Purvas.

Wherein, then, lay the difference between the Purvas and the other scriptural texts which have survived? Many Shvetambara texts suggest that the scriptures as known today were originally promulgated for women and children while only men had the ability to understand the more rarified Purvas.[14] If an explanation of this sort is hardly satisfactory, it is noteworthy that the resilience of the literary tradition about the Purvas is such that no

Jain scholar has seen fit seriously to challenge its validity. Indeed, despite both the absence of specific proof of the existence of these scriptures in the form of manuscripts and the occurrence of obviously fanciful statements calculating the amount of ink required to write the Purvas as equivalent to the volume of a number of elephants,[15] Shvetambara and Digambara texts alike record broadly similar names and descriptions for the Purvas and their contents which points to a common origin of the tradition. The fact that it is not unknown in classical Indian literature for later, better formulated works to render otiose earlier writings suggests that the possibility of some sort of lost precursor of the currently existing scriptures, the memory of which predates sectarian division, should not be completely discounted.

If it seems unlikely that this matter will ever be fully resolved, at least from a philological point of view, an explanation of sorts for these mysterious works can nonetheless be found in the traditional chapter headings of the lost twelfth limb of the scriptures, the *Drishtivada*, where the Purvas were last located before their disappearance. Irrespective of the form in which this text originally existed, there can be no doubt that any accurate knowledge of what its contents might have been had disappeared by about the sixth century CE. This is the only construction that can be put upon the claim that the *Drishtivada*, rather like the Hindu Veda, contained 'everything' and it came to be regarded as a convenient repository where elements of developed Jain literary culture which could not be provided with an impeccable scriptural pedigree, such as the complete version of the Universal History, could be fictitiously stated to have had their origin.[16] In reality, the original text, as its name would suggest, seems to have contained large-scale expositions of views which the Jains considered heretical, and the danger inherent in such a work, at least for the weak monks living in the corrupt age, may have led to its eventual suppression and disappearance.

In the light of this, the third chapter heading of the *Drishtivada*, 'That which relates to the Purvas' (*purvagata*), must refer to 'preliminary statements' (*purva*) of various intellectual opponents which were then refuted, generally known in Indian philosophical texts as *purvapaksha*. This heading was then misinterpreted by a learned tradition which had lost contact with the original *Drishtivada* as referring to a group of 'ancient' (*purva*) texts.[17] Whatever the truth of this, the Purvas are an important component of Jain views about their scriptures, providing the community with some sense of a prehistory for the sources on which the religion is based.

ARDHAMAGADHI AS SCRIPTURAL LANGUAGE

Mahavira, like the Buddha, did not preach in Sanskrit but in some variety of regional vernacular, a Prakrit, found in the Ganges basin and standing roughly in the same relationship to Sanskrit as medieval Italian does to Latin. Shvetambara tradition was to regard Ardhamagadhi, the language of their scriptures, as the dialect in which Mahavira had preached and the language spoken by the gods in heaven. The nature of Ardhamagadhi was supposedly such that, as soon as Mahavira uttered it in his sermons, it became automatically transformed into all the languages of his listeners (Aup p.178).[18]

Ardhamagadhi means literally 'Half Magadhi' and, with the exception of the odd later and deliberately archaising text,[19] it is peculiar to the Shvetambara scriptures. Its phonetic structure shows Ardhamagadhi to be in one or two respects different from the Magadhi dialect spoken in the Magadha region of east India, no extensive sources for which have survived but which was described by ancient Indian grammarians. It can be conjectured that Ardhamagadhi, which in its surviving and apparently somewhat normalised form was certainly not the vernacular in which Mahavira himself preached, evolved from some underlying dialect, presumably a variety of Magadhi, into a specifically Jain scriptural dialect, a sacred language which could be differentiated from Sanskrit, rather as the Jains were later to develop their own systems of Sanskrit grammatical analysis to show their independence from brahman learning.[20]

Jain scholars customarily assert that the existence of the scriptures in a vernacular Prakrit is a sign of the universality of the Jain message since even the uneducated could comprehend it. This may possibly have been so at the outset but, leaving aside the fact that a great deal of the Shvetambara canon is highly technical, it must be asked whether from the beginning of the common era anybody other than learned monks had the capacity to understand Ardhamagadhi. Certainly, a sound scholarly knowledge of the language is by no means widespread among the Shvetambara ascetic community today. The archaic and artificial nature of Ardhamagadhi is implicit in the legendary account of the great logician Siddhasena Divakara (fifth century CE) who was expelled from the Jain community for twelve years for suggesting that the scriptures be translated into Sanskrit, the pan-Indian intellectual lingua franca, as a means of rendering them more accessible (PC 8.108–18). The objections of Siddhasena's monastic superiors to this proposed innovation reflect a desire to maintain the exclusivity and peculiarity of Ardhamagadhi as a badge of sectarian identity.

SHVETAMBARA TRADITIONS ABOUT SCRIPTURAL TRANSMISSION

It is not known exactly when the scriptures were first written down, existing manuscripts not dating from before the eleventh century CE, and the traditional emphasis was originally upon orality and memorisation. Yet, unlike brahman culture where precise mnemonic techniques were able to guarantee the survival of the ancient Vedic literature in near original form for millennia, the Jains from an early period felt their grip upon the scriptural tradition to be at times weak, and Shvetambara accounts of a series of so-called councils, already mentioned in the previous chapter, testify to the efforts of the community to retrieve a worsening situation and consolidate a diminishing textual corpus.

The word *vacana*, usually rendered as council, in fact signifies 'recitation' and the function of these conclaves was ostensibly to establish recensions of the scriptural canon through consulting the memory of authoritative monks. All three are described as taking place after twelve-year famines. The first recitation is supposed to have been held at Pataliputra (modern Patna) 160 years after Mahavira's death, as a result of which knowledge of the twelve-limbed canon was deemed to be imperfect and, with the subsequent disappearance of the *Drishtivada*, it was officially reduced to eleven limbs. The second recitation took place 827 years after Mahavira but, on this occasion, was held at two places simultaneously, at Mathura in the north under the auspices of Skandila and at Valabhi in the west under the auspices of Nagarjuna. These two teachers did not meet to coordinate and compare the respective recitations they presided over and there seems to have been a number of discrepant readings in the respective versions. However, it is clear that the Mathura version of Skandila, collected on the basis of 'whoever remembered something' (Haribhadra on NSH 13), constituted a first 'official' version of the scriptures since all the medieval commentators quote readings from Nagarjuna's recitation only as variants.[21]

The final recitation held at Valabhi in the first half of the fifth century was convened by Devarddhiganin and the accounts of it stress that, to avoid the complete disappearance of the scriptures, the canon was redacted in manuscript form. Copies of this would have been circulated as an authorised version and erroneous readings which are found in every commentary, manuscript and printed edition to the present day must be regarded as deriving from this.[22] According to the seventeenth century writer Samayasundara, the various inconsistencies which appear in the scriptures date from the Valabhi recitation and were preserved because of Devarddhiganin's unwillingness or inability to distiguish among the various readings available (SSh p.86).

The accounts of these recitations are interesting for the insight they give about the Jain view of a gradually disintegrating scriptural corpus but they hardly have eyewitness status. For example, the earliest accounts of any of the recitations date from the second half of the seventh century, while the references to twelve-year famines represent virtually a figure of speech in

Jain literature, not to be taken literally, signifying some degree of discord in the community or political instability.

Many early texts on monastic practice denounce the possession of manuscripts by monks but, by about the seventh century, this custom was no longer stigmatised.[23] In the absence of further evidence, a working hypothesis would be to see the issue at stake in the second and third recitations as not the literal disappearance of the scriptures or the lack of authoritative sources as a result of the death of learned monks through famine but the stabilisation and control of an originally oral tradition whose integrity was being undermined by the proliferation of large numbers of manuscript copies.[24] This can in part be seen from the fact that a commentary written before the recitation of Valabhi by Agastyasimha on the key ascetic text, the *Dashavaikalika*, contains hundreds of variant readings whereas Haribhadra, one of the earliest post-Valabhi commentators, states firmly that variants on that text did not exist.[25]

Occasionally, the influence of the redaction and editing which must have taken place during the recitations can be detected in certain texts. The ancient first book of the first scripture of the canon, the *Acaranga*, was shown by Schubring to have been in origin a kind of mosaic, often consisting of mere fragments of verses and disjointed bits of prose, which had been transformed into, if not a seamless whole, at least a continuum.[26] The complete failure of the medieval Jain commentarial tradition to grasp this fact suggests that it must have been definitively effected at one of the scriptural recitations. Other texts seem to have been finally given up for lost at the later recitations, such as the seventh chapter of the first book of the *Acaranga*, last heard of in the hagiography of the teacher Vajra being used as a magic spell to gain the power of flight (AvNiry 769), while the contents of 'Questions and Answers' (*Prashnavyakarananī*), the tenth scripture of the canon, which must have been finally redacted at Valabhi, are completely different from their description elsewhere in the scriptures. As a result of the varying editorial processes which were at work both before and during the recitation of Valabhi, the Shvetambara scriptures have been compared to an old city in which some buildings have remained exactly the same from the earliest period, some have had extensions built onto them, others have been erected on old foundations while many have disappeared completely and are known only by name.[27]

Looked at objectively, the Shvetambara scriptures can only be dated on a relative basis. No genuinely critical edition of them can be prepared because of the lack of really old manuscripts and serious study of the language of the canon has as yet hardly begun. As regards interpretation, the tendency up to quite recently has been to accept the testimony of the Prakrit and Sanskrit commentators, despite the fact that they are often uncertain or incorrect about the meaning of the linguistic material with which they were working. An often trustworthy, if necessarily limited, guide to chronology is metre.

Chronological strata can occasionally be isolated through the demonstration that certain of the old verse texts largely composed in Vedic metres have been interpolated by verses composed in 'newer' metres.[28]

THE FORTY-FIVE TEXT SHVETAMBARA CANON

Before discussing Shvetambara views about the structuring principles behind their sacred writings, I will enumerate (using, as is customary, Sanskrit names) and briefly characterise the components of what has come to be regarded as the standard version of the scriptural canon which consists of forty-five texts (*sutra*) classified into five groups. The most important texts in this list are the 'limbs' (*anga*) and 'subsidiary limbs' (*upanga*), terms which may have been borrowed from Vedic learning and indicate a desire to organise Jain writings on the model of those of the brahmans. Jain tradition often conceives of scripture as being like a human being and it has been said that scripture and men are alike in that they both have twelve *anga*, which for men would be regarded as being feet, calves, thighs, forearms, arms, neck and head.[29]

Firstly, the twelve limbs (*anga*):

1 The *Acara* ('Behaviour'): doctrinal statements about the nature of reality, concerning particularly the soul and action, a biography of Mahavira and statements about monastic discipline.[30]
2 The *Sutrakrita* ('Relating to Heretical Views'): a variety of doctrinal material, including accounts of the views of opponents, discussions of karma, Mahavira, general recommendations for ascetic behaviour, the evils of women and hells.[31]
3 The *Sthana* ('Possibilities'): an encyclopaedic compilation of lists relating to doctrine, practice, mythology, cosmology etc. grouped in clusters of one to ten.
4 The *Samavaya* ('Combinations'): similar in style to the *Sthana*, while also containing descriptions of the contents of the *angas*.
5 The *Vyakhyaprajnapti* ('Exposition of Explanations'): the largest text of the canon containing material, some of which was in origin independent, relating to the entire range of Jain doctrine and ascetic practice.[32]
6 The *Jnatadharmakathah* ('Stories of Knowledge and Righteousness'): a series of narratives, varying in length and occasionally only vaguely Jain in theme, from which morals about the results of following the religious path are drawn. The eighth chapter gives the story of Malli, the nineteenth fordmaker.[33]
7 The *Upasakadashah* ('Ten Chapters on Lay Attenders'): stories describing the piety of laymen and their fortitude in the face of demonic attack.[34]

8 The *Antakriddashah* ('Ten Chapters on Endmakers'): stories describing those who succeeded in putting an end to rebirth.[35]
9 The *Anuttaraupapatikadashah* ('Ten Chapters about the Arisers in the Highest Heavens): stories describing those reborn as gods.[36]
10 The *Prashnavyakaranani* ('Questions and Explanations'): discussions of a variety of doctrinal matters.[37]
11 The *Vipakashruta* ('The Scripture about Ripening'): stories describing those who experience the results of karma.
12 The *Drishtivada* ('Disputation about Views'): accepted from an early date as being lost.

Along with the twelve *angas* are correlated the twelve subsidiary limbs (*upanga*):

1 The *Aupapatika* ('Spontaneously Arising'): so called because of its descriptions of gods and hellbeings who are born spontaneously. It contains an elaborate account of Mahavira's preaching and descriptions of the mechanism which brings about the attainment of liberation.[38]
2 The *Rajaprashniya* ('Relating to the Questions of King Prasenajit'): centres around a discussion between King Prasenajit and the monk Keshin, a follower of Parshva, about the relationship between the soul and the body (see Chapter 4).
3 The *Jivajivabhigama* ('Understanding of the Animate and Inanimate'): deals with ontological matters.
4 The *Prajnapana* ('Enunciation'): a systematic account of many of the doctrinal matters found in the fifth *anga* and which was in fact at some point incorporated into that text.[39]
5–7 Three works on cosmography, the *Suryaprajnapti*, *Jambudvipa-prajnapti* and *Candraprajnapti*. The first and second which relate to the moon and the sun respectively are virtually identical. The second, the 'Description of the Island of the Roseapple Tree', includes biographical material about Rishabha and his son Bharata.
8–12 Five short narrative texts dealing with the results of actions.

Seven texts constitute the *chedasutras* which deal with 'cutting' (*cheda*) of monastic seniority and contain accounts of the regulation of ascetic behaviour.[40] Of these, the first, the *Dashashrutaskandha* (called in Prakrit the *Ayaradasao*), contains the *Kalpasutra*, not to be confused with the second *chedasutra*, a short text on monastic law, which is also called the *Kalpasutra*.[41] The fourth text in this group, the *Nishitha*, supposedly had its origin as part of the first *anga*, while the basic text of the sixth, the *Pancakalpa*, is now regarded as lost.

The four 'root' or 'base' (*mula*) scriptures (*sutra*) are probably so called because they have to be mastered at the outset of an ascetic's career:

1 The *Uttaradhyayana* ('Later Chapters'): a collection of thirty-six chapters, nearly all in verse, some very old, dealing with legend, practice and doctrine.[42]
2 The *Dashavaikalika* ('Ten Evening Treatises'): a summary treatment of correct ascetic behaviour.[43] Authorship of this text is ascribed to Shayyambhava who intended it to be a summary of the scriptures for the benefit of his son.
3 The *Avashyaka* ('Obligatory'): contains the formulae associated with the six obligatory ritual actions. The mnemonic verses (*niryukti*) on this text have assumed a quasi-canonical status.
4 The *Pindaniryukti* and *Oghaniryukti*, generally taken together, are technical verse texts describing begging for alms and care of monastic equipment such as the alms bowl.

The fifth group contains ten 'mixed' (*prakirnaka*) texts dealing with monastic ritual, religious suicide, physiology, praise of the fordmakers, astrology etc (see next section).

Finally, two texts dealing with hermeneutics, the *Nandi* ('Auspicious') and the *Anuyogadvarani* ('Doors of Disquisition'), situate the scriptures in an epistemological context.[44]

The style of the canon is not uniform. Texts which give simple lists of doctrinal terms or outlines of the teachings alternate with those which contain ornate narrations. The frequently repetitive and stereotyped use of language is in part indicative of an oral origin while the florid style of, for example, the sixth *anga*, reminiscent of the highly compounded Sanskrit poetic prose of the early common era, suggests conscious literary artifice.

ENUMERATION OF THE SHVETAMBARA SCRIPTURES

The enumeration of scriptures given above is strictly speaking that of the Shvetambara *Murtipujaka Sangha*, the 'Image-Worshipping Assembly', and is not accepted in totality by the Sthanakvasis and the Terapanthis, the two aniconic Shvetambara sects who have their own thirty-two text list which, while accepting the *anga* and *upanga* lists, omits thirteen of the remaining texts including some of the *chedasutras* and all of the ten mixed texts. Thus, although the sixteenth century image-worshipping Shvetambara Dharmasagara regarded the fifth *chedasutra* called the *Mahanishitha* as having been produced by Mahavira's disciples and so viewed acceptance of it as one of the touchstones of adherence to a correct form of Jainism (SVVD p.17), sectarian suspicions of the text would have undoubtedly been aroused by the fact that it is written in Maharashtri, a dialect of west Indian belles-lettres, rather than the scriptural language Ardhamagadhi and that it also contains references to goddesses and magic spells not found elsewhere in the canon which suggest a much later period of composition. The story of the rescue and restoration of a dilapidated manuscript of the *Mahanishitha* from a temple in Mathura seems little more than an attempt to manufacture an antiquity for it,[45] and the Sthanakvasis and Terapanthis accordingly refuse to accept its authority. However, the criteria for their rejection of the authenticity of other scriptural texts are not at all clear (see Chapter 9).

The forty-five text list had been communicated in the nineteenth century to Weber, busy in Berlin forming an overall assessment of the Shvetambara scriptures, by Buhler on the basis of fairly restricted information and it is this model perpetuated by Weber, a fixed canon as it were, which has prevailed in scholarly circles as the normative enumeration of the scriptures to this day.[46] Weber nonetheless had enough material at his disposal even in those pioneering days to realise that there were other enumerations of the scriptures available and he concluded that this uncertainty in the tradition possibly reflected a difference in time of composition.[47]

The central difficulty in discussing the Shvetambara scriptural canon is that, while the tradition regarded the recitation of Valabhi as being the moment when it was finally fixed (e.g. SSh p.38), there is nowhere any reference to the actual names of the texts which were redacted there.[48] Moreover, even such an apparently basic correlated division of the texts into *anga* and *upanga* is not referred to before the twelfth century, although the terms themselves are, and the forty-five text list can only be dated back to the thirteenth century or so.[49] This alone should be sufficient to show that the notion of a Shvetambara canon fixed from an early period is not totally convincing and that the list with which Buhler and Weber were confronted in fact represented only a *selection* of old textual material, albeit a selection which eventually seems to have achieved ascendancy among image-worshipping Shvetambaras.[50]

In his brief account of the Mathura recitation, Jinadasa states that Skandila redacted the *kalika* scriptures, that is, texts which have to be studied at an appropriate time owing to their solemnity.[51] This suggests that at a relatively early date there were other ways of grouping the scriptures than the forty-five text list would allow. The *Nandi*, which was perhaps composed around the beginning of the fifth century, describes (NSH pp.70–3) a division of texts into those 'included among the *anga*' (*angapravishta*) and those 'exterior to the *anga*' (*angabahira*, *anangapravishta*), the distinction being based on those texts which were originally redacted by Mahavira's disciples and those, such as the important 'root' scripture, the *Dashavaikalika*, which were written by distinguished monks who came after them, although even on this point there is no firm agreement.[52] This latter group was then subdivided into the 'obligatory' (*avashyaka*) texts and those which are 'different' (*vyatirikta*) from them. The 'different' texts were in turn subdivided into 'those which can be studied at any time' (*utkalika*) and 'those which can only be studied at certain designated times' (*kalika*).[53] The former list is said to include the *Dashavaikalika*, most of the *upanga* texts and the *Nandi* itself, while the latter includes the other important root text, the *Uttaradhyayana*, most of the *chedasutras* as well as the 'Sayings of the Seers' (see Chapter 1) which is not mentioned at all in the forty-five text list. Both these lists also refer by name to a large number of completely unknown texts.

The *Nandi*'s companion hermeneutical text, the 'Doors of Disquisition', on the other hand, reverses this classification and locates the 'obligatory' texts in the *utkalika* group, since it is primarily concerned with their terminological explication, rather than, as is the *Nandi*, with the internal structure of scriptural literature. Different contexts and preoccupations called forth different enumerations, but it is clear that what is generally at issue in these old listings, as opposed to the forty-five text list, is the function of particular scriptures within the practical context of ascetic study and ritual.[54] This can be seen also in the ranking of texts according to the period of years required to master them (SVVD verse 7).

The fluidity of the non-*anga* scriptures is most marked in the mixed *prakirnaka* texts (PNN). There is no firm canonical list of the *prakirnakas*, the oldest citation of them in the *Nandi* suggesting merely that they are outside the *anga* texts and, disconcertingly, numbering them as 14,000 in Mahavira's *tirtha* (NSH pp.73–4). It would thus appear as if *prakirnaka* was a category in which short texts of varying content which had attained some degree of authority could be situated. That this led to confusion is fairly clear from the fact that early enumerations of the forty-five text list are uncertain about the *prakirnaka* component and, although the contemporary canonical list now cites ten *prakirnakas*, there are in fact some twenty texts of this sort currently in existence. In the light of the failure of Sagarananda Suri, the monk who almost singlehandedly revived the study of the scriptures and their commentaries this century by publishing them in the Agamodaya Samiti series, to establish a firm enumeration of these texts, the ongoing 'Jaina Agama' series, which aims to provide as near a critically based version of the Shvetambara scriptures as possible, has decided to hedge its bets and publish all twenty.[55]

The inventories of canonical texts represent attempts to bring order to a complex mass of material produced over a wide span of time, in which elements both of conscious choice in the selection of texts and chance with regard to the survival of types of enumeration, as one suspects with the forty-five text list, played important parts. If the Shvetambara *agama* can be regarded as having a relatively stable core in the form of the *anga* and *upanga* texts (allowing for the disappearance of portions of them), with an often shifting periphery of less significant texts, it should be remembered that it is the uses to which these scriptures have been put within the Jain community which have ultimately defined their importance.

DIGAMBARA SCRIPTURES

The Digambara attitude to scriptural tradition is less complex than that of the Shvetambaras and at the same time more mysterious in that they reject the Shvetambara canon, and yet the circumstances in which this happened are never fully adumbrated. As has already been mentioned, the distinctiveness of the Digambara position can be seen in the view which would assign to scripture a role as little more than a metaphor since the words which once constituted it no longer survive. The Digambara lineage which lists the teachers descended from Mahavira and their familiarity with the scriptures presents a much more drastic picture of decline than envisaged by the Shvetambaras for, by the time of Dharasena, the thirty-third teacher in succession to the disciple Gautama, 683 years after Mahavira, it is held that there was knowledge of only one *anga* and after Dharasena's two pupils, Pushpadanta and Bhutabali, even that disappeared.[56] The two most extensive Digambara sacred texts, the 'Scripture in Six Parts' and the 'Treatise on the Passions', already discussed in this chapter, were regarded as representing the meagre remains, handed down by Dharasena, of an originally vast tradition of sacred literature.

It may be that the Digambaras did lose contact with their scriptural tradition in toto, given that the disappearance of texts at other times is generally agreed to have taken place. An alternative explanation is that the sectarian division, which was brought about by the hardening of attitudes to ascetic practice and by the growing geographical separation of the two ascetic communities, along with the perceived manipulation of the sacred texts by one group in the absence of the other, may have finally led to the promulgation of an alternative, Digambara version of scriptural history in which the 'Scripture in Six Parts' and the 'Treatise on the Passions', which had in origin constituted a Digambara systematisation of parts of an originally undifferentiated textual tradition, came to assume for sectarian purposes the role of sole survivors of that tradition which could otherwise no longer be accepted.[57]

Despite Digambara assertions about the antiquity of the 'Scripture in Six Parts' and the 'Treatise on the Passions', their style and the intricacies of their subject matter suggest a date contemporary with later Shvetambara canonical texts. There are, for example, strong similarities between the fourth Shvetambara *upanga*, the *Prajnapana*, and the 'Scripture in Six Parts', although it is still a moot point as to which was written first,[58] while the 'Treatise on the Passions' is composed in the *arya* metre, a sure sign of its relative lateness.[59] Similarly, two other old Digambara texts on monastic behaviour, the *Mulacara* ('Fundamental Conduct') of Vattakera and the *Bhagavati Aradhana* ('The Revered Accomplishing') share many traits with Shvetambara scriptures and early commentary literature, and the dialect in which they were written, often called by Indian scholars Digambara or Jain Shauraseni, a vernacular supposedly spoken in the region of Mathura, has been shown to have much more in common with Ardhamagadhi than had previously been thought.[60] Everything points to the existence of an original and ancient shared Jain textual tradition which gradually bifurcated.

Whatever the truth of this, the fact is that the Digambaras have always clung tenaciously to the idea of a scriptural canon and their enumeration of the *anga* texts is identical to that of the Shvetambaras, although unsurprisingly they differ with regard to the non-*anga* texts (HVP 10.22–48). The great eighth century logician Akalanka was aware of the contents of the *angas*, although it cannot be said whether they represented an idea rather than a reality for him, and he also seems to have been the first Digambara to have introduced as a valid form of scriptural classification the division into *kalika* and *utkalika* texts which, as we have seen, was also employed by the Shvetambaras (TSRV pp.72–5).

Little work has been done on Digambara attitudes, past and present, to the Shvetambara canon. Prominent Digambaras were certainly familiar with it and cite from it on occasion and, in the nineteenth century, Buhler describes how learned Digambaras whom he had encountered accepted the authority of some Shvetambara texts, while rejecting others.[61] Although the Digambaras do not have a formal canon of their own, they have nonetheless evolved a quasi-canonical grouping of texts into four literary categories called 'exposition' (*anuyoga*), a term associated with the legendary teacher Rakshita who supposedly divided up the scriptures for fear that they would be forgotten (AvNiry 774–7 with Haribhadra; PC 2.231–44). The 'first' (*prathama*) exposition contains Digambara versions of the Universal History; the 'calculation' (*karana*) exposition contains works on cosmology; the 'behaviour' (*carana*) exposition includes texts about proper behaviour for monks and lay people and the 'entity' (*dravya*) exposition contains a wide variety of writings dealing with metaphysics in the broadest sense.

THE FIVE HOMAGES

The Jains share with all other Indian religions a belief in the efficacy of mantras and hold that certain syllables, words or phrases are charged with power and auspiciousness which, if manipulated in the appropriate manner and context, can bring about a positive result for the person who enunciates them vocally or mentally. The most famous of all Jain mantras, indeed the most widely known and used piece of sacred language within Jainism as a whole, is the 'Five Homages' (*Pancanamaskara*). Unlike many mantras, it has specific meaning and consists of five statements in Prakrit addressed to the five central ascetic figures of Jainism, the *parameshthins*, 'those who are situated in the highest stage': 'Homage to the omniscient ones (*arahat*). Homage to the liberated ones (*siddha*). Homage to the teachers (*ayariya*). Homage to the preceptors (*uvajjhaya*). Homage to all monks (*sahu*) in the world.'

There is also found a second explanatory, four line metrical portion: 'This is the Five Homages which destroys all evil. It is the first auspicious statement of all auspicious statements.'

The Five Homages is accepted by all Jains, although there exist some minor differences in versions of the text and the Sthanakvasis reject the authority of the second portion.

Like the scriptures, the Five Homages is generally considered to be beginningless and authorless and as existing during the time of all the fordmakers. However, a history of sorts can be reconstructed for it. The earliest occurrence of a portion of the formula is in a first century BCE inscription where only the omniscient and the liberated are invoked and textual evidence supports the claim of Virasena (ninth century), that it was expanded to five invocations by Pushpadanta (*c.* second century CE) and placed at the beginning of the 'Scripture in Six Parts', its oldest occurrence in literature, although at least one Digambara text claims that he merely inserted the mantra rather than composed it. The Five Homages was virtually unknown to the Shvetambara scriptures. The fifth *anga* does quote it at the beginning but expands it by expressing homage to the alphabet and to scripture also and the commentators on the sixth *upanga* do not gloss it at the beginning of the text, which suggests they regarded its occurrence there as the result of interpolation.[62]

The Five Homages is recited by Jains at all solemn and ritual occasions, such as worship and ascetic initiation, and stories abound in Jain literature from an early period stressing its power even outside these contexts, provided it is used in the appropriate frame of mind. A thief impaled on a stake recalls the mantra and is reborn as a god (BhA 772); even when only partially recalled, the mantra saves a layman from human sacrifice at the hands of a Hindu wizard (DhMV 96); meditation upon the mantra protects from supernatural attack but abuse of it leads to destruction (BKK 52), and recitation of it can even empower flight (BKK 60).

Contemporary Jain writers describe the Five Homages as summing up the essence of the doctrine and as subsuming all other mantras. Recitation of it is reckoned to give worldly success and burn away karma while, through its positive effect upon the mind and capacity to destroy pride and egoism, it can be regarded as a form of integral austerity. It is also said to be a panacea for all physical ills, superior to western-style medicine.[63]

Medieval mystical and ritual texts add the doctrinal principles of right knowledge, faith, practice and austerity to the five *parameshthins* which are together fitted into an abstract ninefold pattern known as the *Navapada* (the 'Nine Stages') or the *Siddhacakrayantra* (the 'Diagram of the Circle of the Liberated') which, with the addition of symbolic colours, syllables, mantras and so on, forms an important component of esoteric and popular ritual alike and is frequently employed on auspicious occasions. One of the most famous of all Jain stories, that of Shripala, shows how worldly and spiritual success can be gained by association with the *Siddhacakrayantra*.[64]

JAIN LIBRARIES

The oldest manuscript libraries in India are those of the Jains and, while their contents can only very rarely be dated to before the eleventh century, their value not just for Jain literature but for classical Indian literature in general is incalculable. The impetus to the large-scale production and collection of manuscripts can be seen by about the eighth or ninth centuries when the idea of laymen being able to gain merit by the commissioning of sacred writings and other texts began to take hold. The first evidence for the emergence of the *bhattarakas*, the clerical heads responsible for the running of Digambara religious institutions, derives from about this time (see Chapter 5) and it was these figures who got libraries erected in the vicinity of Digambara temples to house manuscripts provided by lay people.

The Shvetambaras in Gujarat founded famous libraries at Patan, Cambay and Broach and a checklist of their contents compiled by a monk in 1383 is the oldest Indian manuscript catalogue yet known. However, the most celebrated of all Jain libraries are those at Jaisalmer whose fame to some extent rests as much on on their inacessibility, at least until recently, deep in the Thar desert of Rajasthan, as on their contents. The biggest library there, located in the vaults of the temple of the fordmaker Sambhava, was founded by the monk Jinabhadra in 1551 and it was to there that many precious manuscripts were taken from Patan and Cambay to save them from Moslem depredation. Only after independence were the rich holdings at Jaisalmer, including palm leaf manuscripts from the tenth century and the oldest known Indian paper manuscript dating from 1189, put into order and definitively catalogued by a team led by Muni Punyavijaya. Even today, direct access to this material is difficult to gain, usually requiring the simultaneous presence of all trustees, a rare event.

By about the seventeenth century, management of temple libraries in the north had passed into the hands of prominent lay members of the community who guarded them in the same manner as they did the images in the temples. Manuscripts could be borrowed, under very strict controls only by bona fide members of the sect to which the library belonged and, to avoid total loss, never in complete form. As a result of this, the Terapanthi sect, which was formed in the eighteenth century by a monk who had broken away from the Sthanakvasis, was hindered at the outset by not having its own libraries and an inability to gain access to manuscripts of the scriptures.[65] James Tod, travelling in Gujarat around 1820 and probably the first westerner to see the Jain libraries at Patan, records that entrance was only permitted when his monk-assistant produced an affidavit proving his descent through pupillary lineage from the great teacher Hemacandra who is credited with having collected the ancient manuscripts there in the twelfth century.[66]

With the emergence of printing in India in the nineteenth century, manuscripts lost some of their practical importance, even to those members of the Jain community who could use them with profit, and many of the lay trustees neglected the libraries in their charge, the contents of which often suffered from the assaults of insects, generally only bringing out the manuscripts on those days set aside for the worship of the scriptures. In 1860 the Indian Government attempted to initiate a systematic process of cataloguing but progress was slow, and scholars like Buhler recorded their frustration with trustees who refused to allow inspection of holdings or attempted to fob off the cataloguers with recent paper copies while keeping back old and important palm leaf manuscripts. The conflict of interest here is obvious: for the European, the value of the manuscripts lay in their content by means of which Indian history could be reconstructed, while for the Jain their true worth lay in their role as sacred objects.

Matters have changed in the course of this century where the efforts of a variety of Jain scholars, lay and monastic, have led to the cataloguing of the most important collections (although there is probably still a great deal in private hands) and new libraries have been built such as the *Hemacandracarya Jnan Mandir* at Patan where the manuscripts are now kept safely in steel cupboards. However, the full scholarly exploitation of these treasures has hardly begun.[67]

4 Doctrine

Throughout the centuries there has not been any radical reinterpretation of basic Jain metaphysical teachings. Disputes and disagreements have taken place about certain technical matters and various sectarian groups have sometimes chosen to emphasise some aspects at the expense of others, but the doctrine has remained remarkably stable. However, the source of this stability lies not so much in the Ardhamagadhi scriptural canon, which in its earliest portions lacks many elements which were later to assume importance, as in a collection of aphorisms produced in the fourth or fifth century CE by Umasvati, of whose career the tradition has preserved virtually no information, either historical or hagiographical.

From about the beginning of the common era, prominent exponents of the various Hindu philosophical systems had systematised their teachings in the form of short mnemonic rules (*sutra*) written in Sanskrit, whose full implications were generally impossible to grasp without the aid of a commentary or oral exposition. Umasvati's *Tattvarthasutra*, as it is usually known, the 'Mnemonic Rules on the Meaning of the Reals', was an attempt to sum up the various elements of the Jain path, epistemological, metaphysical, cosmological, ethical and practical, otherwise scattered around the scriptural literature in unsystematic form.[1] The *Tattvarthasutra* is claimed by both the Shvetambaras and the Digambaras (with minor differences in the texts of the rules) and, although a case can be made for Umasvati having been a Shvetambara, it seems better to assume that he was writing at a time before the sectarian traditions had fully crystallised. As the first truly significant Jain text in Sanskrit, the *Tattvarthasutra* signalled the willingness of the Jains to engage with the wider Indian intellectual world and it subsequently achieved such an authority that what is often presented as being Jainism by twentieth century writers is in fact Umasvati's systematisation of it. The commentators on the *Tattvarthasutra*, of whom the most prominent are the Digambaras of Pujyapada (sixth century), Akalanka (eighth century) and Vidyanandin (ninth century), provide a form of extended footnote to a text which came to assume a quasi-scriptural status.

At the start of the *Tattvarthasutra*, Umasvati sets out a formulation of a type occasionally found in the earlier scriptures (e.g. SKS 1.6.17) which enunciates the basic concerns of the Jain religion: 'The way to deliverance is right faith (*darshana*), knowledge and behaviour.'

These came to be known as the Three Jewels and both in name and in their prominence within Jainism can be compared with the Three Jewels of Buddhism (the Buddha, his teachings and the community). There was some lack of unanimity amongst Jain commentators about the relationship between the elements of their Three Jewels. Some argued that faith and knowledge were interrelated and mutually dependent, with behaviour accordingly predicated upon them,[2] while others, such as Shilanka (on AS 1.9.4.17), claimed that it was knowledge and behaviour which were interlocking. Alternatively, according to Akalanka (TSRV p.17), all three were necessarily interrelated since there could not possibly be three different paths to deliverance (cf. UttS 28.29–30).

However, it is the actual presence of faith within this triad which is really noteworthy. For Jainism, faith does not imply some kind of blind belief but is rather the correct way of looking at things, a positive and well-informed disposition (TSRV p.22). By putting faith at the beginning of the first rule of the *Tattvarthasutra* which defines the very nature of Jainism, Umasvati is both drawing attention to its role as an essential component on the path to salvation and at the same time broadening Jainism's range of spiritual reference beyond early Hinduism for whom faith, at least textually, did not have such a central and formally enunciated position.

Similarly, Umasvati's definition of the universe and the creatures living within it as being characterised by origin, disappearance and permanence (TS 5.29; also found at PS 2.3) definitively presented a realist metaphysic of change and stability with which Jain teachings could be contrasted with Buddhism's interpretation of the world as involving change and Hinduism's insistence on the permanence at the root of reality, and as such was to provide the sheet-anchor for subsequent Jain philosophical endeavour.

Before discussing the Jain view of the structure of reality, it will be necessary to remark upon the nature of the authority upon which Jain doctrine rests.

OMNISCIENCE

Jainism views enlightenment as the result of a process of self-cultivation in which an individual gradually progresses with the aid of a variety of religious practices from a state of inadequate perception of the world to the attainment of certain higher forms of knowledge such as the ability to be aware of other people's mental processes until, with the elimination of all negative factors, there arises omniscient knowledge which is totally unique and unconditioned. Some Jain writers, most prominent among whom is the early Digambara Kundakunda, argue for the mystical nature of this experience and suggest that it is primarily directed internally towards realisation of the individual's inner nature. While this is undoubtedly a theme which runs through Jainism, the tradition has from the beginning generally understood the omniscience attained by Mahavira and the other fordmakers to be in the most literal sense the ability to know and see everything in the universe at all times and in all possible modifications simultaneously. Such a claim for a human being was a grand one, and at the outset unique in India, for the omniscience which the Buddhists originally attributed to their founder related to knowledge only of that which was specifically conducive to spiritual advancement.[3]

The fifth *anga* of the Shvetambara scriptures, the 'Exposition of Explanations', conveys some sense of the breadth of the information which Mahavira's omniscience was felt to have encompassed: local knowledge, the actions of gods, the previous and future births of human beings, the unseen ontological categories and creatures living in earth, water, air and fire.[4] Mahavira the liberating teacher does not argue for the truth of what he knows and sees but simply asserts, and conversions are depicted as being effected by his ability, or that of disciples enlightened by him, to describe minutely and give shape to entities which would otherwise remain invisible to the unenlightened. All Jain doctrinal categories, whether ontological, metaphysical, ethical or cosmological, are ultimately validated by Mahavira's immediate and unmediated experience of the totality of reality.

This claim for enlightenment as full omniscience was to prove too much for the Jains' intellectual opponents who subjected it to intense scrutiny. Yet the Jain position is essentially unfalsifiable. By about the sixth century CE, it had come to be accepted that nobody since the disciple Jambu had achieved enlightenment and that the goal of the Jain religion was unattainable during the course of the fifth and sixth spokes of the current world era. While this has obvious implications for the actual practice of Jainism, for polemical purposes it had the advantage of enabling the Jains to dispose easily of one of the main objections of their opponents, namely, that nobody had ever encountered a fully omniscient person. Free, because of the delimitation of omniscience to Mahavira's lifetime, from the obligation to produce an enlightened member of their religion for inspection, the Jains could at the same time assert that there was nothing which militated against the existence of such persons in the past, while on the other hand, it was argued, there was specific proof of their existence in a scriptural tradition which described the omniscient teachers and communicated the otherwise inaccessible truths revealed by them.

Many Jains today, reckoning that recent discoveries of western science, such as relativity and the existence of microbes, were presaged by Mahavira's teachings, find it gratifying to describe Jainism as a 'scientific' religion. Others might be more struck by the fact that Jainism, through its dependence on the teaching of omniscient beings embodied in a fully authoritative sacred scripture which later medieval writers attempted to demonstrate was in full conformity with standard logical procedures, in actuality shows many of the characteristics of a revealed religion of the Judaeo-Christian-Moslem type.

THE *LOKA*

The vast but finite universe in which action, rebirth and the attainment of enlightenment take place and in whose roof the delivered souls find their final abode is called the *loka*, 'world' or, sometimes, the *triloka*, 'triple world'. Although *loka* meant in origin 'open space', Jain teachers generally preferred to derive it from the verbal root *lok* 'see' and explain the term as 'that which is seen by the omniscient ones' (Abhayadeva on Sth 5–6) or, occasionally, 'that which is seen by the soul' (TSRV p.455). The *loka* is both a shorthand designation for the five basic ontological categories of souls, motion, rest, atomic matter and space which permeate the universe (Bh 13.4)[5] and, in its more usual, concrete sense, the massive structure which contains the heavens and the hells, along with the system of island continents divided by mountain ranges and surrounded by oceans which lies at its centre. Outside the *loka*, there is only the non-*loka* (*aloka*) where there is nothing except strong winds.

The *loka* is without beginning or end in time and was not brought into existence through the agency of any divine being. To this extent, Jainism is an atheist religion inasmuch as it regards it as an illegitimate conclusion that there is a conscious creator who can intervene in or control the affairs of living creatures. Such a being, it is argued, would have to be either without a body, in which case a locus for the intention and effort of creation would be lacking or, alternatively, if embodied, unable to fulfil the necessary requirement of being all-pervading, since in that case the ontological categories would not find any room in the *loka*; alternatively, if non-pervading, such a god would have to be an entity possessing component parts and thus non-eternal. In short, for the Jains, deities such as Brahma and Vishnu, whom Hindus credit with a creative role in the universe, are themselves subject to the process of rebirth in the same manner as all other embodied souls in the *loka* (VTP pp.42–67).

Early Jain cosmography, as found in the Shvetambara scriptures, provides only sketchy information about the dimensions of the *loka*. Totally absent is any reference to the 'rope' (*rajju*), the unit of measurement found in the later cosmographical treatises, which is the distance travelled by a god flying for six months at a speed of ten million miles a second. Nor is there any mention of the *lokapurusha*, the universe in the shape of a giant man (*purusha*) measuring fourteen ropes from head to foot, which is frequently depicted in Jain art from about the sixteenth century onwards.[6] However, the classical delineation of the *loka* is recognisable in a passage in the 'Exposition of Explanations' where it is said to be expanded at the bottom, narrow in the middle and broad in its upper dimensions (Bh 8.9).[7] Described in works of fantastic mensural complexity dating from the early centuries of the common era onwards and portrayed in paintings of often striking colour and imagination, the *loka* represents the arena in which rebirth takes place and where, as Hemacandra puts it, all living creatures, brahman or untouchable, Brahma or worm, are actors in the play called transmigration and the manifold types of existence are as temporary and uncertain as living in rented lodgings (YS 4.65–6).

The central strip of the *loka*, the Middle World, represents its smallest area, being only one rope wide and one hundred thousand leagues high, but it is of the greatest significance since it is inhabited by human beings, the only creatures who can attain enlightenment in the course of their lives. The Middle World consists of a system of alternating oceans and continents, with the central continent of Jambudvipa, 'The Island of the Roseapple Tree', forming with the adjacent continent of Dhatakikhanda and half of the continent nearest to it, Pushkaradvipa, the abode of mankind. Within Jambudvipa, there are a series of regions bordered by mountain ranges and rivers, of which Bharata, that is India, Airavata and Mahavideha are *karmabhumi*, lands where fordmakers appear to preach and where motivated religious action can come to fruition. Mahavideha is particularly noteworthy in this respect because it is believed that the influence of the current corrupt world age does not hold sway there, as a result of which it is a perpetual *karmabhumi* where fordmakers are preaching at this very moment (see Chapter 9).

Below the Middle World is a series of hells, each successively darker, more dismal and unpleasant where hellbeings suffer grievously at each other's hands and through the tortures inflicted by their demonic jailers. Underneath the bottommost hell, there are no habitations of any sort, only clouds (Bh 6.5 and 8).[8]

Above the Middle World is a series of heavens of increasing brightness whose divine inhabitants lead lives of pleasure reminiscent of those of earthly monarchs. However, these gods should not be regarded as objects of adoration. Indeed, their situation is ultimately profoundly unsatisfactory since, after the disappearance of their stock of merit which enabled them to be reborn as gods, they will fall from heaven. The torment endured by hellbeings is similarly finite and after lengthy expiation in hell rebirth must at some point ensue.

Above the heavens and at the very crown of the *loka* is 'The Slightly Curving Place' (*Ishatpragbhara*), which is shaped like a parasol and where the liberated and disembodied souls live, experiencing pure knowledge and bliss, without any further rebirth.

This account of the *loka* can scarcely do justice to Jain cosmography, a branch of technical learning of such intricacy that even the polymath Hemacandra seems to have occasionally lost his way within it.[9] However, the incorporation of a stylised representation of the *loka* into the common symbol of the Jain religion which was adopted in 1975 and the recent expenditure of large sums of money by both the Digambara and Shvetambara communities to construct scale replicas of the *loka* at Hastinapur and Palitana respectively suggest that it is not a matter of purely esoteric interest or eccentric theorising run riot but of enduring significance for all Jains.

From a doctrinal point of view, the purpose of the *loka* is obvious. It provides a framework within which the manifold nature of human destiny can be structured, a backdrop for a vast narrative literature of pious exemplification and a focus for contemplation (e.g. KA vv.115–283). The massive dimensions of the *loka* and the insignificant space occupied by the *karmabhumis* also serve as a reminder of the rarity and value of human birth and the limited confines in which serious religious activity can be conducted. However, some broader understanding of the function of the *loka* might be gained by comparing it with another ancient cosmography, that of Manichaeism.

Mani (third century CE), the founder of Manichaeism, is usually associated with the promulgation of a simple ethical model which centres around the struggle between light and darkness, the two positive and negative forces in the universe. Less well known is the fact that the teachings of Mani were located in a complex myth and elaborately described cosmos which represented a truth revealed to him alone, total adherence to which was required of his followers to gain salvation. The records left by Mani's students show that during his lifetime he was continually preoccupied with tinkering with this myth and fitting its details further into an overall cosmic pattern. That later Manichaean teachers spent so much time in mastering this system and communicating it to their followers suggests that it originally played a role as much social as religious in that it enabled them clearly to demarcate Manichaeism in the Mediterranean and Near Eastern areas from rival Judaeo-Christian, Zoroastrian and pagan world views.[10]

A similar process can most likely be seen at work in Jainism. The classical description of the *loka* provided by the Jain cosmographers, while admittedly drawing on material also found in Hinduism, is uniquely Jain and is one which, when linked with the Universal History, provides a fully and internally consistent picture of the universe in which the only values which hold sway are those of Jainism and is thus an emblem of religious identity and separateness through which the Jains could differentiate themselves from other religions.

Jains react to their religion's cosmography in different ways. Some, especially ascetics uninfluenced by western-style education, have been happy to accept it as an exact portrayal of reality, while others have struggled to reconcile their knowledge of terrestrial geography with the statements of the ancient texts (there has been a recent instance of a monk returning to the laity for this reason). However, most Jains would on reflection be happy to subscribe to two cosmographical systems, one relating to the everyday, transactional world, the other to the more profound symbolic realm of religion.

THE FUNDAMENTAL ENTITIES

Jainism claims that there are five ontological categories called *astikaya* (*asti* meaning 'it exists' and *kaya* 'body'), fundamental entities which permeate the *loka* and are the building blocks responsible for the maintenance of life. The most importance of these is the *jiva*, usually translated as 'soul', although a more accurate rendering might be 'life-monad', with the other four, motion (*dharma*), rest (*adharma*), atoms (*pudgala*) and space (*akasha*), collectively forming a category called 'non-soul' (*ajiva*). The Digambaras came to add time as a sixth category to this list.[11]

It must be assumed that an analysis of the world into five entities developed only gradually, for the first book of the *Acaranga* makes no mention of the non-soul category, merely dividing existents into those which have thought and those which do not.[12] The canonical texts do not feel the need to give any serious proof for these entities on the grounds that their truth has been established by the omniscient teachers who alone are capable of witnessing them directly. All other people must infer their existence in the same way that the wind is known to exist despite the fact that it is never seen (Bh 18.7).[13] In general, it is held by Jain teachers that without the fundamental entities there would be universal oneness or, alternatively, all objects would become either totally inexpressible or non-existent, a view of the universe which realist Jainism cannot countenance.

The four *ajiva* entities provide the mechanism by which the *jiva* functions, for its principal characteristics are that it is eternal, although impermanent in respect of its modifications, consisting of pure consciousness with innate will which enables it to act, while at the same time being totally without form. It is the *jiva* which experiences and is responsible for all intellectual and spiritual operations and not the body, which is merely a conglomerate of atoms (KA 188). The *jiva* is nonetheless immediately accessible since it is identical with knowledge and can therefore be internally grasped as an existent entity through that same knowledge (Abhayadeva on Sth 2).

Clearly this view of the *jiva* was one which the Jains felt it necessary to defend and the crude materialist view of the identity of the body and soul is subjected to an early assault in the Shvetambara *upanga*, the 'Questions of King Prasenajit' (RP). This work describes a discussion between Prasenajit, who is presented as a kind of naive empiricist, and the Jain monk Keshin. Prasenajit had been in the habit of carrying out experiments on criminals to test for the possible existence of the soul. For example, he threw one into a tightly sealed cauldron and, as the soul of the suffocated man was not observed to emerge when it was opened, he concluded that soul and body must be identical. On other occasions, he weighed a convicted thief before and after execution and also dissected a corpse but was unable to find any physical evidence for the existence of anything corresponding to a soul.

Keshin replies to Prasenajit's experiments by means of similes. The *jiva*, unlike the body, can be said to be unimpeded in its movements and physically intangible, just as the noise of a drum, although struck within a locked and barred house, will still be heard outside. Similarly, a leather bag will weigh the same before and after being inflated with air, while cutting up a body to find the *jiva* is like chopping up wood to find fire. Prasenajit is finally converted by Keshin's double assertion that certain things can only be witnessed by the omniscient and that the *jivas* of a tiny insect and an elephant are the same size since the *jiva* always expands and contracts according to the size of the body in which it is reborn, just as the light of a lamp always expands or contracts according to the size of the room or receptacle in which it is put.

The *loka* is eternally filled with *jivas* and, despite the immensity of its dimensions, there is not a single space point (*pradesha*: the unit occupied by an atom) in which a *jiva* has not entered or left an existence, just as, according to the 'Enunciation of Explications', there is not one single spot in a pen full of goats which has not been covered with droppings and hair (Bh 12.7).[14] All of these *jivas* are in their purest form identical and fully and equally endowed with the qualities of bliss, energy and omniscience. However, owing to the multifarious operations of karma, they become variously embodied, although the body itself is never seen as anything more than a tool.

Embodied *jivas* are divided into two types, those which are stationary (*sthavara*) such as plants, and those which are moving (*trasa*) such as insects, gods, hellbeings, animals and human beings. There is also a hierarchy of forms of existence depending on the number of senses possessed: one-sensed such as extremely basic and microscopic forms of life known as *nigoda*, earth-, air-, water- and fire-bodies along with plants, two-sensed such as worms, three-sensed such as ants, four-sensed such as flies and five-sensed including hellbeings, gods, animals and humans. The *Dashavaikalika* asserts that, despite the apparently huge discrepancies between these various forms of life, the mark of a great monk is to realise that all of them are essentially like oneself (DVS 10.5).

The idea of motion (*dharma*) and rest (*adharma*) as representing separate ontological categories is peculiar to Jainism among Indian metaphysical systems and it seems probable that these entities developed as a result of the cosmographers' speculations about what lay outside the *loka*. So although the 'Exposition of Explanations', the earliest text to deal with cosmography, says nothing about the possibility of anything moving from the *loka* into the *aloka*,[15] it came to be accepted that souls and atoms could not exist in the emptiness of the *aloka* because of the absence there of the entity of motion, while at the same time the entity of rest was regarded as serving to restrict them to the confines of the *loka* (Abhayadeva on Sth 8 and 337).

The term *dharma* is well known throughout other Indian religious traditions with a general sense approximating to 'salvific truth' or 'the immemorial standards in accord with which individuals should lead their lives'. While *dharma* does have these senses within Jainism, its literal meaning of 'that which carries' better conveys its metaphysical function of providing the support and creating the conditions for souls and atoms whose natural state would otherwise be movement, just as water is the occasioning cause for fish to swim (TSRV on TS 5.17). Conversely, its opposite, *adharma*, creates the conditions for their stasis. The 'Explication of Explanations' broadens the significance of these two entities by stating that *dharma* is responsible not just for ordinary physical motion but also for verbal and mental activity, while *adharma* is involved in the stabilising of the mind through contemplation (Bh 18.4).[16]

Umasvati defines the atoms (*pudgala*) as providing the bodily and non-spiritual dimension for the *jiva* (TS 5.19–20). Through the accumulation of atoms brought about by karma, the *jiva* forms a body which for most creatures is one of flesh and blood (called the *audarika* body), although there are other types of body involved, for example, in the process of rebirth. Language and breath are composed of atoms, and we also owe to them our direct, physical experience of pleasure and pain, birth and death.

Space is the locus in which the other entities perform their proper tasks. According to Akalanka, it functions in the same way as a great pot in which rice is being cooked (TSRV p.477). It is the only entity which interpenetrates both the *loka* and the *aloka*.

These categories obviously provide a model of the contents and dynamics of the universe but it is one without any ethical or soteriological implications and which does not in itself explain why the soul becomes embodied and loses its pristine powers. It was in the context of karmic theorisation that such an explanation was given and it took the form of a series of nine 'reals' (*tattva*) which maps out in abbreviated form the various modifications which can effect change in the spiritual status of the *jiva*. Assent to these ontological categories was to be regarded within the tradition, at least as intellectually formulated, as the mark of the true Jain.

Along with the *jiva* and the four entities which constitute the *ajiva*, the reals consist of the flowing in of karma (*asrava*), *punya* and *papa*, respectively meritorious and morally negative action which effect the quality of karma, the binding of karma (*bandha*), the warding off of inflowing karma (*samvara*), the destruction of karma which has been bound (*nirjara*) and, finally, spiritual deliverance (*moksha*).

This full list occurs in the twenty-eighth chapter of the *Uttaradhyayana* (UttS 28.14), probably a later portion of the Shvetambara scriptures, but all of the reals, with the exception of warding off of karma, are mentioned in the *Acaranga*, although not in any systematised manner, which points to their presence at the very earliest stage of Jain teachings. *Asrava* is in fact an archaic term, found also in early Buddhism, which originally signified the channels which linked a sense organ to a sense object (cf. MA 738). While Umasvati presumably subsumes meritorious and morally negative action under either *asrava* or the binding of karma within his list which contains only seven reals (TS 1.4), Jain tradition in general accepted the necessity of their formal inclusion in order to provide an ethical dimension which was meaningful not just for ascetics but for a community which as a whole also contained lay people and whose concerns were to be increasingly directed towards the gaining of merit rather than the achieving of deliverance.[17]

KARMA

'There is nothing mightier in the world than karma; karma tramples down all powers, as an elephant a clump of lotuses' (BhA 1616).

It is karma which is responsible for the manifest differences in the status, attainments and happiness of life-forms. Yet the manner in which this all-governing force comes into contact with the *jiva* is never fully explained and has to be taken on trust as a matter of inference and faith. Karma for Jainism, unlike other Indian religions, is regarded as being a physical substance and, as such, there ought to be no means by which it could adhere to and modify the *jiva* which is non-substance, formless and pure consciousness. A nexus of similes, in the oldest of which karma is most commonly likened to dust (DVS 12.10), was employed by Jain theoreticians to explain the mechanism of this beginningless relationship. For Akalanka, the *jiva* which experiences the passions attracts karma like a damp cloth does dust

(TSRV p.506) or, more elaborately, the binding of atoms onto the soul brought by about being wetted by false belief develops to karma in the same way as seeds, fruit and flowers thrown into a pot ferment into wine (TSRV p.566). Abhayadeva Suri (comm. on Sth 13) compares the *jiva* to a leaking ship with karma pouring in through the holes, the *asravas*, which have to be caulked by correct religious practice. Images of tying, smearing and staining abound in discussions of karmic influence which, if not providing a fully rigorous explanation of the process, nonetheless convey the negative role which karma plays in Jain ontology.

The notion of karma as a substance pervading the universe and being attracted to the *jiva* by the latter's actions was unknown to the earliest Jain teachings. However, the germs of this view of karma can be seen in the 'Exposition of Explanations' which describes somebody who kills another creature as being 'touched' by enmity towards that creature. Here action is viewed in physical terms and this gradually led to an interpretation of the overall relationship between the *jiva* and action as being a material one. However, the idea of binding particles of karma is hardly found at all in the course of the 'Exposition of Explanations' nor is any interest shown in the effects of morally positive karma.[18]

Umasvati, drawing on canonical sources, regarded physical, mental and verbal activity (*yoga*) as responsible for the flowing in of karmic particles (TS 6.1–2), although the actual binding of them to the *jiva* is said to come about through possession of a variety of negative characteristics: false belief, lack of discipline, carelessness, the passions and mental, physical and verbal activities (TS 8.1). However, earlier sources ascribe particular significance to the passions (*kashaya*) in effecting this process. The initial emphasis here was upon strong attachment and hatred alone, although a fourfold group of passions – anger, pride, deception and greed (found, for example, at DVS 8.37–9) – came to represent the standard enumeration which was to be integrated into the developed karma theory.[19] The term *kashaya* is given several etymologies, including derivations from verbal roots meaning 'plough' and 'injure' (Abhayadeva on Sth 249), but its common sense of 'resin' or 'stickiness' conveys perfectly its perceived function of constituting a kind of glue which enabled karma to adhere to the *jiva*. If the passions are calmed and destroyed, then, states Akalanka, karma cannot come into contact with the *jiva*, just as a clod of earth thrown at a dried-up wall will not stick to it (TSRV p.508). The image of the passion-induced viscosity of the *jiva* being burnt away by the heat of asceticism has remained basic to Jain ideology.

In the earliest teachings, a mental action or intention which was not carried out, or causing someone to carry out an action or merely approving the performance of such an action, were not regarded as different in any way from a fully willed and performed action with regard to karmic retribution (SKS 1.1.2.24–9). Here Jainism differed radically from early Buddhism which was more preoccupied with the quality of the intention lying behind an action. Moreover, while the notion expressed at one point in the 'Exposition of Explanations' that even inanimate objects, such as a bow and arrow, could through being used to kill some creature bind karma, since they were composed of colonies of life-forms, was not seriously pursued,[20] there is no doubt that early Jainism was particularly uncompromising in its insistence that even involuntary actions, inasmuch as they were expressions of a general lack of awareness, had a negative karmic effect.

The origins of this view of human activity lay in an ethical universe in which the principal actor was the brave ascetic striving to ward off and destroy the deleterious effects of that violence which early Jainism regarded as characterising all action of unenlightened people. Such a position, if it ever had any serious basis in reality, was hardly likely to be attractive to prospective ascetic recruits, let alone to the lay followers who supported the ascetic community and whose role as moral agents was to become a subject of increasing concern.[21] So the 'Exposition of Explanations', which represents a transitional stage leading to the formulation of the classical Jain teachings as represented by Umasvati, while accepting that physical movement by an embodied *jiva* inevitably causes harm, also states that the karma attracted by a monk in the performance of physical activity which relates to his spiritual development is experienced and expelled in an infinitesimally short time so that it has no effects (Bh 3.3).[22]

THE TYPES OF KARMA

The description of karma and the modifications which it effects upon the *jiva* came by the medieval period to constitute an autonomous branch of learning which in its amplitude and immunity to controversion was, like cosmography, a mark of Jain intellectual distinctiveness. However, despite its proliferation of subdivisions and combinations thereof, the basic structure of karma in Jainism is comparatively straightforward.

Karma is divided into eight categories, found as early as the 'Exposition of Explanations',[23] which are in turn divided into two categories of four: the harming karmas and the non-harming karmas. The principal harming karma is called the 'delusory' (*mohaniya*) which is the keystone of the whole structure in that its destruction paves the way for the elimination of the other varieties of karma. This type of karma brings about attachment to incorrect views and the inability to lead the religiously correct, Jain life.

The karma 'which covers knowledge' (*jnanavaraniya*) is, to use Abhayadeva Suri's similes, like 'a screen which blocks out the soul which is as bright as the autumn moon' or 'a cloud covering the sun of omniscience' (comm. on Sth 105). At one level, it interferes with the normal functioning of the intellect and senses; at another, it prevents the functioning of the developed mental capabilities of the *jiva* including the omniscience which is otherwise natural to it.

The karma 'which obscures perception' (*darshanavaraniya*) hinders the perception brought about by the sense-organs and the various types of knowledge.

The 'obstacle' (*antaraya*) karma obstructs, amongst other things, the innate energy of the soul.

The four non-harming karmas are, as their name suggests, non-deleterious to the *jiva*.

'Feeling' (*vedaniya*) karma dictates whether the experiences of the soul are pleasant or unpleasant.

'Name' (*nama*) karma determines what sort of rebirth is attained, as well as the state of one's senses and spiritual potential. Its most important subtype is 'fordmaker-name' (*tirthankaranama*) karma, which is brought about by a variety of exceptional circumstances and activities in past lives which ensure that an individual eventually becomes a fordmaker (see TS 6.23).

'Life' (*ayus*) karma decides the duration of one's life which must be in accord with the species to which one belongs.

Finally, 'clan' (*gotra*) karma determines one's status, high or low, within a species and thus, like name karma, has a bearing on an individual's ability to progress on the spiritual path.

This apparently rigidly defined schema gives the impression that the possibility for freedom of action on the part of any individual is near to being excluded. Certainly, the rich literature of exemplification and homiletic which grew up with karmic theorisation contains many examples of specific actions of particular intensity in one life determining events in the next. A king being forced by his captor to eat the flesh of his family as a result of having been an egg seller in a previous existence or the passion of a young merchant for a prostitute bringing about their rebirth as incestuously linked brother and sister are just two examples of the sort of theme which was often used (VPS 3 and 4). One of Haribhadra's most famous works is the 'Story of Samaraditya' (SamK), a long prose romance which describes how one character, tormented by another because of his ugliness, hounds his enemy through a series of existences, and the events in their lives are explained as receiving their impulse from an original intensity of passion.

While it is understandable that ascetics would have used frightening stories to ram home the full karmic implications of morally incorrect modes of life or excessively intense emotional relationships, such narratives were often softened by concluding statements about the protagonists' eventual attainment of liberation, and the transforming effect of pious action is an equally common theme in Jain literature. Jain karma theory is undoubtedly much more elaborately thought out and systematised than its equivalent in Hinduism or Buddhism, but this does not imply lack of free will or the operation of total deterministic control over destinies. Hemacandra points out that at no time has the karma of any two individuals exactly coincided[24] and, indeed, karma as understood generally in Jainism merely establishes the conditions of possibility with an individual's life and should not, irrespective of what the narrative literature might sometimes suggest, be regarded as responsible for every single event which might befall an individual. Unless that individual is *abhavya*, a category of *jiva* which the Jains claim will never attain liberation, there must always remain the possibility of responding to spiritual prompting and awakening or suddenly experiencing fear of the round of rebirth (*samvega*). If this were not so, the entire efficacy of Jainism as a gradualistic religious path would be undermined.

It is unfortunate that no ethnographic research has as yet been carried out into contemporary Jain lay and ascetic attitudes to karma, free will and retribution. All monks and nuns and many lay people are familiar with the eight basic types of karma and there are well-known rituals through which knowledge of karma is mediated to the laity but, although there is general assent to the necessity of burning away karma from the soul in order to make progress on the spiritual path, few study the intricacies of the doctrine and familiarity with it would not be regarded as of any real relevance to most Jains. It would in fact be surprising if karma proved to be the sole explanation available to Jains for the variety of events and experiences which occur in the course of life. Hindus and Buddhists invoke karma as merely one amongst a variety of explanations, such as the evil eye, planetary conjunction and fate, for the vagaries of human fortune and it seems likely that Jainism is no different in this respect.[25]

REBIRTH

At death, the *jiva* leaves its body and progresses to its next place of birth virtually instantaneously. As with other Indian religions, the mental state at the precise moment of death is regarded by Jains as being particularly important for determining the nature of the next body. Sometimes, the medieval writers tell us, this can lead to unpleasant results. Abhayadeva Suri claims that a man who dies in the act of sexual intercourse is reborn in the womb of his partner (comm. on Samav 152), while Haribhadra tells the bizarre story of how a sheep which covered its mother and, being killed by the leading ram of the flock, was reborn in his mother's womb, having as it were engendered himself (SamK p.259). Such grotesque examples apart,

Jainism has always been intent on conveying that a calm death free from rancour, frustration or pain, with mind fixed on religious principles at the end of one life, will ensure a positive rebirth, the length of which, and therefore, partially, the nature of which, will have already been established by life karma bound six months before death.[26]

The rapidity of the *jiva*'s transition from one life to the next, 'leaping like a monkey' (Bh 25.8), enables the Jains to bypass a great deal of speculation, of the sort found in Hinduism and Buddhism, about what happens to the transmigrating entity in the intermediate stage between existences. Little more is said than that the *jiva* is sheathed by subtle and invisible karmic and luminous bodies, linked to the gross physical body of flesh and blood (TS 2.41–3), which facilitate the speedy process of rebirth and provide a degree of continuity in the course of transmigration. Such an interpretation also ensured that the Jains could from a social point of view further dissociate themselves from the Hindus, for it left no scope for the performance of one of the crucial Hindu rites of passage, the *shraddha* ritual, by which a new body is symbolically moulded and created out of riceballs for the next birth of the dead ancestor who would otherwise remain in a state of limbo.[27]

Once the *jiva* reaches its next birth, a process of gestation takes place in the womb. Although when in embryonic form it does not possess fully formed senses or flesh and blood, the *jiva* is is still sheathed by the karmic and luminous bodies with which it transmigrated. It lives off its mother's menstrual blood and father's semen and, nourished by that, builds up a physical body, with its flesh, blood and brains coming from the mother and bones, marrow, hair and nails coming from the father (Bh 1.7).[28] This form of birth is characteristic of humans and animals only and does not apply to gods and hellbeings which appear spontaneously and to many lower forms of life which are born through a process of coagulation (TS 2.32–5).

DELIVERANCE

Spiritual deliverance (*moksha*) is defined in simple terms by Umasvati (TS 10.5) as release from all karma. This should in its finality be clearly distinguished from the attainment of enlightenment which, after the cultivation of morally positive attitudes, the practice of austerity and the gradual suppression of negative discriminative mental processes, involves the uprooting of deluding karma which is then succeeded by the removal of the remaining three harming karmas, thus liberating the innate qualities, such as omniscience, of the *jiva*. Enlightenment, however, does not of itself entail death because the operation of the four non-harming karmas is still unimpaired, with life and name karma guaranteeing the continuation of embodied existence and experience karma ensuring bodily sensations, although the latter point was a source of sectarian dispute for the Digambaras denied that a *kevalin*'s feeling karma could bring about an effect such as hunger. The enlightened person, fordmaker or *kevalin*, may therefore spend a considerable period after enlightenment engaging in mental and physical activities such as walking, preaching and meditation. However, no new karma is bound by these activities nor is it possible in this state to carry out acts of violence, even involuntarily.

It is necessary for life karma to run its course before final deliverance can be gained. From the time of the scriptural texts, Jain theoreticians claimed that it might be necessary for the *kevalin* to perform an expulsion (*samudghata*) of karmic particles in order to equalise experience karma, which has been generally bound more intensely than any other type, with life karma. This strange process is effected by the *kevalin* expanding the *jiva*, for the short duration of eight instants, to the height and width of the *loka* in a variety of temporarily assumed shapes whereupon, after ejecting karmic particles in the same way as dust is shaken off an open sheet which is then refolded, it subsequently returns to the confines of the human body. This ensures that the non-harming karmas will quickly reach their end and the *kevalin* then starts to run down the operation of mind, body and speech until all natural functioning ceases.

The *kevalin* remains in this state for the time taken to enunciate five short verses, upon which the four non-harming karmas disappear and the *jiva* then becomes free from its body and the occluding force of karma until it rises through innate capability in one instant, without coming into contact with any of the entities which permeate the *loka*, to the realm of the liberated *jivas* at the top of the universe where it will exist perpetually without any further rebirth in a disembodied state of perfect joy, energy, consciousness and knowledge (Aup pp.286–314 and TS 10).

The number of liberated *jivas* is infinite: it both remains constant and increases through a steady influx of newly liberated *jivas* which in the case of the current period of the world era will come from one of the parallel regions of Jambudvipa where fordmakers are at present teaching. Despite the fact that these *jivas* interpenetrate each other and are all possessed of the same qualities, Jainism fiercely resists the possibility of their constituting a unified world-soul of the non-dualistic variety found in Hinduism. Non-dualism, according to Haribhadra, makes no sense for, if the world-soul were inherently pure, it would be difficult to explain why the phenomenal world is manifestly impure, while if it were impure, there would then be no point in the liberated *jivas* merging with it (LV p.268).

Despite the infinitude of liberated *jivas*, the world of rebirth (*samsara*) will never become empty, for liberation is regarded as having validity only if its opposite continues to exist. This may well be a metaphysical reflex of a practicality of Jain society, namely that, despite the ascetic community by its example and teaching continually urging the lay community to renounce and become monks and nuns, the possibility of all lay people becoming ascetics, or even of the laity being outnumbered by ascetics, cannot be countenanced since support in the form of alms and shelter for the ascetic community would no longer be forthcoming.

Jainism dichotomises all *jivas* into two spiritual categories: the *bhavya* ('capable') who has the potential to attain liberation and the *abhavya* ('incapable') who at no point in the limitless future will be capable of achieving this goal.[29] Jain storytellers portray the *abhavyas* as manifesting their unhappy state by an inability to concentrate when listening to sermons, doubting the efficacy of basic Jain practices and not offering homage to the fordmakers with full sincerity (MSP 21 and DhMV 13). There was a sectarian disagreement over the fate of the most disreputable villain in Jain tradition, Makkhali Gosala, with the Shvetambaras claiming that as a *bhavya* he would ultimately attain liberation, while to the Digambaras he is *abhavya*, condemned to unending rebirth.

PLANTS AND ANIMALS

The lowest forms of life in the *loka* are the infinitesimally small *nigoda*, which do not themselves have bodies but live for extremely short periods of time in conglomerates in the bodies of other *jivas*. Despite the abject nature of their condition, it was nonetheless regarded as possible for some of these *nigodas* (others are condemned to stay in that existence eternally) to mount the Jain evolutionary scale and eventually gain human birth (KA 284–90).[30] However, little serious interest was taken by Jain karma theoreticians in describing how human beings, the only creatures capable of achieving liberation, could spiral downwards to the bottommost level of existence, with a Digambara tradition about Makkhali Gosala's rebirth as a *nigoda* apparently unique in this respect. Similarly, the type of karma which would lead to rebirth as a one-sensed earth-, air-, water- or fire-body is not dwelt upon, although these *jivas* are accepted as having a certain minimal capacity to act themselves in that they breathe each other (Bh 9.34).[31]

Of all the lowest categories of life, it is plants alone which are deemed to share certain characteristics with human beings. It is obvious that plants develop and decay like all higher forms of life but, more specifically, they are also regarded by Jainism as possessing a form of consciousness and awareness of their surroundings in common with those of animals and humans. This supposedly can be seen from their germinating at certain regular times of the year, while their nature also evinces quasi-human aspects such as desire for nourishment (SKS 2.3) and sexual reproduction and a sense of both fear and possession (TSRV on 2.24 and Shilanka on AS 1.1.5.6–7). They are even capable of the expression of morally negative feelings. Haribhadra describes in his 'Story of Samaraditya' how a greedy individual is reborn as a coconut tree which avariciously extends its roots to a cache of treasure buried beneath it (SamK pp.138–53).[32] The fact that, according to the 'Exposition of Explanations', Mahavira himself predicted that a tree and two separate branches blasted by heat, drought and fire would first be reborn at a slightly more advanced level as sacred trees and subsequently progress to human birth and enlightenment shows that Jainism accepted the real possibility of the spiritual perfectibility of plants (Bh 14.8).[33]

Animals, a designation which includes fish and birds as well as terrestrial creatures, have an obvious advantage over plants for, as well as possessing five senses and a certain degree of discrimination, they are capable with the right prompting of remembering their previous existences and modifying their normal patterns of behaviour by fasting and contemplation so that they can achieve rebirth in heaven (Aup pp.264–7). The narrative theme of the pious animal became a means to exemplify the workings of karma and to foster the principles of compassion and non-violence. One of the 'mixed' texts of the Shvetambara canon, the 'Divisions of Death' (MV 507–24), describes how a variety of animals, such as a fish, lion and snake, all received some kind of spiritual jolt which caused them to give up their predatory lives and take to fasting, the moral being that if animals can practise austerities, it is difficult for humans to justify laxity (MV 512).

Many stories from the medieval period demonstrate how positive or negative character traits acquired during human birth still manifest themselves in animal existence. So Jineshvara Suri tells a charming story of a doctor who has given alms to Jain monks being reborn as a monkey who uses healing herbs to cure a monk who has a wound in his foot (KKP 17). The Jain view of life is expanded far beyond the concerns of human beings alone and is one which encourages respect for plants and animals. However, the true value of these life-forms is ultimately only seen in the human values which are imposed upon them.

KUNDAKUNDA AND THE DIGAMBARA MYSTICAL TRADITION

In the Digambara Kundakunda India found one of its most intense advocates of the centrality of inward experience and the reorientation of all religious practice to focus upon the self. Nothing is known of Kundakunda's life, although he can reasonably confidently be dated to the second or third century CE, and hagiographical accounts of him do not appear until the tenth century. His original monastic name was Padmanandin and he seems to have been called Kundakunda because he supposedly came from a village of that name in south India. Tradition regards him as being the founder of the Mula Sangha, the main Digambara ascetic lineage, and his name is invoked along with those of Mahavira and Gautama in a famous auspicious verse still recited in Karnataka. However, it is his writings which are responsible for his great prestige and several of them have remained among the most influential in the history of Jainism.

Sixteen works are attributed to Kundakunda but caution must be exercised in connecting him with all of them. For example, the group of texts known as the 'Eight Treatises' (*Ashtapahuda*) was shown by Schubring to be later than Kundakunda on metrical and stylistic grounds, while other texts evince clear signs of interpolation.[34] None of these philological considerations have had any impact upon the Digambara community which continues to regard all Kundakunda's writings as genuine and forming a unity.

Kundakunda's most significant works are written in Prakrit and are deceptively simple in style. The 'Essence of Restraint' (NiyS) deals largely with the obligatory ritual practices incumbent upon the ascetic, while the 'Essence of the Five Entities' (*Pancastinikayasara*) seems in origin to have been a loosely connected anthology of verses whose subject matter is obvious by its title. The 'Essence of the Scripture' (PS) is a manual dealing with ascetic and spiritual behaviour, probably directed towards young novices, and the 'Essence of the Doctrine' (SS), the most famous of Kundakunda's works, is largely devoted to a discussion of the real nature of the soul. All these writings, although they generally discuss different aspects of the Jain path, provide an exemplification of Kundakunda's overall soteriological standpoint as involving a radical interiorisation of the religious life.

For Kundakunda, the soul is the only true and ultimate category in existence which, as such, provides a particular standpoint (*naya*), the pivotal point, called either 'certain' (*nishcaya*), 'supreme' (*paramartha*) or 'pure' (*shuddha*), with reference to which all other entities, beliefs and practices can be judged.[35] Jain karma doctrine holds that as a result of the adhesion of karmic particles the soul loses its ability through omniscience to understand the nature of the external world. Much more significantly, Kundakunda suggests, it loses an awareness of its own inner nature as pure knowledge and its status as being already liberated. In reality, the soul cannot be in any meaningful way modified by contact with karmic matter and therefore, on the level of the certain standpoint, the sole object of omniscience is the soul itself (NiyS 159–66). Everything else in the universe has a purely transactional and provisional value and is to be viewed from the perspective of a worldly (*vyavahara*) standpoint. The Jain ascetic should therefore direct his energies to inner experience.

This is one of the earliest examples of the two truths model of reality, better known through being used by Mahayana Buddhism and the non-dualist brand of Vedanta in Hinduism. Kundakunda employs it to suggest that the soul by its very nature cannot have any real physical connection with anything extraneous to it such as karmic matter. It has nothing to do with the state of embodiment and only experiences the *mental* results of karma (NiyS 18 and 42; PS 1.77). Furthermore, the pursuit of merit through the practice of austerities, meditation and so on with a view to improving rebirth can have no serious bearing on the real state of the soul. The idea of polarities, moral or otherwise, is collapsed and Kundakunda asserts that good and bad, pleasure and pain, fasting and non-fasting and so on are of significance solely at the worldly level in the flawed realm of transmigration (e.g. SS 306–7). The continual theme of the 'Essence of Restraint' is that the outward, ritual observances of Jainism are of validity only when carried out in a soul-directed manner, and the Three Jewels of right knowledge, faith and practice, which on the face of it represent the path to deliverance, are in reality reckoned to be merely another means of describing the soul. The worldly level of truth has meaning only in terms of the soul's unfamiliarity with its own nature and is otherwise of no value.

The way to realise the soul is clearly a practical one involving direct knowledge but, in a statement deeply subversive of Jain tradition, Kundakunda declares that scripture and its injunctions, generally regarded in Jainism as the source of correct understanding, are incapable of bringing this about because they cannot be said to know anything (SS 360). However, it has to be conceded that there is also a strand running through Kundakunda's writings which would see the practice of the correct ascetic and moral behaviour described in the scriptures as bringing about the warding off and destruction of karma which then leads the self to a direct understanding of its own nature. It has been suggested that Kundakunda's works deploy both a mystic and a non-mystic pattern, with verses expressing the latter standpoint which relates to conventional Jain theorisation possibly having been interpolated into the 'Essence of the Doctrine'.[36] It is, however, predictable that a two levels of truth model will be manipulated to provide apparently paradoxical statements, for that is part of its function, and we should not expect total 'logical' consistency in its deployment on Kundakunda's part.

Later Digambara commentators greatly elaborated and expanded these ideas. A principal concern for them was the status of the worldly level of truth, the necessity for which the 'mystical' Kundakunda tended to deny completely, and its inherent validity as a vehicle towards the higher truth. The prominent thirteenth century layman Ashadhara succinctly described the person wishing to abandon worldly means in pursuit of mystic understanding of the soul as a fool trying to grow corn without seed (AnDh p.74).

Although Kundakunda's ideas should not be seen as exclusively Digambara in origin, since he was most likely drawing on nascent Jain views about a perspectivist approach to reality which antedated the sectarian split,[37] he nonetheless seems to have established a general idiom for Jain mysticism. His influence can no doubt be seen when the Shvetambara Haribhadra states that on the worldly level of truth the abode of the liberated souls is a physical place while, on the higher level, it is nothing other than the true nature of the soul (LV p.261). However, the Shvetambaras were generally ill at ease with what they perceived as Kundakunda's reductionist approach to reality and, in the seventeenth century, Yashovijaya, perhaps the last truly great intellectual figure in Jainism, whose fame rests largely on his learning combined with a mastery of sophisticated logical techniques but who also later in life developed a strong interest in the mystical side of the religion, criticised the inadequacy of Kundakunda's reliance on only one standpoint and also strongly attacked the laity-based Adhyatmika sect whose de-emphasis of the role of ritual and ascetics derived its inspiration from Kundakunda and his commentators.

GOD

One of the most common terms used in Jainism to describe the self in its purest, unconditioned and karmicly free state as sole object of contemplation is *paramatman*, the 'supreme soul'. The liberated *jivas* have reached their culminating state by a realisation of the *paramatman* and it is therefore an object of reverence for all Jains. While Jainism is, as we have seen, atheist in the limited sense of rejection of both the existence of a creator god and the possibility of the intervention of such a being in human affairs, it nonetheless must be regarded as a theist religion in the more profound sense that it accepts the existence of a divine principle, the *paramatman*, often in fact referred to as 'god'(e.g. ParPr 114–16), existing in potential state within all beings. Jain devotional worship of the fordmakers, who are frequently also referred to by the designation 'god', should be interpreted as being directed towards this and as an acknowledgement of the spiritual principle within every individual.

Jains participated in the culture of the *sants*, the poet-saints of medieval India, and like them produced devotional poetry in emergent vernaculars such as Hindi and Gujarati. The imagery and language of poets such as Banarsidas (1586–1643; see Chapter 7) and his imitator Dyanatray (1676–1727) is often very close in style to that of a figure such as Kabir (*c.* 1440–1518), claimed by Hindus and Moslems alike, who wrote pithy and often highly paradoxical verses about the God who is without qualities, and the Jains did not shy away from using the same sexual and marital imagery as their Hindu and Moslem contemporaries to convey the nature of the attainment of the *paramatman*. However, despite their insistence on the ultimate worthlessness of orthopraxy, at no time do the Jain mystical poets seem to have imitated or advocated the type of antinomian and eccentric behaviour found elsewhere at this time.[38]

5 History: from early times to the late medieval period

To write a conventional history of the Jains is an awkward undertaking. This is not simply as a result of an inadequacy of material on which to draw, for at times the sources available are rich although, paradoxically, it is the eighteenth and nineteenth centuries, so close to us in time, which represent one of the periods of Jain history most difficult to reconstruct, but rather because exclusive reliance on the few 'hard facts' provided by inscriptional or literary texts will result, at least for the early period of Jainism, in little more than a skeletal chronological framework and mere lists of teachers, authors and descriptions of their works. It is unfortunate that the flavour of Jain history has, for all its interest, often remained elusive and I would contend that it will only be possible to gain some sense of it if there is brought into play a wider range of source materials such as stories, legends, belles-lettres, clan and sectarian traditions, hagiographies and so on, not all of which constitute evidence of the sort generally employed in the writing of history but which nonetheless provide a distinctively Jain perspective on the religion's past.

The single most important fact about the development of Jainism as a whole is that, from Mahavira onwards, the obligation to hand down the teachings has created a community and a culture with their own memories and resonances which are not bounded solely by objective historical data, however indispensable it might be to attempt to retrieve them. As a result of this, I will adopt in this chapter a broadly thematic approach to the sweep of Jain history up to the sixteenth century or so, drawing eclectically on a range of sources and concentrating largely and of necessity for much of this period on the ascetic as main protagonist.

MATHURA

From a very early period, the Jain community shifted from its original heartland in the Ganges basin outward towards different parts of India. No doubt the region where Mahavira preached the doctrine was never totally abandoned, for it still remained the location of important sacred spots, but virtually all Jains who live in the states of Bihar and Bengal today are descendants of those who migrated back from the west for economic reasons from the seventeenth century onwards.

The two main directions of movement were along the important trade route to the west and down the eastern litoral to the Dravidian south, and it must be assumed that this process involved both ascetics and lay supporters, the former following the logic of the ideal of wandering mendicancy and the latter in search of greater mercantile opportunity. Early confirmation of Jainism's presence in the east can be found in the famous inscription from Hathigumpha, dating from approximately the first century BCE, of Kharavela, the king of Kalinga in what is now the state of Orissa. In this, Kharavela boasts of having attacked the Ganges basin kingdoms of Anga and Magadha and of having retrieved an image of a fordmaker which had been taken from Kalinga by earlier invaders.[1] It is difficult to say to what extent Kharavela was a devout Jain, since the inscription states that he honoured all sects, and the significance of the description of his raid probably lies in the early evidence it provides both of the existence of Jain image worship and of a practice which was to become particularly prevalent in medieval south India, the seizing of an important image as a means of symbolically stripping a kingdom of its prosperity and wellbeing. Architectural remains point to the continued presence of Jains in Orissa as late as the sixteenth century but that region's contribution to the historical development of Jainism remained comparatively minor.

It is the westward shift to the city of Mathura and its environs which provides the best evidence for generalising about early Jain society. Mathura owed its position from about the fourth or third century BCE as a cultural and trading centre to the fact that it was located on the junction of the caravan routes to the west, east and south of India and it was undoubtedly a cosmopolitan city exposed to a variety of influences. All our knowledge of the archaeological and inscriptional evidence for the Jain connection with this ancient centre polarises around the funerary monument (*stupa*) excavated at Kankali Tila. The Jains themselves maintained a legendary tradition of the antiquity of this site whose fullest expression is given by the medieval Shvetambara pilgrim, Jinaprabha Suri. According to this legend, two monks came to Mathura and lodging in a garden converted its mistress, a goddess, so that she became a Jain laywoman. The goddess, to compensate for her failure to take the Jain community of Mathura to Mount Meru to pay homage to the *stupa* there, constructed a replica of it made out of gold and jewels. The Buddhists and Hindus claimed this great *stupa* for their own, but a miracle demonstrated that it had in reality been dedicated to the seventh fordmaker Suparshva whose image it contained, thus bringing about Mathura's status as a holy place for the Jains. In the course of time, the fordmaker Parshva came to Mathura and warned that the corrupt world age was at hand, as a result of which the goddess, fearing her inability to protect the *stupa*, got it bricked it up and a more normal stone monument was built outside (VTK 9).

There is an inscriptional reference to the *stupa* 'created by the gods' dating from 157 CE, which suggests that by that period it was reckoned to be of considerable antiquity.[2] Jinaprabha's story points to the fact, corroborated by archaeological evidence, that the Jains cohabited in Mathura with other religious groups and also that at an early period there was no great difference between them with regard to religious architecture. A slightly earlier legend about the *stupa* given by the tenth century Digambara Somadeva records how the foundation of the *stupa* took place after considerable rivalry with the Buddhists.[3] It is also likely that around the beginning of the common era the Jains, no doubt in order to accommodate themselves to the Hindu population, started remodelling the story of Krishna, of whose cult Mathura was and still is an important centre, in order to link him with the fordmaker Nemi.

The inscriptions from Kankali Tila offer important evidence of the fission of the Jain ascetic community into troops (*gana*) and branches (*shakha*), descended from specific teachers and often relating to specific geographical areas, information which is essentially in accord with the elaborate details of the post-Mahavira ascetic organisation given in the 'Succession of the Elders' (*Sthaviravali*), an appendix to the *Kalpasutra*. However, much more significantly, donative inscriptions also show that by the turn of the common era Jainism was patronised at Mathura by people such as traders, artisans and jewellers: in other words, the skilled and moneyed middle classes from whom the lay community has usually, although not exclusively, been constituted. This bears clear witness to the fact that Jainism was not in its earliest period a purely ascetic religion and that the patterns of worship and belief which gradually emerged within it proved attractive to lay followers whose interaction with monks and nuns on a formal basis provided the means for the maintenance of the religion.[4]

The fame of Mathura as a great Jain holy place lingered on for centuries. As late as 980 CE, a massive image of Parshva, which was later excavated from Kankali Tila, was dedicated there.[5] However, there is little doubt that during the fourth and fifth centuries CE substantial sections of the Jain community had begun to drift away from the city and migrate further to the west. While this may seem strange in view of the fact that northern India was at this time under the control of the Gupta dynasty, which presided over ancient India's most significant period of political stability and artistic efflorescence, it has been suggested that an important component of Gupta culture was a Hindu revivalism whose effects could be seen in the gradual decline in the production of Jain sculptures and images at Mathura.[6]

Certainly the Puranas, the Hindu mythological lorebooks, some of the most important of which were written during the Gupta period, describe the archetypal heretic, essentially portrayed as an amalgam of the Jain and Buddhist monk, as a demonic and anti-social figure, but this may only reflect the prejudices of the brahman compilers of these texts. There is in fact no serious evidence for Hindu persecution of Jains in north India at this time, and an alternative explanation might be that a substantial part of the Jain community responded to the external and internal political pressures that were being inexorably exerted on the Gupta empire, and which were eventually to bring about its fragmentation, by migrating to the west into the, from the fifth century, prosperous kingdom of the Maitrakas of Valabhi where doubtless new overseas trading opportunities were also available. This gradual relocation of a sizable part of the community is reflected in the fact that the penultimate Shvetambara scriptural recitation was held at both Mathura and Valabhi while the last was held at Valabhi alone (see Chapter 3).

JAINISM IN SOUTH INDIA

A late tradition related by Hemacandra in the twelfth century describes how the son of the famous northern emperor Ashoka (third century BCE), Samprati, a ubiquitous figure in Jain lore whose agency is often invoked to provide temples of uncertain date with a fictive antiquity, having prepared the ground by sending spies disguised as Jain monks to provide instruction in such matters as almsgiving, then dispatched real monks to civilise the barbarian south (PariP p.69).

It must be assumed that this story preserves some distant memory of the gradual infiltration into the south of bands of wandering mendicants who acted as transmitters of a northern, prestigious culture, of which Jainism was a part. Fragmentary inscriptional evidence testifies to the existence of Jain ascetics and lay supporters in the south in the second and first centuries BCE,[7] although for several centuries after this inscriptions are hard to find, and Digambara Jainism gradually assumed a major role for almost a millennium in the south Indian religious imagination. The processes involved in this are certainly obscure, but historians of south India have generally made little effort to explain what the sources of Jainism's popularity were and they have often treated the religion's presence in the south as an aberrance, little more than a convenient focus of supposedly negative and world-denying values against which, from about the sixth century, the renascent forces of devotional and intellectual Hinduism could react and define themselves in order to restore a supposedly pure, life-affirming Tamil culture, underpinned by

Sanskritic values. Yet this is to underrate not only the nature of Jain devotion and doctrine but also the significance of the alternative religious and political ideology which Jainism was able to provide and which can be seen at their most distinctive in the south in two areas, literature and kingship.

JAIN LITERATURE IN TAMIL

Jain texts constitute a significant proportion of ancient Tamil literature and form a legacy which has been lovingly studied and commented upon for centuries by Hindus as well as Jains.[8] The earliest grammar of the Tamil language is generally regarded as having been written by a Jain, while two of the main Tamil epics either are exclusively Jain in subject or contain significant Jain themes.

Not among the very earliest Tamil works, as it dates from about the ninth century, but of the greatest literary importance is 'Jivaka the Wishing Jewel' (*Civakacintamani*) by the Digambara Tiruttakkaterar, a text which is still sung and performed among the Tamil Jain community.[9] Such was the power of this work, so tradition has it, that a twelfth century Hindu king who had become obsessed with its beauties had to be weaned away from it by means of a specially composed epic about the Shaiva saints.[10] Drawing on a pre-existent story and reworking it in the context of Tamil literary convention, 'Jivaka the Wishing Jewel' contains a blend of the worldly and the spiritual in which the erotic and picaresque adventures of its hero Jivaka take their real meaning as no more than a prelude to his eventual renunciation and attainment of spiritual deliverance. Various opposing themes are skilfully intertwined, such as kingship and asceticism, sexual desire and disgust with the world, marriage and renunciation, to create a poetic work of religious propaganda in which a highly developed northern metaphysical structure is integrated into a sophisticated southern aesthetic to demonstrate how worldly values are transcended by those of a higher ideal.

The most famous of all the Tamil epics and the oldest is the 'Lay of the Anklet' (*Silapadikkaram*) which dates from perhaps the fifth century. Here the Jain theme is not predominant, perhaps surprisingly in the light of the author's name, Ilango Adigal (*adigal* denoting a Jain ascetic in Tamil), but it nonetheless has an important structural purpose within the narrative as a whole. The starting point of the 'Lay of the Anklet' is the theme of a patient wife and her philandering but finally repentant husband. Kovalan, in order to escape from a courtesan with whom he has become infatuated, resolves to travel to the city of Madurai with his wife Kannaki to start a new life there. In the course of the journey they fall in with a Jain nun called Kavunti and share the hardships of the road with her. The eventual disastrous denouement of the story, the killing of Kovalan in Madurai and Kannaki's destruction of the city in revenge, is presaged by one of Kavunti's homilies to the couple in which the nun argues at length that the Jain ascetic gains freedom through the absence of the ties of sexual relations and the burden of emotional longings and attachments.

However, Kavunti's main function within the 'Lay of the Anklet' is to proclaim the centrality within human affairs of the law of karma through a demonstration by means of her powers gained from the practice of asceticism that the disasters which befall Kovalan and Kannaki are ultimately the result of their own actions and that the apparently tragic and random course of events can be shown to be explicable in terms of Jain metaphysics. At the same time, the poem also presents Kavunti as being to some extent under the sway of her emotions herself, for she compromises her ascetic vows to aid Kannaki and expresses her admiration for the marital devotion of the couple. As a result, it can be said that the figure of the Jain nun Kavunti is not presented solely as an adjunct to the plot of the 'Lay of the Anklet' and a mere device for the arid transmission of Jain doctrine but as a compassionate and involved commentator on the crises of the epic who attempts to show that Jainism and its explanation of the workings of the world can provide a mollifying influence on the intensities of human experience.[11]

The Jain contribution to Tamil literature demonstrates how a northern and originally alien religious tradition could, through the adaptation of existing literary forms and the deployment of a conscious artistry, both manipulate and feed into south Indian culture and by a process of naturalisation become part of it.

JAIN KINGSHIP IN KARNATAKA

In the course of the 'Thirty-Twos' (*Dvatrimshika*), a series of treatises on philosophical themes by the great logician Siddhasena Divakara (fifth century CE), who is claimed by both the Shvetambaras and the Digambaras, there suddenly occurs a panegyric of an unknown king (Dvatri 11). In fact, it is likely that this encomium is an interpolation but its occurrence in such an unlikely context points to an important theme in Jain history: royal patronage and, in particular, the apparent espousal of Jainism, a religion of non-violence, by aggressive and militaristic south Indian kings and their warrior supporters.

The ancient texts which legislate for ascetic behaviour are adamant that it is improper for monks to take alms from a king (e.g. MA 911).[12] However, Jain monks, especially in the Karnataka region of south India, often seemed to have forged close relationships with kingly patrons and on certain occasions played an important part in the foundation of royal dynasties, if tradition is to be believed. The monk Simhanandin is credited with being one of the agents behind the emergence of the Ganga dynasty in the third century CE (although the main inscriptional evidence for this is late),[13] while the twelfth century Hoysala dynasty supposedly had its origins in a defensive act of violence urged on its founder by a Digambara monk.[14] Indeed, there is no epigraphic mention in Karnataka of Jains of a mercantile or bourgeois background until the tenth century and, although it would be imprudent to deny the existence of such lay followers, the picture of Jainism up to this point is very much of a religion sponsored by kings and warrior aristocrats.[15]

Early Jainism was prepared to countenance the exercise of martial skills in war but only if carried out defensively, and it denied the possibility, frequently stated in Hinduism, that a warrior who died in battle would be reborn in heaven (Bh 7.9).[16] Instead, Jainism redefined the nature of martial valour and violence so that the true warrior was seen as being the fully committed Jain ascetic. The early Digambara writer Shivarya compares the young warrior fighting in battle to the spiritually victorious monk and the gaining of deliverance is equated with the attainment of kingship (BhA 19–23, 199 and 1849–50). Jainism's ideology, particularly marked among the Digambaras who were the dominant sect in the south, of heroic individualism and self-perfection, frequently expressed in images of striving, battle and conquest, which could thus lead to it being seen as a religion of vigour and bravery, is no doubt one of the reasons why it was held in such respect by a large sector of south Indian warrior society.

In addition, it has been argued that the attractiveness of Jainism also lay in its ability to confer a brand of respectable, northern aryan culture upon southern warriors while at the same time time enabling them to distance themselves from peasant, Hindu society. It is from this background that the idealised Jain king, familiar from literature and south Indian inscriptional panegyric, emerges who owed his position to merit and moral qualities rather than to the ritual validation on which the Hindu king depended.[17] However, although Jain scholars have naturally argued for the exclusivity of such kings' Jainness, it is difficult to be so confident about their religious affiliation. The institution of kingship in south India seems to have been one which transcended conceptual or religious boundaries, and the inherent obligation incumbent on all kings to gain plunder and increase the boundaries of their realm through military means at the expense of their neighbours would have carried more weight than any duty to observe the Jain principle of non-violence.

Practical prescriptions for the conduct of the Jain king are found in the 'Lorebook of the Beginning' (*Adipurana*) of Jinasena (ninth century CE). This is the main Digambara source for the Universal History, although Jinasena did not carry it beyond the biography of Rishabha and it was finished by his pupils. The 'Lorebook of the Beginning' was most likely composed to be read in the court of Jinasena's patron, the great south Indian monarch Amoghavarsha Rashtrakuta, and there is a strong didactic element in it, most clearly embodied in the forty-second chapter in which Bharata, Rishabha's son and the first universal emperor of this world age, instructs an assembly of warriors in the duties of kings and the warrior class, all of whom are said to be related to the spiritual warriors, the Digambara monks, through having their birth in the Three Jewels of right faith, knowledge and conduct (AP 42.15). In the course of this discourse, Bharata firmly enjoins all kings to protect not only themselves and their subjects but also the Jain community and doctrine, putting them under an obligation to keep their kingdoms free from heretical teachings and, in particular, the malign influence of brahmans.

The most famous exemplification of the nature of the Jain warrior occurs in Jinasena's description of the conflict between Bharata and Bahubali. Bharata attempted to take over the kingdoms of his brothers which had been bestowed upon them by Rishabha. However, his half-brother Bahubali refused to countenance this, as a result of which the two fought a duel. At his very moment of triumph over Bharata, Bahubali realised the transience of kingship and worldly affairs and renounced, standing in the forest in a meditative posture for a year at the end of which he gained the true Jain victory, conquering the real enemies, the passions and thus becoming, according to the Digambaras, the first human of this world age to achieve liberation. It is this story which inspired the most conspicuous artistic monument in south Indian Jainism, the massive image of Bahubali at Shravana Belgola dedicated by the victorious general Camundaraya in 981.[18]

The 'Lorebook of the Beginning' presents a subtle model of kingship as a necessary but potentially dangerous and flawed institution (Bharata was motivated by anger and attempted to cheat in his fight with Bahubali). All kings are regarded as requiring the controlling presence of Jain principles and Jain, rather than brahman, advisers, and they can ultimately only gain mastery of the world by winning through to the genuine kingship of austerities and becoming a monk. We do not know how many south Indian kings or warriors attempted to put these principles into practice, although the ideal of the righteous Jain monarch remained a powerful one. While the last Rashtrakuta emperor supposedly ended his life in the manner of the true ascetic by fasting to death, it must have also been the case that a generally syncretistic religiosity prevailed, as in the case of Camundaraya who is known to have dedicated temples to the Hindu gods Vishnu and Shiva.

EARLY DIGAMBARA SECTS

An inscription from Shravana Belgola describes how the teacher Arhadbali, fearing the various dissensions which might arise as a result of the influence of the corrupt world age, split up the Mula Sangha, the 'Root Assembly', which had descended from Mahavira through the great Kundakunda, into four sections called Sena, Deva, Simha and Nandin.[19] The sixteenth century writer Indranandin gives a more extended version of this story, referring to a greater variety of subdivisions of the community, with each monk being obliged to incorporate the designation of the sectarian division to which he belonged into his own name (ShruAv pp.88ff). Traditional dating would regard Arhadbali as the twenty-ninth teacher in succession from Gautama, thus locating him in the early common era, although the accounts for his activities might well suggest a later attempt to explain a contemporary situation.[20] Whatever the truth of this story which no doubt preserves a memory of a restructuring of the ascetic community, it scarcely does justice to the complexity of medieval Digambara organisation in which a plethora of sects and subsects, many of them totally obscure to us today, emerged on the basis of preceptorial association and geographical connections with particular regions and towns. A representative, if perhaps slightly unusual, example of this fission is the thirteenth century monk Ramacandra Maladharideva whose full title contained no less than six separate lineage connections.[21]

It was the monks of the Mula Sangha who exerted the dominant and most longstanding influence in the Digambara ascetic community. Digambara tradition views the Mula Sangha as in some way replacing the Nirgrantha Sampradaya, the 'Bondless Lineage', a supposedly pristine line of undifferentiated descent from Mahavira. The first mentions of this signal an awareness of the growing separation of naked and white-robed monks and can most likely be dated to about the end of the fourth century. Shvetambara references to the appearance of a 'Forest-dwelling Lineage' confirm the existence of a particularly austere ascetic community which was eventually to be known as Digambara. The Mula Sangha and its senior monks are referred to repeatedly in inscriptions from about the fifth or sixth century and the name occurs at Shravana Belgola as late as the nineteenth century, although an affirmation of affiliation to it by that late date must have been a hollow one.[22] For Shrutasagara, writing in the sixteenth century, the Mula Sangha was so called because it was the basis (*mula*) of the path to deliverance and those who did not belong to it were only pseudo-Jains (ShP p.11: comm. on *Darshanapahuda* 11). However, claims to represent true lineal descent from the ancient teachers were common in Jainism and it is difficult to avoid the conclusion that the Mula Sangha gradually became little more than a prestigious but artificial designation, redolent of a long unattainable orthodoxy.

References to several Digambara ascetic groupings which the monks who claimed allegiance to the Mula Sangha regarded as deviant are found frequently in medieval inscriptions. The main continuous textual source for these sects is a short work defending the centrality of the Mula Sangha as the only legitimate Jain sect by Devasena, who was most likely writing at the beginning of the tenth century (DS), in which he describes a rogues' gallery of sectarian miscreants, including the Buddha, presented as an apostate follower of Parshva, the Shvetambaras and the Yapaniyas, whose behaviour marked them out, for him, as being beyond the pale.

However, Devasena's real venom was reserved for rival Digambara sects. The first of these is the Dravida Sangha, the 'Dravidian Assembly' founded by Vajranandin (died 469) at Madurai in the Tamil heartland. Devasena accuses Vajranandin of advocating total laxity of conduct in respect of bathing and eating proscribed food. Even more seriously, his followers are said to have virtually abandoned wandering mendicancy and taken to a settled mode of life, tilling the ground and selling the produce.

The Kashtha Sangha, which seems to have been named after a place, was, according to Devasena, founded by Kumarasena at the end of the seventh century. Among his supposed faults was the giving up of the peacock feather whisk, the normal emblem of Digambara ascetics, and the substituting of one made of cow's tail hair. The Mathura Sangha, reputedly founded by Ramasena in the second century CE, is said to have advocated the abandonment of the whisk completely.

These ascetic groups, of which the Dravida and Mathura Sanghas disappeared some time in the late medieval period, were singled out as heretical by Devasena on the basis of their rejection of points of custom and practice which he regarded as reflecting false understanding (*mithyatva*). For their parts, the Kashtha and Mathura Sanghas must have regarded themselves as ultra-orthodox in that the former would have argued that a cowtail whisk would minimise the possibility of injury to life-forms, since peacock feathers are more adhesive and likely to pick up dust and small insects, while the latter would have felt justified in rejecting the whisk completely on the grounds that monks should have no possessions at all. Devasena would appear to have been on firmer ground in expressing doubts about the legitimacy of the Dravida Sangha, which seems to have been an early example of the tendency on the part of many ascetics to yield to the inevitability of contact with the laity and live permanently in monasteries.

THE *BHATTARAKA*

If the Digambara ideal was in origin that of the wandering or forest-dwelling naked ascetic, the realities of the existence of a lay community and altered social and political structures were to ensure that another figure would eventually emerge as a focus of religious authority. From an early period, the institution of *dana*, the giving of alms and temporary shelter by lay people to ascetics, developed in a manner not envisaged by Jainism at its earliest stage to the gifting of rock cut caverns, of a sort that can still be seen at ancient sites in south India, and the eventual building alongside temples of monasteries which were accompanied by substantial land endowments, so that the ancient ideal was in part transformed, with many ascetics gradually accommodating themselves to their lay followers by adopting a quasi-householder mode of life.

This was a practice which later Digambara writers were to stigmatise as a sign of decadence, an unhappy compromise in the corrupt world age when ascetic values were declining. Depictions of Digambara monks being carried in palanquins attended by escorts of soldiers, the gradual shift in meaning of the title *acarya*, which originally designated a senior monk who expounded the scriptures, to denote the functionary who administered a temple, and the inscriptional instruction from ninth century Tamil Nadu that a monk in charge of a monastery had to keep a lamp burning in a temple in perpetuum out of the interest accruing from a donative grant, all represent stages in a process which was to lead to the emergence of the *bhattaraka*, the pivotal figure in medieval Digambara Jainism.[23]

The Sanskrit term *bhattaraka* denotes a 'learned man' and is roughly comparable to the academic title 'doctor'. In origin, he was the head of any group of naked monks which lived permanently in one of the monasteries (*matha*) which had begun to be built near temple complexes from about the fifth century CE. According to Shrutasagara, who was writing when the institution of the *bhattaraka* had become firmly established, a thirteenth century *bhattaraka* proclaimed that owing to Moslem persecution monks could wear clothes when outside the monastery and remove them when they returned to it.[24] Whatever the truth of this, Digambara asceticism came to be associated in the medieval period less with naked monks than with the *bhattarakas*, who were celibate but non-initiated clerics, linked to pontifical centres, taking hereditary names from their predecessor, wearing orange robes both inside and outside the monastery and taking them off in honour of the ancient ideal only when eating and when initiating another *bhattaraka*.

In an age when the community of naked monks was gradually dwindling away, the *bhattarakas* played a vital role, not always based on any conspicuous spirituality, in the perpetuation of Digambara Jainism. This could sometimes take a striking form. For example, at the end of the fifteenth century, a *bhattaraka* in Rajasthan consecrated a thousand images of fordmakers and sent them round India to repair the damage done by Moslem iconoclasm.[25] But, generally, the function of the *bhattaraka* was the parochial one of conducting rituals, supervising the lay performance of vows, overseeing the affairs of his monastery, maintaining libraries and being responsible for religious education. Most importantly, the *bhattaraka* had to represent the local Digambara community as a mediating figure when dealing with Hindu rajas or the Moslem authorities. Indeed, the *bhattaraka* was very much like a king himself. He sat on a pontifical throne, enjoyed trappings of office and a great deal of pomp and ceremony attended his processional activities. The *bhattaraka* of Kolhapur in Maharashtra who built the gate of his monastery of equal height to the city gate was making a specific point about his equality of status with the local raja.[26]

It seems to have been the *bhattarakas* who maintained the lingering vestiges of the Digambara sectarian divisions and at times longstanding antipathies can be detected. There survives, for example, a manuscript copy of Devasena's critique of Jainism from a Mula Sangha perspective which belonged to a seventeenth century *bhattaraka* of Surat, affiliated to the Kashtha Sangha, who deleted every one of Devasena's objections to his sect and substituted the name of the Mula Sangha, adding general abuse of it to make his point clear.[27] James Tod, who encountered a *bhattaraka* of Surat at the beginning of the nineteenth century, was aware of these two Digambara sects, and some *bhattarakas* still have cowtail whisks as a legacy of an original connection with the Kashtha Sangha.[28] However, of much more importance than any sectarian allegiance was each *bhattaraka*'s connection with a specific local caste over whose affairs he adjudicated, thus strengthening his personal relationship and that of his monastery with a particular region.

In the medieval period, there were thirty-six *bhattaraka* thrones in various parts of India but the bulk of them seem to have faded away to insignificance by the nineteenth century. The most important and famous today are the oldest, those at Mudbidri and Shravana Belgola in south Karnataka, while also of significance are two in Kolhapur, each of which is linked with a local caste. Although the medieval role of the *bhattarakas* will never be fully repeated because there is now no serious need for any formal intercession with the government on behalf of the Jain community, they still play an important part in the promotion of Jainism, both through travelling inside and outside India and through general educational and publishing work.

MIXED FORTUNES IN THE SOUTH

Whatever the attractions of Jainism for many of the inhabitants of south India and notwithstanding its striking artistic contribution to the culture of that area, it was merely one element of a complex religious world and its position gradually became embattled in the face of often militant forms of Hinduism, the so-called 'Hindu Renaissance', eventually undergoing a slippage into the marginalised position which it occupies today in the south.

An appreciation of some of the forces at work at the outset can be gained from a brief consideration of the significance of Kalugamalai, one of the oldest Jain sites in south India. Kalugamalai is a small town at the foot of a huge rock outcrop by Jains on an otherwise flat plain in the district of Tirunelveli in south Tamil Nadu. There can be found a cluster of Jain inscriptions, the oldest of which date from before the common era, and some superb carvings which date from around the eighth century CE. Ancient caves with carved rock beds in them testify to the early presence of Digambara monks in the area.[29] However, the name 'Vulture Peak', the literal meaning of Kalugamalai, is also strongly suggestive of Buddhism since it was on a hill of that name outside the city of Rajagriha in the Ganges basin that the Buddha preached many of his sermons and there is in fact a resilient local tradition which would connect Kalugamalai with the Buddha, by which is presumably meant the Buddhists.[30]

Furthermore, the large natural cave at the bottom of the hill seems to have become at a relatively early date a shrine to Murugan, a regional god particularly associated with the Tamil sense of their identity as Hindus, while on the rock itself, which was the main focus of Jain activities, there is also an old shrine to the Hindu god Aiyanar, the cause of some recent disturbances when a group of Digambara monks, for whom Kalugamalai is still a place of pilgrimage, attempted to replace the Hindu image with a statue of one of the fordmakers. It is impossible to reconstruct in detail the early history of this area but it might be noted that Aiyanar is a divinity who sometimes served as a guardian deity in Jain temples and whose main epithet *Shasta*, 'Ruler', is of Jain and Buddhist origin and that he is in many respects the figure who symbolises an eventual shift in Tamil Nadu from a conceptual world where various south Indian religious traditions coexisted and intersected, Kalugamalai perhaps representing a microcosm of this, to an eventual Hindu dominance from about the eighth century onwards in which Jain and Buddhist shrines were increasingly appropriated or destroyed.[31]

The frequently employed expression 'Hindu renaissance' is of course partisan and also of only limited value, for it implies that Hinduism in south India had in some sense become quiescent in the face of the Jains and the Buddhists, which would be difficult to demonstrate. However, a reassertion of Hindu values unquestionably took place in the south at the expense of Jainism and Buddhism, often through members of those religions returning to Hinduism. The position of Buddhism in south India is not relevant for this study and, while the resurgence of brahman theology as embodied in figures such as Kumarila and Shankara was largely aimed at the Buddhists, the attack directed against the Jains is of much more interest for the social history of the far south.

Some sense of what this 'revival' involved can be gained from a reading of the Hindu devotional poets who used the Tamil language to express the intensity of their relationship with the god Shiva. The classic example of such a poet is Appar who lived in the ninth century. He had in fact converted to Jainism and become a Digambara monk, rising to be head of a monastery. Appar's hagiography suggests that during this time he suffered intense psychosomatic pains, perhaps as a result of fasting, until on being received back into his ancestral faith he was cured by the grace of Shiva. Appar's poetry, in which he sings of his love for Shiva and bemoans his wasted years as a monk, gives a remarkable insight into the manner in which many south Indians must have come to regard the Jains. Appar refers to Shiva as 'the god who pierced the delusion/that afflicted me/when I joined the Jains/and became a wicked monk'. He continues:

> Calling it a great penance, everyday I carried/the peacock feather fan under my arm; /a fool, I whirled about like the great bar of a loom... I don't know how to get rid/of the heart that loved/the weak and filthy Jains/with their yellowing teeth.... When I think of the long years spent/in following the contradictory teachings of Jains/I feel faint./When I think day and night/of the honey that dwells in holy Aiyaru [a shrine of Shiva]/town of jasmine groves/I am filled with sweet delight.[32]

Intense bitterness of this sort may well have had unfortunate consequences for many Jains. In Hindu temples in Tamil Nadu today, including the shrine to Murugan at Kalugamalai, one may see lurid mural representations of the massacre by impaling of eight thousand Jains in Madurai for having taken Shiva's name in vain.[33] This event, which is often taken as marking the end of Jainism's influence in Tamil Nadu, is most graphically represented in the great Minakshi temple in Madurai itself and it remains a folk memory among Hindu peasantry who can have only the vaguest idea of what a Jain is. Interpretation of this tradition is uncertain. It is conceivable that in some way it reflects the abandonment of the city of Madurai by the Jains for economic reasons or their gradual loss of political influence. Alternatively, it could be said that the massacre is essentially mythical, the destruction by the Hindu gods of the demonic forces of unrighteousness personified by the Jains, with the stakes on which they were impaled being simulacra of the *yupa*, the piece of wood set up in the Vedic sacrificial compound to homologise earth, heaven and the intermediate space.

No record of a massacre at Madurai can be found in Jain literature or inscriptions. There is, however, one interesting piece of evidence with relevance to the story, although it may do no more than confuse the question. In the hills to the west of Madurai, there was a large-scale Jain monastic establishment, possibly the greatest in the far south of India. This site, which seems to have been occupied by the Jains from before the common era, was clearly of considerable importance, with many temples affiliated to it and connections with Shravana Belgola in Karnataka to the north in the eleventh and twelfth centuries. What is significant is that, after an early group of inscriptions, there is a gap of some six hundred years, in other words, covering the period when the Hindu revival was taking place and when the massacre at Madurai must have occurred, until a further cluster of inscriptions dating from the ninth and tenth centuries.

It is unclear why there is such a gap in the evidence. It may well be that some terrible persecution was indeed inflicted on the Jains around the eighth century or before and it is indicative of the nature of the times that a temple affiliated to this monastery had a shrine to Shiva erected on its foundations around 1000 CE. At the same time, it is apparent that the site of the monastery, if it was indeed abandoned for several centuries, was eventually reoccupied and began to thrive again, testimony to the fact that Jainism in Tamil Nadu was not totally destroyed by the Hindu revival.[34] The religion even continued to receive some degree of patronage from Tamil royal families and a small but steady stream of inscriptions bears witness to the continuing presence of Jainism up to the present day. However, it has to be conceded that the Hindu revival ensured that from about the ninth or tenth century Jainism lost much of its earlier hold on the Tamil imagination and it gradually became restricted to the north of Tamil Nadu where today's indigenous Jain population of some thirty thousand, miniscule in a state inhabited by fifty million people, is largely located.

In Karnataka, the Jains also experienced varying fortunes. From a literary point of view, virtually all early literature in the Kannada language deals with Jain themes. At the same time, as in Tamil Nadu, the Jains were threatened by a Hindu revival, this time in the form of the militant Virashaiva movement which started in the twelfth century, and the hagiographies of its leader Basava describe in often chilling terms how the Jains, who are accused of having used trickery and black magic to intimidate pious Shaivas, were eventually frustrated by Shiva's power and slaughtered in pogroms.[35] However, Jains continued to exercise a degree of influence within the Hindu Vijayanagar empire which was founded in 1336, with laymen often holding prominent ministerial and military positions. One of the Vijayanagar emperors, Bukka Raya, intervened in 1368 in a dispute between the Vaishnavas and the Jains, proclaiming that both their religions were equal and that Hindus had to protect the Jains, while also appointing a state garrison to guard Shravana Belgola.[36]

On the surface, then, Jainism remained a religion of substance in Karnataka and a project such as the erection in 1432 of a great image of Bahubali at Karkala, designed to rival the one at Shravana Belgola, by a donor styling himself the new Camundaraya, and yet another at Venur in 1604, suggests a tenacity, and indeed grandiosity, of purpose which belies any notion of the religion's disappearance in that region. Nonetheless, Jainism went into inexorable, albeit not fully terminal, decline in Karnataka as it experienced the effects of a sea change within society, with many Jain clans converting to Hinduism, and it remained a significant presence perhaps only in the southwest. Even this area did not remain immune, with Shringeri, famed as the place where the great ninth century Hindu theologian Shankara supposedly founded his first monastery, in reality being originally a Jain centre taken over by Hindus in the fourteenth century and then fitted out with a spurious history.[37]

The twelfth century Kannada poet Brahmashiva who lived at the beginning of the Virashaiva onslaught expressed his deep unhappiness with Jainism's embattled position.[38] While making fun of the pretensions of Hinduism, he also chronicled disturbing developments, such as the conversion of a temple in Kolhapur dedicated to the fordmaker Candraprabha into a shrine to the Hindu goddess Mahalakshmi and the existence of families in which the father was a Jain, the wife a Shaiva and the children devotees of the sun god. Brahmashiva, who seems originally to have been a Shaiva himself, argued for the superiority of Jainism on the grounds of its universal appeal but was forced to admit that Jains in the south were becoming few and far between: 'Just as lamps burn in the dark/at the time of [the festival of] Divali, so the Jaina shines/between the hordes of people/who in the age of Kali are blinded by falsehood'.[39]

SHVETAMBARA TEACHERS

It would be possible after a fashion to delineate the fortunes of Shvetambara Jainism in north India up to about 1000 CE, but it would be overambitious to attempt to furnish a full social history. The inscriptional evidence is meagre and sporadic, and the fragmentary records of ascetic lineages, patronage by minor rajas and donative activities by merchants stand very much in the shadow of the intellectual and literary achievements of the great Shvetambara teachers. Extended biographies of the most significant of these figures, so central to Shvetambara tradition, only started to be written about the beginning of the twelfth century, although they are no doubt based in part on earlier material, with brief accounts of some of the more ancient teachers being found in the scriptural commentaries, and it must be remembered that the Shvetambara community viewed its leaders through the lenses of hagiography. As a result, it can be regarded as of no real consequence that the details of the lives of these teachers in the various medieval biographies often differ in detail or are at variance with each other. What is truly important is that the teachers are linked by the common activity of *prabhavana*.

Prabhavana is today the name of the pleasant and informal custom often followed by Jains of giving a piece of coconut or a sweet to those who have been present at a religious ceremony. In its earlier usage, the term refers to what can be roughly translated as 'spreading and exalting the Jain religion by the performance of glorious deeds'. In the standard enumeration there are eight ways in which Jainism can be exalted: through scriptural knowledge, preaching, debating, astrological prediction, asceticism, mastery of spells of invocation and of magic power and, finally, literary skill (YS 2.16 comm.). The most important collection of Shvetambara hagiographies is the thirteenth century Prabhacandra's 'Deeds of the Exalters of the Doctrine' (*Prabhavakacarita*: PC) in which are given the biographies of twenty-two teachers, starting with the near-legendary Vajrasvamin who lived in the early centuries of the common era and concluding with Hemacandra (1089–1172), a figure about whom some serious historical conclusions can be drawn. The emphasis in these hagiographies is on the Shvetambara teacher as performer of *prabhavana* and as hero and protector of the community, with often the very intellectual achievement which gives that teacher his prominence for modern scholarship being underplayed in favour of descriptions of his magical abilities and performance of miracles which represent a kind of debased version of the superhuman powers possessed by the fordmakers and their disciples, no longer attainable in the corrupt world age.

Siddhasena Divakara, who can be approximately dated to the fifth century CE, is one of the most striking examples of this. Famed for his learning, Siddhasena supposedly received his epithet 'Sun' (*divakara*) from the legendary king Vikramaditya to whose court he is portrayed as having been attached. Through writing the first work devoted to logic to be articulated in purely Jain terms, he equipped Jainism with the intellectual tools to engage its opponents in formal debate. In addition, Siddhasena wrote a terse Prakrit work called the 'Examination of the True Doctrine' (*Sanmaitakka*) whose second chapter, in which epistemology and the structure of ommniscience are discussed, generated the only serious intra-Jain dispute about a matter of philosophical doctrine. However, the hagiographies of Siddhasena are not interested in such writings and indeed they use his learned reputation as an excuse for some burlesque at his expense.

The oldest hagiography of Siddhasena available (*c.* twelfth century) depicts him at the beginning of his career as a haughty brahman who agrees while in the countryside to debate with a Jain monk called Vriddhavadin in front of an adjudicating audience of rustics rather than the learned scholars of the royal court to whom he would have been more accustomed. Siddhasena's Sanskrit grandiloquency baffles the yokels and they award the victory to Vriddhavadin, who merely uttered some platitudes about the necessity of leading the righteous Jain life but expressed them in a readily understandable vernacular dialect. As a result of this, Siddhasena has to convert to Jainism.

Siddhasena's learning here rebounds upon him as it does later on in the hagiography when Vriddhavadin rebukes him for his pride which leads him to adopt the trappings of royalty and also, drastically, when his enthusiasm for Sanskrit leads him to offer to translate the scriptures into that language, as a result of which he is given a penance of twelve years' exile. The most dramatic and miraculous event of Siddhasena's career occurred during this period of wandering when he used a Sanskrit hymn to conjure up an image of Parshva from a statue of Shiva. Other versions have the stone phallic emblem of Shiva (*linga*) splitting to reveal the fordmaker within.[40]

The hagiographers of Siddhasena weave a skein of cross-references to create a picture of a representative Shvetambara leader whose learning is set at nought or transformed by the power of the Jain religion. So, if Jaiṇ ascetics are as a matter of custom all addressed with the title 'great king' (*maharaj*), they should not behave like monarchs as Siddhasena did,[41] while the account of his twelve year exile would have resonated powerfully with an audience which was familiar with the many Indian stories describing kings who were sent into the wilderness for this period. Like these kings, Siddhasena returns from exile transformed, in this case into a monk who has become fully aware of the potentialities that can be effected by devotion rather than technical learning.[42]

Many other teachers were the subject of Shvetambara hagiography, such as Kalaka who is credited with having induced the Scythians to invade western India at the beginning of the common era in order to avenge the honour of his sister, a nun who had been raped by a Hindu king,[43] or Jiva who miraculously restored to life a dead cow placed in a Jain temple by malicious brahmans, thus demonstrating that the Jain community would endure an insult from nobody (PC 7.128–53), or Manadeva who saved the city of Taxila from the plague through the magic power of a hymn to the fordmaker Shantinatha and then predicted its destruction by Turkish invaders three years later (PC 13), or the eleventh century scriptural commentator Abhayadeva Suri who was aided by a goddess to find a buried image of Parshva which cured him of leprosy (PC 19). However, of a still greater order of significance for Shvetambara history are the two most eminent of the 'exalters' (*prabhavaka*), Haribhadra and Hemacandra.

The hagiographies describe two main events in Haribhadra's life. We have already encountered one of them, his conversion by the nun Yakini, at the beginning of Chapter 1. The second relates to Jainism's long antagonism towards Buddhism. Haribhadra's nephews are described by the hagiographers as having clandestinely studied in a Buddhist monastery and, on being discovered, as having lost their lives. To avenge them, Haribhadra challenged the Buddhists to debate and, defeating them through his command of metaphysical learning, enforced a penalty of jumping into a vat of boiling oil. As a result of his anger and grief for his nephews, both inappropriate for a Jain monk, he was required by his teacher to undergo penance.[44] This story is somewhat problematic in the light of the many conciliatory remarks about Buddhism to be found in the works ascribed to Haribhadra, a topic I will return to in Chapter 8 but, like the story of Siddhasena, it demonstrates how glory accrued to the Jain community through the defeat of its enemies and at the same time how the learning which brought about that glory is curbed by the obligations of the Jain religion.

Haribhadra is credited by Shvetambara tradition with having written fourteen thousand works. Although this number is obviously artificially high, some of the hundred or so texts with which Haribhadra can reasonably be connected are among the greatest masterpieces of Jain literature. Every area of concern to Jainism or literary genre which can be put within a Jain context – ritual, ethics, ascetic and lay behaviour, doxography, novelistic romance, satire, scriptural commentary and logic – falls within the ambit of this protean writer. The modern scholar Jinavijaya (1888–1976), who did more than anybody else to bring to light and publish many of the sources for medieval Shvetambara history, in fact argued that, on internal grounds, many of the works attributed to Haribhadra had to have been written considerably later than 529 CE, the traditional date of his death. Williams, in a paper published in 1965, took this idea further and suggested that there were two Haribhadras, one using an epithet alluding to his grief for his murdered nephews, 'Having Separation as a Distinguishing Mark' (*Virahanka*), the other styling himself 'Spiritual Son of Yakini' (*Yakiniputra/sunu*). The former could be differentiated from the latter on the grounds of his use of more archaic language and subject matter and according to Williams perhaps lived in the sixth century. Williams also produced evidence that Haribhadra the 'Spiritual Son of Yakini' was in fact a temple-dwelling monk and thus a representative of the group which, as we shall see in the next section, was to represent for later Shvetambaras the worst of all perversions of correct Jain practice.[45]

That Williams' suggestions have remained unknown or ignored by Jain scholars in India is indicative of the high status which Haribhadra continues to occupy amongst Shvetambaras. For them, it is Haribhadra who was responsible for the creation of a truly autonomous Shvetambara literary culture through the integration into Jainism of both the style and some of the substance of the brahman tradition of learning from which he had emerged and, from the eleventh century, Haribhadra was regarded as being the pivotal figure in the Shvetambara teacher lineage, a paragon of orthodoxy standing in the middle of the line of descent from Mahavira's disciples which led to the radical monastic reformers of the later medieval period. The rumour, known in the twelfth century, that Haribhadra was a temple-dwelling monk was easily, if somewhat dubiously, attributed to the fact that there was another, heretical teacher of the same name (GSS 57). One of the most urgent tasks to be undertaken by scholars of Jainism is a full scale investigation into the work of the 'Haribhadra corpus' and the formulation of some system of attribution and chronology.

If Haribhadra, however many teachers there may have been of that name, must remain for the present a somewhat nebulous figure, then Hemacandra is the most tangible of all the exalters of the doctrine. His fame is firmly rooted in a specific historical role with which all Gujarati Jains are familiar and which was in part responsible for establishing Shvetambara Jainism as a resilient and self-confident presence in western India. Of the main writers who describe Hemacandra's life, Prabhacandra is concerned with those of his activities which specifically advanced the cause of Jainism (PC 22), while the fifteenth century chronicler Merutunga locates him in the broader context of a semi-legendary history of Gujarat.[46]

Hemacandra was born in 1089 in the town of Dhandhuka near what is now Ahmedabad to parents of the Modha merchant caste. While still a boy, he was given to a Shvetambara teacher called Devacandra and initiated by him, being given the name Somacandra. The young monk's prodigious mastery of various branches of learning, Jain and non-Jain, led to Devacandra designating him as his successor, and in 1108 he was given the honorific title *suri* and became a teacher in his own right who had authority over a group of monks and entitlement to provide his own exegesis of the scriptures. From that time he was known as Hemacandra.

The dominant concern in the biographies of Hemacandra is his relationship with Jayasimha Siddharaja and his successor Kumarapala of the Caulukya dynasty who ruled Gujarat from their capital at Patan which, although now only a small town, was then one of the finest cities in India. Siddharaja, who ascended the throne in 1092, ruling to 1141, epitomised some of the main qualities of the ideal Indian king. Militantly aggressive towards his neighbours, he was also interested in learning and culture and to further this he appointed Hemacandra as his court scholar and historian, commissioning him to produce a poetic history of the Caulukya family and a Sanskrit grammar. Hemacandra's grammar, called the *Siddhahaima*, enshrining the names of patron and author, is still used by Shvetambara ascetics today.

According to Prabhacandra, Siddharaja, who was without a son, formed a desire to kill his nephew Kumarapala who astrologers had predicted would both succeed him and bring about his kingdom's demise (PC 22.358–60). Kumarapala was only able to escape through Hemacandra hiding him under a pile of manuscripts (PC 22.368) and he had to remain outside Gujarat until with Siddharaja's death he was able to return to claim the throne. The motif of a hero fleeing the evil designs of a relative with the aid of a benefactor and returning to regain his rights after a period of exile is a common one in folk literature throughout the world and may lead some to question the historicity of this episode, especially as the sources differ about Siddharaja's motives. However, there is unanimity about the close relationship formed between Hemacandra and Kumarapala, with the monk validating the prince's claim to the throne and, furthermore, apparently prevailing upon him to run both his life and his kingdom in accord with Jain principles.

Some of Hemacandra's writings were specifically directed at Kumarapala, such as the 'Treatise on Behaviour' (*Yogashastra*), which was designed to show him how to lead the Jain life, while towards the end of his version of the Universal History he portrays Mahavira as predicting Kumarapala's meeting with himself.[47] As a result of this prompting, Kumarapala is said to have given up eating meat and he also issued edicts banning the slaughter of animals in his kingdom. Some accounts of his enthusiasm for Jainism sound a little hyperbolic, such as the vast fine supposedly imposed on a merchant for killing a louse, but the erection of many Jain temples, such as those at Taranga Hill in north Gujarat, would appear to testify to his sincerity.

Yet, as with the south Indian kings whom the Digambaras claimed to be Jains, one suspects that the realities of Kumarapala's religious affiliations were rather more complex. Siddharaja was certainly a Shaiva Hindu and there is evidence of a teacher of that sect being rewarded by Kumarapala for restoring the famous temple to Shiva at Somnath.[48] One of the most celebrated episodes in the hagiography of Hemacandra takes place at Somnath where, in the presence of Kumarapala, the monk summoned up Shiva himself to attest to the superiority of Jainism.[49] This story has the air of an allusion to Kumarapala's partiality for this god, and the most likely interpretation to put on Kumarapala's overall religious stance is that he allowed Jain moral values to inform both his own conceptual universe and the practical running of his kingdom, while also remaining a devotee of Shiva and participating in Hindu ritual kingship and its obligations. One Hindu text describes Kumarapala as re-entering the Hindu fold late in life, which certainly suggests that he was strongly associated with Jainism, and then goes on to describe how his successor persecuted the Jains.[50] If an Indian kingdom run on purely Jain principles ever did exist, then it was shortlived.

Hemacandra's main legacy is his literary works which embrace all the main branches of Indian learning, as can be seen from his epithet 'Omniscient One of the Corrupt Age'. It is not uncommon for scholars to berate him for his lack of originality, but that would be to miss the point about his achievement. Hemacandra's role was as the maintainer and systematiser of Shvetambara tradition rather than a radical innovator. While there may have been later figures such as Yashovijaya of more penetrating intellect, no one subsequent to Hemacandra was able to match his command of Jain learning.

THE TEMPLE-DWELLING MONKS

According to the Shvetambara canonical commentator Shilanka, an ascetic cannot be said to be righteous simply through living in the forest. Righteousness, which comes from the avoidance of the destruction of life-forms, can be found in either a village or a forest but these places are not in themselves the determining elements for it. Mahavira, after all, did not preach with reference to one place of abode or another but to knowledge of the fundamental entities of existence and correct behaviour (comm. on AS 1.8.1.4).

Shilanka is here referring to two styles of asceticism, one based on relative isolation from lay society, the other involving some form of interaction with it, in terms of an ancient polarity going back to Vedic times, where the village represented the social world centred around the domestic fire while the forest stood for the unstructured world lying beyond it. Despite Shilanka's insistence upon the ultimate irrelevance of these distinctions, the idea of the forest as representing the proper domain of the true and upright ascetic life remained an ideal in Jainism, rather as the desert or the hermit's cave once did for Christianity and, although solitary habitation by Jain ascetics in the jungle or other such remote places quickly became exceptional, medieval Shvetambara chroniclers describe how in the eleventh century would-be reforming monks, who saw themselves as fundamentalist in their uncompromising adherence to an ancient way of life, associated themselves with the forest with a view to challenging the temple-dwelling (*caityavasin*) monks who were sedentary inhabitants of temples or monasteries built beside temples in villages and towns and who had arrogated a central institutional role within the Shvetambara community to themselves.

By Shvetambara reckoning, the temple-dwelling monks appeared in about the fourth century CE,[51] but it is impossible to trace their early history beyond the odd reference such as that to the king of Patan who banned non-temple-dwelling monks from his city (PC 19.71–6). However, by about the thirteenth century, chroniclers begin to describe debates which took place in Gujarat between the temple-dwellers and those reforming monks who attacked the entire basis of their mode of life. The main objection to the temple-dwellers was that they ignored the injunctions about following the wandering life and living only in the temporary lodgings appropriate to it, as a result of which they did not exercise any rigour in begging for alms and the avoidance of violence. A further accusation was that the temple-dwellers misused temple funds in order to stage garish rituals involving loud music and dancing girls which were conspicuously similar to Hindu idiom.[52] Their very appearance, with coiffured hair, teeth stained with betelnut, immodest expressions, sleek bodies, feet and hands painted with lac and wearing of garlands and fine clothes, was enough to induce a frisson of revulsion in their upright opponents.[53]

To invoke decadence or a decay in spiritual values in order to explain change comes naturally to Jain scholars but is of only limited explanatory value. The temple-dwelling monks represented an important, possibly majority, strand in Shvetambara Jain practice for several centuries, one which merits an attempt to be understood on its own terms. Its emergence can in fact be seen reflected in the centrally important books of monastic law, the *chedasutras*, and their layers of commentary, which up to the seventh century introduce exceptions to general rules about behaviour with, for example, one text citing a variety of reasons why a monk might be permitted to give up the wandering life and stay permanently in the same place, such as unsatisfactory or dangerous conditions in the surrounding world, or a simple desire to increase knowledge.[54]

The eleventh century teacher Sura justified the behaviour of the temple-dwelling monks as a natural expression of Jain values which, even if appearing deficient in rigour, should not be challenged by the laity. If it were not for the temple-dwelling monks, Sura is portrayed as arguing, then Jainism would have disappeared:

> There would be a lack of temples today if monks did not live in them. Previously lay people took great care and interest in temples, teachers and the doctrine, but now because of the corrupt age they are so preoccupied with providing for their families, they scarcely go to their homes, let alone to the temple. The king's servants also because of their worldly interests no longer concern themselves with the temple. Eventually, the Jain religion will be destroyed. Ascetics by living in temples preserve them. There is scriptural authority for adopting an exception to a general rule to prevent the doctrine falling into abeyance.[55]

It was the intensity of the ascetic's connection with his lay supporters, built into Jainism from early on, which created the conditions for the emergence of the non-wandering monk (as it did for the Digambara *bhattaraka*) who, as a form of reciprocity to the laity, lived in and safeguarded those temples which were an expression of the totality of the Shvetambara community's religiosity.[56]

Sura seems to have been defeated in 1024 by the reforming monk Jineshvara Suri in front of the court of King Durlabha at Patan, and a reading of the descriptions by the medieval chroniclers of the successive humiliations suffered in debate by the temple-dwelling monks at the hands of the reformers suggests that they were all but eliminated by the end of the thirteenth century. However, this would be to accept sectarian polemic. A record of a lost inscription describes how a conclave was held in 1242 involving both senior temple-dwelling monks, designated according to the shrines which they controlled, and 'lodging-dwelling' (*vasativasin*) monks, that is, mendicants of the kind envisioned by the ancient texts, living only in temporary abodes on their wanderings and designated with reference to their teachers. The reason for the assembly is interesting enough in itself, a ban on the ascetic initiation of sons who had been fathered by monks as a result of a breach of celibacy, but the apparent lack of any confrontation suggests that the two groups of monks represented an acknowledged division of labour in the Shvetambara community, with one group managing the sacred places and the other fulfilling the wandering ideal.[57] However, the increasing prestige of the reforming sects ensured that the temple-dwelling monks lingered on for several centuries only in attenuated or mutated form.

THE EMERGENCE OF SHVETAMBARA *GACCHAS*

The *Kalpasutra* makes clear that from an early date the ascetic community was both internally divided into a variety of branches descended from prominent teachers and highly organised in accord with an essentially unified view of what was entailed in the renunciatory path. The oldest and most basic unit of organisation was the *gana* or 'troop', denoting a small group of monks, although there were other organisational designations whose precise significance is often unclear. The uncertainty of the evidence before the eleventh century makes it difficult to locate any mainstream Shvetambara lineage, and indeed there most likely never was one. Shvetambara tradition refers to four pupils of Vajrasvamin (*c.* fourth century CE), supposedly the last teacher to be familiar with any of the *purva* texts, founding four 'families' (*kula*) or ascetic lineages called respectively Candra, Nirvriti, Vidyadhara and Nagendra (PC 1.116–18). Haribhadra is generally regarded as having belonged to the Vidyadhara Family, while there were monks claiming association with the Candra Family as late as the sixteenth century, presumably on the grounds of what was perceived as its antiquity and orthodoxy.[58]

The old designations of *gana* and *kula* came to be replaced amongst the Shvetambaras in the medieval period by the term *gaccha*, an expression found in the latest parts of the Shvetambara scriptures, whose derivation is usually connected with the Sanskrit verb *gacchati*, 'goes' and is generally translated as 'sect' or 'subsect'.[59] From the eleventh century in western India, there appeared a variety of image-worshipping Shvetambara *gacchas*, each claiming to represent a true Jainism as near to that stipulated in the scriptures as possible, although in reality often differing from other *gacchas* in very little respect, and headed by charismatic teachers, invariably entitled *suri*, whose legitimacy was enshrined in meticulously recorded lineage records going back to the disciple Sudharman which are among the most important sources for Jain chronology.

While the bulk of the literary accounts of this period centre around two groups which have survived to this day, albeit with differing fortunes, the Kharatara Gaccha and the Tapa Gaccha, the existence in the past of a large number of other *gacchas* with their own lists of teachers testifies to an extremely diverse Shvetambara ascetic world. One of the chroniclers of the Kharatara Gaccha attempted to account for the origins of this situation by describing how a tenth century *acarya* called Uddyotana had, at the end of his life, consecrated eighty-four (a Jain round number) of his pupils as *acaryas* as a result of which there arose the same number of *gacchas* (KhGPS p.20). If the purpose of this account was to establish the existence of a single quasi-patriarchal figure as founder through whom descent could be traced, it was in reality the accelerating expansion of local affiliations and personal associations amongst Shvetambara ascetics which led to fissions within the community, with the names of some *gacchas* having their origins in a particular region or caste, while others were designated by their founder's name or with reference to some important event in their history or particular ritual modification with which they were associated.[60]

To take one example indicative of the last point: a sect still in existence, but as yet almostly completely unstudied from the historical point of view, is the Ancala Gaccha. This sect maintains that it took its name from the permission given by an *acarya* to a laywoman who had forgotten to bring a mouth-shield to the temple for ritual obeisance to use the edge (*ancala*) of her sari to cover her mouth instead.[61]

THE KHARATARA GACCHA

According to the chroniclers of the Kharatara Gaccha, their sect arose as a result of a monk called Vardhamana abandoning his teacher, a temple-dwelling monk, in disgust with what he saw as his disrespect for the doctrine and starting a lineage of teachers whose sense of sectarian identity initially derived from victory over temple-dwelling monks in public debate.

Vardhamana (died 1031) is a shadowy figure whose authority is rejected by other *gacchas* and about whose origins the Kharatara chroniclers differ. One portrays him as having become Uddyotana's main pupil (KhGPS p.20), while another states that he received the *mantra* which entitled him to become head of the sect directly from Dharanendra, the tutelary deity of the ford-maker Parshva (KhGBG p.1). Certainly, in all the accounts of the central legitimating event in Kharatara history, the defeat of the temple-dwelling monk Sura at Patan in 1024, Vardhamana is pictured either as not being present or as delegating authority to his pupil Jineshvara, whose alacrity in debate was, according to most sources, responsible for the sect receiving the name *Kharatara*, that is, 'Particularly Sharpwitted' or 'Fierce'. The *suris* who came after Vardhamana, including his successor Jineshvara, are, as pictured by the chroniclers, among the liveliest personalities in all Jain history: scholars, installers of images, pilgrims, wizards, even children.[62]

With the exception of the canonical commentator Abhayadeva Suri, whose inclusion in the Kharatara teacher lineage was hotly challenged by other sects, the most famous and representative of the Kharatara *suris* were Jinavallabha and Jinadatta.[63] Jinavallabha (eleventh century) had as a boy been a pupil of a temple-dwelling monk who provided education for the sons of the laity and who, because of the young Jinavallabha's precocity, had bought him from his mother to be his disciple. Once, Jinavallabha was left in charge of the temple library, whose contents were normally kept concealed, and read part of one of the manuscripts, which turned out to be the defining text of Shvetambara asceticism, the *Dashavaikalika*, whereupon he realised that the way of life he and his master had been following was not in accord with the scriptures. He then went to study with Abhayadeva Suri and was subsequently appointed his successor as *suri*, not without misgivings on the part of other monks because of his temple-dwelling background. It is with Jinavallabha that one of the alternative names of the Kharatara Gaccha, the *Vidhisangha*, the 'Assembly based on Scriptural Injunction' is associated.

Not all versions of this story tally in every respect. However, it is agreed that scripture occupied a central place in determining the course of Jinavallabha's career. It was recourse to the literal words of sacred texts which, through furnishing binding behavioural injunctions, governed the entire Kharatara approach to the ascetic life, and the supposedly heretical behaviour of their arch-enemies, the temple-dwelling monks, was specifically linked by the chroniclers of the sect to ignorance, misuse or travesty of the scriptural canon.[64]

Few of Jinavallabha's works have been seriously studied but one which deserves to be better known is the 'Crown of the Assembly' (SP), a pessimistic and gloomy poem about the state of Jainism in the eleventh century which belies the triumphalist tone of the later Kharatara chroniclers and expresses its author's often sardonic views about the corrupt forces with which the then relatively small Kharatara Gaccha felt itself to be contending. Jinavallabha regarded himself as living in bad times, the Kali Yuga with a vengeance, in which the fort of the Jain doctrine had been captured by false ascetics and hordes of barbarians, in other words the Moslems, were perpetrating savage depredations (SP 40). To quote one verse:

> Now that the ascetic community has shown itself to have a body unequalled in ugliness, now that mighty armies of barbarians have appeared like the plague, now that the prophecy of the time when upright monks will not be honoured has come to pass, we are harassed because we expound the true doctrine by those who have united with the growing camp of the king of delusion to do his bidding (SP 40).[65]

It is Jinadatta (1075–1154) who is the most celebrated of the *suris* of the Kharatara Gaccha and a wider range of activity is ascribed to him than to any other. While a boy, he was given by his mother to some Shvetambara nuns who saw in him signs of greatness. During his youth, the chronicler Jinapala records, Jinadatta evinced a degree of impulsiveness and abrasiveness (KhGBG p.14) and in later years, when *suri*, he was to be an energetic and aggressive advocate of the interests of the Kharatara Gaccha, as when he journeyed into Sindh, then a dangerous land under Moslem control, to gain converts. Jinadatta's career is presented by the hagiographers as being replete with miraculous deeds, such as raising the dead, which had little obvious connection with the 'great truths' of Jainism but nonetheless glorified the religion, and they stress his contact with a supernatural world in which divinities come to his aid with warnings and Hindu goddesses overcome by his power grant boons which will ensure the continuity and safety of the Kharatara Gaccha.

Some of the chroniclers describe how a monument was erected to Jinadatta Suri after his death at Ajmer, with the spot becoming known as the *Dadabari*, the 'Garden of Dada'. He and three other later *suris* of the Kharatara Gaccha became affectionately known as the Dada ('Grand-dad') Gurus and are the objects of a cult centred around a variety of Dadabaris, built usually in the vicinity of temples, which is still popular in western India today.[66] Jinacandra Suri (1139–65) was given the epithet 'Jewel-wearing' because he had a jewel in his forehead with which he performed miracles, Jinakushala Suri (1279–1331) through triumphal processions throughout the west gained many converts and Jinacandra Suri (1537–1612), after a vision of his predecessor as *suri*, instituted a reform of the Kharatara Gaccha and won concessions for the Jain community from the Moslem authorities. The Dada Gurus function rather like the saints in Christianity and are credited with the ability to intervene in human affairs when propitiated. One of the later chroniclers describes how Jinasakhya, who was Kharatara *suri* at the beginning of the eighteenth century, was saved from drowning by meditating upon Jinakushala Suri (KhGPS p.36), and many devotees of the Dada Gurus today ascribe their luck and prosperity to the intervention of these holy men.

THE TAPA GACCHA

The image-worshipping Shvetambara sect which is by far the most dominant today both in numbers and significance is the Tapa Gaccha. This was founded in 1228 by Jagaccandra Suri who abandoned out of disgust for its lax behaviour the 'Figtree' (*Vata*) Gaccha, so called because it was supposedly under a figtree that Uddyotana initiated his pupils, which Tapa tradition regarded as the mainstream *gaccha*. On seeing the intensity of Jagaccandra's austerities, a king gave him the epithet *Tapa*, 'Asceticism', which was subsequently applied to the *gaccha*.[67] Jagaccandra is an even more elusive personage than the Kharatara teacher Vardhamana and it is not until the sixteenth century with the great *suri* Hiravijaya that a member of the Tapa Gaccha stands forth as a clearly definable historical figure. It is also at this time that the Tapa monk Dharmasagara produced a variety of writings which represent the main source for the issues at stake in medieval Shvetambara sectarianism.

The language of Indian religious polemic was often extremely fierce but even by these standards Dharmasagara was an unusually dyspeptic controversialist. His main concern was to establish the centrality and uniqueness of the Tapa Gaccha and his writings are relentless exposures of what he saw as flaws in both the lives and doctrinal standpoints of other Jain teachers and the lineages which sprung from them. Indeed, there is evidence of attempts even within the Tapa Gaccha to suppress some of his writings because of their excessively aggressive tone.[68]

Dharmasagara's most important work is called the 'Sun in the Eyes of Owlish Heretics' or, more prosaically, the 'Examination of the Doctrine' (PP). Apart from the Digambaras, who are disposed of with what had become time-honoured Shvetambara arguments, and the followers of Lonka who advocated the rejection of image worship (see Chapter 9), Dharmasagara's greatest ire is reserved for the Kharatara *suris*, Jinavallabha and Jinadatta and, in a manner often strikingly modern in style through its analysis of textual sources, he attempted to show that the bulk of the Kharatara accounts of them were fictitious or self-serving and that no legitimate lineage could possibly have descended through these two teachers. In particular, Dharmasagara concentrates upon Jinavallabha's relationship with Abhayadeva Suri, whose eminence ensured that he was included in both the Kharatara and the Tapa lineages, and he claims that there could be no possible pupillary connection between the two because Jinavallabha, as the erstwhile pupil of a temple-dwelling monk, had never been properly initiated. That this remained an important issue can be seen from the seventeenth century Kharatara writer Samayasundara's clam that in 1560 a conclave of teachers from a wide variety of *gacchas* formally announced that Abhayadeva Suri was a member of the Kharatara Gaccha (SSh p.25).

The attack directed by Dharmasagara against the Kharatara Gaccha is long and involved but his objection, as to all other Jain sects, is clear. Teachers who started new lineages or who introduced, as Jinadatta did, innovations in ritual were in fact setting themselves up as the equals of the fordmakers. There could be only one *tirtha*, one community with one correct form of practice and, although there may be many *suris* within it, it could be based only upon Mahavira with lineal descent proceeding through his disciple Sudharman. Furthermore, a particularly telling point against a sect like the Kharatara Gaccha which claimed to derive its authority from a fundamentalist adherence to the scriptures is that there cannot be any validation of practice through sacred texts alone for, while there is no action of the *tirtha* which is not in accord with scripture, the *tirtha* cannot be based solely on scripture but must take its strength from a properly constituted teacher lineage.

For Dharmasagara, the true and uninterrupted lineage is, needless to say, represented by the Tapa Gaccha, and by arguing for its centrality he was attempting to impose a uniform orthodoxy upon a multifarious Jain identity. Clearly sensitive to the possible accusation that the Tapa Gaccha itself might be regarded as no more than one of a variety of sects which all came into being in the same way, Dharmasagara points out that Jagaccandra seceded from the Figtree Gaccha at the express command of his teacher, and the fact that the name Tapa Gaccha does not occur before him does not, he claims, signify any new doctrine or change of behaviour but a confirmation of the ancient ascetic values upon which Jainism was based.[69]

Controversy continued between the Kharatara and Tapa Gacchas for some considerable time, particularly over the great pilgrimage place of Mount Shatrunjaya.[70] The conflict even proceeded on the supernatural level. One of the Kharatara chroniclers describes how at the end of the sixteenth century a *suri* called Jinacandra gained control of Manibhadra, the tutelary deity of the Tapa Gaccha (KhGPS p.35), while another story describes how the sixteenth century Tapa Gaccha *suri* Anandavimala invoked Manibhadra to defeat the god Bhairava who had been summoned up by the Kharataras.[71] Such controversy seems improbable today when Kharatara ascetic numbers have dwindled to some 19 monks and 193 nuns, nearly all localised in Rajasthan, compared with the 1,179 monks and 3,680 nuns of the Tapa Gaccha.[72]

RELATIONS WITH THE MOSLEMS

The Shvetambara chroniclers preserve a faint echo of the dismay which must have attended the destruction in 782 of the city of Valabhi, the cultural and political centre of western India, by Turkish invaders. This event marked the start of the onset of Islam and a gradual restructuring of Indian polity and society, as a result of which the Jains, although not totally excluded from political power, began to assume the almost exclusively commercial role with which they have been associated to this day.[73]

Jain relations with Moslem rulers were at some times friendly, at other times uneasy and conciliatory as the attitudes of the Moslems varied. One of the earliest examples of this is the despoliation in 1313 of the temples on Mount Shatrunjaya by the Turks. Their restoration was in fact effected quickly by Samara Shah, a servant of Alp Khan, the governor of Gujarat, with the Jain even receiving financial assistance from his master to do so, a sign that the Moslems were on this occasion pragmatic enough not to let religious scruples lead to the alienation of an economically powerful minority.[74] An interesting insight into Jain attitudes towards this whole episode can be found in the account written in 1336 by Kakka Suri which describes the restoration of the great temple of Rishabha at Shatrunjaya. He shows no interest in the motives behind the Moslem desecration, stressing instead that such occurrences are to be expected in the irreligious Kali Yuga, and Kakka Suri's real concern is in describing the lavish renovation of Shatrunjaya by which the Jain community demonstrated its prosperity, thus fitting it into a pattern of previous renovations performed by legendary Jain figures stretching back to the very beginning of the world era (NNJP 3.26ff).

However, the restoration of Shatrunjaya notwithstanding, there can be no doubt that the early period of Moslem rule in western India saw the destruction and disappearance of a large number of Jain holy places and many once great shrines are now no more than names. References by the Kharatara chronicler Jinapala to the escape of one of Jinadatta Suri's disciples from slavery under the Moslems (KhGBG p.18), Jinacandra Suri's magical rescue of some merchants by rendering them invisible to Turkish raiders (KhGBG p.21), and the difficulties involved in carrying out pilgrimages to the main Gujarati holy places (KhGBG pp.62–4) testify to the pressure that was being exerted on the Jain community in the thirteenth and fourteenth centuries.

The greatest manifestation of Moslem power in India, the Moghul empire, was founded in 1526 by Babur, an adventurer from Central Asia, and reached the peak of its glory with his grandson, the emperor Akbar (1556–1605). Akbar was deeply interested in religion and it is often said, in fact incorrectly, that he founded a new religion. Certainly, he did invite many teachers of various denominations, including Jesuits, to his court and Jain sources dwell at length on his relationship with Shvetambara teachers.

Akbar seems to have been in contact with the Shvetambaras from a fairly early age. He was, for example, in possession of a library of Jain manuscripts which had been presented to him by a monk called Padmasundara. However, it was with the great preacher Hiravijaya Suri (1527–95), the head of the Tapa Gaccha, with whom he had the closest relationship. In 1587 Hiravijaya, somewhat late in his career (he had become *suri* in 1566), was summoned by royal edict to the imperial court at Agra. According to the Jain accounts, Akbar interrogated the Shvetambara teacher about the characteristics of true religion and, on being informed that it was compassion for all forms of life which was its most important constituent, he was moved to issue decrees ordering the freeing of caged birds and the banning of the slaughter of animals on the Shvetambara festival of *Paryushan*. When Hiravijaya departed after three years at Agra, he left behind one of his pupils, Shanticandra, who also prevailed upon Akbar to issue edicts banning the killing of animals as well as lifting the tax upon non-Moslems. The monks of the Tapa Gaccha were not the only Jain influences in the Moghul court, for the Kharatara *suri* Jinacandra who visited Lahore in 1591 persuaded Akbar to protect Jain temples from Moslem assault.[75]

However, the Shvetambaras also had enemies at court. Another of Hiravijaya's pupils, Vijayasena Suri, had to defend Jainism from a charge of atheism made to Akbar in 1592 and the attitude of the emperor's successor, Jahangir, towards the Jains was not always as benign as that of his father. Jahangir seems to have developed a strong animus against the Kharatara *suri* Jinasimha, ostensibly because he had predicted an early end to his reign, while on another occasion he apparently banned all Jain monks from his kingdom. Jahangir's behaviour was unquestionably erratic since there is no doubt that at other times he viewed Shvetambara monks very favourably, appointing one to teach his son and in 1616 issuing an edict granting Jains freedom of worship. Indeed so inconsistent does the Moghul emperor's attitude towards the Jains seem to have become that it has been suggested that they represented for Jahangir, who had taken a vow of non-violence earlier in his life in repentance for a murder, a focus for his own turbulent and ambivalent feelings towards killing which, in the form of hunting and military activity, he was never really to abandon.[76]

None of the Jain teachers who attended the Moghul court exercised any really serious influence over Akbar and Jahangir, and their main significance lay in their position as spokesmen for an economically powerful but politically impotent group of imperial subjects. While many exploits by members of the Moghul royal family in the seventeenth century were financed by Jain bankers, this was no guarantee of immunity from persecution. In 1645, while governor of Gujarat, Aurangzeb (later to become emperor) desecrated, and turned into a mosque, an ornate temple to Parshva dedicated at colossal expense by Shantidas Jhaveri, the richest and most influential merchant and financier of Ahmedabad. Although Aurangzeb's father, the emperor Shah Jahan, ordered the temple to be given back to Shantidas (in fact, it could never be used again), this event must have been a stark reminder to the Jains of their powerlessness in the face of a dominant Islam.[77]

SHVETAMBARA CASTE CONVERSION

The metaphysical doctrine that all souls are essentially the same and the constant reiteration in the literature from an early period that rank depends upon moral qualities rather than purity of birth ought to have ensured a thoroughgoing egalitarianism within Jainism. However, the Jains have over the centuries evolved a caste structure in the sense that each individual belongs to a social group, originally endogamous, which ranks itself in respect to other groups. While the origin of such differentiation in part lay in claims of relative purity based around marriage alliances and interdining, today the prime determinant for Jain caste ranking is essentially economic status, with some castes being accepted as manifestly more prosperous and powerful than others and, despite some lingering conservatism, caste prescriptions do not play a vital role in Shvetambara Jain life any more. In the last resort, purity for Jains is a matter of religion rather than society, something to be achieved, unlike brahman purity which is perceived as innate and governing all social relationships.[78]

Many Shvetambara Jain castes have their origins in the patronage by particular families of a Jain teacher who in turn assumed a ritual role and recorded the history of that family's relationship with his *gaccha*. Such castes generally take their names from the town or region in which legend suggests they arose and this gives a sense of 'roots' to the caste members, who have very often migrated far from their place of origin, which supplements their identity as Jains. It is also significant for merchant society in north India that some of these castes also contain Hindus so that, depending upon context, religious affiliation can at times be subsumed under the broader caste designation of *bania*, 'merchant'.

For the chroniclers of the deeds of the great teachers of Shvetambara sects like the Kharatara Gaccha, the conversion of Hindu clans, particularly in Rajasthan, and their subsequent linkage to and perpetuation of the *gaccha* of the converting monk is one of the major hagiographic themes. The motivation for such conversions to Jainism is not always connected by the chroniclers with any awareness of the truth of the tenets of Jain doctrine but is often brought about by the persuasiveness of a miracle-working Shvetambara monk who is able to compel allegiance through the obvious superiority of his powers.[79] It is also likely that the willingness of Jain teachers to link their teaching with emerging regional vernaculars and popular poetic modes played a part in this process.

One of the most famous and successful castes is the Oswals who, although containing Hindu Vaishnavas, are predominantly Jain and have spread outside the Marwar region of Rajasthan to be found wherever Jains conduct business. The Oswals originate and take their name from the town of Osian near Jodhpur and, according to Shvetambara history, they were lay followers of the Upakesha Gaccha, a lineage which seems to have died out at the beginning of this century. The chronicle of the Upakesha Gaccha describes how a monk called Ratnaprabha Suri who died eighty-four years after Mahavira was responsible for the conversion of the Oswals. In fact, despite attempts based on highly questionable interpretations of fragmentary inscriptions to locate Jainism in Rajasthan before the common era, there seems little doubt that Ratnaprabha Suri lived considerably later, possibly in the twelfth century.[80]

The accounts of the activities of Ratnaprabha Suri contain motifs common to other conversion stories. According to the chronicle, he both restored to life the son of a prominent brahman who had been bitten by a snake, thus creating the climate for other inhabitants of Osian to convert, and confirmed his power by his conquest of the town's tutelary goddess Saccika who was compelled to abandon her carnivorous habits and become a Jain vegetarian deity. The sanctity of Osian was further guaranteed by the miraculous discovery of a buried image of Mahavira which was installed in a temple. The chronicle also describes how the attempt to remove the prominent nipples of this image, which brought about a miraculous flow of blood, led to Saccika predicting the eventual loss of Osian's prosperity and the scattering of the Oswal caste.[81]

6 The ascetic

Early Jain literature describes a religious world in which deliverance would automatically ensue from the correct performance of Mahavira's prescriptions concerning the ascetic way of life. However, this view gradually became qualified, as can be seen in the assertion of an old Digambara text that three further existences could intervene until the attainment of deliverance (MA 97), and the emphasis gradually changed within Jainism to the possibility of the gaining of an appropriate rebirth, usually as a god in one of the heavens, which could provide the platform for a suitable, human continuation of existence. It is likely that the reason for this shift was the growing distance of the ascetic community from the physical presence of Mahavira and his disciples which had provided the unique environment for escaping from rebirth, and there was eventual recognition that a variety of advanced spiritual attainments, of which enlightenment was one, were no longer possible in this era after the death of the disciple Jambu. Thus the supposed goal of Jain teachings lost its immediacy and religious practice became directed not just towards the burning away of karma but also, increasingly, to the gaining of sufficient merit to ensure the continuity of rebirth rather than its extinction.

At the same time, the ancient scriptural texts also bear witness to a movement from an original situation in which the bondless ascetics were simply contrasted with all those who did not follow the same mode of life, alms being taken only from those householders who manifested obvious moral qualities, to the acceptance of the necessity of an accommodation with what had become a specifically Jain community of almsgiving supporters, laymen and laywomen who formed with the monks and nuns the 'fourfold assembly' (*caturvidhasangha*).

It is true that Jain writers in the past occasionally attempted to downplay the significance of the laity. For Haribhadra, even a religiously minded lay person continually experiences to his detriment the pull of familial and social ties, like a turtle which rises up from the depths of the ocean to catch a glimpse of the sky, only to sink down again (comm. on AvNiry 97) and elsewhere the same writer states that the true characteristic of the layman is his desire to become a monk (LV p.180). At the same time, the use of the term *sangha*, 'assembly' or 'community', to include both ascetics and laity points to an acceptance of their interdependent relationship and shared aspiration to an ideal goal, however distant it might be.

THE STAGES OF QUALITY

The commonality of human experience as envisaged by Jainism was given expression in the list of fourteen 'stages of quality' (*gunasthana*) which appears for the first time in Digambara texts at the beginning of the common era and delineates how every individual can in gradualistic manner proceed over one life through a series of levels to final deliverance. Starting from superstition and ignorance and proceeding to the gaining of faith and the consequent performance of the full range of lay duties, the career of each individual is depicted as potentially leading to initiation as an ascetic which will then, after the practice of austerity, meditation and suppression of the passions, bring about the elimination of karma and the attainment of deliverance.[1]

The stages of quality, although representing a form of continuum, were not regarded as in any way mechanical or inevitable in their progression: rather they provided a model of the fluctuating nature of human spiritual capabilities within which, even in the highly advanced eleventh stage where the passions have been calmed but not fully eliminated, it was possible to relapse back into the lower stages. Moreover, through the acceptance of non-Jain views as being located in the stages of quality, if only at the very beginning where they are designated as 'false belief' (*mithyatva*), Jainism demonstrates a willingness to encompass, yet also transcend, all other religious and philosophical paths.

Some Jain writers today invoke the stages of quality as if they threw some genuine sociological light on the way Jains envision their position in the world. However, the fact that it is generally accepted that lay people and ascetics in this age cannot progress beyond the fifth and sixth stages respectively shows that this model of the development of spirituality has only a theoretical value. Nonetheless, it demonstrates general approval of the validity of the householder's role and its linkage to that of the ascetic.

MONKS AND NUNS

The use of the terms 'monk' and 'nun' to describe male and female Jain ascetics is both convenient and conventional, and I employ them in this book, using 'ascetic' where possible as an approximately gender-free expression. However, these categories can cause a degree of confusion to those familiar with them in a Christian context. The early designations *shramana*, 'striver' and *nirgrantha*, 'bondless' are no longer employed today, male ascetics being called *muni*, also an ancient term, which is derived from the root *man*, 'think, be silent' and is thus similar in origin to English 'monk', while female ascetics are generally called *sadhvi*, the feminine of *sadhu*, 'good' or, among the Digambaras, *aryika*, 'noble'. Monasticism in Christianity signifies the following of a mode of life which is settled, enclosed and generally contemplative whereas Jain monks and nuns, unless they have received some kind of dispensation from a senior ascetic for reasons such as illness or old age, lead lives of mendicant wandering, although by no means of a random nature, punctuated by greater or longer periods of residence in the vicinity of the lay community and interaction with it. Jain ascetics are homeless and without any attachments and the possibility of living permanently in one place is today associated only with, for the Shvetambaras, the *yati*, descended from the medieval temple-dwelling monk or, for the Digambaras, the *bhattaraka*, neither of whom is an initiated ascetic.

The oldest textual material cannot provide an exact guide to the required behaviour of Jain monks and nuns today, and modifications and adaptations have occurred over the centuries. The most ancient scriptures, for example, often insist upon the social isolation of the individual ascetic, exemplified by the solitary Mahavira, as reflecting the ontological isolation of the soul and thus representing an acknowledgement that every ascetic is responsible for his or her own destiny. But solitary endeavour proved to be uncongenial to Jain ascetics from an early date and, as we have seen, they organised themselves in groups which provided security and solidarity. For an individual to leave the ascetic band to which he was attached and wander alone was regarded as highly inappropriate. Isolation became in the early medieval period a form of temporary austerity or a much feared penance for misdemeanour and has remained only an admired ideal, albeit one that has to some extent been revived today by Digambara monks.[2] Nonetheless, the overall ethos has remained much the same for some considerable time, despite the existence in medieval times of redefinitions of ascetic behaviour and the severe decline in ascetic numbers in the early modern period, and the exclusivity of the Jain ascetic path is still perceived as deriving from adherence to certain principles enshrined in ancient prescriptions.

REASONS FOR RENUNCIATION

The interpretation of the stages of quality model of Jain religious life as a continuum would present the change from the lay to ascetic vocation as a smooth transition. In reality, such a radical reorientation of behaviour would require some kind of motive factor, a jolt which gives rise to disgust with the world (*vairagya*) and a consequent change of attitude. The diversity of human nature will, furthermore, dictate that there must be a variety of reasons why an individual might be shaken into altering his perspective and seeking renunciation. One Shvetambara scripture recognises this diversity of motive in a list of ten reasons for renunciation, few of which have any reference to overt religiosity. They include the individual's own desire to renounce, anger, poverty, the promptings of a dream, a promise to leave the world, the memory of previous births, sickness, lack of respect, being enlightened by a god and following one's child into the order (Sth 712). Not all of these reasons, which are connected by the commentator with legendary exemplar, would necessarily be regarded as commendable – Shivabhuti, for example, whom the Shvetambaras regard as the founder of the Digambara sect, supposedly became a monk out of anger – but they show an awareness that what is of real significance is what is done *after* becoming an ascetic.

The motive for renunciation on the part of an individual is not a question with which lay people would normally concern themselves. Nonetheless, a recent survey of Shvetambara nuns has produced an interesting mixture of spiritual and social reasons for rejection of the world and subsequent initiation. Out of answers garnered from one hundred nuns interviewed about why they had chosen to reject the world, twenty-one expressed themselves as having been attracted to this attitude for personal reasons, fourteen were impressed by the general ambiance of the ascetic community, nineteen were spiritually drawn to a prominent female teacher, nineteen were spiritually drawn to a particular nun, seventeen were orphans who regarded ascetic life as preferable to that with relatives, and five were attracted by the outward appearance of ascetic life, such as the initiation ceremony itself. With regard to reasons for initiation, fifty-nine nuns stated themselves to have been spiritually motivated, eleven sought increase of knowledge to gain a specifically religious end, ten wanted to be of service to the community, three to escape from marriage and seventeen to find some sort of refuge, presumably because they were widows.[3]

The Hindu philosopher Bhasarvajna (*c.* 900 CE) speculated that one of the main attractions of religions such as Jainism for potential converts was the possibility which they offered those of low caste and the poor of an escape from the harshness of society.[4] Leaving aside the fact that admission to the Shvetambara ascetic order has never been entirely open to all and that Digambaras do not allow low caste people to take initiation,[5] it would seem fruitless to seek some kind of grand, unifying theory to explain the attractions of the Jain ascetic path, either in its beginnings or at any other time. One thing seems certain. Nobody today becomes a Jain ascetic to enter a state of contemplative solitude, for the lives of monks and nuns seldom offer an opportunity for sustained privacy,[6] while reasons for renunciation may range from a deeply personal, spiritual commitment to a simple desire to emulate a particular act of asceticism which has been witnessed, such as the regular ascetic practice of pulling out the hair from the head.[7]

The scriptures often refer to the impossibility of family relationships enabling the achievement of serious religious goals, and initiation as an ascetic is predicated upon the severing of such worldly ties, although the intensity of this can vary: for example, many Shvetambara nuns today receive and welcome visits from their relatives. Theoretically, renunciation should be carried out in a manner least likely to cause distress to one's family. Shvetambara tradition regards Mahavira as having resolved to renounce only after his parents were dead and as being persuaded by other relatives to postpone this for a further two years lest he compound their grief. The potentially unfortunate results of not settling one's affairs prior to renunciation can be seen in the well-known story of Gajasukumara who, the day before his marriage, renounced to become a follower of the fordmaker Nemi and subsequently, while seated in meditation, was tortured by his enraged prospective father-in-law.[8] If in general families regard the renunciation of a relative as a source of great merit, it is also clear that many young women can experience a degree of opposition from their relatives prior to becoming nuns.[9] The reformed Shvetambara Terapanthi sect insist upon the written permission of the immediate next of kin before anyone can become an ascetic.

INITIATION

Diksha, 'initiation', was a term originally used in the context of Vedic ritual to describe the symbolic second birth of the patron of the sacrifice. Although the specifically sacrificial connotation of *diksha* is not present in Jainism, the use of the word to describe the ceremony of ascetic initiation is nonetheless appropriate, for *diksha* is the only purely Jain rite of passage by which a formal change of status of an individual is ritually signalled and acknowledged, other life-cycle events, such as birth, marriage and death, being marked by ceremonies which are essentially Hindu in shape, if not in interpretation. Indeed, *diksha* can, through its creation of a new set of relationships within the ascetic community, to some extent be regarded as the event which replaces the social bonding brought about by marriage, and the dress and demeanour of a monk or nun prior to their initiation are overtly those of a person about to be married. This is perhaps of some particular significance today given that newly initiated nuns tend to be young women who prefer to enter the order rather than get married.[10]

Diksha varies across sectarian boundaries and certain historical modifications have unquestionably taken place within the ritual over the centuries, although there remain fixed elements within the ceremony, and its performance to some extent also exemplifies the ideals of a particular sect. The Digambara ceremony, for example, seems in origin to have been comparatively simple in accordance with the particularly austere mode of life being adopted, with the postulant approaching the initating teacher after bidding farewell to his parents and, on being given permission to enter the order, abandoning his clothes, uprooting his hair and taking the ascetic vows and a new name, along with a whisk and a water pot handed over by the teacher. Today, however, no doubt partly as a result of the breakdown of the lineage system in the nineteenth century, male Digambara initiates, as well as taking the five Great Vows in the presence of their teacher, are painted with symbols by a caste priest (*upadhye*) within a temple in the same manner as an image being consecrated while a *bhattaraka* oversees and legitimises the event.[11]

Strictly speaking, full initiation into the order should be preceded by a preliminary period which Shvetambaras today call 'little' (*choti*) *diksha* as opposed to the formal 'big' (*bari*) *diksha*, although the classical texts use the expressions 'going forth' (*pravrajya*) and 'ordination' (*upasthapana*) to describe the separate stages involved.[12] For the Shvetambaras, the initial period, starting from a formal declaration of sincerity about entering the order and, in the case of the image-worshipping sects, the adoption of a new name, is followed by a probationary period lasting about one month (for the Terapanthi sect this can last as long as two years) in which fasting and the study of basic scriptural texts are undertaken. The Digambaras formalise this preliminary period by allowing for the existence of two types of lower order male ascetic who may in fact never proceed to take full initiation as a naked monk. The *kshullaka*, a term meaning 'lesser', may wear a robe, keep an alms bowl, is not obliged to pull out his hair, and may bathe, while the more advanced *ailaka*, a term of uncertain etymology which may possibly mean 'partly clothed', wears a loincloth and eats sitting down but, like a naked monk, without a receptacle for his food. The *ailaka* also pulls out his hair and cannot wash himself.[13]

The Shvetambara 'big' *diksha* ceremony, while containing processional elements involving the lay community, is solemnised by a range of rituals and exchanges in Prakrit between the ascetic-to-be and the initiating teacher which take place in the ascetic lodging house (*upashraya*) in front of an image of a fordmaker. The hairpulling ceremony, which takes place at this time and is not witnessed by the lay community, signifies austerity and the abandonment of sexuality. This may involve the actual removal of the hair by tearing it out in handfuls as is often described in the old literature, although there is also ancient warranty for the custom sometimes found today of the head being shaved in advance with some small tufts being left which are removed in the course of the initiation.[14] It is also during the big *diksha* that the newly initiated Shvetambara ascetic receives his robe, whisk (used for gently brushing away insects) and alms bowl (and if Terapanthi or Sthanakvasi, the *muhpatti* or mouth-shield) which, apart from their practical use, serve as emblems of sectarian allegiance.[15] At the conclusion of the ceremony, he will then spend some time in fasting before going out to seek alms for the first time.

If the *diksha* ceremony obviously celebrates both the consummation of a particular spiritual or social choice and the continued reproduction of the ascetic community, it also provides a means of fostering a sense of Jain identity amongst the community as a whole, a feeling enhanced during its course by the hortatory speeches of ascetic leaders, and participation in the ceremony enables Jains to make a public statement about their uniqueness with regard to the larger Indian community in which they live.

The Digambaras hold that only adults can become initiated ascetics. However, the minimum age for initiation into the various Shvetambara orders is as low as eight years and there is even evidence for it having been permitted in the past at the age of six.[16] While the laity has not always been united about the validity of child initiation, the ascetic community seems unanimous in approval and the sight of very young novices amongst monks and nuns is not uncommon. This matter became a source of controversy in 1931 when the Government of Baroda, in response to the views of Jain social reformers, attempted to pass an act effectively banning the custom. Many prominent monks opposed it strenuously and, although the act was eventually passed, it ceased to have any force after independence.[17]

Advocates of child initiation could point to ancient scriptural justification. The 'Exposition of Explanations' describes how the boy-monk Atimukta is found engaged in the somewhat unmonastic activity of playing at boats in a stream with his alms bowl. Rather than rebuke him, Mahavira interprets this as a sign that Atimukta will cross the river of rebirth in one lifetime (Bh 5.4).

THE GREAT VOWS

The word *vrata* in its earliest use in Sanskrit meant not just a 'temporary vow', as was to be its general later significance in Indian religions, but also conveyed the notion of a 'calling' in the sense of a solemn dedication of oneself on a permanent basis to one single purpose.[18] It is the adoption of the five *mahavratas*, the 'Great Vows', and their integration into what must after ascetic initiation become a totally realigned way of life which is the central defining characteristic of the monk and nun, governing their external, observable behaviour and providing a system of internal, spiritual control.

According to a Kharatara Gaccha ritual manual (VMP p.39), the presiding ascetic at a ceremony of initiation should read out the scriptural story of Rohini, the girl who, unlike her sisters, planted and reaped the rewards of five rice grains given to her by her father, to demonstrate how the five Great Vows should not just be formally acceded to but put to good use.[19]

The oldest Jain literature is not familiar with the five Great Vows in any formal sense, identifying only possession and violence as the main causes of rebirth, and more detailed specification of five areas of inappropriate activity which the ascetic has to abandon came only gradually.[20] Another model of faults to be rejected, consisting of those designated by the five Great Vows amplified by the four passions and a further series of deleterious activities, is much more prevalent in the 'Exposition of Explanations' than the Great Vows alone, reference to which appears to be found only in the later portions of that scripture.[21] Nonetheless, irrespective of the history of their development, the Great Vows are accepted by Shvetambaras and Digambaras alike as lying at the heart of Mahavira's ethical teachings and a discussion of them is necessary to understand the restrictions which bound the Jain ascetic's life and fully bring about the state of homelessness for him.

The classic account of the Great Vows is to be found in the second book of the *Acaranga* where they are directly linked with Mahavira's description of life-forms (AS 2.15).[22] The statement of the renunciation entailed in each vow is followed by five 'realisations' (*bhavana*) which outline more detailed implications, the observance of which will ensure that the vow is fully and correctly executed (TS 7.3).

In the first Great Vow, the ascetic rejects the act of killing any life-forms whatsoever and undertakes that for the rest of his life he will confess, repent of and avoid violence, whether performing it himself, compelling another to perform it or approving another carrying it out, mentally, vocally and physically. The succeeding realisations then delineate particular areas in which violence might occur and with regard to which the ascetic must take special care. Firstly, he must closely observe how and where he walks lest he injure life-forms on the way. This is institutionalised in the form of *caturmas*, the four-month rain retreat, for during the monsoon there is a great burgeoning of plant and insect life which might otherwise be injured in the course of ascetic wandering. The next two realisations are implicit in the vow itself, enjoining the ascetic to control mind and speech lest they be agents of violence. Fourthly, the ascetic has to take care about how he puts down his alms bowl and, fifthly, all food and drink has to be inspected to ensure that there are no life-forms within it.

The other Great Vows are predictable enough, given Jainism's origins within a common Indian renunciatory culture.

According to the second, the ascetic is obliged to abstain from lying, underlined by the realisation that he should be deliberate in his speech and not subject to anger, greed, fear or mirth.

The third Vow in its literal sense states that the ascetic should not take what has not been given. This is generally interpreted as rejection of theft (e.g. TS 7.10) but, as the realisations show, relates also to the excessively prolonged occupation of any space of ground or the consumption of alms without the teacher's permission.

The fourth Vow states that the ascetic should renounce sexual activity, which the realisations reinforce by advising against any contact, mental or physical, with women or eating or drinking anything likely to stimulate the sexual drive.

Finally, the fifth Vow entails the renunciation of any attachment which the realisations take as relating to the objects of the senses and which later tradition was to regard as referring to possessions in general.

A further sixth Vow, forbidding eating after dark, came to be added on to the basic list of five. Its first occurrence (SKS 1.2.3.3) describes it as supplementing the Great Vows, and its incongruous inclusion in prose in the *Dashavaikalika* (DVS 1.4) within what is otherwise a verse passage suggests that it assumed importance only relatively lately, presumably because it was in origin little more than a subdivision of the first Great Vow of non-violence.[23] The injunction about not eating at night has binding force upon all ascetics and technically applies to lay people as well, although very few of them would follow it to the letter other than during festivals. The reason for this particular stipulation is that ascetics cannot go out to seek alms at night because this would inevitably involve inadvertent trampling upon small life-forms (Aparajita on BhA 1179), while the cooking of food by the laity would inevitably attract insects which would be drawn into the flames (NBh 3399–400). Hemacandra claims that consuming insects which have fallen into food can lead to loss of intelligence and that nocturnal ghosts can pollute food. However, a more convincing reason for the ban, although without textual authority, is the popular belief that the proper digestion of food can only take place in sunlight.[24]

Broadly speaking, the purpose of the Great Vows, and indeed of the other ancillary vows which a Jain ascetic undertakes, is to bring about a state of internal purification. Although, on the face of it, they would all appear to relate to a variety of different activities, the Vows are in fact understood in Jainism as developing from the first, the renunciation of violence. Thus, not speaking falsely draws its real significance not only from a positive commitment to truth but from an assessment of whether an enunciated statement will lead to violence. A common narrative theme in Jain literature relates to the monk who refuses to tell a hunter the whereabouts of an animal being pursued and as a consequence endures torture in silence rather than reveal the truth.

Minimal verbal activity is a sign of ascetic commitment to non-violence and, while lying should be avoided, a truth should not be spoken which harms another (YS 2.61).

The third Great Vow of not taking what has not been given, if obviously ensuring the ascetic's honesty of dealings with all people, signifies on a more profound level not taking the lives of other creatures (Shilanka on AS 1.3). Attachment to possessions and the sense objects, rejected by the fourth Great Vow, engenders the passions, the prime cause of violence (YS 2.110), and sexual activity is prohibited not only because of the distraction and passion it causes but because innumerable life-forms are destroyed in each ejaculation of semen (YS 2.79).

THE NATURE OF NON-VIOLENCE

'Non-violence is the highest religious duty' (*ahimsa paramo dharmah*) is a phrase which many Jains would regard, along with the motto 'all living creatures must help each other', as encapsulating what their religion stands for. Without the abandonment of violent activity, all religious behaviour, no matter how correct, is worthless (YS 2.31). The ideal of the primacy of non-violence is not, of course, unique to Jainism,[25] but for Jains the failure of Hinduism and Buddhism to provide a truly thoroughgoing analysis of reality ensures that they must forfeit any claims to be regarded as non-violent religions. In the laconic words of the *Dashavaikalika*, 'first knowledge of the world, then compassion for it' (DVS 4.10). The ability to conduct oneself in an appropriate manner towards one's fellow-creatures can only come from a correct understanding, provided by the Jain religion, of the manner in which reality is structured and of the nature of the relationship between body and soul. As a result, the ascetic must accede to delimitations placed upon his way of life: he cannot light fires, dig or plough the ground, must drink filtered or boiled water, inspect his surroundings carefully to avoid injury to insects and avoid any exaggerated movement of the body.

Thus, though non-violence may not have been a concept which emerged in an exclusively Jain context, the urging of humans to realise that all souls are like onself in that they suffer distress, cling to life and do not wish to be destroyed (AS 1.2.3; DVS 6.16 and 10.5) was a unique message which shaped and defined a Jain ascetic culture which made strong demands upon its members but which also, if activated properly, was regarded as bringing about quiescence of the senses and eventual deliverance (SKS 1.3.4.20). Moreover, *ahimsa*, 'non-violence' (although perhaps in origin literally 'non-intention to kill'), if a negative expression, is also interpreted within Jain tradition in strongly positive terms as involving such qualities as friendship, goodwill and peace which manifest themselves through gentleness and lack of passion.

The first Great Vow in fact enjoins the ascetic to abstain from destruction of living creatures rather than to adopt non-violence, and it would be easy both to interpret this vow as having a strictly prohibitive import and to speculate as to how at all it could provide for a practical mode of life. According to one prominent twentieth century Shvetambara monk, while non-violence is the natural human condition to which violence is totally inimical, man is nonetheless in thrall to violence because he is continually obliged to engage in the essentially destructive activities of eating and drinking in order to support his body.[26]

The continual likelihood of destroying organisms on the ground and in the air would appear to create an intolerable burden for the ascetic trying to follow the Jain path but, leaving aside the fact that karma generated in the performance of religious duties disappears instantaneously (Bh 18.8; PS 3.17) and that the destruction of less developed organisms brings about much less karma than killing a five-sensed creature,[27] Jainism came in time to see action as truly violent only when accompanied by lack of care (*pramada*). Carelessness is stated in an early scriptural text to be action itself (SKS 1.8.3) and one of the most famous passages of the scriptures describes Mahavira at the point of death exhorting Gautama not to be lacking in care (UttS 10). If the general tenor of the most ancient portions of the Shvetambara scriptural canon was uncompromisingly to regard all acts of violence, whether performed, caused or approved, as the same, Umasvati, reflecting a somewhat less intense atmosphere, provided what has become the standard definition of violence (*himsa*) as the removal of life through a careless action of mind, body or speech (TS 7.8).[28] Any propensity towards carelessness must therefore be controlled by observation of oneself and the exercise of restraint.

Jainism holds that the soul of the perpetrator of a violent action is negatively affected in the same way as the life-form which has been destroyed, the only difference being the time when retribution takes place (BhA 796). Thus, 'if one does not wish to destroy one's soul, then one should not destroy living creatures'(MA 923). Inasmuch as violence is brought about by passion, it therefore becomes a primarily internal, psychological matter. Moreover, later Jain tradition eventually came to accept that even somebody who destroyed life did not suffer karmic effects if lacking in carelessness while, at the same time, failure to carry out a violent action did not necessarily militate against severe karmic retribution if violent intention already existed. In the words of Jinabhadra (sixth century), who is concerned to show that the omnipresence of life-forms in the world need not totally inhibit normal behaviour:

> It is the intention that ultimately matters. From the real point of view, a man does not become a killer only because he has killed or because the world is crowded with souls, or remain innocent only because he has not killed physically.... Even if a person does not actually kill, he becomes a killer if he has the intention to kill; while a doctor has to cause pain but is still non-injuring and innocent because his intention is pure.... For it is the intention which is the deciding factor, not the external act which is inconclusive. From the real point of view, it is the evil intention which is violence whether it materialises into an evil act of injuring or not. There can be non-violence even when an external act of violence has been committed and violence even when it has not been committed.[29]

This willingness to accept inner motivation and intention as a necessary component of any action meant that the Jains could, depending on the context, justify as self-defence certain acts of violence committed by monks, and examples from medieval texts show that pragmatism could determine responses to external threats. If, for example, a lion were to attack a band of monks, it would be justified for one of them to kill it (NBh 289), while no violence at all would be involved in monks fighting to protect nuns.[30] Jinadatta Suri, writing at a time when Moslem destruction of temples and interference with pilgrimage was causing the Jain community great trouble, stated bluntly, in a manner more reminiscent of Islam itself, that anybody engaged in a religious activity who was forced to fight and kill somebody would not lose any spiritual merit but instead attain deliverance (UR 26). While such examples are admittedly rare compared with those extolling non-violence, they do show that elevated doctrinal principles do not necessarily render the Jains passive in the face of danger and that when their religion or community experiences any serious threat, such as in this century at the hands of militant anti-Jain groups in Rajasthan, they have been willing and able to take active countermeasures against violence.[31]

ASCETICISM

The early literature provides a picture of the ascetic's life which, while still broadly recognisable, does not entirely overlap with customary practice today. What is perhaps the oldest attempt to provide for a fully organised monastic day, without any reference to mendicant wandering, divides the daylight hours into four parts devoted to study, meditation, seeking for alms and study again, the night-time into four parts devoted to study, meditation, sleep and study again, while also allowing time for various aspects of monastic ritual such as paying homage to the teacher and practical tasks such as inspecting and cleaning the alms bowl (UttS 26).[32] However, few ascetics would attempt to adhere rigidly to such a model today and it also does not allow for interaction with and preaching to the laity, an important element of ascetic life, particularly during the four-month rain retreat, or the fact that, on a more mundane level, Shvetambara monks and nuns can now wash and repair their robes. As ethnographic studies of Jain ascetics are as yet extremely rare and understanding of the texture and practicalities of their lives imperfect, I will confine myself to consideration of those elements which the textual tradition considered to be of prime importance and of which contemporary ascetics are still aware.[33]

In the widest sense, the entire range of ascetic behaviour is aimed towards both the imposition of mental and physical constraints in order to ward off the influx of new karma and the cultivation of ascetic practices which, if exercised with sufficient intensity, will destroy that karma which is already clinging to the soul. These two areas are defined as being 'restraint' (*samyama*) and 'asceticism' (*tapas*).

Protection from karma (*samvara*) can be gained through a controlled and informed stance towards the surrounding world. Care in all actions, harmonisation of personality traits and forebearance in the face of the inevitable difficulties of the ascetic life play a part in this. Basic are the three 'Concealments' (*gupti*) and the five 'Careful Actions' (*samiti*). All of these are implied in the Great Vows and, given the relative lateness of the latter, seem to represent a parallel pattern of ascetic restraint, apparently formalised for the first time by Umasvati, which was subsequently superseded in importance by the ritually binding Vows.[34]

The Concealments involve the general curbing of the three modalities of mind, body and speech so that they are not employed for frivolous or spiritually irrelevant purposes (TS 9.4). The Careful Actions provide a form of etiquette according to which Jain ascetics can conduct themselves in the world. The first of these, 'care in motion' (*iryasamiti*), is also included among the 'realisations' of the first Great Vow and must have been originally of major importance, for it was in the sphere of physical movement that the sincerity of Jain attitudes towards their teaching of non-violence could most easily be scrutinised by their opponents. The 'Exposition of Explanations' describes how Gautama, to Mahavira's great approbation, confounded some heretics who accused Jain monks of destroying by the very act of walking insects and small life-forms through an appeal to the manifest care which the Jains took as they proceeded along (Bh 18.8). Watchfulness is thus a quality which should characterise the Jain ascetic above all others.

The next two Careful Actions relate respectively to speech, through the prevention of malevolent statements or excessive laughter which is one of the minor passions, and seeking for alms (*eshana*), the ascetic always having to be sure that the food offered to him is not inappropriate. The fourth Careful

Action relates to care either in receiving something or in putting it down so that, after proper inspection, the ascetic can be sure that there is no possibility of violence to tiny life-forms. The fifth Careful Action dictates that the ground should be checked before voiding the bowels (TS 9.5; BhA 1181–94).

In addition, the development of positive moral qualities, reflection upon the nature of the situation of human beings in the world of transmigration (*anupreksha*), conquest of the endurances (*parishaha*), those disagreeable social, psychological and physical factors which are the inevitable result of leading the ascetic life in an often hostile environment, and the maintenance of pure and correct behaviour all bring about restraint and, therefore, protection from karma (TS 9.6–18). However, difficult though these may be to practice, a different order of physical and spiritual cultivation is required to bring about the elimination of karma already accrued (*nirjara*) and it is here that asceticism assumes a dominant position.

To many westerners, the words 'austerity' and 'asceticism' conjure up images of grim and fanatical physical privation undergone to attain artificially heightened experience. Leaving aside the failure of such a reaction to do justice to the way that self-mortification fits into a variety of religious traditions, there can be no doubting that the ascetic experiencing self-imposed physical hardships (as opposed to the 'endurances' which occur randomly) which bring about a 'heating up' (*tapas*) of the body has always been a representative figure within Jainism bringing glory upon himself, his family, monastic group and the religion as a whole (BhA 244).

Austerity was certainly regarded as something difficult to perform. A classic description of the idealised Jain ascetic is found in one of the later narrative portions of the Shvetambara scriptures which, in a grim parody of the conventions of Sanskrit erotic poetry, lingers lovingly on each emaciated part of the fasting monk Dhanya's body, withered and dried up, showing 'a beauty of mortification', moving only through force of spirit, yet glowing with lustre, 'like a fire confined within a heap of ashes'.[35]

However, to insist upon the painfulness of austerity (which the description of Dhanya does not) or to suggest, as did early Buddhists, that it was both fruitless and the result of bad karma, would be to fail to grasp how in Jainism ascetic practice is underpinned by a spiritual and doctrinal rationale. In his 'Victory Banner of Relativism', Haribhadra defends the integrity of Jain austerities as being characterised not by physical suffering but by knowledge and sincere religious prompting, a course of action undertaken when bad karma can no longer have any serious effect and which cannot cause pain because the mind is under control and fixed upon a pure goal. Just as a doctor might prescribe fasting and medicine to cure a malady, so the spiritual doctors, the fordmakers, have prescribed austerity to cure the illness of transmigration (AJP p.218).

Austerity then is viewed in very positive terms: it is a cool house for those burnt by the fire of transmigration (BhA 1457), a refuge for those afflicted in mind and body (BhA 1464) and a city with walls in the form of restraint which the passions cannot storm (MA 879–80). If anybody considers austerities a source of pain then, as Abhayadeva Suri has it, he should consider the future torments of hell (comm. on Sth 338). Yet, in itself, austerity is of no value, for it must be accompanied by faith in Jain principles and lack of attachment (BhA 7) and be infused with friendship towards all living creatures. This interpretation of asceticism as requiring doctrinal understanding, ethical qualities and, also, a general avoidance of ostentation enabled the Jains to criticise Hindu ascetic practices, such as sitting on corpses or staring into the rays of the sun, for not being directed towards any serious religious goal. Even the austerity of Vasishtha, the archetypal Hindu ascetic, was, so one Digambara story has it, disfigured by violence, for in performing the most celebrated of all Hindu penances, sitting in the middle of four blazing fires while exposing himself to the heat of the midday sun, he burnt his guru who had been reborn as a snake (BKK 106).

The bipolar nature of Jain austerity can be seen in its conventional division into six external and six internal types. External austerity involves a variety of withdrawals and denials: complete fasting, reduction of food intake, deliberately making the process of seeking alms difficult for oneself, giving up any substance which might impart flavour to one's food, temporarily entering a period of solitude and performing bodily mortification. The quintessential form of external austerity is to fast for a predetermined period of time, either cutting out food completely, omitting alternating meals or interspersing a longer period with limited consumption of the unattractive and unflavoured food known as *ayambila*. Various other patterns of ascetic fasting can be followed.

Internal austerity brings about a diminution of egocentricity and involves atonement for any faults committed, respect both for one's ascetic superiors and for the truths embodied in the Jain religion, service to one's fellow ascetics, study and reflection, the giving up of personal attachments, and meditation (TS 9.19–20).[36]

MEDITATION

Jain literature is full of statements asserting the necessity of meditation (*dhyana*) as a weapon or armour in the battle with the passions (e.g. BhA 1886–7). Yet Jainism, unlike Theravada Buddhism, has never fully developed a culture of true meditative contemplation, no doubt because early Jain teachings were more concerned with the cessation of mental and physical activity than their transformation, and meditation did not lose its original role as little more than an adjunct to austerity until the early medieval period, by which time it had become a subject of essentially theoretical interest. Certainly, it is difficult to avoid the conclusion that later Jain writers discussed the subject only because participation in the pan-Indian socio-religious world made it necessary to do so.

Like the Buddhists and the Hindus, the Jains adhered to a view of the mind, which is regarded as one of the senses and therefore linked to the body, as inherently unstable, incapable, like a monkey, of standing still for a moment (BhA 763). However, instructions about how to bring it under control are either vague or excessively abstract, no doubt because the culminating stages of the meditative path were from early on restricted solely to those who knew the now lost *purva* scriptures and the omniscient *kevalins* (TS 9.39–40). Even the basic meditative activity of fixing one's mind upon something is stated to be possible only for those of a highly developed bodily physique, the result of karma (TS 9.27). In other words, the Jains can be said to have lost contact with a substantial part of their ancient meditative structure at an early date. Hemacandra, whose account of the subject is normative for the Shvetambaras, revealingly admits that the only reason he describes the latter stages of meditation is because descriptions of them have come down to him through tradition, for his contemporaries were otherwise totally incapable of attaining them (YS 11.4).

The idiosyncracy of the early systematised pattern which uses the term *dhyana* is indicative of the somewhat unfocussed manner in which the topic of meditation was handled by the Jain scriptures. The basic schema is fourfold, each element being referred to as a *dhyana*: the anguished (*arta*), the angry (*raudra*), the religious (*dharma*) and the bright (*shukla*).[37] The first two, as is evident from frequent reference to them in the story literature, are bitter and negatively intense emotions which result from loss, separation or some kind of ill-treatment and they are thus detrimental to the attainment of a spiritually positive rebirth. They hardly qualify as meditative states or even as preliminary stages to them and the fact that an early source (SKS 1.11.26–8) uses the term *dhyana* with reference to carnivorous birds contemplating fish and heretics considering sensual pleasures suggests that the term in origin implied for the Jains not so much calm meditation as unhealthy and obsessive brooding.

In fact, the religious *dhyana* amounts to little more than the reflections on the mechanism of rebirth (*anupreksha*), already mentioned as one of the means of warding off karma (cf. TS 9.7), and it must be concluded that the later doctrinal systematisers concocted an artificial path leading up to the bright meditation, no doubt under the stimulus of the general Indian acceptance that meditation and *yoga* must lead to deliverance and by analogy with the common Indian pattern of three plus one in which the last element is regarded as the most significant. For it is only the bright meditation which is placed in a strictly soteriological context in the early texts (SKS 1.6.16–17), being specifically associated with Mahavira's burning away of karma and attainment of enlightenment which, judging from the sources, was taken as involving a gradual reduction of activity to the extent of cessation of breathing. Umasvati acknowledges the inadequacy of the fourfold *dhyana* model when he states that only the last two, the religious and the bright, have anything to do with the gaining of deliverance (TS 9.30). Later, Abhayadeva Suri stated that the anguished and the angry *dhyanas* were specific causes of the binding of karma (comm. on Sth 511) and, indeed, Hemacandra was to omit them completely in his account.

Nonetheless, as the significance of meditative and yogic attainments for other Indian religious paths increased, so did the expansiveness of Jain treatments of these subjects, with the culmination being Shubhacandra's 'Ocean of Knowledge' (JnA; eleventh century?), a work to which Hemacandra seems to have been indebted. Shubhacandra was situated very much within the Digambara mystical tradition, stressing the goal as being penetration to the innermost soul, while at the same time insisting on the necessity of faith in basic Jain tenets. The 'Ocean of Knowledge' contains a further fourfold division of meditation which Shubhacandra and later Jain writers were to set alongside the older pattern of four *dhyanas*. It consisted of, respectively, contemplation of particular images and objects (*pinda*) which the meditator mentally summons up and which are then dispelled and destroyed as symbols of the eight types of karma; contemplation of words (*pada*), that is, the mystical manipulation of mantras and power-filled syllables as summations of the knowledge embodied in the scriptures; contemplation of form (*rupa*) by which is meant visualisation of the physical appearance of the fordmakers through which the meditator can gain an understanding of his own potential omniscience; and, finally, the contemplation of that which is beyond form (*rupatita*) in which the meditator concentrates upon his soul in its purest and most positive sense (JnA 34–7).[38]

Although Shubhacandra places this new fourfold pattern as a preliminary to the attainment of what is still designated as the pure meditation where the harming karmas are eliminated, the idiom in which he describes the meditative path suggests the broadening of the resources of Jain spirituality into areas previously foreign to it. Here there are clear signs of a restructuring, if only theoretically, of the Jain contemplative model to incorporate elements of Hindu provenance, for the system of four objects of contemplation (object, word etc.) seems to have had its origin among the influential Shaiva mystical ritualists of Kashmir.[39] This, and the medieval Shvetambara literature involving ritual circles, diagrams and mantras, in which Gautama plays a central role as a kind of king of the yogins, demonstrates an eventual Jain assimilation of a mystical and ritual style which had long been existent in Hinduism and Buddhism.

Meditation does not seem to be practised today by Jain ascetics in any meaningful way and contemplative activity would most naturally take place during the ritual performance of the Obligatory Actions described in the next section. Although this century has seen a definite revival of interest in meditation among the Terapanthi sect, with the development of a new form of meditation (see Chapter 9) and the use of Theravada Buddhist techniques,[40] it seems likely that the focus of Jain ascetic attention will remain the transforming power of fasting and devotion.

ASCETIC RITUAL: THE OBLIGATORY ACTIONS

Jainism took considerably longer than its coeval, Buddhism, to develop a full ascetic ritual and liturgy, and the adjustment of behavioural traits to take account of the surrounding environment was the main concern of the Jain ascetic at the outset. However, some sort of formal mechanism for the confession and repentance of faults clearly developed at a relatively early stage, judging by the frequent prediction in the 'Exposition of Explanations' of dire consequences in the next birth for those who die without performing these actions and, indeed, the tradition also came to credit Mahavira with refining Parshva's Jainism by their introduction. No doubt a growing need to emphasise solidarity was responsible for the emergence of the *Avashyakas*, the six daily Obligatory Actions and the Prakrit ritual formulae associated with them, the performance of which according to Haribhadra (comm. on AvNiry 2) forms the essential precondition for that knowledge and practice which lead to salvation.[41]

The *Avashyakasutra* is not one of the old texts of the Shvetambara scriptural canon but its importance can be seen from its near submersion under layers of commentary and other more loosely affiliated types of text which have been attracted into its orbit. The complex phenomenon of *Avashyaka* literature was a pre-sectarian one and there are close parallels between certain Shvetambara and Digambara texts, especially the Prakrit mnemonic verse commentary (*niryukti*) on the *sutra* text and the seventh chapter of the early Digambara Vattakera's 'Fundamental Behaviour' (cf. MA 503).[42]

The six Obligatory Actions, which are incumbent on ascetics, are equanimity (*samayika*; sometimes *samata*. Cf. MA 22), praise of the fordmakers, homage to the teacher, repentance (*pratikramana*), laying down the body (*kayotsarga*) and abandonment (*pratyakhyana*).[43] If the contemporary situation is examined, it becomes impossible to talk about any entirely unified ceremony, for there are variations among Shvetambara sects with regard to the order of the ritual and the wording of the formulae, while Digambara ascetics would appear to have abandoned the performance on a daily basis of some of the rituals.[44]

The term *samayika* seems to have originally meant little more than 'correct behaviour'.[45] What is entailed in it within the context of the Obligatory Actions can best be seen in the formula with which the ascetic addresses the teacher:

> I perform, sir, the rite of equanimity. I abandon all bad activity for the course of my life, threefold by threefold, in mind, body and speech. I will not perform nor cause anybody to perform nor approve anybody performing any bad action. I repent of it, sir, I censure, reject and abandon myself.
>
> (AvS 2)

As described by Vattakera, equanimity is a quasi-meditative state of mind, consciously achieved in a motionless standing position for a short period of time (traditionally forty-eight minutes), in which the passions and negative mental traits are suppressed and a sense of goodwill to all creatures is developed (MA 518–38). '*Samayika* is that state in which the ascetic is the same towards himself and another, to his mother and to all other women, to pleasant and unpleasant things and to honour and disrespect' (MA 521). Strictly speaking, the entire ascetic life is regarded as an act of *samayika* so that its ritual performance is in fact merely a temporary actualisation of it.

The *Avashyakasutra* delineates the second Obligatory Action in terms of a hymn of praise to the fordmakers which demonstrates how devotional activity (*bhakti*), although non-existent in the oldest texts, was from an early period a necessary part of the Jain path (BhA 748) and was credited with the ability to destroy karma.

The third Obligatory Action is a formalised act of homage (*vandana*) to the ascetic's teacher in which are included a request for forgiveness of offences and an enquiry concerning the teacher's welfare. The responses of the teacher are given in the commentary literature which suggests that the exchange had soon been ritualised to such an extent that no articulated response was necessary or expected, especially if the teacher was not present.

The act of repentance, the fourth Obligatory Action, stands at the centre of the *Avashyaka* ritual by its emphatic concentration on non-violence and the fact that it must be performed in the presence of the teacher twice daily as well as at other times (fortnightly, four-monthly and annually). Although not specifically allowed for by the *Avashyakasutra*, the act of repentance should be preceded by *alocana*, usually rendered by 'confession' but with a more precise sense of 'inspection' or 'acknowledgement' of faults. *Pratikramana* itself means 'going back' to the correct form of behaviour which has been interrupted by transgressions in study, practice and so on. As well as involving meditative elements, *pratikramana* revolves around the recitation of six passages enumerating faults, each ending with the expression *miccha mi dukkadam*, 'may evil which has been done by me be in vain'. For example, the formula for repenting of injury to creatures while walking runs:

> I want to make *pratikramana* for injury on the path of my movement, in coming and in going, in treading on living things, in treading on seeds, in treading on green plants, in treading on dew, on beetles, on mould, on moist earth, and on cobwebs; whatever living organisms with one or two or three or four or five senses have been injured by me or knocked over or crushed or squashed or touched or mangled or hurt or affrighted or removed from one place to another or deprived of life – may all that evil have been done in vain.[46]

After further formulae including a formal expression of trust and confidence in the Jain doctrine, the monk is obliged to utter what has become one of the most famous of all Jain statements: 'I ask pardon from all living creatures. May all creatures pardon me. May I have friendship for all creatures and enmity towards none' (AvS 32).[47]

The fifth Obligatory Action (for the Digambaras the sixth since they reverse the order of the last two), the abandonment of the body (*kayotsarga*), refers to one of the best known of Jain ascetic practices, frequently portrayed in art, performed by assuming a motionless position, with arms hanging down without touching the sides of one's body. Also involved are requests for forgiveness and expressions of homage. The repetition of the formula for the second Obligatory Action prior to this suggests that the fordmakers are being imitated, if only for a short time.

Finally, abandonment, the sixth Obligatory Action, involves the undertaking to abstain from a wide variety of transgressions and to refrain from the consumption of various sorts of food and drink. While *pratikramana* has reference to faults committed in the past, abandonment relates to the present and the future and can also involve the giving up of even harmless substances as a form of austerity.

The performance of the Obligatory Actions has obvious spiritual significance through the internal harmony it brings about and the regular commitment required to devotion and the principle of non-violence, but it also marks an important stage in the broader socialisation of Jainism for, apart from its cohesive role for ascetics, it established for the first time a liturgy and ritual which could be used by lay people. The expansion in the early medieval period of the *Avashyaka* literature with its strong emphasis on edifying narrative reflects an increasing acceptance by ascetics of the validity of the lay path.[48]

The beginning of this can be seen in the 'Exposition of Explanations' which otherwise knows nothing of the *Avashyaka* ritual in any formal sense but refers to the *samayika* being performed by a layman, while also stating that because of his continuing worldly attachment he cannot be transformed by it in any way (Bh 7.1).[49] Somewhat later, the emphasis changes as the following statement found in identical wording in both Shvetambara and Digambara sources shows: 'Since through the performance of *samayika* the layman becomes like a monk, for this reason it should be performed often' (MA 533; Av Niry 801).

This sixth section of the *Avashyakasutra* opens with specific reference to the layman who is instructed to assert his unwillingness to pay homage to any other religion, a formula which seems to have been the earliest means by which a non-ascetic could align himself with Jainism.

By the time of the medieval handbooks of lay behaviour, we find the *Avashyaka* formulae and the description of their significance slightly adapted to take account of the, if only temporary, merging of ascetic and lay ritual. However, whatever the idealised textual picture, it is unlikely that the *Avashyaka* ritual was ever definitively integrated into lay life and there is evidence that the *samayika* had lessened in importance by the fifteenth century,[50] while the Digambaras seem eventually to have restricted the performance of the Obligatory Actions to the ascetic community only. Failure to perform the Obligatory Actions would never prejudice a lay person's position as a Jain as it would for a Shvetambara ascetic and, although the pious will often perform the *samayika* on holy days or during sermons, perhaps the most meaningful regular contact which the Shvetambara laity has with the Obligatory Actions is the communal *pratikramana* which takes place at the festival of *Paryushan*.[51]

INTERACTION WITH THE LAITY

The earliest Jain literature shows no awareness of the possibility of a formal relationship between the ascetics and a body of lay supporters. However, the institution of the enforced four-month ascetic rain retreat due both to the difficulty of travelling and to the greater possibility of destruction of life-forms during the monsoon must have been of key importance in the emergence of such a laity. Regular contact with their supporters inevitably involved a degree of compromise for ascetics. One important text describing normative ascetic behaviour points out the potential danger of the relationship with lay people by describing the monk as a deer and the layman as a hunter (NBh 1649: *curni* comm.), while the ancient and straightforward injunction, shared with Hindu renunciants, that an ascetic should stay for only one night in a village and five in a town came to be modified by the introduction of a large number of rules about how the monk should deport himself in relation to the laity which provides temporary lodging.[52] At the same time, the benefits to the laity of contact with the ascetic community became an important theme of the medieval literature of exemplary narrative, and image-worshipping lay Shvetambaras have in fact been organisationally attached to ascetic *gacchas* from about the eleventh and twelfth centuries.

In more recent times, lay–ascetic relations have altered somewhat compared to the old textual prescriptions. For example, monks, rather than travelling from place to place in self-sufficient small groups, are today usually accompanied by lay followers who form an almost triumphal procession and see to their needs en route in a variety of ways. Again, ascetics cannot always impose their authority upon the laity in the way which might be suggested from the literature. So, although an ascetic may often be able to prevail upon a lay person to take a religious vow or donate money towards some pious purpose such as the building of a temple, this will tend to be a matter of the ascetic offering advice to which the lay person is under no formal obligation to acquiesce. Conversely, the lay community has at times been able to exercise control over the ascetics to the extent of compelling expulsion from the order if it is felt that an individual has not been conforming adequately to his vows.[53]

However there is one basic and essential institution which brings ascetics and laity together and at the same time defines their radically different positions in the world: religious giving.

GIVING

At its most basic levels, *dana* (cognate with English 'donation') is the giving of food by a lay person to a monk or nun and is thus the institution which sustains the ascetic community, for monks and nuns cannot be involved in any way in the preparation of food nor can they possess money with which to buy it. Furthermore, ascetics can only drink water that has been previously boiled or filtered for them to ensure that it contains no organisms. The real beneficiary of the transaction of giving, however, is the lay donor for *dana* is accepted as being a means of gaining merit and improving the quality of his destiny. Giving has come to be regarded as the form of religious activity most appropriate to the current world age and the easiest for the lay person to perform. Yet it is also a practice which involves more than the mere passing on of food and various Jain preoccupations, public and spiritual, intersect within it. Acts of giving, for example, very often set the seal on important Jain ritual and ceremonial events.

The process of giving involves an etiquette to which both ascetic and lay person must conform. Central to it is the fact that the ascetic who has gone out to get alms does not beg in the sense of importuning people but rather is humbly requested by the lay person to accept food. This is something which the ascetic need not always do since he may have imposed a vow upon himself to delimit his opportunities for getting alms, resolving to accept food under certain predetermined conditions which may sometimes mean alms are not obtained at all (Aup pp.70–3).

The *Dashavaikalika*, one of the basic texts to be studied by all Shvetambara ascetics, gives a detailed account of how the monk should conduct himself in this potentially dangerous situation. While engaged in the search for alms, the ascetic has to take the most scrupulous care not to breach the principle of non-violence and must gain food as the bee gets honey from flowers without damaging the blossoms (DVS 1.2–5). As well as exercising all care in the way he walks, the monk is instructed not to receive food from a woman who treads on plants or whose hands are wet or dusty and on returning he must perform *pratikramana* for any inadvertent transgression which might have been committed (DVS 5.1.33 and 88–9). Continual equanimity must be exhibited and there must be no attempt to visit prosperous families at the expense of the more humble (DVS 5.2.25–6). The monk must enquire about the origins of the food to ensure its purity and not take anything which has been specially prepared for him (DVS 5.1.55–6), although this latter point is often ignored in practice today since, it is argued, only careful advance preparation could ensure that totally pure food and properly filtered water are available to be offered.[54]

Shvetambara ascetics seek alms twice a day (in the morning and the late afternoon). The food will be taken back within alms bowls, with usually one or two ascetics collecting for their fellows within the group, and will be consumed in privacy in whatever place of lodging the group is staying, eating being one of the few occasions during the day when the Shvetambara ascetic is totally insulated from the attentions of the laity.

However, it is perhaps the Digambara monk eating only once in the morning and meagrely at that, using his cupped hands as a receptacle into which food is deposited, who best exemplifies the full significance of giving. Totally silent, eyes carefully fixed on the ground, the fingers of the right hand placed upon the shoulder signifying the intention to seek alms, he will be directed, if possible after visiting the temple nearest his place of abode, to the house of a lay person who will greet the monk, ask him to stay, proclaim the religious purity of his family and the suitability of the food and water to be offered, and then invite him to enter his house. If the monk accepts, he will be circumambulated in worship and then, having entered and inspected what is to be offered, he will stand upon a small wooden stool designed to protect food falling onto the ground and attracting small creatures. Food will be placed in his cupped hands, thirty-two mouthfuls in all, followed by water, by the lay family, and the monk should then eat 'without tasting the food's savour' (MA 816). After the monk has finished, the lay people will pay homage to him whereupon he will bless them and go, although sometimes he will also deliver a homily or give advice.[55]

Various themes come together in this highly public series of actions: the non-violence, restraint and inwardness of the Digambara monk, solitary even among the throng of lay people, who is worshipped as if he were an image of a fordmaker, while the concern of the lay people for the smooth running of the ritual reflects the personal prestige which is to some extent at stake in every act of giving which takes place within the Jain community, for if the ascetic were to take umbrage for some reason and refuse to accept alms, then that could only be because of some moral flaw on the part of the donor and his credibility, socially, in business or otherwise, would be greatly diminished.

Religious giving can also involve the ascetic receiving, as well as food, lodging, medicine and, among the Shvetambaras, robes.[56] The ascetic himself also gives, not so much because he has any formal obligation to the lay person, but because his every action is permeated by his attitude of non-violence. Teaching about the doctrine, for example, is a form of giving while, above all, the ascetic gives the highest of all forms of *dana*, safety and protection to all living creatures (*abhaya*; SKS 1.6.23 and MA 941).

VEGETARIANISM

It is of course open to question whether there can be a totally pure act of giving in which donor and recipient are free from any sense of expectation and there is no possibility of any act of violence. However, the wide range of dietary prescriptions and exclusions found in Jainism to a greater extent than in any other Indian religion suggest that purity of food, at least, was regarded as being an achievable goal. This is a matter which affects all Jains, not simply the ascetic community, and goes beyond simple vegetarianism, for the notion of meat is extended by the Jains to include not just animal flesh, fish and eggs also but types of vegetables which were felt to contain life-forms. So, although total consistency should not be expected, the Jains have felt it necessary to prohibit the consumption of vegetables such as onions and garlic (although the fact that many Indians ascribe aphrodisiac powers to these may also be significant) and fruits with large numbers of seeds within them. Alcohol is proscribed as much because the fermentation process leads to the destruction of life-forms and the ascetic is instructed to eat only bland food and avoid any substance, such as milk products, which undergo change.[57] Hemacandra goes so far as to claim that those who eat honey are worse than butchers (YS 3.37).

In the light of this, it may seem strange that there is evidence that in ancient times Jain ascetics consumed meat. The most controversial example of this is the account in the 'Exposition of Explanations' of Mahavira's recuperation after his duel of ascetic power with Makkhali Gosala in which the fordmaker is portrayed as asking a woman to send him as food a cock which has been killed by a cat rather than the two pigeons which she had prepared, on eating which he recovered. Such an interpretation became abhorrent by early medieval times and either this passage is interpreted to give a vegetarian gloss or words signifying types of fruit are substituted.[58] Similarly, Schubring's translation of the *Dashavaikalika*, published in Ahmedabad by the Shvetambara charitable trust of Anandji Kalyanji, was tacitly censored at the verse where the monk was enjoined to avoid meat with too many bones in it (DVS 5.1.73).

Nonetheless, it seems clear that the early Jains were not totally strict vegetarians and that, like the Buddhists, they would accept meat as alms if an animal had not been specifically killed for them.[59] Shvetambara monastic law also suggests that in certain exceptional circumstances such as famine or to cure an illness the consumption of meat was permitted.[60] However, a medieval story (DhMV 153) describing how a sick layman refuses to eat meat even though he will regain his health is an obvious reaction against this dietary pragmatism and ascetics are today not allowed to eat meat under any circumstances, while for a lay person to breach the rule of vegetarianism would in India almost inevitably lead to his rejection as a Jain by the rest of the community.

RULES ABOUT SHVETAMBARA ASCETIC BEHAVIOUR

'Discipline is the root of religious practice' (DVS 9.2.2). From a relatively ancient period, the Jains produced collections of rules which were designed not just to instruct the ascetic how to carry out the obligations entailed in his vows but also to regulate inter-monastic relationships, delineate acceptable forms of connection with lay supporters, and enable senior monks to impose penances for misdemeanours. Of the *chedasutras*, the texts of the Shvetambara canon which describe these matters (see Chapter 3), three have developed particularly extensive commentaries, stemming from oral sources based both on scripture and learned consensus, which provide very detailed evidence for Shvetambara monastic law.[61]

Jain monastic law does not attempt to connect its injunctions with episodes in the life of Mahavira in the way that the Buddhists linked all their ascetic rules to the Buddha. It does, however, abound in narrative illustrations which are intended to convey the positive and negative results of following a particular rule rather than give a technical account of its full ramifications.[62]

In particular, the commentaries on the disciplinary texts develop a characteristic found elsewhere in the Shvetambara canon, as in, for example, the third *anga*, of providing exceptions to general rules of conduct, often on the basis of local custom, and it could be said that, as a result, by the seventh century the required rigours of the ascetic life had been diluted and weakened by these exceptions which thus paved the way for the temple-dwelling monks whose behaviour the Kharatara Gaccha was to find so objectionable. Certainly, there are signs that the Shvetambaras wished to restrict access to the *chedasutras* on the grounds of their possibly being misunderstood. The name of one of the most important of them, the *Nishitha*, means 'secret' and only experienced monks were allowed to study it. The force of these texts has diminished somewhat today, since instructions about ascetic behaviour are generally imparted orally, but it is noteworthy that the nuns of the Tapa Gaccha are expressly forbidden to read the *chedasutras*.[63]

Rather than see the expansion of monastic law through the introduction of exceptions in the early medieval period as being symptomatic of a growing laxity, it might be better to interpret this as a practical attempt to broaden, without surrendering basic principles, the boundaries of the Shvetambara community by acknowledging and allowing for differences in ability among its ascetic members The *chedasutras*, while condemning transgressions, do not so much prescribe punishment or suggest ways of circumventing rules as offer a context in which an ascetic can be guided and assisted by his fellows. Indeed, a mechanism was provided by which even an individual who had broken his vow of chastity could be accommodated within the order, provided there was sufficient repentance and willingness to strive to improve.[64] Rather than arguing that the fordmakers laid down a fixed and immutable set of rules, the Shvetambara tradition of monastic law held that they had offered a general indication of areas of concern, leaving it open to successors to evaluate their validity and, if necessary, recast them.[65]

However, the stern and unbending monk who cleaved firmly to ancient scriptural injunction was the ideal among practice-based sects such as the Tapa Gaccha, as can be seen in the reply which the handsome young monk Siddhicandra gave to the Moghul Emperor Jahangir who had, while drunk, invoked the supposed flexibility of Shvetambara monastic rules in an attempt to persuade him to marry:

> All this may be all right for the ears of a coward. A man of courage and conviction never breaks a vow once he has taken it, even if his adherence to it means certain death for him. The least deviation from the path once chosen results in utter worthlessness and failure.... Exceptions are meant for those who have not power enough to stick to the absolute rules. They

are loopholes through which the weak-minded seek relief from the severity and inexorableness of the absolute principles.[66]

SALLEKHANA: THE RELIGIOUS DEATH

In the light of the general Indian belief that the last moment of life has a decisive bearing on the state of an individual's next birth and the specifically Jain teaching about the possibility of the destruction of karma through gradual withdrawal from mental and physical activity, it is hardly surprising that Jainism views the ideal mode of death as being a form of highly controlled wasting away through fasting. This process is known as *sallekhana*, in which the central austerity of cutting down the consumption of food is taken to its logical conclusion so that the body is 'scoured out' (*sallikhita*) of its negative factors and the mind can focus solely upon spiritual matters as death approaches.

Jain writers have always been adamant that the voluntary death of *sallekhana*, which is exclusively directed towards the soul and must be performed with a sacred formula on one's lips (MA 94), is in no way equivalent to an act of suicide and they contrast it with various forms of the 'fool's death', types of suicide carried out through despair or inadequacy which involve violence to one's body.[67] *Sallekhana* cannot be suicide, Akalanka argued, because it would have to involve the passions, as well as the probable use of poisons or weapons (TSRV p.550).

The earliest statement about the religious death emphasises its solitude and difficulty (AS 1.7.8). However, the paradigmatic Shvetambara canonical description, the account of the death of the brahman convert Skhandaka Katyayana found in the 'Exposition of Explanations' (Bh 2.1), puts *sallekhana* into its full ritual context. Skhandaka, a pupil of Mahavira, is initially portrayed as having engaged in severe bodily mortification but also as still maintaining full energy and mental lucidity, as a result of which he resolves to perform *sallekhana*. On being given permission by Mahavira, Skhandaka takes the five Great Vows again and then, surrounded by other monks, finds an appropriate spot of ground and recites the appropriate ritual formulae. After taking the five Great Vows once more, he abandons food, drink and his body and, 'without actively waiting for death', omits sixty meals until, having confessed and repented, he dies in meditation, controlling his life until the very last minute.[68] Skhandaka's *sallekhana* is presented as a structured form of progress towards death in which the double taking of the Great Vows represents an initiation into the final human rite of passage. The ritual nature of this *sallekhana* is confirmed by the fact that Skhandaka spreads *darbha* grass, an important component of the Vedic sacrifice, on the ground where he fasts to death.

Whereas the older Shvetambara texts are primarily concerned with the force which *sallekhana* derives from being performed by heroic monks at the height of their physical and mental powers, a slight shift in emphasis can be found in the later texts of the scriptural canon. *Sallekhana* (also called *samthara*, 'death-bed', its designation among Shvetambaras today), is presented as requiring the controlling involvement of a teacher as presiding guide during the whole process and, furthermore, as being a form of death accessible to lay people.[69] Early medieval writers suggest that when bodily illness or infirmity prevents anybody performing the Obligatory Actions, then *sallekhana* can be an appropriate end to life (TSRV p.551). One Digambara story describes how a Jain soldier decided, as a result of wounds sustained in battle, to fast to death and so went to heaven (BKK 124).

The extension of an originally ascetic practice to the laity is vouched for by inscriptional evidence from south India attesting to the voluntary religious death of prominent lay people, but *sallekhana* seems to have ceased to play even an ideal role in lay spirituality by about the twelfth century.[70] Similarly, *sallekhana* in the sense of fasting over a long period along with ascetic reinitiation has not been a general or practical goal among the Shvetambaras for some considerable time and it is perhaps only the revived Digambara ascetic body, taking its lead from the great Acarya Shantisagar who performed *sallekhana* in 1955, which would regard fasting to death as a wished-for conclusion to a monastic career. Pious lay people, when advanced in years and encouraged by ascetics, will still occasionally decrease their food intake with a view to bringing about a religious death. However, the recent interest and excitement elicited by a Sthanakvasi nun who died at the age of eighty-seven after a fast of fifty-one days is testimony to the relative rarity of the religious death.[71]

THE ROLE OF THE *ACARYA*

The Jain ascetic community had from an early period its own network of relationships and power structures, just like the social world which had been left behind. Unfortunately, the full import of some of the ranks of the senior monastic officers which ancient texts and inscriptions have recorded cannot always be understood. The five most common in whose absence, Vattakera warns, a monk should not remain in a particular group (MA 155) are the teacher (*acarya*), the preceptor (*upadhyaya*), the promoter (*pravartaka*), the elder (*sthavira*) and the leader of the troop (*ganadhara*, later also called *ganin*). The preceptor was responsible for teaching the wording of the scriptures and still exists as a separate rank among the Shvetambaras, although there are few monks with this title. The promoter, the monk responsible for enforcing discipline, seems to have had little more than a formal role by the early medieval period and, along with the elder, is not found today.[72] The *ganin*, the monk who has authority over a small group of ascetics, is a rank still in use among the Shvetambaras.

However, it is the *acarya* who holds the central position in Jain monastic polity and, by the combination of correct behaviour, learning and charisma, provides the cohesive force within the community. To quote Vattakera: 'As a ship full of treasure but without a captain can easily sink, so a monk who has correct faith but is without a good teacher can drown in the ocean of rebirth' (MA 88).

Among the image-worshipping Shvetambaras, the importance of the *acarya* can be seen even on the symbolic level in the form of the *sthapanacarya*, the 'representation-teacher', a small structure of three wooden sticks bound in the form of a tripod around which is slung a pouch usually containing conch shells symbolising the holy persons enumerated in the Five Homages formula and which, when placed in front of the monk when preaching, performing the Obligatory Actions, teaching or studying, signifies, in the absence of the real teacher through death or otherwise, the continuing presence of the spiritual guide.

The minimal requirement for becoming a Shvetambara, according to one of the *chedasutras*, was, along with unimpeachable moral conduct, a period of eight years as a monk and full familiarity with the third and fourth *angas* of the scriptures.[73] While the latter, scholarly requirement is not quite as exiguous as it might appear since both the texts involved require a great deal of supporting knowledge to understand them, the relatively short period of qualification meant that in the medieval period in particular, when child initiation was more prevalent, quite a few monks became *acaryas* when little more than teenagers. A further relevant factor in this appointment of *acaryas*, according to the medieval chroniclers, was the presence of auspicious marks on the bodies of young monks.

The installation of an *acarya* is in certain respects equivalent to the succession of a king, as is seen by the fact that the *acarya* is called the 'bearer of the *patta*' (*pattadhara*), the turban used at the time of a regal consecration in ancient India. That the new *acarya* becomes a participant in a continuing tradition is emphasised in the medieval accounts by the handing over to him of the *surimantra*, a sacred and secret formula supposedly taught by Mahavira to Gautama and the other disciples from whom Shvetambara ascetics claim descent, by the *acarya* or senior monk who is performing the installation (SMKS).[74] From the moment of his appointment, the *acarya* is qualified to oversee a group of monks, appoint a successor, provide his own interpretation of the scriptures and impose penances. On the other hand, ordinary monks were occasionally empowered to expel an *acarya* who was felt to be deficient in moral standards. A medieval chronicler recounts the rather sad story of an *acarya* of the Upakesha Gaccha who was compelled to relinquish his post because of his fondness for playing the lute.[75]

All the Shvetambara *gacchas* which emerged from the eleventh century onwards had at their head one dominant *acarya* or *suri*, also often styled the 'principal man of the age' (*yugapradhana*: UR 41–50) from whom descent was traced by a series of succeeding *acaryas* and, although secessions might take place and collateral lineages develop as a result of disputes over practice or successions, his authority was seldom effectively challenged. However, by the eighteenth and nineteenth centuries, image-worshipping Shvetambara numbers had gone into serious decline and it has been estimated that by about the end of the first half of the nineteenth century there were only about twenty-five monks and no *acaryas*.[76] Ritual and ceremonial tasks, as well as custodianship over records, were the responsibility of the somewhat mutated descendants of the temple-dwelling monks known as *yati* (literally 'ascetic') who were approximately comparable to the Digambara *bhattaraka*. Although some were celibate, wore white robes and had a certain degree of learning, especially in areas such as astrology and medicine, their non-mendicancy and control of money meant that they were scarcely comparable to fully initiated monks.[77]

No serious research has yet been undertaken into the revival of the image-worshipping Shvetambara ascetic order in the nineteenth century and early twentieth centuries. Suffice it to say that the teacher lineage was reactivated, largely through the agency of the lay community which temporarily assumed responsibility for creating *acaryas*, and ascetic numbers started to expand, partly assisted by an early influx of Sthanakvasi converts. A succession of prominent *acaryas*, both scholars and moral exemplars, such as Buddhisagara Suri (1874–1925), Sagarananda Suri (1875–1950) and Vijayavallabha Suri (1870–1954) were responsible for the dominant position which the Tapa Gaccha has assumed amongst image-worshipping Shvetambaras today, particularly in Gujarat.

Various sublineages (*samudaya*) have sprung up within the Tapa Gaccha, each descended from a recent prominent teacher of the sect. While there is now no head *acarya*, claims to the contrary are made by each *samudaya*. So the lineage of Vijayaindradinnasuri presents him as the seventy-sixth teacher in succession from Mahavira's disciple Sudharman and thus overall head (*adhipati*) of the Tapa Gaccha, whereas he is more correctly the chief *acarya* of the Vallabha Samudaya, the subgroup descended from Vijayavallabha Suri, whose members originally wore saffron-coloured robes, adopted to distinguish them from the white-robed *yatis*. The proliferation of *acaryas* which have been installed within the various *samudayas* means that the Tapa Gaccha has today become somewhat fragmented.[78]

If the image-worshipping Shvetambara lineage underwent straitened circumstances in recent times, then its Digambara equivalent can be said to have been effectively obliterated by the nineteenth century, with all the evidence suggesting that the numbers of naked ascetics had started to go into serious decline from the seventeenth century, and the focus of religious activity for the laity of necessity became temple ritual and the performance of vows such as fasting. The only nineteenth century Digambara monk in south India for whom there is clear evidence is Siddhasagar (1928–1903) who initiated himself by removing his clothes in front of an image of a fordmaker. Hagiographies of Siddhasagar do not refer to his interaction with other monks, but concentrate instead on his solitary forbearance in the face of psychological and physical dangers and his ability to perform miracles. Siddhasagar was a prime exemplar for Acarya Shantisagar, the great twentieth century reviver of Digambara ascetic culture, but there was certainly no pupillary connection between the two and the latter's achievement was of a completely different order in the implications which it had for recent Digambara history.

Shantisagar was born in 1873 in north Karnataka, an area which is the place of origin of most Digambara monks today. Thwarted in his desire for ascetic initiation by parental refusal (and, presumably, by the absence at that time of anyone competent to confer it), the young Shantisagar spent much time performing minor acts of austerity and in going on pilgrimage to a wide range of holy places which confirmed his sense of Jain tradition and civilisation. Having himself taken the *ailaka* vow, the preliminary stage to full Digambara initiation, in front of an image of the fordmaker Nemi, he was eventually at the age of forty-seven able to take initiation at the village of Yarnal.

The manner in which this happened is not entirely clear. According to one source, the individual who conferred initiation was a monk called Devendrakirti but, as this is the fixed name of every *bhattaraka* of Humcha in the Shimoga district of south Karnataka, it seems more likely that it was a *bhattaraka* who in some manner initiated Shantisagar. Devendrakirti had apparently come to Yarnal to preside over a *pancakalyana* ceremony, in which the five main events (*kalyana*) of every fordmaker's life (conception, birth, renunciation, enlightenment and final release) are acted out by members of the lay community on the occasion of the installation of an image. Shantisagar took *diksha*, abandoning his loincloth and pulling out his hair in front of the lay community, on the same day as the new image ceremonially also received initiation, thus confirming the lineal descent of all Digambara monks from Mahavira himself. Photographs of the elderly Shantisagar impart an almost iconic quality to him, and no doubt the solitude of his early career would have brought the parallel with the fordmaker to the minds of the Digambara community.

From the spiritual point of view, Shantisagar was concerned with self-development of the mystical, soul-oriented variety found in Kundakunda's writings which had formed the substance of his reading when he was starting to think seriously of taking initiation. He seems to have attempted to familiarise himself with the technicalities of Jain metaphysics only later in life through conversations with lay scholars, and the title of *acarya* was bestowed upon him by general lay acclaim as a token of his charisma and asceticism rather than because of any profound learning. Shantisagar's greatest significance lay in his willingness to reproduce the Digambara Jain ascetic community by initiating pupils, and he regenerated and heightened the Digambara sense of identity through repeated pilgrimage and public preaching and by defending Jain interests as in the controversy over the Temple Entry Bill of 1948 which would have given Hindus unrestricted access to Jain temples.

In addition, and ironically for somebody who in his own life was consciously aiming to revive an ancient ideal, Shantisagar was an important part of the process which in this century has seen a shift from traditionally minded *bhattarakas* to more modern forms of religious dissemination. He was, for example, instrumental in getting the Mudbidri manuscripts and other literature published and made generally accessible, at least in theory, through translations into modern Indian vernaculars, despite conservative opposition.

Since Shantisagar's death in 1955, the community of fully initiated naked Digambara monks has grown to something over one hundred, with a similar number for those in lower orders. Distinguished by and large for asceticism rather than scholarship, for their background is generally rural with an attendant low level of educational attainment, and usually renouncing late in life, they nonetheless represent a remarkable legacy to the Digambara community. Virtually all of them trace their lineage back to Shantisagar, with perhaps a vague acknowledgement of a link with Kundakunda, and it is solely due to this great contemporary *acarya* that Digambara monks actually now exist and are not ranked below the *bhattarakas* as they were in the medieval period.[79]

7 The lay person

THE SOCIAL MILIEU

The gradual consolidation of Jain identity and the necessity for an expanding ascetic community to be supported on a regular basis led to an early acceptance of the lay estate as constituting a vocation in its own right. The 'Exposition of Explanations' contains only sporadic references to lay practice,[1] but the acknowledgement in the *Avashyakasutra* of a distinction between monk and layman and the existence in the later portions of the Shvetambara scriptural canon of extensive narrative material describing the pious deeds of *upasakas*, 'lay attenders', demonstrates that this was a matter of some importance for the ancient teachers.

The lay path as described in the Shvetambara scriptures is heavily imbued with ascetic values. The seventh *anga* of the canon, the 'Ten Chapters on Lay Attenders' (UD), describes how the rich layman Ananda gradually withdrew from his wealth and, following precepts dictated to him by Mahavira, died the religious death of *sallekhana*. Elsewhere in the same text, there are accounts of the fortitude of meditating laymen in the face of supernatural beings who attempt to distract them. All the figures in the 'Ten Chapters on Lay Attenders' climax their lives by taking lay vows and assiduously practising religious exercises and they become, in essence, monks who have not received ascetic initiation. The idealised course of the layman's life was formalised in this text and elsewhere (Samav 11) into eleven successive stages, called *pratima*, in which the layman progressively abandons worldly needs and finally, after leaving his household, devotes himself to fasting and contemplation.[2] This spiritual model was, however, to become otiose by the medieval period.

Much more interesting for an understanding of the development of the layman's role within Jainism is the gradual supplanting of the term *upasaka*, which signified the individual who performed the *pratimas* by another term for the Jain layman, *shravaka*.[3] *Upasaka* in its sense of 'one who attends, serves' reflects an ancient view of the layman as only having true significance through catering to the needs of monks and partial imitation of them. *Shravaka*, on the other hand, means 'hearer' and signifies the layman as someone who not only listens to the doctrine being expounded and acts upon it but who is also a listener by virtue of performance of worship in the temple, each example of which replicates the preaching assembly (*samavasarana*) of the fordmakers. However, the original sense of *upasaka* is preserved by many Jain writers in a popular etymology of *shravaka* which would explain it as meaning 'someone who attains (*shri*) faith in the Jain doctrine, sows (*va*) wealth unceasingly upon appropriate objects and makes (*ka*) merit by serving good monks'.[4]

In the ninth century, the Digambara monk Jinasena described a series of life-cycle rituals for the use of lay people which he linked with the first fordmaker Rishabha (AP 38–41).[5] These rites of passage, although recast and 'sanitised' through being placed in the context of Jain legend and liturgy, appear distinctly Hindu in idiom and, while largely unknown to Shvetambaras in the north and certainly lacking any overall prescriptive force for the carrying out of births, marriages and funerals amongst Jains as a whole, are nonetheless still of significance to Digambaras in the south of India.

If it might be said that most Indian life-cycle rituals are of a general provenance anyway, being subsequently rationalised as Hindu, Jain or whatever, the important point about Jain rituals, Shvetambara as well as the Digambara rites described by Jinasena, is not so much their origin or outward appearance, which may vary in detail from sect to sect or between region and region, but the fact that they are specifically lay in character and devoid of direct ascetic participation. The ascetic ideology of Jainism, as texts continually emphasise, is oriented towards spiritual deliverance through the removal of karma, and many generations of monastic theoreticians have tried to make the lay path conform to this. In reality, the lay person, albeit accepting on certain holy days and festivals the primacy of ascetic values, is concerned in the main with leading the prosperous, good and morally auspicious life to gain merit which will effect further prosperity and human birth in the next life.[6] Deliverance, if never denied as the theoretical aim of existence, is very much a far-off goal.

WHAT SHOULD A LAYMAN DO?

From the 'Ten Chapters on Lay Attenders' onwards, the textual tradition defined the non-monk as a Jain to the extent that he adopted a series of lay vows which mirrored the various mental and physical checks which governed the ascetic life and, in the course of time, specialised delimitations came to be placed upon his freedom of action and professional calling. By the thirteenth century, an extensive literature had emerged, Shvetambara and Digambara, which meticulously delineated the duties and obligations of the Jain layman (no serious interest is taken in the laywoman), situating him in a world based as much upon monastic abstraction as practical reality, for all the authors were, with one exception, monks. Nonetheless the model they presented still remains a ubiquitous one in accounts of the Jain laity and their religious and commercial activity.[7]

The lay vows are presented as being twelvefold, the core being the five *anuvratas*, the 'Lesser Vows', which parallel the five ascetic Great Vows both in their content and in the lifelong commitment which they require.

With regard to the first, while the ascetic is required to eschew any act of violence whatsoever, the layman must instead try to the best of his ability to avoid any pointless destruction of life-forms. The most appropriate manner to achieve this is by the regulation of possible ways of gaining a livelihood. The monastic theoreticians thus prohibit a variety of occupations, all of which in some way involve destruction of life and the causing of distress to humans and animals, such as gaining a livelihood through destroying plants, digging, milling, excessive use of fire or water, and breeding livestock or selling their products.

The second Lesser Vow of truth applies to an individual's social and business dealings and involves the necessary avoidance of sharp business practice such as wilfully misrepresenting the qualities of the goods one is selling.

The third Lesser Vow of non-theft obviously prohibits any form of stealing and is also extended by some modern writers to include such anti-social practices as avoidance of paying taxes.

The fourth Lesser Vow of chastity recognises that it would be impossible for the layman to practise complete celibacy in the same way as a monk and instead makes it incumbent upon him to restrict himself to one wife and curb his sex drive and, if possible, renounce sexual activity completely after the birth of a son who will be able to carry on his business.

The fifth Lesser Vow states that, rather than completely abandoning possessions, the layman should not be overattached to his wealth and instead of hoarding it or glorying in it, he should lead a simple life and dispose of any surplus money by religious giving.

The three 'Subsidiary Vows' (*gunavrata*), which supplement the Lesser Vows, involve the restriction of excessive travel and random and untrammelled movement in order to minimise the destruction of life-forms, the avoidance of excessive enjoyment of, for example, food or clothes, and the general abandonment of deleterious forms of activity such as futile speculation, moping or idle and self-indulgent practices.

The four 'Vows of Instruction' (*shikshavrata*) relate to positive and obligatory religious practices: the restriction of one's activities to a certain area for a certain period of time (essentially a variation of the first Subsidiary Vow), the regular performance of the *samayika* ritual, the undertaking of fasts on fixed days of the lunar calendar, and the performance of all sorts of religious and charitable giving.

The apogee of this monastic idealisation can be found in Hemacandra's depiction of the layman par excellence (*mahashravaka*) who intensely pursues the twelvefold vow in its totality, with particular reference to religious giving both to ascetics and to the community by means of the building of temples and the installation of images, and carefully compartmentalises every moment of his day for religious purposes.[8] Hemacandra's account of the lay life was to prove particularly influential and still forms the basis of publications produced by image-worshipping Shvetambara ascetics for lay consumption today.

For example, 'What Should a Layman Do?' is the title of a crisply written and reasonably widely disseminated work, available in Hindi and Gujarati, by the Shvetambara monk Muni Muktiprabhavijaya.[9] The book's cover, depicting a layman dressed in the robes often worn by pious lay Jains for important ceremonial occasions and standing in homage before a variety of articles used by ascetics, such as an alms bowl, whisk and sacred books, makes clear that the attitude towards Jainism the author is trying to inculcate is based on reverence for and a desire to attain the transcendent goal which the ascetic represents. However, the schedule of daily, monthly and annual vows, rituals and obligations mapped out for the layman by Muktiprabhavijaya hardly leaves room for the pursuit of any sort of professional or mercantile career and, although the necessity of earning money is acknowledged, the place of business is characterised as being like a dark hole inhabited by a poisonous snake.[10]

Although not discounting the role of the handbooks of lay behaviour, medieval and modern, in moulding and confirming a particularly Jain moral ethos, it would be unwise to use them as a touchstone for assessing the orthodoxy or deficiency of the activities of Jain lay people as observed today, for the preoccupations of the monks who produced these handbooks and the laity by no means always coincide. Perhaps the most obvious example is the respective ways in which lay people and ascetics envisage non-violence. The layman is typically portrayed by the ascetic writers as being by his very nature continually implicated in violence and destruction, even when he is acting for ostensibly pious motives. As one Digambara writer almost comically puts it, giving food to monks cannot be undertaken without killing life-forms owing to the need to light fires, boil water and so on, building a temple involves activities like digging the ground and chopping down trees while worship within the temple is performed by cutting flowers and pouring liquids, all activities which by the strictest standards involve destruction of life-forms. In addition, we are told, the curbing of the sexual drive will have an unfortunate psychological effect upon one's wife, while even fasting is likely to upset somebody in the household (KP p.90).

The monk would of course advocate renunciation of the world as the best means to escape the dilemmas of lay existence. Yet Jain lay people, although maintaining a respectful attitude toward animals and lower forms of life, taking care to conform to traditional dietary prescriptions and following trades and professions which do not blatantly infringe the principle of non-violence, seldom exercise their imaginations greatly about the religious implications of their normal day-to-day activities, placing the emphasis instead, if challenged, on their purity of intention. Thus, agriculture, while hardly a typical or prestigious pursuit and one largely confined to those Digambaras living on the border of Maharashtra and Karnataka, is not today stigmatised for the destruction it causes to organisms in the earth. Jain industrialists do not speculate about the possible infringement of non-violence in their factories and workshops or through the transport of their products, nor do they agonise about their possible place in a manufacturing process which might culminate in, say, the production of military weaponry. Furthermore, the Jain laity does not generally regard its attitudes towards matters of government policy, international politics or capital punishment as being conditioned by the doctrine of non-violence.[11]

What is important in Jain lay behaviour is not precise conformity to a canonical pattern of religiosity (it is very rare today for anybody to take the Lesser Vows formally) but the manifestation of pious intentions and correct ethical dispositions through public participation in religious ceremonies, worship and community affairs, the enhancement of the prestige of oneself and one's fellow Jains through religious gifting and the correctness of one's business affairs and family alliances.

Before proceeding to discuss some of these areas further, it will be useful to consider at this point the career of one layman who in earlier times stands out as a clearly defined individual.

BANARSIDAS

Banarsidas is not the first Jain layman to emerge as a distinct historical personage. Vastupala, for example, a minister of the Vaghela kings of Gujarat during the first half of the thirteenth century, performed many of the activities which are still standard among prominent members of the Jain community: sponsorship of large-scale pilgrimages, the building of libraries and temples such as the celebrated Lunavasahi (erected in memory of his elder brother Luniga) at Mount Abu in south Rajasthan, and general acts of philanthropy including the construction of wells, travellers' rest houses and so on. Banarsidas's career was somewhat different and less overtly glorious than Vastupala's but it remains unique in its interest.

Banarsidas recorded the events of his life in a memoir called 'Half a Story', the title referring to the fact that he completed it at the age of fifty-five which he describes as being half the normal span of a man's life, and it was most likely an apologia written for the edification of his close personal associates.[12] Born in 1586, Banarsidas was the son of a Jain merchant of the Shrimali caste who may have belonged to the Kharatara Gaccha. After a youth in which he pursued amorous affairs and learning, both of which the elders of the Jain community regarded as inappropriate to the mercantile life, Banarsidas adopted the habits of a pious layman, worshipping the fordmakers, performing the *samayika*, undertaking the dietary restriction of giving up green vegetables and so on, an attitude which intensified in his thirties when he became particularly attracted to various forms of lay ritual.

Much of the interest of 'Half a Story' lies in Banarsidas's account of the insecurities of the merchant's life in north India in the seventeenth century and, in particular, the vicissitudes which he himself experienced, for his business affairs could hardly be said to have been an outstanding success. However, towards the end of his autobiography, Banardidas's interest in recounting commercial transactions wanes. In 1623 he became associated with the Adhyatma movement, a group of like-minded merchants of Agra who were attracted to mystical exploration of the inner self (*adhyatma*) of the kind advocated by Kundakunda and his Digambara successors. Banarsidas was persuaded to read a Hindi commentary on Kundakunda's 'Essence of the Doctrine' and, although initially baffled by the two-level of truth approach to reality, he experienced a crisis of faith as a result, which he described in memorable terms:

> My studies had the effect of completely shaking my faith in rituals and in everything else in religion which was just a conventional, outward form. I had wandered into a spiritual void, for although I lost faith in form, I was unable to savour spirit. I hovered between earth and heaven, befouling the air like a camel's fart.[13]

Gradually, Banarsidas underwent a spiritual transformation, evinced in part by the writing of poetry but this time in a mystical vein as opposed to the erotic variety he had practised when young:

> I renounced all rituals, giving up every form of ordained, conventional precept I had so long been religiously observing.... I even broke my vow of never eating green vegetables. In fact there was no end to my

> disillusionment with outward forms. I felt strangely isolated and everything began to seem alien to me.[14]

The result of this abandonment of previous ritually oriented habits was that the structure of Banarsidas's life temporarily collapsed. He fell in with three cronies, passing the time with them in performing dubious pranks and mockeries of religion such as stripping naked in private and pretending to be Digambara monks, and his generally irreverent behaviour led to the dissipation of his credibility as a Jain and a businessman. By 1636, however, Banarsidas had begun to make sense of the two different approaches to the Jain religion to which he had been exposed in the course of his life. A famous scholar who had come to Agra expounded at the request of the members of the Adhyatma movement a celebrated Digambara doctrinal digest called the 'Essence of Gommata'. This work, which had been written in the ninth century by the monk Nemicandra, caught Banarsidas's imagination, despite its difficult and technical style, by its description of the fourteen stages of quality (*gunasthana*: see Chapter 6) in which the soul is portrayed as remaining in essence the same while external actions, which could range from the basest form of false belief to the most highly developed mystical experience, altered according to the individual's spiritual and intellectual situation. To Banarsidas, this provided a justification for his practice in early life of various forms of lay ritual which he could now regard as forming a valid part of the spiritual path as preliminaries which the true seeker after enlightenment could confidently move beyond. Banarsidas scorned the conventional Jain view that the higher states of spiritual development had become impossible:

> The poems I wrote now were written in the true light of the spirit. I realised too that in the ultimate sense, there was no contradiction between what I was writing now and what I had written earlier. There had been a dark spot on my soul, a canker on my faith; it now disappeared. I achieved a vision with which I could see everything with the same untroubled eye: everything was equal, nothing high or low. As God is my witness, I had indeed attained a knowledge akin to supreme realisation.[15]

Banarsidas died in 1643, leaving behind an important corpus of Hindi poetry. The neo-Digambara Adhyatma movement, of which he was the most prominent member, lingered on for no more than a century, although its principles are still to be found in the minority Digambara Terapanthi sect (not to be confused with the Shvetambara sect of the same name). Banarsidas is the best documented early example of a trend within Jainism, albeit not a dominant one, which authorises lay people to take charge of their own spiritual affairs without reference to ascetic influence. He does not depict himself, even in his pre-Adhyatma period, the bulk of his life, in fact, in which he followed a relatively conventional lay path, as having had any serious dealings with ascetics, although admittedly he did study briefly with a Shvetambara monk when young. This should alert us to a basic fact of lay experience in Jainism, namely that, contrary to ascetic ideology, the lay person does not gain identity solely through interaction with ascetics and that a satisfactory and fully Jain religious life may be constructed around events and practices in which ascetics play a minimal or non-existent part.

WEALTH, HONOUR AND PIETY

Even in an ancient scriptural text such as the 'Exposition of Explanations', the nature of action was analogously compared with mercantile activity (Bh 5.6) and for the last millennium trade has been the traditional occupation associated with the Jain layman.[16] It is, however, only by the seventeenth century with a source such as Banarsidas's autobiography that we can gain some direct understanding of how Jains conducted business in north India. But, prosperous as some of the individuals described by Banarsidas were, they in no way prepare us for the scale of the wealth of the great Jain merchant grandees of Gujarat who flourished at roughly the same time.

The world in which tycoons such as Shantidas Jhaveri (died 1660) and Virji Vorah (died 1675) moved was a complex one. By the sixteenth century, the Portuguese, to be followed a hundred years later by the English and Dutch, had become a significant factor in trade in the Indian Ocean and ports like Surat, from which Virji operated, became centres of burgeoning economic activity, with the Gujaratis acting as middlemen, brokers and bankers for the Europeans. The financial leverage and influence of west Indian merchants at this time became very great indeed. In 1657, for example, Murad Baksh extorted a loan from the family of Shantidas to finance a revolt against the Moghul throne. After defeating the rebel, the emperor Aurangzeb willingly undertook to repay in full Murad's debt to Shantidas, no doubt calculating that he also might need monetary assistance at some later date. Virji Vorah, for his part, commanded such wealth that he has been reckoned to have been among the richest men in the world at the time and without his financial support the English would not have been able to trade in west India.

Both Shantidas and Virji also played a prominent role in community life, with the former being regarded as the head of the merchant guild in Surat, while Shantidas was accepted as the *nagarsheth*, the honorary chief merchant of Ahmedabad who could informally intercede on behalf of the city with the Moghul authorities and interpret and mediate their edicts to his fellow citizens. At the same time, both men were the dominant lay figures in the Shvetambara *gacchas* to which they belonged, sometimes exercising an authority near to that of an *acarya*. Shantidas was particularly famous for his lavish temple building.[17]

It is true that Shantidas and Virji were because of the size of their wealth to some extent exceptions even among the highly prosperous Gujarati merchant community. Yet other great magnates were to succeed them in north and west India so that by the nineteenth century it was estimated, no doubt with some slight exaggeration, that half the commercial money in circulation from Rajasthan to the Bay of Bengal was under the control of Jains who, then as now, constituted a miniscule fraction of the population,[18] and the obvious question to ask is whether religious affiliation played any part in this remarkable worldly success.

It has often been suggested that the reason the tiny Jain community wielded and continues to wield so much economic power in India is that the religion it follows, rather like Protestant Christianity, naturally inculcates principles of self-reliance and responsibility which create an appropriate environment for commercial activity. This theory cannot be totally rejected but it fails to take account of the manner in which Jain businessmen throughout India and beyond have succeeded in being able to expand their financial resources through consistently fitting into particular commercial niches and making use of ready-made networks of capital, credit and social relationships based on religious, regional and caste origin.[19] Nor does it adequately assess the nature of the ethical and social milieu in which these businessmen have moved since the massive expansion of trade in west India from about the fifteenth century.

One of the main concerns of Indian merchants, Jain and Hindu alike, in the early modern period was the gaining of *abru*, a Persian word signifying 'prestige' or 'reputation' (the equivalent Sanskrit term *pratishtha* was also used). It was *abru* which was the test of whether a merchant was creditworthy and competent and such respectability, when confirmed, served to generate further *abru* and still more credit and concomitant financial success. Reputation was based on publicly observable correct behaviour, itself regarded as an index of inner piety, which had to take the form of the organisation of one's life and those of one's immediate relatives in accordance with certain essentially conservative principles. These would include lack of ostentation or scandal in the conduct of private and commercial affairs, strict vegetarianism and temperance, avoidance of overt involvement in political matters, carefully regulated marriage alliances and a cautious approach to business enterprises in which financial credit was generally advanced only on the basis of short-term returns, and active support of the religious sect to which one belonged.

Furthermore, it was consistently accepted that a particularly efficacious way of gaining honour and reputation was to direct one's wealth outwards as religious giving (*dana*) in the form of expenditure upon the construction and upkeep of temples (which could also have a positive effect upon local economies), the financing of communal festivals and the endowment of animal hospitals, the latter being a tangible sign of commitment to non-violence. By the nineteenth century and after, religious giving had also broadened to take the form of a general philanthropy and charity through which social credit could be further enhanced in the community as a whole. To take one recent example: in 1988, during a period of extreme drought in Gujarat, it was estimated that over 60 per cent of the state's voluntary relief agencies were controlled by Jains, a mere 2 per cent or so of the area's population.[20]

The values of such a merchant culture were not exclusively Jain in origin, for the *mahajans*, the merchant guilds, were composed of both Jains and Hindu Vaishnavas, the latter being traditionally vegetarian and often linked maritally to the Jains, and, in particular, the insistence on religious giving as one of the prime means of gaining *abru* was common to both groups.[21] However, it has always been the Jains who enacted the requirements of this frugal and disciplined mode of life with the most assiduity, and religious giving has generally assumed for them a dimension of meaning lacking among their Hindu counterparts. The proliferation, from about the fifteenth century, of often lavishly illustrated manuscripts of Sanskrit and Old Gujarati versions of the most famous of all religious giving stories, that of the still proverbial Shalibhadra, shows the Jain acceptance of *dana* as a potent force within an individual's financial and spiritual destiny.[22]

The basic kernel of this story, which perhaps dates back to the sixth century CE, is that Shalibhadra, a merchant of fabulous wealth, owed his prosperity to having in a previous existence, while living in poverty, given food to a monk, as a result of which action he eventually went on in a later rebirth both to become rich and to take initiation from Mahavira himself. The point of this story, which would not have been lost on laymen such as Shantidas and Virji who must have commissioned manuscripts of it, is that religious giving can generate both worldly and religious success. While the Old Gujarati version switches the emphasis of the original story from Shalibhadra's gift of food to the monk to his careful divestment of his riches prior to renunciation, few Jain merchants at any time would have regarded becoming a monk as a natural development in their lives. Nonetheless, there was general acknowledgement that commerce and Jainism alike would only flourish if money was used for religious purposes and be thus transformed into social and spiritual credit.

Outward piety and restraint, a propensity towards religious giving in the form of building hospitals, temples and educational establishments, and a general reticence about family and business affairs have tended to remain features of Jain lay life until comparatively recently and, although changes in social behaviour have taken place, the lives of the prominent laymen of this century exemplify interests and qualities little different from those of an earlier era.[23]

BIDDING

The enmeshing of religious giving and the need for a creditable reputation takes a form peculiar to the image-worshipping Jains in the institution of bidding for the right to perform certain ritual actions. This bidding represents one of the most public activities which a Jain layman can perform within the community and serves as a means by which his moral and financial status can be established, while at the same time the idiom of the activity, which is that of the marketplace, acknowledges the centrality of business in Jain society.

Bidding takes place at the time of important ritual occasions and is usually elicited by a request emanating from an ascetic or a local elected lay committee formed of prominent members of the community that a certain sum of money be raised for some religious, educational or social purpose.[24] Laymen will then gather and compete with each other, urged on by members of the committee who function approximately as auctioneers and often under the supervision of ascetics, for the right to engage in some ceremonial activity such as anointing an image, performing the *arati* ritual of waving a lighted lamp in homage in front of an image of a fordmaker or, in the course of the Shvetambara *Paryushan* festival, garlanding silver images of the fourteen dreams of Mahavira's mother before his birth. The right for an individual and members of his family to act out various roles such as Indra, his consort and the parents of the fordmaker in the course of the *pancakalyana* ceremony prior to the installation of an image could also be established by bidding. While ascetics may provide the initial suggestion about a project for which money could be collected, bidding is exclusively the concern of the Jain layman enabling him to demonstrate both his religious commitment, in the form of unwillingness to succumb to attachment to possessions, and the standing of himself, his family and business through ritualised competition with his fellow laymen.[25]

FASTING

If bidding is very much a male practice, a more marked demonstration of the pious ideals of Jainism can be found amongst laywomen in the activity which has become their special province, fasting. Although the medieval literature makes clear that this practice was in the past regularly undertaken by both men and women, it is now unusual for men to fast other than on holy days, the standard explanation being that they are too preoccupied with business affairs, and women therefore have to assume responsibility for this.[26]

Fasting is the principal ascetic activity which has found a place in lay behaviour. It is not a private matter nor is it imposed as a form of penance to expiate a misdemeanour. Rather the taking of a vow (*vrata*) which involves some kind of fasting is the most significant of a range of religious activities willingly adopted by a woman, often at the suggestion of an ascetic, which will confirm the seriousness of her commitment and, by extension, that of her near relatives, towards the Jain religion and it can also establish the moral purity of her family through the channelling of her potentially dangerous sexual energy into a practice which involves physical restraint and control of the senses. As such, fasting, like bidding, functions in part as a means of bringing about social prestige.[27]

The practice of fasting is generally associated with *parvan* days when the moon changes, three of these occurring each lunar fortnight, while there are three further eight-day periods (*ashtahnika*) which occur in the course of the year.[28] In Gujarat, there are also two periods known as *oli*, 'succession' of fasts, and fasting is also very prevalent amongst the laity during the four-month ascetic rain retreat of *caturmas*. The term *poshadha*, used to refer to these periods, derives from the Sanskrit word *upavasatha*, 'attendance', the fast performed by the patron on the evening before a Vedic sacrifice. It is on these occasions (lasting twenty-four hours for the Shvetambaras, forty-eight for the Digambaras) that fasting, ranging from cutting down the number of meals eaten during the day and simple abstention from fruit and green vegetables to more severe forms of dietary denial, are most commonly practised. Brief periods of fasting without liquid or, among the Shvetambaras, the restriction of one's diet in the *ayambil* fast over a longer span of time involving the consumption of food, usually prepared in a communal kitchen, in which substances such as oil, milk, sugar, salt or anything imparting a piquant flavour are omitted, are regarded as particularly meritorious. Fasts can also be structured over a considerable period of time. The fast of nine successive Sundays, for example, involving abstention from water, has to be followed for nine years.[29]

Fasting is not an activity carried out in isolation and, if the abstention involved is relatively arduous, it will be conducted in the community hall (*upashraya*), with the woman's household duties being taken over by other female relatives. It will also generally be accompanied by a variety of religious activities such as regular visiting of the temple for worship, the performance of *pratikramana* and listening to ascetics preaching. Very often, if the type of fast is particularly well known, there will take place reading and contemplation of traditional narratives which explain its origin and efficacy.

The public nature of fasting is underscored among the Shvetambaras by the elaborate processions, feasting, acts of worship and giving of robes to ascetics, if they are present, which generally greet the conclusion of this activity and which are in sharp contrast to the abnegation assumed during the fast itself.[30] The honour which accrues to the fasting woman's family is celebrated by the taking of photographs which are bound in a book which functions rather like a marriage album, although in this case it is the woman's post-marital piety which is being commemorated.

In the life of the Jain laity, religious giving and fasting are two activities which complement each other. Both are public undertakings which lead to the conferral of prestige, with the former supporting and perpetuating outward, institutional aspects of Jainism, while the latter relates to its more spiritual dimension of inner purity.

WORSHIP

BACKGROUND

Fasting, either through direct participation in the act itself or through celebration of the merit and honour which flow from it, is the religious activity which is the most familiar to Jains of all sects. To the outsider, however, it is the temple-centred cult involving worship (*puja*) of images of the fordmakers which appears to be the most prominent and conspicuous element in the practice of the Jain faith. Although such a view would be encouraged by the existence of a large number of temples, some of great fame and ornateness, found the length and breadth of India and beyond, it nonetheless would be in part mistaken since two Shvetambara sects, the Sthanakvasis and an offshoot from them, the Terapanthis, define themselves to a large extent by rejection of worship of iconic representations of fordmakers. Nonetheless, despite both these sects being important components of contemporary Jainism, their adherents are numerically in a minority when compared with those Jains, both Shvetambara and Digambara, who describe themselves as *murtipujaka*, 'image-worshipping', and, despite the controversies it has aroused since the medieval period, there can be no doubt that the image-cult represents one of the major historical continuities in Jain civilisation.

Jain tradition claims for the practice of temple building and the worship of images installed within temples an eternal and universal presence which lies outwith the bounds of conventional chronology and geography. It has long been a standard belief, for example, that on the continent of Nandishvara, the eighth island of the Middle World which is uninhabited by human beings or animals, there are fifty-two temples housing images of the fordmakers which have been in existence for all eternity and to which Indra and the rest of the gods travel at regular intervals to offer worship. Other such eternal images are scattered around the universe, in various heavens or on mountain tops. According to the Universal History, the first emperor of this world age, Bharata, installed millions of years ago a large number of images, including one of his father Rishabha, on the greatest of all Shvetambara sacred places, Mount Shatrunjaya in the Saurashtra region of Gujarat. Accounts given by twentieth century monks of ancient images of Mahavira found in Australia and of Jain temples in Mecca and Medina are regarded, in some eyes, as providing historical authority for the antiquity and widespread presence of both Jainism and an image-cult eternally associated with it.[31]

The first century BCE inscription of Kharavela mentioned in Chapter 5 provides the first clearly datable piece of textual evidence for the existence of an image of a fordmaker, for the oldest portions of the Shvetambara scriptures show no knowledge of this phenomenon, while the sporadic references in the rest of the canon tend to occur in the later, mainly narrative parts. A naked and headless stone torso excavated at Lohanipur near Patna and which has been dated to the third century BCE would, if the claim that it represents a fordmaker is correct, constitute the most ancient piece of archaeological evidence so far available although, since it lacks any precise artistic or iconographic context, little more can be deduced from it. Nonetheless, Mathura provides clear corroboration of the early appearance of Jain images, for a shrine to a fordmaker dating from the second century BCE has been found there.[32] A necessary historical conclusion from this evidence, although one insufficiently stressed, is that devotional worship of the fordmakers was from the very earliest times an important element of Jainism.

It seems likely that Jain image worship may have evolved under the influence of or in connection with the cult of the spirits (*yaksha*) who lived in sacred trees.[33] The *Aupapatika* (Aup) depicts Mahavira preaching in the vicinity of such a tree which was an ancient cult site outside the city of Campa, the term used for the site being *caitya*, a word which came in Jainism to designate both an image and a temple. A sacred spot of this sort was characterised by enclosing fences around the tree and an altar along with engraved stone tablets called *ayagapata* at its trunk. Similar tablets dating from before the common era have been found at Mathura, the earliest of which display auspicious signs which seem to have functioned as symbols of the Jain religion, while the later examples show figures of fordmakers sitting crosslegged or standing in the *kayotsarga* ascetic posture, supposedly the bodily positions in which they died and which have remained the two standard iconic poses to this day.[34] Some of these images also show a fordmaker sitting under a tree, no doubt a device to facilitate the assimilation of the *yaksha* cult, and it has been argued that it was wooden and terracotta effigies of *yakshas* which provided the model or prototype for the fordmaker image proper.[35] The worship of at least one *yaksha* has had a remarkable resilience in Jainism: Manibhadra, known at Mathura as a deity who protected trading caravans, has been since about the fourteenth or fifteenth century the tutelary deity of the Shvetambara Tapa Gaccha.[36]

At the same time, the evidence from Mathura also shows that at this early period a style of temple architecture appeared, common to both Jains and Buddhists but, as the Jains took greater care to differentiate themselves from their opponents, this style was superseded, as were the ancient rock-hewn cave temples which probably drew their original inspiration from the cave-retreats of ascetics,[37] so that by the early medieval period the style generally familiar to us today had emerged in the north and west, often sharing elements in common with Hindu architecture such as the tower symbolic of Meru, the mountain which in Indian cosmography forms the axis mundi, and also heavily influenced by the elaborate literary descriptions of the fordmaker's preaching hall, the *samavasarana*, first described by about the fifth century CE (AvNiry 539–69).[38] Today, Jain temples are most obviously recognisable through the gleaming marble out of which they tend to be constructed.

PUJA

Puja in its broadest sense in south Asian religion signifies an act of devotion or obeisance directed towards a divinity and some kind of interaction with that divinity by means of making an offering to its iconic form. Such an act of worship may sometimes take place at home, where many Jains maintain small domestic shrines, but if it is conducted in a temple, then depending on the sect some sort of ritual specialist might play a part. The Digambaras in south India, for example, generally do not touch the image in the temple and any *puja* which involves decorating or anointing it is carried out by a priest called an *upadhye*. In Shvetambara temples, however, the lay people carry out such ceremonies themselves and temple servants called *pujari*, who are usually non-Jains, are employed to clear up after any ritual, taking as their fee the various foodstuffs which have been offered. If for some reason no Jain comes to the temple, they carry out the *puja* themselves.

Neither the *pujari* nor the *upadhye* are in any way regarded as mediators or intercessors with the fordmakers, being solely ritual functionaries. While Jain *puja* has a range of permitted forms and styles, all image-worshipping Jains accept that what is really important in *puja* is to have an appropriate inner, spiritual disposition (*bhava*) so that, to this extent, an act of worship can only be carried by an individual on his own behalf. In Jainism, as also in

Hinduism, the simplest and most common form of devotion is the act of 'looking' (*darshan*) at the image with a suitable outward show of homage and mind directed towards the qualities which the image embodies. Temple worship of this sort, called *caityavandana*, is included in the third Obligatory Action and involves attitudes of obeisance and formalised expressions of homage in front of the image.

Only lay people (or *pujaris* and *upadhyes*) can carry out *dravyapuja*, the type of *puja* in which the image is anointed with various types of substance (*dravya*). Ascetics are confined to inner worship (*bhavapuja*) and merely contemplate the image without having any direct contact with it, being debarred from this because of their impurity, the result of their abandonment of the normal social activity of washing, while their lack of possessions entails that they can neither own nor buy anything with which to make an offering. This does not mean, however, that ascetics necessarily denigrate the making of offerings to images as a 'popular' or inferior form of religiosity. Certainly, early medieval writers sometimes attempt to stress the superiority of internal worship over the making of offerings in that the former is deemed to lead to spiritual deliverance, while the latter can only bring rebirth in heaven at the most and is therefore secondary.[39] However, as early as the first century at Mathura, there is inscriptional evidence of lay people installing images at the instance of monks and in more recent times monks and nuns are often not only the 'instigators' (*prerak*) of the decision of a wealthy layman to endow the building of a temple or to install an image but can also be enthusiastic advocates of all the image-related practices in which they themselves cannot engage.

Thus Muni Bhadrankaravijaya, one of the most prominent twentieth century monastic interpreters of the Jain message for a Shvetambara lay audience, asserts that image-worship involves some of the central concerns of the religion and forms an integral part of correct spiritual disposition (*samyaktva*). He argues that making offerings to the image is an act of religious giving, the necessary curbing of the senses during *puja* cultivates morality, the giving up of food and drink immediately before and during *puja* is an act of austerity while praising the qualities of the fordmaker is akin to meditation. He also claims that in this current age ordinary people cannot focus adequately upon the fordmakers without some kind of mental prop or support and that, as well as bringing merit to the worshipper, image-worship will actually destroy a wide variety of karmas.[40]

While the origins of *puja* in Jainism are obscure, it seems most likely that the practice of making offerings to images of the fordmakers took its form as a logical extension of the Obligatory Actions, involving as they did meditative contemplation, inner worship of the saving teachers, and the formal act of reverence which the ascetic was required to show to the teacher, along with the adoption or sharing of some of the characteristics and idiom of Hindu *puja* which had developed contemporaneously.

The original and basic form of ritual involving physical contact with an image of a fordmaker is impossible to reconstruct but seems, according to references in the Shvetambara scriptures, to have been a simple act of lustration consisting of the bathing of the image.[41] From about the sixth century CE, the textual focus is directed towards the enumeration of a variety of materials which are used in the conduct of the ritual, and there emerged a broad consensus among both Digambara and Shvetambara writers that there were eight 'substances' (some sort of perfumed material such as camphor, flowers, rice, incense, light, sweets, fruit and water)[42] which provided the basic elements for the most common form of *puja* described in the literature, the eightfold worship of an image.

The conduct of the ritual has not always been stable and many of its characteristics, some of which are no longer practised while others are still current, emerged in the medieval period. There is, for example, evidence that the eightfold form superseded an earlier version of the ritual involving only the first five substances, while an examination of the literary evidence makes clear that a much larger variety of substances could be employed in medieval *puja* than is found today.[43] Moreover, certain innovations in practice were also introduced which seem to have derived from Hindu patterns of worship. Hindu-style dancing in front of the image by young women, for example, was prevalent in Shvetambara shrines controlled by temple-dwelling monks in the eleventh and twelfth centuries but, being roundly criticised by monks of reforming sects such as the Kharatara Gaccha, is no longer practised. The waving of lights in front of the image which might be expected to have been censured by reference to Jain teachings about the existence of life-forms in fire, is nonetheless a ubiquitous form of *puja* in South Asia and seems to have been integrated into Jain ritual from early medieval times.[44]

THE *PUJA* OF EIGHT SUBSTANCES

The *puja* of eight substances is the only Jain ritual which has received extended scholarly description and interpretation.[45] Such accounts do make clear that there are certain reasonably fixed modes of procedure within it, but the ritual when witnessed often displays a strongly improvisatory character and it should not be regarded as an event which is identically replicated on the basis of a standard codification on each occasion it is performed. Nor is there necessarily any unanimity amongst Jains about the significance of the actions in which they engage during the course of this ritual. This is understandable both in the light of the historical variation found in *puja* and of the fact that Jain image worship is not communal, for it is generally accepted that the individual performing *puja* should proceed without reference to or acknowledgement of any other of his fellow Jains who might be present.[46] I will now describe in approximate terms the eightfold *puja* (as performed by Shvetambaras) which embodies an extremely wide variety of the ritual actions which are available to Jains.

The performance of the eightfold *puja* should normally take place in the morning and should be carried out in a state of purity, clean unstitched clothes being stipulated as the required apparel. The layman (or laywoman) when entering the temple should utter the word *nisihi*, 'abandonment', signifying a move from the profane world into the sacred space of the *samavasarana*, the preaching assembly of the fordmaker. Similarly, he should also utter this word when he moves from the outer concourse of the temple proper into the inner shrine which houses the image of the fordmaker.

As a necessary preliminary to the eightfold *puja*, the layman should perform a circumambulation (*pradakshina*) of the image three times and then, with substances in part brought from home and in part provided by the temple, he should commence the ceremony. Firstly, the image is bathed to clean it of any accretions from the previous day's worship and then anointed with a mixture of milk and water. Textual descriptions of this phase of the ritual urge the layman to imagine himself as Indra, the king of the gods, who carries out just such a lustration on the newborn fordmaker on the top of Mount Meru. Next, the worshipper should apply *gandh*, a mixture of camphor and sandalwood, both expensive cooling substances, to all the main parts of the image's body, and then make an offering with flowers, usually garlanding the image.

After these three ritual actions which require immediate contact with the image, the layman withdraws from the inner sanctum to the main hall of the temple to engage in ritual which is directed at rather than performed upon the image. This stage of the *puja* involving the offering of the remaining five substances requires considerably less time than the anointing and, as it also lacks the necessity of physical contact with the image and therefore the need to observe scrupulous purity, can often be performed as a self-contained ritual. The first two of these offerings consist of the waving of incense and lamps in the direction of the image, after which the lay person proceeds to complete the *puja* by offering the three types of food-substance, rice, sweets and fruit respectively.

The most distinctive part of this phase of the ritual is the lay person's arrangement of the pile of rice, placed along with the other two types of offering, on a low table facing the inner shrine, into a design which conveys in emblematic form the major doctrinal principles of the Jain religion: firstly, a *svastika*, the pan-Indian sign of auspiciousness, whose four corners signify according to conventional Jain exegesis the four main states of existence, human, animal, god and hellbeing,[47] then above that, arranged horizontally, three dots standing for the Three Jewels of right knowledge, faith and conduct, while above that is placed a crescent within which is a single dot signifying the liberated souls at the top of the universe. After this, the lay person puts aside his offerings, which will later be collected by the temple staff as payment (there is usually a small sum of money which is used in the offering) and, after uttering for the final time the word *nisihi* to indicate a movement to a further stage, completes the ritual by contemplation of the image, inward worship and the muttering of prayers and sacred formulae.

The ritual of the eightfold *puja* has been endowed with a layer of exegesis over the centuries which would interpret it as symbolising some of the key ascetic and spiritual goals of the Jain religion. As early as Haribhadra, the eight substances were taken as standing for the five Great Vows, devotion to one's teacher, knowledge and austerity (Asht 3.6) while, in the seventeenth century, Yashovijaya in his account of the ritual interiorised many of the offerings, the garland of flowers on the image being interpreted as forgiveness, the incense as auspicious thoughts, the waving of the lamp as the suppression of the mental, vocal and physical activities and so on, the whole *puja* being taken as an exercise in self-control (JnS 29).

Today, a rather similar symbolic interpretation of the offerings can be found in the accounts of *puja* written by ascetics for lay people, according to which they represent either the attainment of positive spiritual goals or the elimination of negative ones, and some variation of this is generally repeated in scholarly analyses of the meaning of Jain worship. Accordingly, the water is taken as signifying the purity of the soul when free from karma, the cooling sandalwood the quieting of mental and worldly turbulence, the flowers the attainment of the fragrance of the Three Jewels, the incense the burning away of the karmic matter which clings to the soul, and the light of the waved lamp the attainment of enlightenment, while the rice, sweets and fruit supposedly symbolise respectively the intention to use one's human birth in a religiously meaningful way, the abandonment of worldly pleasures and the attainment of spiritual deliverance.[48] However, in reality, a wider variety of meanings can be and is assigned to each of the eight substances by Jain worshippers and, rather than look for some non-existent, 'official' interpretation of each constituent element of the ritual, it seems more appropriate to consider the overall purpose of Jain *puja* as a totality.

THE PURPOSE OF *PUJA*

The general idiom of *puja* is that of devoted attention of the sort which might be given to a king, a baby or a welcome guest. But why engage in such worship in the first place? For the fordmakers, having died and attained deliverance from the world of rebirth, are by definition outwith human affairs and thus have no ability to respond to an act of worship, nor are they ever depicted as having during their lives courted such worship. As Vattakera puts it: 'What is to be given by all the excellent Jains has in fact already been given by them, namely, the instruction in the threefold doctrine of faith, knowledge and behaviour' (MA 570).

For the fordmakers to be so gratified by praise and worship directed towards them that they would grant the request of a devotee would imply that they have not cast away the passions and are in some way physically present.

Devotion to the fordmakers is frequently described in the ancient literature as something which can bring about a favourable rebirth and generate sufficient merit to lead to deliverance (e.g. BhA 745), and statements in hymns and the activities of present day Jain worshippers in front of images would superficially suggest that the fordmakers are indeed believed to bestow some sort of grace upon their devotees. However, ancient tradition, which in this case has clearly informed current practice, is emphatic that worship of the fordmakers does not actually elicit a response from them but rather brings about an internal, spiritual purification in the worshipper (e.g. LV p.352). So, while it might be the case that worship destroys karma, such an effect is regarded as having been brought about by the inner transformation which worship effects.

This is where the image of the fordmaker serves as an important aid. Although there is no divinity actually within a wooden or stone image, it nonetheless represents a locus for the whole range of moral and spiritual attainments associated with the fordmakers which are, as it were, superimposed upon the image.[49] According to one writer, just as the sight of somebody's son might bring to mind one's own son, so an image of a fordmaker brings about remembrance of the qualities of the fordmakers (Aparajita on BhA 46).[50] Through his offerings and praise, the worshipper gains both merit and inner purity in accord with the intensity and sincerity of his devotion. Moreover, since the image represents the embodied form of a soul which has attained deliverance and since all souls (with the exception of those who are *abhavya*, without the capacity of true religious devotion) have the potential to burn away karma and attain that same state themselves, worship of the image of the fordmaker represents an acknowledgement of the divinity of one's own innermost self.

The distinctively Jain nature of the values which are embodied in this mode of worship can be seen in the area where Jain and Hindu *puja* differ most clearly. After offerings of food have been made to the image of a Hindu deity, they are distributed among the worshippers as *prasad*, the 'goodwill' of the divinity. There has been scholarly controversy as to precisely what this *prasad* signifies but if, as seems most likely, it represents some kind of assimilation to the deity by consumption of food which the deity has already 'eaten', it will be readily apparent why *prasad* is not distributed at the end of a Jain *puja*, for the dead and liberated fordmaker cannot in any way be said to eat the rice, sweets and fruit offered to his image. The significance of these offerings derives rather from the fact that they are generally perceived by Jain worshippers not so much to have been *given* with the expectation of some divine boon being bestowed in return as to have been *abandoned* by them, in a manner similar to the throwing of rice and money into the crowd of onlookers by an ascetic prior to initiation as a token of a rejection of the material world.[51] The various stages of the eightfold offering thus represent a confirmation by the lay person of the renunciatory ideal which lies at the root of Jainism and an expression of willingness to further one's spiritual development.

The fordmakers are objects of reverence because devotion to them removes obstacles to faith. Prayers are therefore not offered for mundane success such as prosperity in business affairs or luck in marriage. This is the province of the various divinities such as the goddess Padmavati who are linked to the fordmakers and whose representations are generally located outside the inner shrine where offerings to them can be made. Amongst the Shvetambara Kharatara Gaccha, worldly requests can also be directed to images of the sanctified medieval teachers, the Dada Gurus. The fordmaker Parshva has a wide reputation as a saviour but, on closer examination, intercession as a result of devotion to him is regarded as being effected by his guardian deities or, rather more mysteriously, by the special power which is associated with particular images of him in particular shrines.

Jainism is far from being a cold or bloodless religion and there is a rich literature of praise and devotion to the fordmakers which, in the vernacular literatures of north and west India, reached a particularly impressive extent during the late medieval period. At times, the language of the medieval Jain devotional poets assumes an almost Hindu tinge in which the fordmakers are often addressed as if they were Hindu gods, able to bestow grace and favour. However, there has never really been in Jainism the fervid ecstacy which is associated with certain types of Hinduism and, whatever the language in which praise of the fordmakers might be expressed, Jain doctrinal tenets are deeply ingrained and have not been radically modified by the introduction of a devotional theology.[52]

GODDESSES

The eleventh century Shvetambara storyteller Devacandra describes how a Jain layman who had been converted from Hinduism by a monk was persecuted by the goddess whom he had previously worshipped in an attempt to get him to revert to his previous religious practices. She carried off his cattle and his son and threatened him in the form of an old woman whom she had possessed but, in spite of all this, the layman told the goddess to do her worst and refused to worship her as before. Persuaded of his strong resolve, the goddess then asked him to show a modicum of faith towards her, which the layman stated that he was prepared to do if she would undertake to stand beneath the image of the fordmaker in the temple. Agreeing to this, she returned his son and cattle (MSP pp.71–2).

This story is primarily intended to be an example of the virtues of maintaining correct faith and not yielding to superstition. However, it also attempts to provide an explanation of a phenomenon which was without scriptural warranty but had become prevalent by the early common era, namely the absorption of local goddesses into the Jain religion and the specific linking of some of them with particular fordmakers. It would be easy to see this as solely the outcome of a process of Hinduisation and the capitulation of Jain teachings in the face of external pressure. In fact, these goddesses, while continuing to play an important role in Jain devotional and ritual activity, do not fall into any strictly religious or soteriological category, for that is the realm of the fordmakers alone, and instead they represent, through their ability to grant requests and offer protection, an infusion of worldly values and a willingness on the part of Jainism to make some concessions to the more mundane aspirations of lay followers and potential converts alike. Moreover, the goddesses, as devotees of the fordmakers, exemplify the quintessentially Jain principles of non-violence and restraint, being benevolent, vegetarian and unmarried, unlike the often inauspicious and meat-eating Hindu goddesses.

The origin of the practice of linking each of the fordmakers with a *yaksha* and *yakshi*, a divine male and female attendant respectively, is difficult to date. Some of these deities no doubt go back to Jainism's beginnings in eastern India and it has been suggested that others were introduced as the community gradually spread towards the west and south and adopted regional deities, some associated with powerful local clans and families, as part of a process of integration and adaptation.[53] An image from Akota in western India dating from about 550 CE depicting Rishabha with attendant goddesses represents the earliest iconic example of this phenomenon, and textual and iconographic evidence points to the introduction of a full complement of twenty-four *yakshas* and *yakshis* by the end of the first half of the eighth century CE.[54]

By about the tenth century CE, the worship of the *yakshis*, as opposed to the rather bland male attendants (with the possible exception of Parshva's attendant, Dharanendra), as *shasanadevatas*, tutelary goddesses of the Jain religion, reached such a prominent position that some of them became the objects of cults which had only a limited connection with the fordmakers with whom they were nominally connected. Padmavati, for example, is the goddess associated with Parshva, although there is not much evidence of the relationship before the tenth century, and various elements go to compose her mythical personality, deriving both from her function as a curer of snakebites and a goddess of wealth and beauty.[55] In Karnataka, Padmavati is an object of such devotion among Digambaras that she can often be found in association with fordmakers other than Parshva and those who do not visit the temple every day will often take care to worship her on Fridays.

Ambika is the goddess who, according to standard enumeration, accompanies the twenty-second fordmaker Nemi, although there is evidence that she was of independent status in Karnataka in the seventh century.[56] She is of particular importance among the Shvetambaras of Gujarat and the legend associated with her, while also found among south Indian Digambaras, associates her with that region. The 'Little Mother', the literal meaning of the name Ambika, was driven from her home along with her two sons by her brahman husband because she had given alms to a Jain monk. Miraculously, a withered mango tree gave forth fruit and a dried up lake filled with water for her hungry and thirsty children. When her husband, who had realised his mistake as a result of further miracles which occurred at home, came after her, she tried to escape from him by jumping into a well with her two sons and died, being reborn as the attendant goddess of Nemi. Iconographically, Ambika is generally depicted with two children and mangoes, indicative of her role as a goddess associated with childbirth and prosperity.[57]

Leaving aside the mass of female deities connected with magical invocation for whom no particular cult has developed, there are a variety of other important goddesses found within Jainism. In common with Hindus, Jains worship the pan-Indian goddess of wealth, Lakshmi, while the oldest known image of Sarasvati, who is revered by the Hindus as the goddess of wisdom, is in fact Jain, and dates from early in the first century CE. The Jain Sarasvati is depicted squatting in the same position in which Mahavira attained enlightenment with a sacred book in her hand, indicative even at that early stage of her position as the tutelary deity of the Jain scriptures and the goddess who is invoked to help dispel the darkness of knowledge-concealing karma.[58]

YEARLY FESTIVALS

Like all religious traditions, Jainism has developed a sacred calendar which either defines certain periods of the year as especially sacred or relates to particular individuals or events in the religion's past. This in part provides a focus for communal celebration and an opportunity both to gain merit and to demonstrate to other social and religious groups some of the ideals embodied in Jain history and culture. However, Jain festivals are noteworthy for the muted and restrained demeanour of the participants and there is little of the extreme exuberance which often characterises Hindu festivals. The Jains have, for example, generally tried to distance themselves from celebration of Holi, the Hindu Spring Festival, which can often take on near-anarchic dimensions and is for many a time of temporary abandonment of normal sexual and social constraints.

It is, perhaps, typically Jain that there should have emerged amongst the Shvetambaras a religious day solely devoted to silence, called Maun ('Silence') Eleventh (*ekadashi*) which falls on the eleventh day of the bright half (i.e. when the moon is waxing) of the month of Margashirsha (western November/December) and which supposedly takes its origin from a request by busy merchants to have their own day to compensate for their inability to find the time to engage in religious vows and ceremonies.[59] Although this is not strictly speaking a festival, it demonstrates the Jain view that holy days should be very much occasions for reflection and pious activities. This is not to say, however, that Jainism totally lacks an overtly festive side for, as we have seen, just such a dimension appears in the various activities such as processions which greet a successfully completed course of fasting or the end of a festival such as Mahavir Jayanti, Mahavira's birthday, and which today probably represent for most Jains the most obvious public expression of their religious adherence, apart from the Shvetambara *Paryushan* and Digambara *Dashalakshanaparvan* festivals which climax the four-month ascetic rain retreat.

There is no complete unity between the Shvetambara and Digambara sacred calendars, nor is there much synchronicity of dating, with the most notable exception being Mahavira Jayanti, which both sects celebrate at the same time, on the thirteenth day of the bright half of the month of Caitra (western March/April). The festival in honour of the scriptures, for example, is celebrated by the Shvetambaras as 'Knowledge Fifth' (*Jnanapancami*) on the fifth day of the bright half of Karttika (October/November) while the Digambaras celebrate it as 'Scripture Fifth' (*Shrutapancami*) on the fifth day of the bright half of the month of Jyeshtha (May/June). If both sects are at one in emphasising the merit to be gained both from dusting and repairing books and in getting new manuscripts copied at this time, the respective orientations of the festivals are nonetheless different since for the Shvetambaras Knowledge Fifth represents the merging of the religious and the worldly which takes place towards the end of *caturmas*, for this is also the time when businessmen reopen their shops at the end of what is the new year period, while for Digambaras the festival also involves commemoration of the monks Pushpadanta and Bhutabali who copied down the 'Scripture in Six

Parts' at the beginning of the common era. Even in such an essentially local festival as that to the goddess Gauri Abba followed by Hindus and Jains alike in Mysore in south Karnataka, the Digambaras celebrate by feasting while the Shvetambaras fast.[60]

The entire Jain sacred calendar is potentially extremely large in extent, if regional festivals and fairs are taken into account.[61] Although it would be an unusual Jain who did not take part as a matter of social course in a good number of the ceremonies during *caturmas*, participation in festivals during the rest of the year is not enforced upon Jains as an obligatory duty and is essentially a matter of personal preference and piety and, therefore, I will single out only a few of the more important yearly events.[62]

As *caturmas* is the period when a Jain's response to the demands of his religion is usually at its most charged, the ceremonies which take place during this time can largely be regarded as the events around which the ritual year pivots, for the extended presence of ascetics, at least for the Shvetambaras, ensures a greater preoccupation with fasting, listening to sermons and the temporary abandonment of worldly concerns than at other times. During this period and in partial imitation of the mode of life of the ascetics who are now living alongside the lay community, a much larger number of laymen will attempt to fast or restrict their diet in some way than would be usual during the rest of the year

The most auspicious period within *caturmas* is the block of eight days called *Paryushan*, 'Abiding', by the Shvetambaras (although there are differences among the various sects about its dating) when great efforts are made, at least by the serious minded, to carry out activities such as confession and fasting which theoretically should have been performed during the rest of the year. We have already seen in Chapter 3 how one of the central events of Paryushan is the recitation of the *Kalpasutra* by monks. The final day known as *Samvatsari* involves a ceremony of communal confession and the seeking of pardon from all living creatures for any injury inflicted. At this time of the year, letters asking forgiveness are generally sent to friends and business associates, while local authorities have often been prevailed upon to place a temporary ban upon the slaughter of animals for food. *Paryushan* concludes on the day after *Samvatsari* with a communal meal eaten by all members of the local community.

The equivalent Digambara ceremony, known as *Dashalakshanaparvan*, the 'Festival of the Ten Religious Qualities', is rather different in emphasis, both because the Digambara rejection of the Shvetambara scriptural canon means that the *Kalpasutra* cannot be recited and because the paucity of monks in the last two centuries has necessitated essentially temple-centred practice during this period. *Dashalakshanaparvan* starts immediately after the completion of the Shvetambara *Paryushan* and lasts for ten days. It revolves around the recitation of the ten chapters of the *Tattvarthasutra* and homilies delivered by members of the community on successive days on each of the ten religious qualities enunciated at TS 9.6 (viz. forbearance, gentleness, uprightness, purity, truth, restraint, austerity, renunciation, lack of possession and chastity). The most auspicious day is 'Endless Fourteenth' (*Anantacaturdashi*), which comes at the end of *Dashalakshanaparvan* and is associated with the fourteenth fordmaker Ananta, when fasting and image-worship is universally carried out and *puja* is performed with fourteen flowers. The final day is called *Kshamapana*, 'Asking for Pardon'.

The festival which ends the ritual year in mid-October is *Divali*, 'Row of Lights'. Whereas the Hindu *Divali* is connected with the return of Lord Rama after exile, the Jain festival commemorates the final liberation of Mahavira and the lighting of lamps by various kings of the Ganges area in tribute to the light of knowledge which had gone out with his death. At this time there is generally no fasting, despite monastic arguments that there is great merit to be gained from abstention on this day,[63] for *Divali* is for Jains as for Hindus very much a worldly festival in which *puja* is offered to Lakshmi the goddess of wealth in order to promote prosperity. The day immediately after *Divali* commemorates Gautama's attainment of omniscience and also marks the beginning of the new ritual and commercial year when merchants open a new set of financial books.

'Undying Third' (*Akshayatritiya*), a festival which occurs on the third day day of the bright half of Vaishakha (April/May) and is common to Shvetambaras and Digambaras, provides a link to the next section which deals with sacred places. This festival is essentially a commemoration of the initiation of the first fordmaker Rishabha and, in particular, of the gift of sugarcane juice to him by Shreyamsa which represented the first act of religious giving of this world age, the name 'Undying' referring to the merit generated by this. The ceremonial completion of fasting and the recounting of the story of Rishabha's fastbreaking represent the substance of Undying Third and those who have completed a series of fasts over the course of a year are given sugarcane at this time. The most suitable spot for this to take place is regarded by Shvetambaras as being Mount Shatrunjaya in Gujarat, whose tutelary goddess is Cakreshvari, the helper of all women who fast and the attendant divinity of Rishabha to whom the main temple on the mountain is dedicated. However, Hastinapur, to the north of Delhi and the legendary scene of Shreyamsa's gift, is now regarded by many as a highly appropriate site for the ceremonies involved in Undying Third and in 1978 a fastbreaking temple (*paranamandir*) with lifesize images of Rishabha and Shreyamsa was consecrated there.[64]

PILGRIMAGE AND HOLY PLACES

The length of Jainism's history and the extent of its geographical outreach over the whole of India make it hardly surprising that there are a large number of places scattered over the subcontinent which image-worshipping Jains consider to be sacred and journeying to which is felt to confer particular merit on the pilgrim. The Sanskrit name for a holy place, *tirtha*, we have already encountered in the specifically Jain sense of the 'community' which Mahavira and the other fordmakers create to enable the crossing of the ocean of rebirth. The literal sense of the term, 'ford', conveys the purity and holiness which Hindus regard as being the principal characteristics both of water and pilgrimage places. However, while certain of the greatest Hindu holy places of north India such as Benares, Prayaga and Hardwar are both literally and spiritually fords through their association with sacred rivers, the Jains have always rejected as utterly spurious brahman claims about the possibility of ritual purity as a result of bathing in such places and no Jain *tirtha* has had sacrality conferred on it through proximity to water.

Pilgrimage, like the performance of the *samayika* ritual, enables a Jain lay person to become an ascetic for a short period. If modern transport now ensures that the rigours and privations of journeying to a holy spot are negligible compared to earlier times, the circumstances in which pilgrimage is performed have changed little since the medieval period. The central figure on the occasion of a large-scale pilgrimage (smaller-scale journeys by individuals and families are of course permitted) is the prominent layman who organises the entire event both through sending out letters to other members of the community inviting them to participate, although the original impetus will often come from ascetics who in the Shvetambara case will themselves sometimes join the pilgrimage if it is being conducted on foot, and by meeting the bill for lodging, travel expenses and community feasts held in the course of the journey. In medieval times, he would generally also have had to negotiate with the Moslem authorities for official permission to mount a large pilgrimage. Such meritorious actions have traditionally gained for the sponsor the honorific title *sanghapati*, 'lord of the assembly', which, according to one medieval writer, is the equivalent of taking monastic initiation (DhAMK 1.73).

There is no formal requirement for Jains to engage in pilgrimage, but it remains a consistently popular activity owing to its combination of the religious and the recreational. However, the ideal of the temporary suspension of the householder's life to journey as a pilgrim remains before lay Jains even when they go to worship in their local temple. Most Shvetambara temples contain painted representations of the great holy places, depicted without any normal artistic perspective and in the standard garish style of contemporary demotic Indian religious art, which can serve as ancillary focuses of devotion after homage has been paid to the main temple image. It should also be noted that monks and nuns, particularly among the Shvetambara Sthanakvasi and Terapanthi sects who do not have a system of holy places, are generally regarded as being pilgrimage spots themselves and lay people will make journeys to visit an ascetic in the same way as they might to a celebrated shrine.[65]

HISTORICAL BACKGROUND

The origin of Jain holy places did not stem from the worship of relics, as seems to have been partly the case with early Buddhist pilgrimage sites. The remains of the Buddha's body were, after cremation, supposedly distributed throughout the Ganges basin whereas the stories of Mahavira's funeral describe how his bone relics were collected together by Indra and taken to heaven where they were worshipped by the gods (YS 1.8.670).[66] This emphasises the Jain insistence that the fordmakers, having attained deliverance, are no longer physically accessible to humans. Instead, Jain holy places are very often linked to the attainment of enlightenment or liberation by a fordmaker or some other ancient ascetic, although there can be other reasons, such as miracles or the presence of a powerful image or tutelary deity, which might lead to a site being regarded as a place of pilgrimage.

A particularly common theme in the legends about the origins of holy spots is the miraculous discovery of an ancient but long buried image of a fordmaker whose presence is often revealed by the spontaneous lactation of a cow in its immediate vicinity. This was suposedly the origin of a medieval image of Parshva at the Rajasthani town of Phalodhi (VTK 60). Another famous image of Parshva at the small Gujarati town of Shankheshvar, one of the most important Shvetambara regional pilgrimage spots, the earliest reference to which dates from 1099, also reappeared in the same way, after an illustrious history in which it had been given to Krishna by Parshva's guardian deity Dharanendra in order to confound his enemies, subsequently being lost after the sack of the *tirtha* by the Moslems.[67] The seventeenth century monk Samayasundara, writing after the most intense period of Moslem persecution, lends some credibility to this sort of story by describing how many old images, previously buried to save them from sacrilegious despoliation, were in his time excavated from the ground (SSh p.97).

From an early period in the development of the Universal History, the Jains linked the careers of several of the fordmakers and other legendary ascetics with some of the leading Hindu sacred places. A long Jain connection was claimed, for example, with the holiest of all Hindu cities, Benares, whose role as Parshva's place of birth and pre-renunciation life as described in the

Kalpasutra came to be expanded to include the early careers of four other fordmakers and a link with Mahavira, while Ayodhya, famous as the birthplace of the Hindu hero-god Rama, also became connected with a variety of fordmakers and was, according to the Universal History, the capital of the first Jain monarch, Bharata. However, none of the sources for these appropriations of Hindu holy spots can be said to be truly early and the incorporation of these cities into the Universal History can best be regarded as part of the process by which the Jains, in the course of migrating from the Ganges basin, staked a claim to be regarded as an ancient component of the north Indian religious environment.

Benares and Ayodhya are of little real significance to the Jain pilgrim, but another Hindu holy spot has been fully absorbed into Shvetambara consciousness and contains some of the most important examples of Jain architecture. Mount Abu in south Rajasthan was the location of the ceremony held, according to tradition, in the eighth century whereby the Rajput clan was ritually purified by fire and admitted into the Hindu warrior caste. For the Shvetambara Jains, however, Abu became famous from the eleventh century for the spectacularly beautiful marble temples with elaborate filigree carving situated on the top of the mountain in the village of Dilwara. According to the chroniclers of the Kharatara Gaccha, the Jain minister Vimala (eleventh century) formed a desire to build a temple there but was rebuffed by local Hindu holy men who claimed that the Jains had no right to be on the mountain. The teacher Vardhamana discovered, after invoking a deity through the power of his fasting, that there was an image of Rishabha beside the temple of Arbuda, the tutelary goddess of Mount Abu and after whom it is named. Despite this revelation, the Hindus only allowed Vimala to build a temple after he had covered their land with gold coins (VP 1; KhGPS p.43).[68] This story makes clear that the presence of the buried image of the fordmaker authoritatively established the validity of Jain claims to a presence on Mount Abu but that, at the same time, the ground on which the temple complex was erected had to be bought. To this day, the Jains still share Abu with a variety of Hindu shrines.

The most important guide to Shvetambara holy spots is the 'Description of Various Tirthas' (VTK) by the thirteeenth/fourteenth century Kharatara monk Jinaprabha Suri. This work records origin legends about the *tirthas* along with many topographical details, but its particular value lies in the fact that Jinaprabha, who journeyed extensively in north India and also into the south, was an eyewitness to the destruction of many Jain shrines by the Moslems. By his own account, he played an important role in restoring to the Jain community the famous miracle-working image of Mahavira originally at Kanyanaya and which had been forcibly taken by the Moslems to Delhi and deposited in the sultan's treasury (VTK 22; see also VTK 29 for the destruction of an image by the Moslems).

Prominent *tirthas* such as Pava near Patna, the site of Mahavira's death, or Mount Sammeta in Bihar are sacred to both Shvetambaras and Digambaras and the two sects have equal jurisdiction over the main temples there. Other sites, as was seen in Chapter 2, are the subject of continuing dispute. However, with the exception of Mount Girnar in Gujarat from which the Digambaras claim to have been wrongly expelled, the most prominent Jain holy places tend to align themselves according to a geographical, and therefore a sectarian, pattern, with the great Shvetambara holy places being in Gujarat and Rajasthan whereas the most famous Digambara *tirthas* are in Karnataka and Maharashtra. In order to contextualise the significance of pilgrimage places in Jain history, I will give brief accounts of what are unquestionably the two most famous for the Shvetambaras and the Digambaras respectively, Mount Shatrunjaya and Shravana Belgola.

MOUNT SHATRUNJAYA

The hill 'which conquers enemies' (*shatrunjaya*) outside the small market town of Palitana in Gujarat is one of the five holy mountains of Shvetambara Jainism.[69] It has the distinction of being mentioned several times in the Shvetambara scriptural canon, albeit in the later parts, which would suggest some sort of familiarity with this most famous of *tirthas* by the fifth century. The legendary history of Shatrunjaya is pushed back towards the beginnings of this world age by the *Saravali*, one of the 'mixed' texts of the canon, which probably dates from about the elventh century and reflects a time when the hill was beginning to gain major prominence as a holy spot.[70] According to the *Saravali*, Rishabha's grandson Pundarika travelled to Shatrunjaya after being told by the fordmaker that he would gain final release there, thus giving the hill its alternative name of 'White Lotus' (*pundarika*). Bharata, his father, is said to have built a temple there and Rishabha himself supposedly visited the *tirtha*, ensuring that it be regarded as the first of all holy places. The *Saravali* also claims that Bharata attained deliverance there, as did some of the great hero figures of Hinduism incorporated into Jain tradition such as Rama and Sita and the five Pandava brothers, the main protagonists of the Hindu epics. Furthermore, the *Saravali* points out how effortlessly spiritual attainments are gained on Shatrunjaya and that merely installing one image there will lead to rebirth in heaven. Perhaps a vested interest in the expansion of the site is shown by the anonymous author when he states that pilgrimage to Satrunjaya is the equivalent of pilgrimage to all other holy places and that religious giving there is particularly excellent.

A near supernatural atmosphere is associated with this holy mountain.

Cycles of legends about the Jain wonderworker Nagarjuna attempt to link him with Shatrunjaya which with its magical streams and wells provided a suitable backdrop for his miraculous activities.[71] Jinaprabha Suri, whose account in the 'Description of Various Holy Places' dates from a time when Shatrunjaya had fully entered into historical reality, for the temples on the hilltop had, as he says (VTK 1.119), been sacked by the Moslems in 1311, describes how even wild animals living there gave up their savage and carnivorous ways and took to fasting under the influence of the atmosphere of non-violence which prevailed there (VTK 42).[72]

For Shvetambaras, Shatrunjaya exists outside the dimensions of normal chronology. It has supposedly been renovated sixteen times by devotees in the course of this world era and in the future nineteen fordmakers will preach there.[73] Leaving aside the few scriptural references, the first piece of clear historical evidence for a lay Jain presence on the hill is an image of Pundarika and a preaching monk set up by a merchant in honour of his guru and dated 1006 CE, while a slightly later image dated 1075 depicts a prosperous layman.[74] The lay practice of lavishly endowing temples (the original wooden structures were replaced by stone ones in the twelfth century) and gifting money and jewellery for the images within which seems to have started about this time was no doubt in part responsible for the Moslem assault on the site at the beginning of the fourteenth century. Although renovation took place within two years under the sponsorship of Samarashah, the temples on the summit seem to have remained relatively limited in number for over two centuries, and it is likely that it was the massive pilgrimage to Shatrunjaya organised in 1593 by Hiravijaya Suri, the head of the Tapa Gaccha, and the probable consecration by him of the temple to Rishabha dedicated by the merchant Tejpal Soni, which gave the impetus to the remarkable proliferation of shrines and temples which has characterised Shatrunjaya to this day.[75]

In 1656 the Moslem governor of Gujarat gave custody of the village of Palitana at the foot of Shatrunjaya to the great merchant Shantidas Jhaveri, the effective leader of the Shvetambara community, and subsequently exemption from all taxes connected with the site was granted. Eventually, Shatrunjaya came under the control of Anandji Kalyanji, the trust which was set up around 1730 to manage a variety of Shvetambara temples and holy places, and although prior to independence the Jains often had difficulties over the payment of taxes to various maharajas of Bhavnagar who had gained control over Palitana after the disappearance of the Moghul Empire and who refused to accept the legal validity of the Jains' dealings with the Moslems, the hill has remained an inviolate and thriving place of pilgrimage which, with nearly one thousand shrines, some admittedly little bigger in size than a British mailbox, provides remarkable testimony both to Jain architectural style to and to the commitment of the laity to gain merit through the glorification of their religion.[76]

SHRAVANA BELGOLA

The 'White Lake of the Ascetics', as the Kannada name Shravana Belgola can be translated, is a rural town of about ten thousand people situated in the southern state of Karnataka, roughly equidistant between the cities of Mysore and Bangalore. Its principal feature is a small lake on each side of which lies a hill, known colloquially as the Big Hill and the Little Hill, although their classical names are Indragiri and Candragiri respectively. The fame of Shravana Belgola stems from the fifty-seven-feet-high image of Bahubali, according to the Digambaras the first person of this world age to achieve liberation, which stands on the summit of the Big Hill. This colossal monument was erected in 981 by Camundaraya, a general of one of the kings of the Ganga dynasty, and it was unquestionably intended to allude to the accommodation which a Jain warrior had to make between the claims of his religion and his necessary engagement in acts of war, for Bahubali, the son of Rishabha, after defeating his half-brother Bharata in a duel, drew back from killing him and instead renounced the world and performed austerities in the forest (see Chapter 5). The image erected by Camundaraya portrays the naked and motionless warrior ascetic fighting the solitary, spiritual battle with arms hanging down by his sides in the *kayotsarga* position and with jungle creepers twining round them, while anthills cover the lower part of his legs and snakes slither at his feet.

The summit of the Big Hill has been since at least 1398, subject to astrological circumstances but generally every ten to fifteen years, the scene of one of the most spectacular of all Indian religious ceremonies, the 'head-anointment' (*mastakabhisheka*), in which the head of Bahubali is anointed with a variety of substances, such as milk and liquified saffron, poured from 1,008 pots by prominent members of the lay community who have bid for the privilege and who stand on a balustrade erected behind the image. In recent years, this event has drawn hundreds of thousands of pilgrims to the little town and novelties such as bombarding the image with flowers from a helicopter have been introduced.

Shravana Belgola had, however, attained a degree of sanctity for Digambaras several centuries before the consecration of the great image on the Big Hill and Camundaraya's choice of the site in fact represented a confirmation of the eminence of the Little Hill which had by his time long been for generations of Digambara ascetics a hallowed spot for the controlled religious death by fasting (*sallekhana*). It is the Little Hill, with its concentration of temples and memorials to ascetics and lay people greater than that found in any other Digambara holy spot, which remains the true goal of the committed pilgrim to Shravana Belgola.

The earliest reference to Shravana Belgola is an inscription of 600 CE on the Little Hill commemorating the supposed journey from the north of the great teacher Bhadrabahu and his disciples to escape famine and which, as we saw in Chapter 2, is often regarded as having some bearing upon the origins of the Digambara sect. It is impossible to determine the veracity of this account but the dispassionate observer might well suspect that this claim of a connection with an event which could only have occurred centuries before, along with the later identification of a fissure in the rock of the Little Hill as 'Bhadrabahu's Cave', in fact represents an anachronistic attempt to enhance the prestige of an emerging holy place. Certainly, the feature of this first inscription which has most bearing on the early history of Shravana Belgola is its commemoration of a monk, supposedly one of Bhadrabahu's followers, who fasted to death on the Little Hill and it is from about the seventh to the tenth centuries that there occur the memorials called *nisidhi*, in the form of stone reliefs, pillars, images and temples, which testify to the religious death of ascetics and, after the tenth century, lay people also. It is these which give Shravana Belgola its particular aura of holiness as do, more humbly, the marks scraped on the surface of the summit of the Little Hill by nameless ascetics to record the periods of their fasting.

The attraction of Shravana Belgola for warriors such as Camundaraya can be seen from the setting up there in the tenth century of hero stones, of a sort still to be seen today on the outskirts of many Indian villages, commemorating those who had died a violent death in battle and which were placed near the memorials to those brave ascetics who had fasted to death on the Little Hill. The erection at this time of memorials to kings demonstrates Shravana Belgola's connection with local royal courts, and it emerged as the most important ritual centre of south Indian Jainism, with the subsequent founding of a monastery whose successive clerical heads (*bhattaraka*) claimed descent from Camundaraya's guru, Nemicandra, and the attendant promotion of the cult of the local tutelary goddess Kushmandini who, according to legend, had appeared in the guise of an old woman to complete with the contents of a tiny pot the first ritual lustration of the image of Bahubali which Camundaraya had been unable to carry out fully.

The twelfth century onwards saw the development of Shravana Belgola as a religious foundation with large-scale endowments such as villages being made by lay people and, according to the inscriptional evidence, the continual presence of monks of the Mula Sangha, the leading Digambara ascetic lineage. The focus of religious concern about this time also began to shift away from the Little Hill and its various monuments to the glory of the religious death. An inscription of 1118 describes the gathering of a large number of prominent monks to perform the ceremony normally associated with the installation of an image of a fordmaker, thus seemingly inaugurating the beginning of the real fame of the Big Hill by a reconsecration of the image of Bahubali.

However, the fortunes of Shravana Belgola were also to fluctuate in the succeeding centuries. While its continuing prestige in the south Karnataka region can readily be seen by the erection of other massive images of Bahubali in the region and by the fact that the maharajas of Mysore have always been closely associated with the head-anointing ceremony, there is evidence that the ascetic community began from the thirteenth century to lose some of its authority over the site and inscriptions allude to what would appear to be embezzlement by merchants of the large sums of money being contributed by pilgrims. Little serious building of temples took place after 1300, land holdings began to be mortgaged off and by the seventeenth century the *bhattarakas* seem to have lost their ability to influence lay people to make substantial donations. At the same time, Shravana Belgola also experienced difficulties due to altering political circumstances. During the seventeenth century the site was attacked by one of the Telugu chieftains who had moved into the area in the wake of the disintegration of Hindu polity in south India through the onslaught of Islam and the *bhattaraka* was forced to flee (although head-anointing ceremonies are recorded as taking place in 1612, 1659 and 1677). In the following century, zealous Moslem rulers placed an interdict on the performance of the head-anointing ceremony.

It is difficult to say how regularly the head-anointing ceremony was carried out in the past and its performance may have ultimately depended upon the availability of funds for the costly ritual. This would most likely explain why in 1887 it was the *bhattaraka* of Kolhapur who performed the ceremony at the expense to his foundation of 30,000 rupees. Today, however, it is the State Government of Karnataka, with the assistance of the Digambara community, which is responsible for the management of the ceremony.[77]

8 Jain relativism and relations with Hinduism and Buddhism

Whatever the sectarian differences which might divide them, the Jains have in the twentieth century usually attempted to present themselves within the wider spectrum of the world's religions as advocates of harmony, conciliation and the essential equality of spiritual traditions. The prominent Shvetambara monk and social reformer, Vijayavallabha Suri, for example, who was particularly associated with this standpoint, stated that he was 'neither Jain nor Buddhist, Vaishnava nor Shaiva, Hindu nor Moslem, but rather a traveller on the path of peace shown by the Supreme Soul, the god who is free from passion'. Another leading Shvetambara monk of this century, Vijayadharma Suri, took the view that all religions were essentially the same and that adherents of different faiths had to have respect for the truths which were to be found in other traditions.[1]

While a cynic might suggest that a community whose members gained their livelihood primarily through business activity could hardly afford to antagonise the adherents of other religions, such an eirenic attitude was in fact also a characteristic feature of recent neo-Hinduism which, starting in the nineteenth century and gaining momentum in the twentieth, espoused under the influence of the non-dualist form of Hindu Vedanta a view of the unity of the world's religions whose implicit purpose, in the course of the struggle towards independence, was the essentially political one of bringing about communal solidarity and the promoting of the moral and intellectual prestige of a newly emergent India. It is natural that many contemporary Jains should share such sentiments.

It would be easy to point to unconciliatory attitudes both from this century and earlier periods of Jain history which derive from a keen awareness both of Jainism's uniqueness and of the inadequacies of other religious paths. Todarmal, for example, writing near the beginning of the modern period, insisted on the impossibility of anybody from another faith achieving the correct attitude (*samyaktva*) necessary for the ultimate achievement of spiritual deliverance owing to an inevitable inability to accept the authority of monks or the veracity of the Jain analysis of the workings of the universe.[2] Nonetheless, the eirenic attitude to other intellectual standpoints can unquestionably be traced back through Jain history to great teachers such as Hemacandra who recommended the honouring of all religious systems and, most conspicuously, to Haribhadra.[3]

It is no exaggeration to state that Haribhadra (assuming for the sake of argument that he was a teacher who lived around the eighth century) possessed the most wide-ranging mind in Jain history, and several of his works evince an at times remarkable willingness to evaluate rival intellectual systems on the basis of their logical coherence alone. In a famous verse, he states: 'I do not have any partiality for Mahavira, nor do I revile people such as Kapila [the founder of the Hindu Sankhya system]. One should instead have confidence in the person whose statements are in accord with reason'.[4]

This assertion of a commitment to the inherent validity of correct logical procedures in abstract argumentation may owe something to Haribhadra's original mastery, insisted on by Shvetambara tradition, of a wide variety of branches of brahman learning, but nonetheless it was not an empty boast. Haribhadra was the first classical author to write a doxography, a compendium of a variety of contemporary intellectual views which, rather than espousing narrowly partisan judgements, attempted to contextualise Jain thought within the broad framework of possible intellectual orientations available to Indian thinkers around the eighth century CE.[5] He also wrote two works on *yoga* (YB and YDS), a term which signifies Haribhadra's own individualistic mode of conceptualising the world, which demonstrate a strikingly liberal approach to alternative, non-Jain attempts to map out spiritual paths.

Haribhadra suggests that those who live a moral life and do not infringe the dictates of their own scriptural tradition, whatever it might be, are worthy recipients of religious giving (YB 122), a statement which is directly contrary to the authority of another influential Shvetambara, Jinadasa (seventh century), who argues that giving to those following non-Jain religions is totally inappropriate (NishithS 1 p.19). There is continual emphasis placed by Haribhadra on conformity to reason as being the prime determinant of what has truth (YB 525). At the same time, he suggests that certain things are beyond the realm of sensory perception, for otherwise logicians would have come to some degree of correct understanding of them (YDS 143 and 146) and thus, in the last resort, wrangling over metaphysical questions can be said to be self-defeating (YB 310). Religious doctrines as propounded by the great teachers in fact differ only according to the capabilities of the people to whom they are addressed (YDS 134–9) and so 'the ultimate truth transcending all states of the worldly existence and called *nirvana* is essentially and necessarily one even if it be designated by different names' (YDS 129 and 130). The various terms which denote the enlightened or liberated being in fact involve no more than simple differences of nomenclature (YB 302 and 308). On this basis 'it is impossible for thoughtful persons to quarrel as to how to express one's loyalty to this truth' (YDS 132) and, as a consequence, whoever stands at the centre of a religious path, whether teacher, deity, brahman or ascetic, ought to be honoured (YDS 151).

Haribhadra's espousal of this relativistic approach is unique in its forcefulness within the Shvetambara learned tradition (there is nothing truly comparable among the Digambaras) but it would be incorrect to view it as purely an eccentric legacy of his background within brahman erudition, for Haribhadra's upholding of the integrity of Jainism is never in doubt. The remarkable scholar Sukhlal Sanghvi, who overcame the handicap of blindness contracted very early in life to became one of the most incisive of recent interpreters of Jain philosophy, described Haribhadra in tribute as *samadarshi*, 'viewing everything on the same level', and his eminence derives to a large extent, as Sanghvi saw, not just from the breadth of his intellectual command but from his willingness to articulate more clearly than any of his predecessors the full implications of Jainism's main claim to fame among Indian philosophical systems, the many-pointed doctrine.[6]

THE DOCTRINE OF MANYPOINTEDNESS

Respect for all religious paths of the sort often expressed in Jainism can to some extent be taken as an extension of the principle of non-violence to include the opinions of other people. However, the central Jain intellectual position that a variety of approaches and standpoints have to be incorporated into any ontological judgement can better be regarded as evolving from two factors: the claim of full omniscience for the fordmakers, the authoritative teachers who mediate a correct understanding of the nature of reality to the unenlightened, and the interpretation of that reality as being characterised by both permanence and change.

Jain epistemology is concerned with the means by which mundane knowledge is acquired. At a basic level, this is viewed in conventional terms with the sources of knowledge being direct perception, inference, analogy and scripture. There are also two varieties of suprasensory knowledge but these came to be regarded as having died out in this world age with Mahavira's disciple, Jambu. As was shown in Chapter 4, in its purest and pristine form the individual soul which is the agent of cognitive activity is omniscient but, owing to the occlusion brought about by the influx of karmic substance, its innate capabilities are impeded and, as a consequence, the immediate knowledge simultaneously apprehending all possible points of view which characterises omniscience is impossible, and thus any epistemological judgement made by the soul, while perfectly adequate for the purposes of ordinary, transactional activity, is flawed. The necessary outcome of this for the Jains is that a multifaceted approach which synthesises and integrates a variety of contradictory viewpoints, as opposed to a dogmatic insistence on a mode of analysis based on a single perspective only, is the sole means of gaining some kind of understanding of the complexity of reality.

The germs of this idea can be found in the Shvetambara scriptures. The 'Exposition of Explanations' (Bh 2.1) portrays Mahavira as converting the brahman Skhandaka Katyayana by a perspectivist approach in which a variety of entities, the world, the soul, spiritual deliverance and the liberated soul, are shown to be finite or infinite depending on the perspective from which they are approached, although the standpoints which are adduced, namely an entity's physical and spiritual structure along with the time and space in which it is located, are not in any strict sense mutually contradictory.[7] As for the early Digambaras, we have already seen how Kundakunda employed a two levels of truth model using the term *naya* which was to stand at the centre of fully developed Jain relativism.

The catalyst for the emergence of philosophical relativism was the condensing by Umasvati in the *Tattvarthasutra* of the often inchoate and unconnected remarks found in the early scriptural tradition concerning substance and its modifications and the standpoint from which they should be approached into the definitive expression of a distinctively Jain model of reality as simultaneously involving the two apparent contradictories of permanence and change. It seems, however, to have been the Shvetambara Mallavadin who lived in perhaps the fourth CE who was the first to have formulated what became a standard system of seven *nayas*, standpoints through which judgements could be made about this complex reality, applying them with merciless rigour to intellectual systems which were opposed to the Jains.[8]

The most significant point about the *nayas* is that each of them is incomplete as an independent judgement and cannot in itself form the basis for a correct apprehension of the world. The first three relate to the fact that entities must in ontological terms be interpreted as being conjoined either with both general and specific properties, or with general properties only, or with specific properties only. The fourth *naya* relates to entities as necessarily rooted in the present when judgements are being made about them, while the last three demonstrate the manner in which language is implicated in ontological analysis. Thus, according to the sixth and seventh *nayas*, verbal statements have to be carefully differentiated on the basis both of an understanding of the way in which their sense can be modified through tense and grammatical inflection, and through a consideration of the etymology of words as a means of gaining information about their meaning or nuance. The seventh *naya* delimits individual words to one particular meaning: that is, a word only has its proper meaning when something is carrying out the function designated by it (TSRV p.99). A judgement can only be valid if it encompasses all these perspectives and is 'many-pointed' (*anekanta).*[9]

In Jain hands, this method of analysis became a fiercesome weapon of philosophical polemic with which the doctrines of Hinduism and Buddhism could be pared down to their ideological basics of simple permanence and impermanence respectively and thus be shown to be one-pointed and inadequate as the overall interpretations of reality which they purported to be. On the other hand, the many-pointed approach was claimed by the Jains to be immune from criticism since it did not present itself as a philosophical or dogmatic view. Nor did its juxtaposition of irreconcilable standpoints betoken an irrationalism which infringed established norms of logical procedure. Akalanka defended the coherence of manypointedness with reference to the method's insistence upon adherence to linguistic precision and its ability to convey the true, multifaceted nature of things on the basis of direct sensory perception alone (TSRV p.36).

The inevitably provisional nature of any ontological judgement based on knowledge short of that omniscience which alone can encompass reality can be seen most clearly in the Jain prescription, found in nascent form in the 'Exposition of Explanations',[10] that all statements should include the word *syat*, the optative of the Sanskrit root *as*, 'be', meaning 'may be', to signal the need for linguistic qualification of metaphysical judgements by putting the statements in which they are framed into the conditional mode.

Syadvada, 'the doctrine of may be', in its classical form delineated seven possible judgements which could be predicated of an entity, involving positive and negative attribution, an acknowledgement of its possible inexpressible nature, and combinations of these so that, to take the seventh type of predication, it might under certain circumstances be said of that entity that it simultaneously existed, did not exist and was inexpressible.[11] For Jain philosophers, this was not a form of scepticism, merely an acknowledgement that linguistic expressions relating to the world ought to be structured with appropriate awareness of the nature of the reality being described.

It must be stressed that, whatever the recommendations of philosophical writers, Jains do not now nor, as far as I can tell, did they ever, qualify every statement they utter with the words 'may be', and it might well be argued further that the level of abstraction at which the doctrine of manysidedness functions takes little or no account of the various motivations which lead an individual in everyday life to espouse one particular viewpoint as opposed to another. As a consequence, manysidedness could ultimately be regarded as operating in a moral vacuum.[12] However, this does not diminish the force of the Jain intellectual argument that systems such as Hinduism or Buddhism which claim to interpret reality, while genuinely containing partial versions of the truth, cannot do full justice to the manifold nature of the world in which we live and that judgements about that world must necessarily vary according to the observer's perspective. As a result of this insight and their strong commitment to non-violence, the Jains feel able to claim the moral high ground among the world's religions.

THE JAINS AND THE HINDUS

The Veda and animal sacrifice

The attitudes of the Jains to Hinduism were never uniform, albeit today relationships tend to be generally amicable, and throughout a long literary history they employed a variety of idioms and strategies, including accommodation, rejection, satire and transmutation, in an attempt to come to terms with the most all-embracing of the world's religions. Certainly, the pull of Hindu culture exerted at times an intense influence. There can be no doubt, for example, that the greatest of Jainism's literary enterprises, the Universal History, was gradually manufactured in order to provide a corpus of tradition which would be comparable with the accounts of the legendary royal dynasties found in the Hindu epics and mythological lorebooks on which the Jain writers unquestionably drew.[13] From the eighth century, we also find the fordmakers being linked with the gods of the Hindu pantheon through the use of Hindu names and epithets, while the elaboration of a full-scale Jain iconography of guardian gods and goddesses shows extensive Shaiva influence.[14] The Hindus for their part incorporated the first fordmaker Rishabha as one of the minor incarnations (*avatara*) of the god Vishnu.[15] In the tenth century, the Digambara Somadeva appears to have been near to acknowledging the existence of a type of Hindu–Jain syncretism when he conceded that Jains could engage in any form of popular or regional custom provided it did not infringe any of the basic tenets of Jainism.[16]

Yet, despite such evidence of social and religious interaction, the Jains consistently attacked the foundations upon which Hinduism rested. The prestige of the Veda, the supposedly revealed collection of scriptures whose mastery enabled the brahman class to exercise ritual and social authority, was challenged by the Jains on the grounds that it was of the same human provenance as any other type of literature and that the brahman claim of absence of an author for it could no more be sustained on any logical grounds than an argument that anonymous poems were not written by anybody. The Jain scriptures, on the other hand, through being conveyed by the omniscient teachers, were deemed to be of human origin and manifestly greater worth (VTP pp.72–101). Some Jain writers even claimed that the Hindus did not know their own scriptures because they were unfamiliar with references to the fordmakers in the Veda (e.g. KKP 35 pp.170–1).

Conclusive proof for the Jains that the Veda was a false scripture which purveyed evil doctrine lay in its association with animal sacrifice. The Jains refused to accept that, even in the controlled and delimited context of ritual action, the use of sanctified language in the form of mantras could neutralise the inevitable evil brought about by the slaughter of animals and lead both sacrificer and sacrificed to heaven. Hemacandra quotes verses by the principal Hindu lawgiver, Manu, which argue for the validity of sacrifice as examples of *himsashastra*, 'the science of violence'. In reality, the Jain teacher asserts, a dreadful rebirth can be the only possible result for those who destroy animals under the pretext of worship (YS 2.33–40). The entire Jain attitude to ritual violence is summed up by Akalanka's scornful remark: if killing can bring about a religious goal, then one should best take up a life of hunting and fishing (TSRV p.563).

Hindu mythology

For Hemacandra, the term 'god' (*deva*) denoted an omniscient being who had conquered the passions, was honoured by the entire universe, and described things as they really were. Such a being was to be meditated upon, served, regarded as a refuge and his teachings were to be accepted as the truth. Only the fordmakers could match up to this (YS 2.4–5 with comm.). The gods of Hinduism, on the other hand, he regarded as forfeiting any claim to divinity through their mythological association with a variety of worldly activities such as fondness of women and fighting, their encouragement of improper sectarian insignia such as rosaries and their general engagement in dancing, music and uproarious behaviour, none of which the Jains could regard as conducive to spiritual deliverance (YS 2.6–7). While a mystical writer such as the Digambara Yogindu (sixth century) might refer pityingly to the great Hindu gods Vishnu and Shiva because of their ignorance of the supreme soul located within their own bodies (ParPr 42), the general tone adopted by Jain literature towards these deities was one of mockery, often through a recasting of their mythical careers within the context of the laws of rebirth and retribution applicable to all creatures.

Shiva was an easy target for Jain iconoclasm through his role within Hinduism as sustainer and destroyer of the universe and because of the phallic cult associated with him. Jinadasa, one of the first Jain writers to point the finger of scorn at this mighty figure, describes how in reality Maheshvara, the 'Great Lord', one of the names of Shiva, was the son of a nun who had been magically impregnated by a wizard seeking a suitable repository for his powers and subsequently came into possession of a spell which caused a hole in his forehead, the third eye of Shaiva mythology. As a result of his violent and lascivious behaviour, he was killed by a prostitute called Uma, one of the names of Shiva's wife Parvati (AvCu vol.2 pp.174–6).

The Digambara storyteller Harishena gives a still more lurid account of Shiva's background, portraying him as the offspring of a Jain monk and nun who had broken their vow of chastity. Because of his unpleasant disposition while still a boy he was given the name Rudra, 'Terrible', another of Shiva's epithets. Rudra became a monk, practising austerities through which he gained power on Mount Kailasa, which the Hindus believe to be sacred to Shiva, but he became infatuated with a group of girls who had come to bathe in a pool near him, and who were the daughters of a *vidyadhara*, a semi-divine being who had been cheated out of his inheritance by his brother. In order to win them, Rudra killed the girls' uncle and restored their father to his throne. However, the heat of his semen burnt up the girls after he married them and he killed a further hundred women offered by other *vidyadharas* through the massiveness of his penis.

The only *vidyadhara* woman not destroyed by Rudra's potency was Uma who in a previous existence as a nun had become infatuated with Rudra, then a fisherman. As a result of sexual ecstasy with her, Rudra considered himself to be the creator of the universe and spread the Shaiva doctrine throughout India. Alarmed at the possibility of losing their kingdoms, the *vidyadharas* tricked Uma into revealing a means of overcoming Rudra and murdered the couple as they slept together. The prevalence of the *linga*, the image of Shiva's penis, throughout the northwest of India is ascribed by Harishena to a Jain monk who advised a king to set them up to exorcise the malign effects of the magic powers of the murdered Rudra (BKK 97). In this story, Harishena performs the remarkable feat of devalorising Shiva by presenting him as a degraded Jain monk and at the same time giving Jainism the credit for the universal presence of his phallic emblem throughout India.

If Shiva is viewed in purely negative terms, the Jain attitude towards the other major Hindu deity, Vishnu, is rather more ambivalent, no doubt because of the close ties which the Jains came to form with the Vaishnavas, as can be seen from the early association of Krishna, one of Vishnu's most important incarnations, with the fordmaker Nemi (the two came to be regarded as being related). Although the Jains felt able to poke fun at Hindu claims about the omnipresence of Vishnu (cf. KKP 29: if the supposedly omnipresent Vishnu exists in water, it would seem inappropriate to drink and wash with a god!), their reworking of the famous myth in which he assumes the form of a dwarf to take three massive steps through the universe in order to destroy the demon Namuci and measure out the cosmos does Vishnu the honour of presenting him as a mighty Jain monk, albeit a human one, who uses his magic power to overthrow a brahman minister who has attempted to expel the Jains from his master's kingdom (BKK 11 and DhMV 93).

The whole range of Hindu mythology as found in the *Puranas* was sent up remorselessly by authors such as Haribhadra in mordant satires which were peculiar to Jainism. In his 'Rogues' Story' (DhA), Haribhadra describes how a gathering of lowlife characters, cheats and confidence tricksters of both sexes compete with each other in the recounting of tall stories and outrageous anecdotes which are then capped by reference to the bizarre antics of the gods as described in Hindu tradition. The point is clearly made that if the gods are depicted as behaving in a disreputable manner, it is hardly surprising when humans do the same. Such satires were not just for entertainment but a means of inculcating piety amongst the Jain community and subverting the authority of Hinduism.

The Hindu epics

The *Nandisutra*, one of the Shvetambara canonical texts which deals with scriptural hermeneutics, links the two great Sanskrit epics, the Mahabharata and the Ramayana, with the Veda as examples of *mithyasutra*, false scriptures which convey a message of violence (NSH p.64). Although the precise sense in which these epics can be regarded as scripture is problematic, they are both of central significance for Hindus through their delineation of ideal types and exemplary situations and provision of perennial sources of reference for the manner in which Hindu civilisation has articulated its sense of self-perception. Adaptations of epic narrative of the sort produced by Jain writers would have been a necessary strategy for a socio-religious group which felt itself to be in certain respects both different from and yet at the same time part of a larger culture.

In fact, the Jains seem at times to have employed the epic to engage in confrontation with the Hindus. In the sixteenth century, Jain writers in western India produced versions of the Mahabharata libelling Vishnu who, according to another influential Hindu text, the *Shivapurana*, had created a fordmaker-like figure who converted the demons to Jain mendicancy, thus enabling the gods to defeat them. Another target of these Jain Mahabharatas was Krishna who ceased to be the pious Jain of early Shvetambara tradition and instead is portrayed as a devious and immoral schemer. This Jain response seems to reflect a particularly bitter period of sectarian struggle during which, according to the chroniclers, large numbers of Hindus in Rajasthan were being converted to Jainism.[17]

The Mahabharata, the story of the five Pandava brothers who are cheated out of their kingdom by their relatives the Kauravas and return from exile in the forest to defeat them in battle and reclaim their rights, was never as elaborately treated by the Jains as the Ramayana. Nonetheless, its hold on their imagination from a relatively early period can be seen from the fact that one of the central characters of the Mahabharata, Draupadi, the wife of all five Pandava brothers, is described at length in the 'Stories of Knowledge and Righteousness' (JnDhK 1.16), the fifth Shvetambara *anga*. This scriptural story claims greater insight into the character and motivation of Draupadi by fitting them into an exclusively Jain context in which she herself is portrayed as a potentially pious but flawed Jain. There is also found here the misogyny which generally characterises Jain treatments of the epics (cf. BKK 83 and 84), for the violence and savage war in the Mahabharata are shown to be ultimately the result of Draupadi's foolishness in a previous birth in which she had given poisoned food to a monk.[18]

The most famous portion of the Mahabharata is the *Bhagavad Gita*, 'The Song of the Lord', in which Krishna gives the Pandava hero Arjuna advice about the necessity of fighting his relatives among the Kauravas in order to fulfil his obligations as a member of the warrior class, going on to elaborate a theology of action, knowledge and devotion which was to gain significant status among orthodox Hindu philosophers and eventually become an emblematic text in the twentieth century because of its association with Gandhi and others. Jain writers occasionally quoted from it and it is unquestionably referred to by Kundakunda when the 'Essence of the Doctrine' echoes its famous statement about the impossibility of killing or being killed by reference to the fordmakers' claim that no person can die until their due and karmicly allotted span of life is completed (SS 247–9). In the seventeenth century the great scholar-monk Yashovijaya seems in the latter part of his life to have fallen under the influence of the Gujarati mystical poet Anandaghana (1603–73) and as a result wrote a work called the 'Essence of the Inner Soul' which cites the *Bhagavad Gita* extensively and assimilates, without entirely endorsing, many of its views and at times approaches non-dualistic Vedanta. It is not unknown today for Jain ascetics to compare the *Bhagavad Gita* favourably with Mahavira's teachings.[19]

It was, however, the Ramayana which underwent the most remarkable and extensive transmutation at the hands of Jain writers in literary works of substantial artifice. The hero Rama, called by the Jains Padma, 'Lotus', in the Hindu epic the quintessential exemplar of the cardinal virtue of duty, exiled himself in the forest along with his wife Sita and brother Lakshmana to enable his half-brother to succeed to the kingdom and subsequently rescued with the aid of an army of animals Sita who had been kidnapped and held captive on the island of Lanka by Ravana, the king of the demons. This story gave full scope for a succession of poets to reshape and 'Jainise' an increasingly prominent Hindu theme, point to the causes and disastrous effects of sex and violence and, significantly for a religion which in the early centuries of the common era courted aristocratic support, correlate martial vigour and religious piety.

The first Jain version of the Ramayana was written in about the fourth century in Prakrit by Vimala Suri. Here are found for the first time some of the major themes of the Jain treatment of the story: its location within an essentially Jain world which through the principle of rebirth is projected beyond the temporal limits of the Hindu epic, the distancing of Rama from deeds of violence, the lack of serious interest in any of Ravana's demonic qualities, and an insistence on the negative nature of women.

The fullest and artistically most impressive Jain treatment of the Ramayana is to be found in the seventh century Digambara Ravishena's Sanskrit 'Lorebook of Lotus' (PadP), where the whole story is put into the mouth of Gautama who tells it to King Shrenika who is dismayed at the nonsensicality of the Hindu Ramayana (PadP 2.249). Various ideological statements are made about kingship and brahmanical authority throughout the work. Thus, the entry of Rama, Sita and Laksmana into the forest and their stay there is portrayed as representing an acknowledgement of the primacy of asceticism over kingship, a point clearly made by Rama when he contrasts his state as a forestdweller with Ravana's as an earthly king (PadP 66). The forest itself is portrayed as being full of Jain temples and Digambara monks and the brahmans who live there, rather than being holy men and sages who require Rama's protection, are malevolent and mean-spirited (PadP 35).

The 'Lorebook of Lotus', like the Hindu Ramayana, turns around the kidnapping of Sita, an event which is attributed to the lust and lies of the *vidyadhara* woman Durnakha who falsely claims to have been raped by Lakshmana and by her story causes Ravana who is king of the semi-divine *vidyadharas* to become infatuated with Sita (PP 44).[20] Ravana himself is presented as a devout and thoroughly undemonic Jain ruling a Jain kingdom (PadP 67) who does not force himself upon Sita because he has taken a vow in front of monks not to have sexual relations with other men's wives (PadP 44.98–9 and 46.54–66). Prior to battle with the heroes he prays to Sḩanti, the fordmaker associated with peace (PadP 68.22), but his egoism compels him into combat where, despite his remorse for the seizing of Sita (PadP 72), he is killed by Lakshmana. Rama tells his relatives not to weep for him for that is how the world works (PadP 77.48ff).

It is in the latter portions of the 'Lorebook of Lotus' that Ravishena draws out its full significance as a Jain story. As in the Hindu epic, Rama builds a pyre to test Sita's chastity but as the fire blazes up around her, she praises the fordmakers at which the flames turn to water and she then pulls out her hair in token of her intention to become a Jain nun (PadP 105.21ff). A monk who has attained enlightenment at the same time as this miracle tells Rama that the whole course of events described in the epic stemmed from Sita's insulting in an earlier birth a Jain monk, while Rama and Ravana have hounded each other through a variety of existences out of desire for her (PadP 106).

Sita takes the religious death of *sallekhana* and is reborn as a god and Rama, after ruling for a while, renounces the world on Lakshmana's death to become a monk. Observing the power of Rama's austerities from heaven, Sita returns to earth in her old form to tempt Rama back to their old relationship, but he remains steadfast and attains enlightenment (PadP 122). Sita then travels to hell in order to visit Lakshmana who has carried out all the acts of violence in the story, and he and Ravana, also in hell, lament their actions which they now realise were committed out of delusion (PadP 123). In conclusion, Rama predicts that Sita will be reborn as a universal emperor, while Lakshmana and Ravana, after working out their bad karma in hell, will be her sons and they will all eventually attain spiritual deliverance (PadP 123).

THE JAINS AND THE BUDDHISTS

There is no record of Mahavira and the Buddha ever having encountered each other, although they were near exact contemporaries and lived and taught in the same region. The Buddhist texts of the Pali Canon were familiar with Mahavira, whom they called Nigantha Nataputta, and his claim to omniscience, and one of them (*Digha Nikaya: Sangitiparyayasutta*) describes how his death and the squabbling which ensued amongst his followers were reported to the Buddha. The general attitude of the Buddhists towards the Jains was one of disdain for their insistence on the practice of asceticism as a means to enlightenment.

The early texts of the Shvetambara scriptural canon seem to have had some limited familiarity with Buddhist teachings. The *Sutrakritanga* clearly alludes to the standard Buddhist analysis of the human personality into five factors, although the people holding this view are described only as fools (SKS 1.1.1.17).[21] However, what little can be connected with the Buddhists elsewhere in the same text suggests that the Jains did not have, or did not wish to have, any accurate understanding of Buddhist ideas about the important question of karma, no doubt because they felt that denial of the soul could logically leave no room for it (SKS 1.12.4). Indicative of this is a most curious travesty of Buddhist teachings in which a Buddhist monk is made to argue that cannibalism can be acceptable if carried out through error (SKS 2.6.26–9).[22]

No early Jain text shows any knowledge of the Buddha himself and the tenth century Digambara Devasena dismisses him as a lapsed follower of Parshva who could not accept that living entities were embodied souls and so, having taken to the wearing of orange robes, promulgated a path in which there were no dietary restrictions and a doctrine which stated that the man who performed an action is not the same as the man who experiences its results, as a consequence of which he went to hell (DS 6–9). Classical Jainism refused to credit the Buddha with any authority because his knowledge was only partial and not complete like that of the omniscient fordmakers (Asht 1.3–4), and the epithet *jina*, 'conqueror', which the Buddhists also applied to their founder was regarded as totally inappropriate. It was only the Jain fordmakers, it was argued, who through conquering the passions, the senses, difficulties of the ascetic life and harming karmas could be regarded as the true *jinas*, whereas the Buddhists, who for the Jains had an excessively mentalist and therefore illusionist approach to reality, could not accept the real existence of these negative factors (LV pp.223–7).[23]

Certainly, the most prevalent Jain view of the Buddhists was that their code of monastic law, which was less stringent about matters which the Jains considered to be important such as diet and austerities, showed them to be lax and corrupt and the standard claim in the medieval period was that the Buddhists were habitual meat-eaters, although this most likely derives from the fact that Buddhist monastic law states that an ascetic can eat anything which is put into his alms bowl provided it has not been especially prepared for him.[24] A well-known verse satirising the Buddhist monastic life as involving 'a soft bed, food and drink, gambling and at the end of it all deliverance' (Abhayadeva on Sth 607; cf. MSP p.65 and YS 4.102.10) encapsulates the Jain contempt for a tradition whose followers they regarded as no more than householders.

This hostility can be found throughout the medieval hagiographies which frequently describe great Jain teachers vanquishing the Buddhists in debate or regaining control over holy places, and evidence of tension between the two communities is also to be seen in the Jain narrative literature where there are stories of Buddhists falsely converting to Jainism to contract marriages with pious Jain girls (BKK 68; KKP 22; MSP pp.72–3), seeking revenge upon those who have genuinely converted (BKK 156) and generally fomenting trouble against the Jain community (KKP 26).

The Jains interpreted the Buddhist doctrine of impermanence and, as it later became formulated, the momentariness of things as the classic example of a one-pointed (*ekanta*) and inadequate standpoint. Denial of the continuing presence of some kind of permanent entity could only destroy the ethical and soteriological validity of any religious path (YB 464). Change, by which according to the Buddhists the truth of impermanence can be seen, makes no sense without some underlying essence which can provide a locus for modification, and moral anarchy would come to prevail as a consequence of this erroneous belief for, without a permanent experiencer of the results of action who could be deemed to be identical with the performer of the original action, karma would make no sense as an explanation of the process of retribution. The very goal of Buddhist practice, *nirvana*, would seem to be illogical if momentariness dictated that there was no person who could experience such a state (VTP pp.285–306).

Such criticisms were, in fact, hardly strange to the Buddhists and some of them had been voiced from within the Buddhist intellectual community itself as over the centuries it tightened up or modified the categories with which it worked. That the Jains did not wish to consider whether the Buddhist justifications of their position had any force bears witness to an interpretation, hardly relativistic, of Buddhism as forming with Hinduism the two sides of the coin of false belief, with incorrect conceptualisations of reality regarded as combining with a generally immoral conduct of life in both religions.

However, there is also evidence of more ambivalent Jain attitudes to Buddhism and they inevitably centre around Haribhadra. In his two works on yoga, Haribhadra evinces a willingness to acknowledge the areas in which Buddhism and Jainism show similarities, and at times his attitude to Buddhism is a respectful one. For example, he suggests that the Jain who has attained correct belief and the *bodhisattva*, the figure whom Mahayana Buddhism regarded as exemplifying the main Buddhist ethical values, were essentially the same since both were characterised by a willingness to do good to others (YB 270, 273 and 274). Furthermore, one of Haribhadra's most famous works, although not one which displays any noticably pro-Buddhist sentiments, is a commentary on that part of the *Avashyakasutra* dealing with temple-worship called the 'Extension of Play' (*Lalitavistara*) which, apart from a difference of gender, is the same title as a well-known biography of the Buddha.[25]

The medieval hagiographers appear to acknowledge Haribhadra's interest in Buddhism by turning him into a scourge of the Buddhists and, in a story which does not appear to antedate the twelfth century, they describe his violent revenge on the Buddhists who had killed his nephews (see Chapter 5). Such a story may have been intended to 'reclaim' Haribhadra fully as a prominent Jain teacher at a time when Jainism was trying to establish a firm identity to facilitate conversions which might otherwise have been jeopardised through an excessive stress on relativism.[26] Certainly, the account of the murdered nephews has a great deal in common with the hagiography of the great Digambara Akalanka, whose writings were of vital importance in the creation of a near-definitive Jain epistemology and logic achieved largely through incisive controversions of Buddhist logicians such as Dharmakirti. It was also during the medieval period that the story began to circulate that Haribhadra had written the 'Extension of Play' to bring back to Jainism a monk who had been studying Buddhism so intently that he had begun to be convinced by it.

Yet, despite the polemical tenor of such stories, there can still be seen occasional vestiges of the fascination which Buddhism has at times had for the Jains.[27] The following eerie story by one of the chroniclers of the Kharatara Gaccha is perhaps representative of the way many medieval Jains saw Buddhist teachings, as something both alluring and dangerous:

> Once King Kumarapala said to Hemacandra, 'Master, if you could give me the means of making gold, I could inaugurate a new era like the legendary King Vikramaditya'. The teacher replied, 'Such a means is to be found in a Buddhist book brought back by Haribhadra's pupils, but it now belongs to the Kharatara Gaccha'. Then the king arrested certain laymen who came from various regions and had come to his capital of Patan on business, saying, 'If you get the book brought to me, then you will be released'. So the laymen sent word about the matter to the head of the Kharatara Gaccha, who then went to Chittor, took the book from a pillar within the temple of Wishing-jewel Parshva, brought it to Patan and gave it to the king. But when the king saw the following warning written on the book (by Jinadatta Suri), 'This book is not to be opened or recited, but to be worshipped in a library', he said, 'I will not open this book'. Hemacandra said, 'One must not infringe the instructions of great men'. Then Hemacandra's sister, a nun called Hemashri, said, 'I will open it, for I do not fear the words of Jinadatta Suri'. So the king gave the book to her, but as soon as she opened it her eyes started out of her head and fell on the ground. When the king saw how she had become blinded, he put the book away in his library. But during the night the library caught fire and was completely burnt, and the book flew up to heaven where it belonged.
>
> (KhGPS p.28)

9 Recent developments

Reform is on the face of it a convenient enough rubric under which to group the various attempts which have taken place within the Jain community over the last thousand years or so to establish, generally on the basis of textual authority, a fundamental and pure brand of Jainism. However, the Hindi and Gujarati term *uddhar*, which is often seen as the equivalent of English 'reform', signifies literally 'a raising up' (it can also be used to describe the restoration of a ruined temple) and is employed by sympathetic Jain writers in the sense both of a retrieval and reactivation of a basic doctrine of non-violence and renunciation taught by Mahavira and a concomitant rejection of what are regarded as the debased practices which attend this particular period of the world era. The word 'reform', with its connotation of reshaping an existing structure, is scarcely adequate to convey the radical nature of what the monks and laymen to be described in this chapter felt they were doing, namely, cutting away the accretions of sectarianism and false doctrine to lay bare in its stark and simple grandeur a 'true' Jainism situated outside the exigencies of historical time and social circumstance.

This true Jainism was felt to be obtainable in a variety of ways depending on the context: through rejection of image-worship on the grounds that it was not described in scripture, breaking free from the ties of ascetic lineage which were associated with inability to conform to scriptural injunction and the subsequent creation of new chains of pupillary descent, the affirmation on the grounds of the primacy of non-violence of practices such as the compulsory wearing of the mouth-shield by ascetics, the denial of any overriding ascetic authority, the opening up of scriptural writings to the laity and so on.

However, in trying through their purification of Jainism and recourse to the ancient texts to do away with sectarianism, these fundamentalists merely succeeded in perpetuating and expanding it. A true Jainism emanating directly from the mouth of Mahavira, whether reconstituted on a philological or a practical basis, is a chimera, for the textual and social history of Jainism is far too long and complex to facilitate such a reconstruction and diverse modes and idioms of sectarian belief and practice, regional or otherwise, have through the centuries become too deeply rooted within the Jain community to be swept away.

A delegate at the World Jain Congress held in Leicester in 1988 recounted ruefully how a young Jain of his acquaintance, on being asked to define the constituent elements of the *caturvidhasangha* (the fourfold community of monks, nuns, laymen and laywomen), had described them as the four main sects, the Shvetambaras, Digambaras, Sthanakvasis and Terapanthis. It is, of course, natural that many contemporary Jains who regard themselves as progressive would view the variety of Jain sects, each of which claims to purvey the true doctrine, as restricting Jainism's ability to display itself as a mature and universal religion. Nonetheless, the manner in which Jainism has persistently renewed itself by confronting and rearticulating its past is testimony to its continuing vigour.

LONKA

There are few more mysterious individuals in Jainism than Lonka (also known as Lonka Shah), the figure from whom the two main Shvetambara aniconic subsects, the Sthanakvasis and the Terapanthis, ultimately derive their inspiration, although they do not trace their pupillary descent directly back to him. Little can be said about his life with any real confidence other than that he lived in Gujarat in the fifteenth century, and tradition is unanimous that an inspection of the Shvetambara scriptures led him to deny that image-worship could have any place in true Jainism. A standard picture of Lonka has emerged in the last century or so among the Sthanakvasis who would see him as a rich, mighty and learned layman, with powerful connections among the Moslem authorities in Ahmedabad, whose skills in calligraphy led to an invitation to copy the scriptures, as a result of the serious study of which he became convinced that the practice of Jainism he saw around him was without any textual basis and totally corrupt. Accepting the authority of only thirty-two of the scriptural texts and rejecting a great deal of ritual of all kinds, he took some sort of ascetic initiation and became a charismatic teacher who weaned away large numbers of Shvetambaras from their image-related practices.

A great deal of this account of Lonka's life is the product of little more than wishful thinking and the fact that this version has prevailed is in part a result of the failure of the Sthanakvasi community to undertake a thorough critical examination of the sources upon which it is based. However, such an examination was carried out in 1936 by the image-worshipping Shvetambara monk, Muni Jnansundar, in a book about Lonka written in Hindi.[1] Jnansundar was as a historian of Jainism a pugnacious controversialist and something of an eccentric (he claimed as a member of the Oswal caste to belong to the Upakesha Gaccha, a monastic lineage which died out at the end of the nineteenth century), and his book must be viewed in the context of the sectarian polemics which took place between the image-worshippers and the Sthanakvasis in the early decades of this century. Nonetheless, Jnansundar did display a genuine critical acumen for textual analysis and he exposed many of the inadequacies in the traditional Sthanakvasi account of Lonka.

He points, for example, to the basic problem that the earliest accounts of Lonka are given by opponents such as Dharmasagara who lived some time after him and that none of his contemporary followers produced any sort of biography of their teacher. Moreover, the Sthanakvasis spurned the biographical tradition of the Lonka Gaccha, the lineage which claimed immediate descent from him, on the grounds of its lax behaviour and betrayal of its founder's teachings and they did not themselves start writing about Lonka until the beginning of the nineteenth century. As a result, there is no clear tradition even about the date of Lonka's birth (it could be anywhere from 1418 to 1425) or his place of birth, which Jnansundar considers on the balance of evidence to have been Limbdi rather than Ahmedabad. Jnansundar further argues that the key source for the construction of the standard Sthanakvasi picture of Lonka as a great and unusual personage, a biography supposedly dating from the sixteenth century and written by a Tapa Gaccha monk, is on linguistic and circumstantial grounds most likely a forgery.

Jnansundar's conclusion is that Lonka was driven by necessity to Ahmedabad after the death of his parents and was compelled through poverty to earn his living in an *upashraya* as an undistinguished scribe of whose work nothing has survived and whose lack of learning precluded any ability to understand the Ardhamagadhi language of the Shvetambara scriptures which he was copying. Through the contempt in which he was held by his monastic employers and as a result of contact with Moslems, he subsequently formulated his doctrine of rejection of image-worship and all the rituals such as the *samayika* which had become standard amongst the Jain community, although nothing can be reconstructed of this, Jnansundar argues, because neither Lonka nor his immediate followers wrote anything. There is no early evidence for Lonka taking initiation as twentieth century Sthanakvasi ascetics would have it; rather he falsely assumed the role of *acarya* to teach what he claimed was the true religion of the fordmakers and gathered only a miniscule band of followers. Lonka most likely died about 1475 but not by the religious death of *sallekhana*, as many Sthanakvasis have claimed.

A less drastic interpretation of Lonka's career than that of Jnansundar has been provided more recently by Pandit Dalsukh Malvania, a Sthanakvasi layman and one of the most distinguished twentieth century interpreters of the Jain intellectual tradition.[2] Malvania is, like Jnansundar, sceptical about the value of traditional Sthanakvasi accounts of Lonka but feels that some trustworthy historical evidence about him can still be retrieved. He accepts on the basis of the unanimity of popular tradition that Lonka must have been a scribe and that he had some sort of connection with a minister for whom he copied manuscripts. Having studied the *Acaranga* and *Dashavaikalika* and compared them with the undisciplined behaviour he saw around him, Lonka broke off relations with the ascetic community.

Malvania suggests that Lonka's rejection of image-worship was articulated in part under the influence of Islam, although this may have been a pragmatic response to witnessing the destruction of Jain shrines which Moslem iconoclasts were carrying out at this time. This is all still largely inference, but Malvania also adduces the testimony of two works, the manuscripts of which are held in the library of the Lalbhai Dalpatbhai Institute of Indology in Ahmedabad, which he claims were written either by Lonka himself or by somebody close to him. These works, which not only adumbrate an anti-image stand on the basis of the violence which is caused by building temples but, in addition, take issue with the exceptions to general rules found in the texts dealing with monastic law, in fact evince a close familiarity with the Shvetambara scriptures, as can be seen from copious quotations from them, and therefore give the lie, Malvania claims, to the canard that Lonka was little more than an ignorant manuscript copyist with some sort of grievance.

Malvania goes on to argue that Lonka's fundamentalist views developed over a period of time, with his initial rejection of image-worship being succeeded, as his familiarity with the scriptures increased, by a refusal to accept the relevance of other aspects of Jain religious practice for a doctrine whose exclusive concern ought to have been with non-violence. Lonka himself never took ascetic initiation but there can be no doubt that he gave up the householder's life and became some kind of mendicant. His disciples did not initially define themselves as a group with reference to any monastic lineage but instead styled themselves as 'the followers of the path of Mahavira'.

It is unlikely that the uncertainties about Lonka's life will be resolved until careful research is undertaken into the contents of Sthanakvasi libraries. There is, however, no real need to invoke, as do both Jnansundar and Malvania, Moslem influence to explain his aniconic tendencies. From a strictly doctrinal point of view, Lonka was in a sense correct both because image-worship is hardly an important theme in the scriptures and there are scriptural statements pointing to the destruction of life-forms entailed in the construction of any building.[3] There is also some evidence that image-worship was regarded as controversial from fairly early in the medieval period. A frequent analogy used by Shvetambara writers, found as early as

Haribhadra, which has the appearance of a rebuttal of anti-image tendencies, is that building a temple is like digging a well in that the violence of the action involved is far outweighed by the benefits, both spiritual and material, which ensue.[4] Another piece of evidence is the story of an image of Mahavira supposedly carved during his lifetime and known as *Jivantasvami*, the 'Living Lord'.[5] This is usually interpreted by Jain scholars as positive evidence for the existence of image-worship from Mahavira's day but, as the story does not seem to predate the fifth century CE, it is possible to read it as an attempt to provide image-worship with an authoritative pedigree in order to refute those critics of the practice who claimed that it had no place in an authentic, textually based Jainism.

Tradition presents Lonka as rejecting the authority of thirteen texts which had become accepted into the image-worshipping version of the Shvetambara scriptural canon and, as a consequence, both the Sthanakvasis and the Terapanthis claim that only thirty-two texts have genuine authority. There is, however, a basic problem about this truncation of the canon in that image-worship is mentioned on more than a few occasions within these same thirty-two texts. Apparently, the standard interpretative strategy employed by those who followed Lonka was to claim that the Ardhamagadhi word *ceiya*, which has a basic sense of 'holy place' and is generally accepted as meaning in the scriptures 'temple', in fact signified 'monk' or was given some other sense that satisfied sectarian criteria (PP vol.2 pp.32–3, 44, 199 and 210), and there is evidence of recent Sthanakvasis changing the accepted readings of texts to harmonise them with their views.[6] In fact, the possibility is that Lonka's basic contention that image-worship and temples should not play a part in Jainism was based on that core group of scriptural texts with old layers of exegesis (*niryukti*), such as the *Acaranga*, *Dashavaikalika* and some of the *chedasutras*, which have always tended to form the basis of monastic study and in which image-worship is of minimal importance. As image-worship is hardly an elaborately described theme in the scriptures anyway, being mentioned mainly in the narrative portions and the subsidiary *upangas* to which the Shvetambara ascetic community has traditionally ascribed less importance, references to it could easily be explained away without any large-scale jettisoning of scriptures.

Unfortunately, this does not explain why thirty-two texts were retained and, while those which were rejected belong mostly to the class of mixed (*prakirnaka*) text which are in many respects demonstrably late, there is in fact no clear evidence to associate Lonka with this. Indeed, for about a hundred years after Lonka's death, there was no unanimity among his followers about the number of scriptures and, according to Dharmasagara, enumerations of 27, 29 and 30 texts were found amongst them.[7] As yet, there is no better explanation than that of Jnansundar, according to whom the list of thirty-two texts derives from the translation made for the first time into Gujarati by the image-worshipping monk Parshvacandra and which therefore reflects both the choice of enumeration of his *gaccha* and the lack of learning of Lonka's followers.[8] Malvania also refers to the reliance of Lonka's followers on Gujarati glosses on the scriptures and points to the weakness in understanding of Prakrit and Sanskrit amongst the Sthanakvasis and Terapanthis, with the exception of a few scholars, until recent times.[9]

The aniconic ideal of Lonka's followers did not long survive the death of its inspiration. Tapa Gaccha hagiographies recount gleefully how the Lonka Gaccha gradually reverted to image-worship, the culmination of this being the public conversion in 1572 in Ahmedabad by Hiravijaya Suri of a prominent Lonka Gaccha *acarya* called Meghji along with several hundred monks (VijP 18).[10] As a result, the Lonka Gaccha, while keeping the name of its founding teacher, abandoned his teachings about a century after his death and there is a great deal of subsequent inscriptional evidence for the consecration of temples and installation of images by *acaryas* of that *gaccha*.[11] Vestiges of its original doctrinal stance lingered on, however, as when a Lonka Gaccha *acarya* on entering a town with a group of ascetic followers would first go to the monastic lodging house (*upashraya*) and only afterwards visit the temple, whereas *acaryas* of other Shvetambara *gacchas* would pay their respects at the temple first.[12] The fact that in 1644 the Moghul emperor issued an edict in answer to a complaint that the lay members of the Lonka Gaccha were not permitted to engage in communal meals with the guild (*mahajan*) of Shantidas Jhaveri, the leader of the Shvetambara community in Ahmedabad, which thus no doubt seriously impeded their business activities, suggests that they were not fully assimilated into the image-worshipping community.[13] The Lonka Gaccha today has no fully initiated ascetics and exists only at the fringes of Shvetambara society.

THE STHANAKVASIS

In time, the Lonka Gaccha was subjected to scrutiny by its own members. A merchant called Lavaji, who was a relative of the great Surat magnate Virji Vorah, broke away along with another merchant Dharmasimha from the Lonka Gaccha in about the third decade of the seventeenth century.[14] As with Lonka, there is some dubiety about whether Lavaji took formal ascetic initiation,[15] but there is no doubt that the substance of his criticism of the Lonka Gaccha was directed to its general laxity and he consequently expressed a wish to revert to the model of monastic behaviour found in the *Dashavaikalika* which did not, of course, include image-worship.

The three monks who came after him in pupillary succession followed the practice envisaged in the earliest scriptures of lodging in ruined and deserted buildings as a result of which the ascetics of this nascent subsect were called *Dhumdhiya*, 'Searchers' (for suitable lodgings). The Sthanakvasis, as they are known today, evolved from these monks, the name meaning 'Living in Lodging Houses (*sthanak*)', a reference to the fact that the monks of this sect shunned the *upashraya* lodgings which the image-worshippers erected in the vicinity of temples. Lonka himself is not regarded by the Sthanakvasis as their founder but is rather held to be a great precursor of the Sthanakvasi interpretation of Jainism.

It was Lavaji who was responsible for the introduction of a practice which has continued to distinguish Sthanakvasi and Terapanthi ascetics from those of other Shvetambara sects and which many westerners regard as characteristic of all Jains: the permanent wearing of a strip of cloth across the mouth, tied behind the ears, known as a *muhpatti*, 'mouth-shield' (square in shape for the Sthanakvasis, rather more narrow and elongated for the Terapanthis), which by minimising the destruction of air-bodies and tiny insects through the outflow or inflow of breath is an outward sign of the ascetic's commitment to non-violence. There is no evidence to link the advocacy of this with Lonka, as the Sthanakvasis would contend.[16] However, there are references to the wearing of the *muhpatti*, in early and medieval texts and Lavaji clearly saw himself as reviving an ancient custom which the growing indiscipline of the corrupt world age had caused to fall into abeyance. The disciple Gautama is mentioned in the 'Exposition of Explanations' and the 'Sutra of Fruition'[17] as having a *muhpatti* while another Shvetambara scripture presents it as a necessary part of a monk's equipment and describes the appropriate means of cleaning it (UttS 26.23–7). Early medieval writers such as Haribhadra (LV p.337) also mention the *muhpatti* and one of the chroniclers of the Kharatara Gaccha describes how the leprosy contracted by the canonical commentator Abhayadeva Suri led to his nose falling off so that he was unable to tie on his *muhpatti* properly (KhGPS p.45). As reference to the *muhpatti* is so ubiquitous and as early western travellers mention it as one of the most striking features of the Jain ascetics they encountered,[18] it is difficult to see what was controversial about Lavaji's advocacy of it.

Shvetambara image-worshipping ascetics today all possess *muhpattis* and one of their most conventional poses in portraits and photographs is with a book in one hand and a *muhpatti* in the other, symbolising knowledge and compassion. However, the *muhpatti* is only tied by them over the mouth on particular occasions such as reciting the *Kalpasutra* at *Paryushan* or when preaching, and then not always, for many ascetics are content with holding it in their hands or placing it in the vicinity of their mouths while speaking. Laymen also, when performing *puja* which involves coming into contact with an image or sometimes when holding up the illustrated copy of the *Kalpasutra* for the congregation to inspect at the *Paryushan* recitation, will often temporarily wear a handkerchief knotted over their mouths to prevent pollution of the sacred objects by their breath. It must therefore be concluded that it was Lavaji's stipulation, reflecting his fundamentalist attitude, that the *muhpatti* be worn *permanently* by ascetics which was innovatory, for all the indications are that, in practice, this had not been the case at an earlier period.

The Sthanakvasis are the least studied sect of a little studied religion. Although the ostensible reason for their emergence was a process of ascetic reform initiated by Lavaji and Dharmasimha, it has been suggested with some plausibility that their members were in fact trying to break away from high caste domination and in reality the origins of the sect may well lie in the realm of lay business competition, a subject about which the ascetic writers are predictably reticent.[19] As with other Jain sects, the Sthanakvasis split at a fairly early stage into branches, in this case as many as twenty-two, based on regional and preceptorial connections whose history is difficult to reconstruct.

During the nineteenth century, the Sthanakvasis underwent a crisis with a series of monks apostatising from what could not have been a numerous ascetic community to the ranks of the Shvetambara image-worshippers, the most significant of these being Buterayaji and his pupil Atmaramji (1837–96) who in what would appear to have been the reverse of Lonka's experience decided, after study, that the scriptures justified image-worship. Atmaramji, although continuing to be known generally by this name, attained eminence as the Tapa Gaccha *acarya* Vijayananda Suri and was one of the most important reinvigorators of the image-worshipping ascetic tradition and a scholar who provided invaluable assistance to many of the early western investigators into Jainism.

The Sthanakvasis have remained a resilient component of the Jain community whose reputation for adherence to the principles of non-violence and compassion is high. A recent attempt to unite the various ascetic groups and their various *acaryas* under one aegis foundered in part because of disputes about whether the use of microphones in public meetings would lead to the destruction of organisms in the air. The Sthanakvasis have also continued to argue that image-worship is a feature of the corrupt world age and devotional activity is focussed, as it is with the Terapanthis, upon mental worship (*bhavapuja*) and also, in the case of the laity, upon individual ascetics. In the past, the Sthanakvasis were located mainly in the north and the west in towns such as Ludhiana in Punjab and Limbdi in Gujarat. Now, however, as a result of increasing internal migration by the Sthanakvasi laity in India, they have become more widespread and Sthanakvasi ascetics can often be found passing *caturmas* in the south of the subcontinent. Recently, the Sthanakvasi monk, Sushil Kumar Muni, has gained comparative fame in public life for his attempts to intervene positively in the various communal disputes which plague contemporary Indian society and the ascetic group to which he belongs have even permitted him to travel outside India to spread the message of non-violence.

ACARYA BHIKSHU AND THE TERAPANTH

If Lonka remains frustratingly obscure, then the eighteenth century Shvetambara reformer and founder of the Terapanth sect, Acarya Bhikshu, is one of the best documented figures in the history of Jainism. The Terapanthis have preserved extensive records of Bhikshu's early life, his criticisms of current Jain practice, his teachings and reforms, the area of his mendicant wanderings, and the places where he spent every *caturmas,* along with a large number of ancedotes about him, so that it is possible to form a more accurate picture of Bhikshu than any other figure before him in Jain history, with the possible exception of Banarsidas.[20]

Bhikshu (often known by the Rajasthani version of his name, Bhikhanji) was born in 1726 in the desert region of Marwar in Rajasthan and it is difficult not to conclude that the rugged and often harsh nature of the landscape of this area imparted something of itself to the uncompromising and vigorous Jainism which he preached. Certainly, while presenting itself in universalist terms, the Terapanth has remained particularly Rajasthani, and indeed Marwari, in ethos and most of its adherents are members of the Bisa Oswal caste to which Bhikshu himself belonged and which is particularly numerous in Marwar and the adjacent region of Mewar. The repeated references in Bhikshu's preaching to the rich and honest-dealing merchant and the feckless bankrupt as being analogous to the upright and the backsliding monk were clearly directed to an audience which came from the sort of rural or small town trading and shopkeeping background common in the Oswal caste.[21]

Bhikshu's family had a history of renunciation within it, as is often the case in the families of Shvetambara monks and nuns to this day, so that it was to some extent natural that he would enter upon the ascetic life himself. After concluding that the subsect which his parents followed was deficient in moral qualities, he gravitated towards a leading Sthanakvasi *acarya* called Raghunathji and took initiation from him in 1751. However, Raghunathji was himself to prove unsatisfactory and Bhikshu's later writings convey a wide range of objections to the Sthanakvasis which suggest that they had, like many Jain sects before them, become entangled in their relationship with lay supporters and had started to build up power bases within local communities and alliances with particular families. Bhikshu railed against Sthanakvasi ascetics living permanently in lodging houses built specially for them, taking food from the same families every day and compelling lay people to take initiation from them exclusively. No serious interest, Bhikshu claimed, was taken by them in their vows or in the quality of potential recruits and the Sthanakvasi ascetic community had become so distanced from its origins that it even saw no wrong in owning money.[22]

In one of the anecdotes recorded about Bhikshu's early career, Raghunathji is depicted as arguing that, since the time in which they lived was the fifth spoke of the wheel, the corrupt world age, everything was inevitably in a state of decline and that as a consequence anyone who could maintain fully correct ascetic behaviour for as little as an hour would become an omniscient *kevalin*. Bhikshu mockingly retorted that if that was the way to achieve the goal, he would sit and hold his breath for that period.[23] For Bhikshu, the Jain path could involve nothing less than total commitment. As he is reported to have told Raghunathji, he had taken ascetic initiation to do something about the state of his soul.[24]

Bhikshu remained with Raghunathji as a disciple for eight years despite the latter's inability to remove his many doubts. It is interesting that the catalyst for his final decision to break away from the Sthanakvasis was the uncertainty expressed by members of the lay community about the authenticity of current ascetic practice. Bhikshu had been sent by Raghunathji to spend *caturmas* at a town where the lay people had refused to pay the prescribed obligatory homage to Sthanakvasi ascetics. On being presented with a list of complaints by these lay people, Bhikshu initially tried to placate them with dissembling answers but, subsequently filled with remorse, he spent the rest of that *caturmas* in an intensified study of the scriptures which convinced him of the justice of the points which had been raised. Returning to Raghunathji, Bhikshu claimed that Jain monks had forgotten the path taught by Mahavira and, on his teacher's refusal to read the scriptures to prove this, he formally broke away from him in 1759 by cutting his commensal relationship (*sambhoga*) and leaving the *sthanak*, subsequently reinitiating himself and the six monks who originally seceded with him.[25]

Although the Terapanthis, as they were to become, share aspects of the Sthanakvasi teachings, such as their insistence on the permanent wearing of the *muhpatti* and their rejection of image-worship and certain scriptural texts, they do not regard themselves as lineally descended from the Sthanakvasis. Raghunathji is viewed as Bhikshu's teacher only in the most provisional sense and the Terapanthis do not acknowledge the authority of any Jain teacher before Bhikshu apart from Mahavira and his disciples. As with Lonka and Lavaji, the only true authority was vested in the scriptures, the expression of the eternal truth taught by the fordmakers.

The name Terapanth was not new. It had already been used in the seventeenth century by a Digambara sect which rejected the authority of the *bhattarakas* and the image-related practices associated with them. The Shvetambara Terapanthis explain the name of their sect in three ways based on the fact that in Rajasthani the word *tera* can mean both 'thirteen' and 'your'. The most well-known of these explanations takes the form of a brief anecdote describing how thirteen followers of Bhikshu were seen by the minister of the maharaja of Jodhpur carrying out the *samayika* ritual in a vacant shop in the bazaar. Knowing that Sthanakvasi Jain laymen would normally do this in a *sthanak*, the minister enquired as to their sect, to which they replied that they were followers of Bhikshu who had broken away from the ascetics who lived in *sthanaks* and that they comprised thirteen laymen and thirteen monks in all. Struck by the symmetry of this, a poet then spontaneously composed a couplet praising them as the Terapanth, the 'Thirteen Path'.[26]

The other two explanations are overtly pious, thirteen being the number of the basic constituents of ascetic practice which Bhikshu was attempting to restore to primacy, namely, the five Great Vows, the five Attentive Actions (*samiti*) and the three Protections (*gupti*), while the Path could also be interpreted as being 'your' since it emanated from 'you, Lord Mahavira'.[27]

Bhikshu and the small band of Terapanthi monks initially had to operate in a difficult social environment and one of them was later to describe the group as embattled defenders holding out in a besieged fort, with their sole strength being the scriptures. There was initially some antipathy on the part of lay people towards them, partly stirred up by Raghunathji, which made it difficult to get alms and lodging, and the first *caturmas* was spent in a cave.[28] One anecdote, which dates from a slightly later period since it concerns a nun (female ascetics were not found in the Terapanth at the outset), describes how a Jain laywoman took away food from the nun to whom she had given it when she discovered she was Terapanthi.[29] Bhikshu exulted in these difficulties, however, viewing them as part of the inevitable trials of the ascetic's life described in the scriptures, and many anecdotes portray him as a stern and often harsh teacher who demanded exacting standards of behaviour and obedience from his followers and who was unwilling to give initiation to those whom he felt to be mentally and physically inadequate.[30] In line with this, elaborate and lengthy fasting remains an important feature of Terapanth ascetic life.

Bhikshu's unbending nature was mirrored in his fundamentalist interpretation of doctrine and, in particular, in his rigorous attitude towards non-violence which he regarded as being the essence of Jainism, not to be diluted in any way. Taking his cue from a scriptural statement (DVS 6.9) which states that the first thing which Mahavira had taught, non-violence, involved restraint towards all creatures, Bhikshu insisted that it was not compassion and giving and the merit which arose from them which lay at the heart of the religious path but continual self-discipline, based on a correct understanding of the nature of life-forms, which alone could stop karma being bound to the soul and eventually effect spiritual release.[31] By this standard, Bhikshu viewed any act of violence, irrespective of whether it was performed out of necessity or not, as bad. Since all souls were essentially equal, to destroy even less advanced one-sensed souls to advance the cause of the more advanced, as for example in the cutting down of trees for buildings, could not be justified.[32] As Bhikshu put it, a one-sensed creature would be no more happy about being robbed of its life for the good of the many than anybody would be to be robbed of his coat so that it could be given to someone else.[33]

In addition, Bhikshu made a firm distinction between two realms of value, the worldly (*laukika*), which included virtually all the types of merit-directed religious practice commonly followed by Jains, and the transcendent (*lokottara*), purely religious sphere which, he held, had no connection of any sort with the worldly. There was, for Bhikshu, no possibility of buying merit, as it were, by religious practices.[34] It is this which can make his brand of Jainism seem particularly severe when compared to other Jain sects. The Terapanth, for example, places no value on a practice which many Jains believe to be both meritorious and indicative of their non-violence, the buying of animals from butchers and subsequent freeing of them, and it claims that this is a purely social action.[35] True, *lokottara* compassion for other creatures and non-violence towards them must be conjoined with correct understanding and ascetic restraint. Giving a poor man money and food out of charity is ultimately no more than a social act, as opposed to *lokottara* giving, the teaching of the path of restraint to all creatures.[36] Bhikshu's message is that of the very oldest Jain scriptures: it is not the duty of the true monk to rescue other creatures but rather to concern himself with his own spiritual development. The purpose of non-violence is purification of the soul.[37]

Gradually, over the forty-four years in which Bhikshu followed the mendicant life in Marwar and Mewar, preaching his radical interpretation of Mahavira's doctrine with an almost evangelical fervour as he moved from village to village, the originally Sthanakvasi splinter group evolved into a community in its own right, with its own lay supporters (the full community was formally constituted in 1764) and, when Bhikshu died in 1803, he had initiated fifty-six nuns and forty-nine monks which, in the light of what little is known of Shvetambara ascetic demography at the time, probably represents a reasonably substantial number. However, it is doubtful whether the Terapanth would have long survived the death of its founder had it not been for the provision which he made to ensure the organisation and continuity of the sect.

Like most radicals, Bhikshu was essentially a conservative and his framing of the *maryada*, a fixed code of practice for Terapanthi ascetics, shows both his dissatisfaction with the fluidity and flexibility of much Shvetambara monastic law as it had evolved from the early medieval period and his firm desire to establish the means by which the true ascetic could be recognised.[38] A series of *maryadas* was put together gradually by Bhikshu from 1772 to 1794 and was to be amplified by the immediately succeeding Terapanth *acaryas* until the fourth *acarya* Jaya brought them together and produced a condensed version, a copy of which an ascetic has to read every day and sign with his name to demonstrate that he understands the implications of the rule which binds him. An annual festival takes place at the end of each rain retreat in commemoration of Bhikshu's issuing the last of his rules, when as many Terapanth ascetics as possible gather to renew their allegiance to the *maryada* and to receive instructions from the current *acarya*.

The Terapanth *maryada* is to a large extent unsurprising in its strict delineation of regulations governing begging, dress, possessions, and the permitted relationships between monks and nuns and the laity (Terapanthi ascetics are not allowed to get any assistance beyond alms and lodgings from lay supporters). What is distinctly new, however, is its insistence on the total centrality of the *acarya*, the assumption by him of all monastic offices and the total subordination of all Terapanth ascetics to him. It is the *acarya* alone who is responsible for the administration of discipline, for the appointment of his successor, for the giving of initiation (although today senior monks can do this in the name of the *acarya*) and it is the same figure who every year instructs each ascetic about his mendicant itinerary and the location of his place of rain retreat. Through this total concentration of power in the hands of the *acarya*, Bhikshu hoped to prevent the tendencies towards fission and the emergence of rival ascetic lineages which he saw as leading to the corruption of the Jain community and the impeding of a correct understanding of Mahavira's teachings. Although there has been in recent years the occasional breakaway by dissident Terapanthi monks reflecting rival lay interests, the authority of the *acarya* has remained central and the lineage initiated by Bhikshu and passed down through his successor and closest disciple Bharimalji, whom Terapanthi tradition compares to Gautama, is still intact.[39]

Of the eight *acaryas* who have succeeded Bhikshu, the most significant, with the exception of the current one, was the fourth, Jaya (often known by his name as *acarya*-designate, Jitmalji) who died in 1881. Jaya was the consolidator of the Terapanth who, among a variety of writings including a translation of the fifth *anga* of the scriptures into Rajasthani verse, collected all the various anecdotes which related to Bhikshu and also introduced sacred days celebrating the bestowal of the *maryada*, the death of Bhikshu and the accession of the *acarya* to the pontifical throne, thus giving the Terapanth a clear sense of its past and spiritual direction. In order to compensate for the sect's lack of libraries, Jaya instructed the ascetic community to start copying manuscripts, with a daily levy of verses being raised on a regular basis. He was also responsible for important organisational reforms of the ascetic community as it expanded. The office of *sadhvipramukha*, the chief nun, subordinate to the *acarya*, was introduced in 1853 and the Terapanthi nuns, who by the time of the third *acarya* had come to stand to the monks in a ratio of about two to one as they do today, were divided into forty-three groups of four or five members which could be reconstituted when the *acarya* saw fit.[40]

The ninth and current *acarya* (from 1936), Tulsi, has presided over a recent remarkable expansion of Terapanthi activity and has been responsible for the high profile of the sect in post-independence India. Apart from carrying out the largest number of initiations of any Terapanthi *acarya*[41] and the inauguration of a development programme at his birthplace of Ladnun in Rajasthan which includes plans for the first Jain university, Tulsi has contrived both to maintain the exclusivity of the ascetic ideal and to lead his sect towards a fuller engagement with the surrounding social world.

In 1949, he founded the Anuvrat movement, dedicated to raising the moral tone of Indian public and commercial life by taking Jainism beyond the Jains, which was to become the best known Terapanthi enterprise in India and an outward expression of the sect's identity. Tulsi's initial statement of intent suggests how it came to overlap with and assume, at least among the more westernised Terapanthi laity, some of the trappings of an internationalist western-style peace movement:

> If an atom (*anu*) has in it the monstrous power to destroy the world, amply demonstrated in the unprecedented holocaust at Hiroshima and Nagasaki, I want to tell the world that we have its counterpart in *anuvrata* – a small or atomic vow – which alone has the power to ward off and counter the threat of an atom bomb.[42]

A member of this movement, as conceived by Tulsi, would take both a general and, depending on his or her status and walk of life, a modified version of the *anuvratas*, the lay Lesser Vows, which through effecting a moral reformation would 'inspire people to cultivate self-restraint irrespective of their caste, colour, creed, country and language, to establish the values of friendship, unity, peace and morality, to create an unfettered society free from exploitation'.[43] Tulsi's attempt to provide a code of moral conduct which would penetrate all areas of Indian, and indeed world, society and revolutionise ethical behaviour was of course obviously utopian and, while it has not yet run its course, a cursory examination of contemporary Indian life would suggest that the Anuvrat movement has hardly had any serious impact. Nonetheless, it should be stressed that Acarya Tulsi is very much the heir of Bhikshu, who refused to engage in sectarian disputes, in his eirenic attitude towards other Jain sects and his attempt to bring about the unity of the Jain community, and the Terapanth has in general accepted that all religions share certain basic ideals and aspirations.

Another Terapanthi innovation, associated in particular with Acarya Tulsi's successor-designate, Yuvacarya Mahaprajna, is the development of a modern form of Jain meditation known as *prekshadhyana*, 'insight meditation', which is designed to 'engage the mind fully in the perception of subtle, internal and innate phenomena of consciousness'.[44] This system, which takes its inspiration from scattered scriptural statements about perceiving the self with the self, while also drawing eclectically on a wide range of sources in other traditions, provides a meditative structure, similar in style to Buddhist insight meditation, for a religion which seems to have lost contact with its original system of contemplation at least one thousand years ago.

The practice of *prekshadhyana* is obligatory for Terapanthi ascetics and, supposedly, for members of the Anuvrat movement, but it is too early to say what its long-term significance will be, although there is evidence of growing interest in it outside India. Of unquestionably greater importance, however, at least for the world-wide Jain community, is the Terapanthi leadership's willingness to break with Jain tradition's longstanding prohibition of ascetics travelling into 'non-aryan' lands and to countenance in the last decade the training of lower-order male and female ascetics called *samans* and *samanis*, at present some forty-four in number, who are granted special dispensation to travel abroad. Although they take the five Great Vows, they are unlike normal ascetics in that to facilitate their activities outside India they are allowed to use mechanical means of transport and to accept food which has been specially prepared for them.

SHRIMAD RAJACANDRA

Like his predecessor Banarsidas, the mystic Shrimad Rajacandra was a layman who attempted to point to the truth of Jainism on the basis of direct personal experience. Raichandbhai Mehta (the honorific name Shrimad Rajacandra was to be bestowed on him by his followers) was born in 1867 in the small Gujarati port of Vavania in a family which was part Jain (on his mother's side) and part Vaishnava Hindu and, although it is difficult to see Rajacandra as anything other than a Jain, the influence of Hinduism was to colour his writings and he often talked about God in the vocabulary of Vaishnava theism.

The accounts of his youth predictably present Rajacandra as a paragon but his short career nonetheless does show him to have been highly precocious. He claimed to have attained memory of his former births at the age of seven as the result of seeing the funeral cremation of a family friend and his extensive reading in Jain and other religious literature led him to the conclusion by the time he was sixteen that, given the imperfections which all religions inevitably evince, Jainism was the best and most true, and he produced a variety of writings before he was twenty which show his familiarity with the technicalities of Jain philosophy.[45]

Rajacandra was most influenced by Digambara texts and, in particular, by Kundakunda's writings about the true nature of the soul. He also subscribed to the view that Jainism had gone into decline as a result of its preoccupation with sectarianism and rituals which were, he claimed, sterile and divorced from any understanding of the spiritual teachings of the religion. In a letter of 1887, he affirmed what his position was with regard to Jainism: 'To be entirely free in whatever way from attachment and hatred is my religion.... Don't forget that I do not belong to any *gaccha* but only to my soul'.[46]

However, it is noteworthy that, despite his initial dubiety, Rajacandra came to accept the validity of image-worship as an aid to spiritual advancement.

The corpus of Rajacandra's writings includes about eight hundred letters written throughout his life which chart clearly his spiritual development.[47] Seldom can there have been a correspondent of such unremitting seriousness of intention. Rajacandra's concerns were solely focused upon his own self-development and the enlightenment of a small coterie of friends and associates. By 1886 he was already making grand claims for himself as a spiritual leader and as a saviour who intended to develop and propagate the true religion, and in 1890 he achieved what he held to be a state of realisation which is described in a letter of 1897: 'I am distinct from everything in all respects. I am only most pure consciousness, most exalted and unthinkable and an unadulterated pure experience-self.... I direct my resultant consciousness to my soul. I absorb myself deeply within it'.[48]

Rajacandra summed up his interpretation of Jainism in his 'Attainment of the Soul' (*Atmasiddhi*), a short verse treatise written in the course of one night in 1896. This was intended as a clarification of a more elaborate letter which he had sent earlier to his close friend Sobhagbhai in which he adumbrated six principles which he held to be central to true religion: the soul exists, the soul is eternal, the soul is the agent, the soul is the experiencer of its actions, the state of deliverance exists and the means of gaining it also exists.[49] For Rajacandra, spiritual deliverance and experience of the self were the same:

> On the cessation of the identification of the soul with the body, you are neither the performer of the action nor the experiencer of its result. This is the secret of true religion. By this religion, there is liberation; you are liberation itself. You are infinite insight and knowledge; you are undisturbable bliss itself.[50]

Despite, or perhaps because of, his commitment to the deeper meaning of Jainism, Rajacandra never thought seriously of taking ascetic initiation. He was a jeweller by profession and a married man with three children who regarded the householder state both as more arduous than that of the monk and as having been brought about by his own karma so that he could engage more fully with inner experience. Although his views about the marital state were essentially negative, it was only towards the end of his short career that he took a vow of celibacy and tried in part to imitate the life of a monk.

The spiritual climax of Rajacandra's life is regarded by his followers as having taken place on a hill outside Idar, a small town in north Gujarat. There he practised intense austerities and preached to seven Shvetambara monks who had become his disciples, one of whom had broken his monastic vows to follow Rajacandra, expounding his mastery of his inner being. A photograph of Rajacandra taken at about this time shows him, eyes shining with ascetic fervour, in an advanced state of physical emaciation, more so than any monk would have aspired to, and he died in 1901 in Rajkot, worn out, one suspects, by the effects of continual fasting.

Rajacandra is best known outside the Jain community for the brief relationship he formed with the young Mohandas, later Mahatma, Gandhi and it is still not uncommon in Gujarat to hear Rajacandra described as Gandhi's guru. The two young fellow-Gujaratis were introduced in Bombay in 1891, just after Gandhi returned from studying in Britain, and he recorded his impressions of Rajacandra in his autobiography, paying tribute to the role the Jain played, at least in part, in his spiritual development:

> I have tried to meet the heads of various faiths, and I must say that no one else ever made on me the impression that [Rajacandra] did. His words went straight home to me. His intellect compelled as great a regard from me as his moral earnestness, and deep down in me was the conviction that he would never willingly lead me astray and would always confide to me his innermost thoughts. In my moments of spiritual crisis, therefore, he was my refuge.
>
> And yet, in spite of this regard for him I could not enthrone him in my heart as my Guru. The throne has remained vacant and my search still continues.[51]

While working in South Africa, Gandhi became attracted to Christianity and he was to credit Rajacandra with providing him through letters with the spiritual counsel which was to lead him back to Hinduism. Three letters survive, which have little specific reference to Jainism, in which Rajacandra proffers Gandhi extensive advice about basic religious and metaphysical matters such as the soul and the existence of God. Of particular interest is the third letter, written in 1895, in which Rajacandra advises Gandhi to follow the duties and obligations, particularly the dietary restrictions, of the merchant caste to which he belonged on the grounds that they were a necessary adjunct to correct moral behaviour.[52] Gandhi was to argue later in his career that the performance of caste duties was an important element in bringing about both social cohesion and self-respect for Indians, his source for this generally being taken as the Hindu scripture, the *Bhagavad Gita*. Rajacandra was certainly familiar with the *Gita*, although he does not refer to it in his letter, and it may well be that Gandhi was recalling Rajacandra's advice when he came to formulate his ideas about Indian society. Certainly, the sources of Gandhi's thought were diverse, as much western as Indian in inspiration, but there can be no doubt that his understanding of the nature of religion and non-violence at times shows a Jain tinge which was possibly imparted to it by his early contact with Rajacandra.

Although it is difficult to gauge the number of Rajacandra's followers today, most Jains would regard him as a great teacher and there are Shrimad Rajacandra temples throughout India and in East Africa, Britain and North America. Rajacandra's emphasis upon self-experience suggest that his teachings will continue to maintain their appeal.

THE KANJI SVAMI PANTH

The most successful twentieth century Jain movement has unquestionably been the Kanji Svami Panth. Kanji Svami was born in 1889 into a Sthanakvasi family in a small village in the Kathiawar region of Gujarat. Orphaned at an early age, he gradually became inclined towards the ascetic life and after a long search for a suitable teacher he took initiation as a Sthanakvasi monk in 1913. Later in life, Kanji was to describe how, riding on an elephant during his initiation celebrations, he accidentally and extremely inauspiciously tore his robe.[53]

That this was indeed an ill omen was to be borne out in the course of Kanji's monastic career. Despite the fact that he quickly became a learned and famous monk, whose nickname among the Sthanakvasi community was the 'Koh-i-noor of Kathiawar', he was never able to engage fully with the Shvetambara scriptures which he was to claim lacked a sense of soul. By his own account, the event which changed the course of Kanji Svami's life was his discovery around 1921 of Kundakunda's 'Essence of the Doctrine'.[54] After studying this text in seclusion, he went on to read the writings of other Digambaras such as Todarmal and Shrimad Rajacandra, as a result of which he became convinced that Digambara Jainism was the true path.

From that moment Kanji Svami led a kind of double life, nominally a Sthanakvasi monk but regarding himself as a Digambara. He began to incorporate Kundakunda's ideas into his preaching and his assertions that vows, giving and fasting were ultimately worthless if performed without any understanding of the soul could hardly have been likely to endear him to the Sthanakvasi community.[55] Eventually Kanji Svami's spiritual crisis came to a head and resolved itself when in 1934, during the celebrations of *Mahavir Jayanti* at the small town of Songadh not far from the great Shvetambara holy place of Shatrunjaya, he threw away his *muhpatti* and proclaimed himself to be a Digambara layman, claiming that he had discovered the true, eternal Jainism which was not dependent on transmission through pupillary descent and which, unlike Shvetambara Jainism, gave access to the real nature of inner being.

It is difficult to reconstruct exactly what happened immediately afterwards in Songadh. Although Kanji Svami did have some devotees at this time, the local Sthanakvasi community was enraged by his apostasy, doubly so since Digambara Jainism would have seemed to many of them to be un-Gujarati, and his very life appears to have been threatened.[56] He took refuge in a dilapidated house owned by a follower on the edge of Songadh known by the English name 'The Star of India', which had been given to it by the British who had used it at an earlier period for collecting taxes, and stayed there for some time in study and contemplation. 'The Star of India' is regarded as the place where the Kanji Svami Panth started and members of the Panth visit it for *bhavapuja* every year on Kanji Svami's birthday. Eventually the local Sthanakvasis seem to have become reconciled to Kanji Svami and indeed virtually all of the three hundred or so families who today live at Songadh and belong to the Kanji Svami Panth claim to be of Sthanakvasi background.

The main source of Kanji Svami's fame was his charismatic preaching, much of which was recorded on tape. He never wrote any books or treatises and indeed did not claim to be saying anything new but merely to be reiterating the words of Mahavira and Kundakunda.[57] His discourses often took the form of running commentaries on Kundakunda's writings and a typical day at Songadh still centres around an exposition of this sort at morning, noon and night. Kanji Svami's ideas were very much those of the mainstream Digambara mystical tradition in which Jainism was presented in purely spiritual terms and the 'Essence of the Doctrine' was regarded by him as indeed being the essence of all Jain teachings.[58] He ignored mundane topics, such as dietary prescriptions, in his preaching on the basis that all Jains would inevitably know about such matters, and his teachings were directed solely to the subject of the soul and Kundakunda's representation of it as the one eternal and unconditioned entity, the correct understanding of which gave human existence meaning and constituted the only true religion.[59]

To a large extent, however, Kanji outdid even Kundakunda in his insistence on the primacy of the higher level of truth (*nishcaya naya*) over the lower one of ordinary life (*vyavahara naya*). For him, the Three Jewels of right faith, knowledge and practice could only function properly on the basis of a *prior* experience of the soul, and the various rituals and merit-making practices of Jainism were regarded as subordinate and essentially irrelevant through their being linked to the passions. According to Kanji, it was only the pure soul which could bring about spiritual deliverance.[60]

Kanji Svami never took any form of Digambara ascetic initiation, although he remained celibate throughout his life, and it is understandable that his stress upon a spiritual inwardness which is theoretically attainable by all should have led to a de-emphasising of the ascetic path, despite the revival of Digambara monasticism in the twentieth century. In an interview which he gave in 1977,[61] Kanji denied that he was hostile to monks since he regarded them as personifying the fundamental principles of Jainism. However, he also pointed out that the abandonment of clothes and other possessions could not make an individual a monk if he had not abandoned internal possessions and he seems to have felt that the taking of the five Great Vows was little more than another means of attempting to gain merit.[62] Despite the respect with which eminent Digambara monks such as Acarya Shantisagar spoke of Kanji, the Kanji Svami Panth has always been a lay movement and initiated ascetics are accorded no special status. In this respect, Kanji Svami stands firmly in the tradition of earlier figures such as Banarsidas.

For his followers, Kanji Svami was the inaugurator of a new spiritual era and the reviver of Digambara Jainism not just in Gujarat but in the whole of India through his turning away of Jains from the quest for merit from ritual and directing them towards the words of Kundakunda. A building programme was started by his devotees at Songadh in 1937 with the founding of the *Digambara Svadhyaya Mandir* ('Study Temple') which has continued up to this day and the complex of massive marble buildings, effectively the sacred place of the Kanji Svami Panth, can be seen from the road by Shvetambara pilgrims journeying from the north to the holy mountain of Shatrunjaya at Palitana. The centrality of Kundakunda for the movement was embodied in the main temple, inside which the words of Kundakunda's five main treatises have been engraved on the walls and embossed with gold leaf. However, Kanji Svami did not reject worship of images of the fordmakers, although he claimed that he tried to distance himself from it as he grew more spiritually advanced.[63] In the course of his extensive pilgrimages (by motor vehicle) to Digambara holy places throughout India, he himself consecrated a large number of temples and images, and *puja*, involving *darshan* and a simple anointment of the image with water rather than the more elaborate forms found among other image-worshipping sects, is carried out regularly by members of the Panth.

Kanji Svami did not see himself and his neo-Digambara version of Jainism in sectarian terms because for him, as for all religious reformers and radicals, there was only one true path, in this case the allegedly pure Digambara Jainism of the soul found in the teachings of Kundakunda and his medieval commentators. What marks Kanji Svami out as both singular and, at the same time, part of the broader Jain tradition, certainly when compared with one of the influences upon him, Shrimad Rajacandra, whose message is somewhat similar, is the means by which he tried to validate his authority to transmit these teachings despite not participating in any Digambara ascetic lineage claiming pupillary descent from Kundakunda. This was effected in 1937 when, at the consecration of the *Digambara Svadhyaya Mandir* at Songadh, he announced that he had in a previous existence been living in the region of Mahavideha and had been present when Kundakunda had visited there to hear the fordmaker Simandhara preaching.

Surprisingly little has been written by Jain scholars about the historical development of the cult of Simandhara. While he has never been central within the religion and does not seem to be popular today among south Indian Digambaras, devotion to him on the part of the Shvetambaras is widespread and one of the biggest temples erected in Gujarat in recent years, that at the town of Mahesana, is dedicated to Simandhara (who is generally known as Simandhar Svami).

According to Jain cosmography, Mahavideha is located at the centre of the island of Jambudvipa and lies between the two great mountain ranges which traverse it from east to west. As Jain tradition gradually reconciled itself to the disappearance of the possibility of enlightenmemt in the region of Bharata after the death of the disciple Jambu, there emerged the possibility, as described in the Shvetambara scriptures, of being reborn in the region of Mahavideha, 'Greater Videha' (Videha being the name of a region in the ancient Ganges basin), and achieving enlightenment there. The 'Exposition of Explanations' describes how time is stable in Mahavideha and does not fluctuate, so that there is no corrupt world age, and that twenty-four fordmakers preach there the doctrine of the Fourfold Restraint (Bh 20.8; cf. Chapter 1).[64]

Fairly quickly, it came to be accepted that there were fordmakers preaching in various regions of the Middle World, the number of them possibly reaching as high as 170 depending on the chronological circumstance. During this particular moment of time, there are twenty fordmakers in existence, known as the 'wandering ones' (*viharamana*), with four being found in various parts of Mahavideha, eight in Dhatakikhanda, a part of the island of Jambudvipa, and the rest in Pushkaravartadvipa, another island of the Middle World. Of these fordmakers, the most popular is Simandhara.[65]

The tenth century Digambara Devasena was the first writer to mention how Kundakunda had gained his knowledge directly from Simandhara (DS v.43) and later writers were to give a fuller account of his journey to Mahavideha with the help of gods. Kanji Svami was drawn to link himself with this legendary event by Campabahen Mataji, currently the spiritual head of the Kanji Svami Panth and the only woman to lead a Jain sect. The biographies of Campabahen, who was born in rural Gujarat in 1924, unsurprisingly stress her propensity for religiosity from an early age and describe how, after mastering a great deal of doctrine and having engaged in contemplation, she followed Kanji around Gujarat while he was still a Sthanakvasi monk to listen to his preaching. In 1932 she claimed to have gained full experience of her soul and, four years later, memory of her previous births, and she eventually informed Kanji that she had been present with him in Mahavideha during his then birth as a prince and that they had both listened to Simandhara expounding the true doctrine to Kundakunda during his stay of eight days, as a result of which the latter returned and composed the 'Essence of the Doctrine'. In token of the veracity of this, she gave a full account of Simandhara's *samavasarana*, an elaborate reconstruction of which based on this description can be seen at Songadh.

Kanji Svami was to regard this story as literally true, reportedly often weeping because of his separation from Simandhara,[66] and one of the temple murals at Songadh depicting scenes from his life shows knowledge of the true doctrine flowing like streams of water from Simandhara to Kundakunda and downward to Kanji Svami, thus providing a mythical charter which authenticated his message. Campabahen was to make an even more startling claim after Kanji's death in 1980 when she stated he would be reborn as a fordmaker called Suryakirti in the continent of Dhatakikhanda.[67]

The Kanji Svami Panth and the great deal of money which has flowed into it from its supporters are administered by a board of trustees with a president elected every five years. The movement is a missionary one which claims an extremely large following throughout India, often Digambara or Sthanakvasi in origin but many of whom also are in Gujarat converts from the relatively low Jain caste of the Halari Oswals, and it carries out extensive publishing and educational projects, perpetuating itself by its willingness to train preachers and run a network of schools. The Panth also contains some sixty or so lower-order ascetics called *brahmacaris*, nearly all of whom are women who took vows from Kanji Svami. Their life at Songadh is a celibate one, but comparatively unrestricted in that they are allowed to travel freely and own property.

It is common to hear Gujarati Shvetambaras speak disparagingly of the Kanji Svami Panth, particularly with regard to the claims made about Kanji's next birth, and a great deal of rumour and criticism circulated about him during his lifetime.[68] Yet it is difficult to avoid the conclusion that a substantial part of the future of Jainism may well lie with the Kanji Svami Panth, at least outside India. Kanji himself travelled to Mombasa and the teachings of the Panth, with their emphasis on direct contact with an ancient scriptural tradition, skilful promulgation of a myth of origin, scaling down of ritual requirements, rejection of the ascetic lineage system, and advocacy of a direct, 'do-it-yourself' form of Jainism based on texts which translation has made accessible to all, would seem to be well suited to the Jain community in Africa and the west, which has largely lost contact with the ascetic interpretation of the religion.

THE JAIN DIASPORA

Like other South Asian religions, Jainism has attempted to alter some of its social institutions in response to the twentieth century and the encounter with western ideas, albeit often in the face of resistance from more conservative and traditional elements of the community. From the early decades of the century there have been vigorous debates about questions such as the right of low caste Jains to worship in higher caste temples, the printing of sacred texts and the ascetic initiation of children and, while attitudes have not always been uniform, particularly with regard to inter-caste marriage, interest in social reform has hardly been moribund.

Nonetheless, what might appear to be a particularly striking example of social change and modernisation, the *Dakshin Bharat Jain Sabha*, the 'South Indian Jain Association', founded in 1899, which invests authority in prominent lay members rather than ascetics and which has through assiduous publication heightened the Digambara sense of identity as both Jains and Indians and mobilised the southern community to build schools and improve education, in fact represents a perpetuation of a traditional institution, that of the *bhattarakas*. Their function, exercised until relatively recently, as spokesmen for the community and promoters of Jain learning has effectively been taken over by the Association. Ostensibly modernising Jain institutions in actuality often represent abiding continuities in the Jain community.[69]

It is predictably among the diaspora, the seventy to eighty thousand Jains now living outside India (25,000 in Britain/Europe, 21,000 in Africa, 20,000 plus in North America and 5,000 in the rest of Asia),[70] whose second and third generation members may have little or no direct contact with the land of their origin but who nonetheless perceive themselves as Jains, that the most obvious signs of change and adaptation to a different environment are to be found. Large-scale migration of Jains, almost all Gujaratis and Shvetambara image-worshippers, to East Africa started in the last decade of the nineteenth century. The prime motive was economic, often being prompted by a desire to escape the uncertainties of rural life, and few of these migrants had sufficient capital to set up in business immediately, solidarity usually being offered to successive groups of arrivals by networks of their caste fellows. Caste connections played a more important role in the gradual rise to wealth of these migrants than their identity as Jains. It was not until 1926 that a Jain temple was constructed in Nairobi while the present temple in Mombasa was completed as recently as 1963, with religious rituals previously being conducted at home or in caste social centres.

Although the Jain community in East Africa participates in a variety of rituals and festivals, these seem to be more a means of maintaining a link with the ancestral homeland and the traditional way of life, for there would appear to be little understanding of the philosophical or ethical rationale which lies behind Jainism. Many connect Jain doctrine and practice with old people and thus feel able to postpone any attempt to come to grips with the religion till later in life. Alternatively, Jainism is associated with monks with whom there can, of course, be no contact in Africa since Shvetambara image-worshipping ascetics are not permitted to travel outside India. Symptomatic of all this is the fact that, while vegetarianism remains the norm at home, many male Jains see nothing reprehensible in eating meat elsewhere, and dealing in tinned meat products by Jain wholesalers is regarded as perfectly acceptable.[71]

East African Jains began to move to Britain in numbers from about 1968 to the middle of the following decade in the aftermath of a series of political crises. As in East Africa, caste membership remained an important component of identity. In Leicester, for example, where a significant proportion of Jains settled, after an initial rapprochement between members of the Shrimali and Oswal castes which led to the setting up in 1973 of a Jain *Samaj* ('Association') which functioned as a centre for the community and which was to become in 1982 the 'European Jain *Samaj*', most of the Oswals broke away and they now compete with the Shrimalis to be the dominant Jain group in the city, another piece of evidence for the inappropriateness at any time of homogenising the Jains into an undifferentiated unity.[72]

While an important festival such as *Paryushan* maintains its centrality, Jainism inevitably cannot be practised in the same manner in Britain as in India. Banks has suggested that the attitude of Leicester Jains towards their religion manifests itself in two different modes or categories of belief, very seldom explicitly articulated, which he describes as heterodoxy and neo-orthodoxy. Orthodoxy, against which heterodoxy and neo-orthodoxy would have to be defined, is the type of Jainism which would be recognisable to traditional followers of the religion in India, involving ritual, recitation of prayers and mantras, full acceptance of the authority of Mahavira and his teachings, and a concern with correct practice and sectarian exclusivity, all typically associated with women and old people. However, since the interaction with ascetics which would be a regular feature of orthodoxy in India is impossible in Leicester, it is an attitude which can only be sporadically expressed there.

Heterodoxy involves an interpretation of Jainism as theistic and free from the metaphysical complexities which many feel to be a feature of the religion, with the fordmakers being viewed as in some way the manifestations of a supreme deity and endowed with the capacity to intervene directly in human affairs and offer assistance. Here, God-focused devotion plays an important part and the Jains who have espoused this heterodoxy see no incongruity in, for example, worshipping in Hindu or Sikh temples.

Neo-orthodoxy, on the other hand, presents itself as modern and progressive, with an emphasis on those aspects of Jainism which can be interpreted as scientific and rational and can therefore be accommodated to and encompass western modes of thought. Representative examples of this idiom of Jainism would be strong advocacy of vegetarianism and the advantages of a balanced and healthy diet, non-violence and relativism, the value of meditation, a rejection of ritual and sectarianism, and a belief in the possibility of unaided self-perfection of the sort achieved by Shrimad Rajacandra.[73]

Whether these two categories exhaust the possible types of belief available to Jains in the west is difficult to say, given the absence so far of any serious research into the community in North America. Nonetheless, an inspection of the literature published by western Jain associations suggests that the neo-orthodox approach is prevailing and there are also signs that sectarian boundaries, the maintenance of which does not make so much sense in an extra-Indian context, are being eroded or breaking down.

THE FUTURE

As we saw in the Introduction, there have been times when the terms 'Jain' and 'Hindu' have not always been totally distinct and there is evidence that Jain numbers declined in the ninteenth century, with many members of the community becoming Vaishnavas. In 1930 Charlotte Krause, perhaps the best informed western observer of Jainism in pre-independence India, published an article in which she discussed the social atmosphere of the religion in the north and the west of the country. She drew attention to what she saw as the predomination of stifling and fiercely observed caste regulations which hemmed in every Jain from birth and the disappearance or conversion to Hinduism of smaller Jain castes through inability to establish marriage alliances with larger castes which excluded them.[74] Although Krause somewhat weakened her case by contrasting this situation with what she claimed was the unified and 'pure' Digambara Jainism of south India, and despite the large-scale reforms and changes which the Jain caste system has undergone since Krause wrote, there are still those who conclude that Jainism by its nature as a minority religion must inevitably disappear as a discrete social phenomenon and mutate into little more than another Hindu caste.

The present writer cannot endorse such a gloomy prognostication. The Jain religion will undoubtedly change further in certain respects but the current sense of identity of its adherents, whatever vicissitudes the community may have experienced in the past, the cumulative weight of a specific historical experience, the richness and coherence of the multidimensional world of learning, ethics, art, ritual and social interaction in which Jains have always moved, and the continuity of so many basic institutions and practices will ensure that Jainism does not succumb, even if it does not dramatically expand in numbers.

Jains have always maintained that their religion is by its very nature and the demands it makes on its adherents more serious than any other (e.g. DVS 6.4–5). Not only that, but the odds against being born a Jain and obtaining the opportunity to put the doctrine into practice are extremely long. As one Shvetambara text puts it, there are six things which are difficult for all souls to obtain: existence as a human being, birth in a socially appropriate, aryan country, birth in a good family, hearing the doctrine preached by a *kevalin*, trust in it when heard and putting it into physical action if one has gained faith and taken pleasure in it (Sth 485; for a similar Digambara statement, see KA 290–9).

According to the Universal History, the numbers of Jains in this world era will dwindle until the end of the fifth spoke of the wheel when scriptural knowledge will be restricted to the *Dashavaikalika*, the ability to engage in ascetic practices will be minimal, and the only survivors will be the shortlived last monk and nun, Duhprasabha and Satyashri, along with the last layman and laywoman, the merchant Nagila and his wife Phalgushri, and the last Jain king Vimalavahana. After their death and rebirth in various heavens, the sixth spoke of the wheel will culminate in a conflagration in which human beings who have degenerated to dwarves living in caves, having forgotten the social skills, will disappear and the current world era will come to an end.[75]

But, during this time, Mahavira's contemporary King Shrenika will have been in hell expiating the karma brought about by his suicide in depression at having been imprisoned by his son and, in the third spoke of the succeeding world era, he will be reborn as Mahapadma, the next fordmaker and the first of a new chain of twenty-four (Sth 693, BhA 739 and BKK 55 vv.304–15). The Jain religion is eternal.

Glossary

Acaranga: the first *anga* of the Shvetambara scriptural canon.
acarya: 'teacher', leader of a group of ascetics.
agama: scriptural tradition.
ajiva: insentient categories of existence.
anga: 'limb', designation for each of the twelve main texts of the Shvetambara scriptural canon.
Ardhamagadhi: Prakrit dialect in which the Shvetambara scriptures are composed.
asrava: channel through which karma flows in.
avasarpini: downward motion of the wheel of time, world age.
Avashyaka: Obligatory Action.
Avashyakasutra: Shvetambara scripture describing the ritual involved in the performance of the Obligatory Actions.
bhattaraka: cleric with authority over Digambara institutions.
bhavapuja: mental worship.
brahman: member of the priestly and learned Hindu caste.
caturmas: four-month ascetic monsoon retreat.
chedasutra: Shvetambara texts containing regulations about ascetic behaviour.
dana: religious giving.
darshan: reverential looking at a sacred object or person.
Dashavaikalika: Shvetambara scripture describing ascetic behaviour.
Digambara: 'Sky-clad', sect whose male ascetics are naked.
diksha: ascetic initiation.
Drishtivada: the lost, eleventh *anga* of the Shvetambara scriptures.
Exposition of Explanations: the fifth *anga* of the Shvetambara scriptural canon.
Five Homages: sacred formula of invocation.
fordmaker: one of the chain of twenty-four omniscient teachers who promulgate the Jain doctrine; known in Sanskrit as *tirthankara*.
Fourfold Restraint: ascetic vow associated with Parshva.
gaccha: ascetic lineage.
ganadhara: fordmaker's disciple.
ganin: leader of a small group of ascetics.
Gautama: Mahavira's principal disciple.
jina: 'conqueror', epithet of the fordmakers.

jinakalpa: mode of life, involving nakedness and austerities, imitative of the fordmakers.
jiva: soul, life-monad.
kalika: scriptural text which can be studied only at specific times.
Kaliyuga: the Corrupt World Age.
Kalpasutra: Shvetambara scriptural text containing biographies of Mahavira and the other fordmakers, along with ascetic regulations.
Kannada: language of the south Indian state of Karnataka.
karmabhumi: land where religious action can lead to deliverance.
kayotsarga: ascetic or contemplative posture.
kevalin: individual who has attained omniscience.
Kundakunda: early Digambara teacher.
loka: the universe within which rebirth takes place.
Mahavira: 'Great Hero', name of the last fordmaker of the current world era.
Mahavir Jayanti: festival celebrating Mahavira's birthday.
Marwari: coming from the region of Marwar in Rajasthan.
muhpatti: mouth-shield.
Mula Sangha: the 'Root Assembly', the most celebrated Digambara ascetic lineage.
muni: general designation of Jain monk.
naya: logical standpoint.
Nemi: the twenty-second fordmaker.
Obligatory Actions: six actions incumbent upon ascetics.
Pancakalyana: ceremony prior to the installation of an image in which the five centrally auspicious events in the life of a fordmaker are acted out by members of the Jain community.
Parshva: name of the twenty-third fordmaker of the current world era.
Paryushan: Shvetambara festival held during *caturmas*.
prabhavana: glorification of the Jain doctrine; giving of a piece of coconut or a sweet after a ritual.
Prakrit: term for a variety of ancient Indo-Aryan vernacular dialects.
pratikramana: ritual confession.
puja: worship.
Purana: Hindu mythological lorebooks imitated by Jain writers.
Purva: category of lost scriptural texts.
Rajput: member of a Hindu warrior clan.
Rishabha: the first fordmaker.
sallekhana: the religious death through fasting.
samavasarana: preaching assembly of the fordmakers.
samayika: 'equanimity', one of the six Obligatory Actions.
Sanskrit: language of ancient Indian learning and culture.
Shaiva: devotee of the Hindu god Shiva.
Shravana Belgola: most important Digambara holy place.

Shrenika: king contemporary with Mahavira.
Shvetambara: 'White-clad', sect whose ascetics wear white robes.
sthanak: lodging-hall for Sthanakvasi ascetics.
Sthanakvasi: Shvetambara non-image-worshipping sect.
suri: honorific title given to a prominent *acarya*.
sutra: Shvetambara scriptural text; short mnemonic rule.
Telugu: relating to what is now the south Indian state of Andhra Pradesh.
Terapanth: Shvetambara non-image-worshipping sect.
Terapanthi: member of the Terapanth.
Three Jewels: right faith, knowledge and practice.
tirtha: 'ford', the Jain community.
Universal History: Jain legendary history of the world.
upanga: subsidiary scriptural text.
upashraya: ascetic lodging house maintained by the laity.
utkalika: scriptural text which can be studied at any time.
Vaishnava: devotee of the Hindu god Vishnu.
Veda: most ancient and authoritative Hindu scriptures.
vidyadhara: semi-divine being.
Yapaniya: defunct sect whose characteristics were similar to both the Digambaras and the Shvetambaras.
yati: non-initiated Shvetambara cleric, often associated with ritual and worldly knowledge.

Notes

INTRODUCTION

1 *Epigraphia Carnatica* (1973: no.117).
2 Jain, M.K. (1986). There are about 70,000 Jains presently living outside India. The statement occasionally made that the worldwide Jain community numbers in the region of 12 million probably represents an attempt to achieve parity with the other major indigenous Indian religious minority, the Sikhs.
3 Bayly (1983: 390).
4 Varni, G. (1967: 1–10).
5 Derrett (1976: 5) and Saldanha (1981: 36).
6 Kapur (1986: 22).
7 Saldanha (1981: 86).
8 Derrett (1976: 4–5) and Jain, C.R. (1926a: 6–12).
9 Mahias (1985: 38–9).
10 Cottam-Ellis (1991: 105–6) and Jones (1991: 136–7).
11 Cf. Williams (1977).
12 Cf. Bender (1976).
13 Banks (1986).
14 Weber (1883–5). 'Uber die Heiligen Schriften' was translated into English in the *Indian Antiquary*, volumes 17–21 (1888–92).
15 Jacobi (1880). See also Leumann (1934).
16 *Indian Antiquary* (1892, volume 21: 14).
17 Barnett (1907: viii–ix).
18 Stevenson (1915). To be contrasted with this is von Glasenapp (1925), still perhaps the most successful book written by a European about Jainism. It never found an English translator, although it was apparently rendered into Gujarati.
19 Jaini (1979).
20 Eliade (1987).
21 Folkert (1989a).
22 Mahias (1985). Cf. Cort (1990). Unquestionably the most significant study of Jain lay practice to date is the Harvard dissertation of John Cort (Cort 1989). Dr Cort is currently preparing this work for publication.
23 Cf. Schubring (1935) and (1977).

1 THE FORDMAKERS

1 For the biographies of Haribhadra, see Granoff (1989b). See also Chapters 5 and 8.
2 For the fullest version available, see Hemacandra (1931–62).
3 Cf. Deleu (1970: 257).
4 Gombrich (1988).
5 Cf. Collins (1982: 29–64).
6 For a version of this ubiquitous story, see Granoff (1990: 118–39).
7 Cf. Deleu (1970: 140–2).
8 Cf. Bollee (1981) and Dundas (1991: 173–4). The terms *gana* and *sangha* were also used of some of the quasi-oligarchies which were eventually swallowed by larger kingdoms.
9 Cf. Collins (1988).
10 Cf. Norman (1983).
11 For the structure of the Jain universe, see Chapter 4.
12 They also differ in the type of karma they have accrued. See Hemacandra (1931–62, volume three: 7 and 346). An important and unique theme in the biography of the twenty-second fordmaker Nemi is his renunciation of the world on his wedding day on seeing the wretchedness of the animals who were to be killed to provide food for the feast. See UttS 22.14–24.
13 Jain women will often refer to the popular belief that Mahavira's non-violence was such that he did not kick out even in his mother's womb.
14 Cf. Bechert (1983).
15 Malvania (1986: 89–95).
16 Cf. Deleu (1970: 163).
17 Jacobi (1884: 79–87).
18 Cf. Bruhn's introduction to CMPC: 6.
19 Wujastyk (1984).
20 For Shvetambara references to the endurances, see Dundas (1985: note 55).
21 Cf. Deleu (1970: 214–20). For the Ajivikas, see Basham (1951).
22 Jaini (1980: 228–9).
23 Cf. Dixit (1978: 7).
24 Reprinted in Mukhtar (1956: 67–79).
25 Jaini (1979: 15–20).
26 Compare DVS 4.1 (trans. Schubring 1977: 125). Jaini's sole textual corroboration of the fourfold restraint is the reference from the *Sthananga* mentioned above. The term used there is *samjama*. Note that probably the very earliest Jain source, the first book of the *Acaranga*, connects Mahavira with *three* restraints (AS 1.8.1.4). The ninth century commentator Shilanka's explanation involves taking them either as representing the Great Vows of abstention from violence, lying and possession, with taking what has not been given and sexual intercourse being included within possession, or, anachronistically, as referring to the Three Jewels of right faith, knowledge and practice.
27 Cf. Deleu (1970: 117).
28 Cf. Deleu (1970: 162–3). See also Bh 2.5 where Mahavira concurs with the doctrine preached by Parshvite monks. Cf. Deleu (1970: 92).
29 Note that IBh 31, apparently one of the early sources for Parshva, is somewhat problematic since it connects him with the eightfold karma which does not otherwise seem to be a feature of Jain doctrine in its earliest form.

30 Cf. Dundas (forthcoming).
31 Cf. Shah, U.P. (1987: 171–2). For the legend of Parshva, see Bloomfield (1919).
32 Shah, U.P. (1987: 171–2). The seventh fordmaker Suparshva is also iconographically distinguished by cobra's hoods over his head.
33 But note the odd exception such as Queen Marudevi, according to the Shvetambaras the first person of this world age to achieve liberation (*moksha*), who did not practice austerities.
34 Hemacandra (1931–62, volume one: 190–4).
35 For the *samavasarana*, cf. Shah (1955b).
36 Hemacandra (1931–62, volume six: 62–4).
37 Bollee (1983: 238–40).
38 Cf. Barnett (1907: vii).
39 Cf. Mukhtar (1956: 60–1).
40 Cf. Deleu (1970: 209).
41 One of the medieval Shvetambara ascetic lineages, the Upakesha Gaccha, now defunct, was unique in tracing its origin back to Parshva.
42 Vinayasagar (1987: 66).
43 Cf. Shah, U.P. (1987: 87).
44 Joshi (1989) and Shah, U.P. (1987: 83).
45 The twenty-four fordmakers are Rishabha, Ajita, Sambhava, Abhinandana, Sumati, Padmaprabha, Suparshva, Candraprabha, Suvidhi (also known as Pushpadanta), Shitala, Shreyamsa, Vasupujya, Vimala, Ananta, Dharma, Shanti, Kunthu, Ara, Malli, Munisuvrata, Nami, Nemi, Parshva and Mahavira. For the emblems associated with them, see Shah, U.P. (1987: 112–204).

    The twenty-first fordmaker Nami occurs also in Buddhist tradition as a king who renounced the world and may represent an ancient figure, authoritative for the various religious groups of the Ganges basin. For the Jain version of his life, see UttS 9 and compare Alsdorf (1974: 215–24) and Norman (1983).
46 Shah, U.P. (1987: 86).
47 Cf. Dixit (1978: 1–21).
48 Cf. Malvania (1981: 152).

2 THE DIGAMBARAS AND THE SHVETAMBARAS

1 For references to the early Jain heresies and the origin of the Shvetambaras and Digambaras, see Dundas (1985: notes 8–12) and Jaini (1979: 5–6).
2 Disgust is taken by the commentator Abhayadeva Suri as possibly coming about through diseased monks exposing their naked bodies.
3 Ohira (1982: 130) and Shah, U.P. (1987: 114).
4 Joshi (1989: 347 and 358).
5 SNKBhP written by Shakatayana (ninth century). For the Yapaniyas, see Upadhye (1983: 192–201). There has been a tendency on the part of some scholars to claim a Yapaniya provenance for works which seem to display a mixture of Shvetambara and Digambara traits. However, it is likely that such works were written before sectarian identities emerged.
6 Another Shvetambara commentator, Shilanka, commenting on AS 1.6.3.2, a passage which describes naked monks, suggests that by invoking a rule of Sanskrit usage the word *acela*, 'naked', can in fact be interpreted as meaning 'partially clothed'.

7 Dundas (1985: note 163).
8 For another version of Jiva's biography, see Granoff (1990: 149–53).
9 Cf. Dundas (1985: notes 20–22) for references.
10 Premi (1956: 244–5). Cf. Misra, R. (1972: 24) for Shvetambaras and Digambaras in Mysore not visiting each other's temples or gatherings at which ascetics preach.
11 Cf. Chatterjee (1984: 353) who suggests that the earliest Jain inscription on Girnar dates from the tenth century.
12 Premi (1956: 245–6). For references to Mount Girnar and a discussion of its significance from a Digambara standpoint, see Jain, Balbhadra (1978: 144–66).
13 Carrithers (1988).
14 See Jain, Balbhadra (1978: 288–303) for the story of the demon Kharadushana hiding the image in a well where it was miraculously discovered by the king who founded the shrine at Sirpur.
15 Krause (1952, introduction, second section: 12).
16 For Shilavijaya, see Premi (1956: 454).
17 *Satyadarshan* (n.d. : 13–14).
18 Carrithers (1988: 817).
19 For this whole subject, see Dundas (1985).
20 Shanta (1985). See also Reynell (1985), (1987) and (1991) for the role of both nuns and laywomen in the Shvetambara community in Jaipur.
21 Jacobi (1884: 268). The leader of the nuns was Arya Candana.
22 Roth (1983) and Shah, U.P. (1987: 160).
23 MA 196 and Malvania (1986: 81). Statements denying female capacity for enlightenment associated with the early Digambara teacher Kundakunda derive from apocryphal works and should be regarded as indicative of somewhat later attitudes. See Schubring (1977: 344–61).
24 SNKBhP, appendix two: 78.
25 Shrutasagara (ShP p.313) and Todarmal (1987: 417). Note, however, the unusual statements of the Digambara Somadeva (ninth century) who in a work otherwise conventionally critical of women refers to their intellectual superiority over men. See Handiqui (1949: 106).
26 SNP 27.
27 Cf. Dundas (forthcoming).
28 Shanta (1985: 513–21).
29 For a nineteenth century example of lay prejudice against nuns, see Bhandari (1976: 127). In the Shvetambara image-worshipping Kharatara Gaccha, the regular preaching by nuns reflects the small number of monks within the sect.
30 Shanta (1985: 525), drawing on research by Bordiya.

3 SCRIPTURES

1 Cf. Graham (1987).
2 Compare the use of the term 'basket' with the Three Baskets (*Tipitaka*) of traditional Theravada Buddhism scriptural enumeration.
3 See Haribhadra on AvNiry 735 and ViAvBh 1119–24.
4 Cf. Varni, J. (1970–3, volume one: 235).
5 Cf. Dundas (forthcoming). For differing Digambara opinions about the advisability of lay people reading the scriptures, see Shastri (1987: 10–12).
6 Cf. Jhaveri, M.B. (1949).

7 Todarmal (1987: 10–11).
8 For the manuscripts at Mudbidri, see Alsdorf (1965: 88–92), Shastri (1987) and SKhA, volumes one and three, introductions.
9 Jacobi (1884) and (1895).
10 Cf. Folkert (1989b: 175).
11 As suggested to me by Muni Jambuvijaya during *caturmas*, Carup,1989. Today specially trained young Jain laymen sometimes conduct the ceremony in the absence of monks.
12 See Folkert (1989b) and (1989–90), the latter with Cort's introduction and notes, and Cort (forthcoming b). For illustrations to the *Kalpasutra*, see Brown (1934).
13 Prajnap, introduction: 206.
14 Ibid.
15 Kapadia (1941: 86).
16 Alsdorf (1974: 113 and 253–6).
17 Ibid. See also Bruhn (1987a: 104–5) and Ohira (1980) for a rather different emphasis.
18 The Digambara denial of the authenticity of Ardhamagadhi and their view that the 'divine sound' (*divyadhvani*) emanating from the preaching fordmaker has to be interpreted by his disciples must be linked to their rejection of the Shvetambara scriptures.
19 For example, the anonymous *Pancasutraka* ed. Muni Jambuvijaya (Delhi),1986.
20 For Ardhamagadhi, see Alsdorf (1965: 12–21) and von Hinuber (1986).
21 Cf. Shah and Bender (1989: 209). See also Kapadia (1941: Chapter 3) and Muni Jambuvijaya's Sanskrit introduction to AS: 28–9.
22 Tieken (1986: 7).
23 Sen, M. (1975: 240).
24 Cf. Alsdorf (1977: 2).
25 Sandesara (1959: 19). Cf. also Caillat (1981–2).
26 Schubring (1910).
27 Schubring (1926: 2). For the Shvetambara scriptures as a whole, see Kapadia (1941).
28 Exemplary in this respect are the papers of Ludwig Alsdorf. See Alsdorf (1974).
29 Malayagiri, quoted by Muni Jambuvijaya in his Sanskrit introduction to AS: 18.
30 Trans. Jacobi (1884).
31 Trans. Jacobi (1895). See also Bollee (1977) and (1988).
32 Cf. Deleu (1970) for a summary of contents.
33 See Schubring (1978) for a German summary of the contents. Roth (1983) provides an edition, German introduction and commentary on JnDhK 1.8, while Bollee, in Granoff (1990: 7–16), gives a translation and commentary on JnDhK 1.3.
34 Trans. Hoernle (1890b).
35 Trans. Barnett (1907).
36 Ibid.
37 See Sen, A.C. (1936) for a summary of the contents.
38 For a translation, see Aup.
39 See the introduction to Prajnap for a description of its contents.
40 See Schubring and Caillat (1966).
41 Edition and German translation in Schubring (1977: 3–69).
42 Trans. Jacobi (1895).
43 Edition by Leumann and translation by Schubring in Schubring (1977: 111–248).

44 For a translation of the 'Doors of Disquisition', see Hanaki (1970). For other descriptions of the canon, see Kapadia (1941) and Schubring (1935).
45 See Deleu and Schubring (1963: 2) for references to different versions of this story. The aniconic sects view references to image-worship within the *Mahanishitha* as decisive evidence of its dubiety.
46 Cf. Bruhn (1981: 12–13) and (1987a) and Cort (forthcoming b).
47 *Indian Antiquary*, volume seventeen (1888: 285).
48 Cf. Kapadia (1941: Chapter 3).
49 NS, introduction: 24 and 29.
50 Bruhn (1981: 12–13).
51 Kapadia (1941: Chapter 2, especially 23).
52 Kapadia (1941: 22).
53 Cf. Bruhn (1987a: 102) and Kapadia (1941: 43).
54 NS, introduction: 23–6 and Folkert (1989b: 176).
55 PNN, introduction: 71–7.
56 Shastri (1987: 15–17).
57 Cf. Ohira (1982: 130–3) and see also Dixit (1971: 79) who suggests that some of the later Shvetambara scriptural texts and the Digambara 'Scripture in Six Parts' were produced with the intention of replacing the earlier, less systematic scriptures and that only the Digambaras succeeded in totally supplanting them.
58 Prajnap, introduction: 235 and SKhA, volume three, introduction: 4–10.
59 Alsdorf (1965: 92).
60 Okuda (1975: 30–1).
61 Buhler (1878). See also Aparajita on BhA 423 and Todarmal (1987: 162).
62 See Jain, Nemicandra (1964: 62), Prajnap, introduction: 238–9, Roth (1986: 129–46) and Shah, U.P. (1987: Chapter 3).
63 Cf. Jain, Nemicandra (1964).
64 For the *Siddhacakrayantra*, see Shah, U.P. (1987: 44–5).
65 Bhandari (1976: 134).
66 Tod (1839: 233–4).
67 See Alsdorf (1974: 160–6), Kasliwal (1967) and Tripathi, C. (1975).

4 DOCTRINE

1 Cf. Ohira (1982) and Sanghvi (1974).
2 Sanghvi (1974: 4) on TS 1.1.
3 Cf. Jaini (1974) and Singh, R. (1974).
4 Cf. Deleu (1970).
5 Ibid: 195.
6 Caillat and Kumar (1981: 20 and 53) and Schubring (1977: 421).
7 Cf. Deleu (1970: 117). For a good artistic representation of the *loka*, see Caillat and Kumar (1981: 55).
8 Cf. Deleu (1970: 123–4 and 127).
9 Hemacandra (1931–62, volume three: 92, 110 and 134 and volume four: 353).
10 Lieu (1985: 22–3).
11 For the various characteristics of the fundamental entities as described in the 'Enunciation of Explanations', see Deleu (1970: 93–5).
12 Cf. Malvania (1981: 152–3).
13 Cf. Deleu (1970: 241–2).

14 Cf. Deleu (1970: 189).
15 Cf. Dixit (1971: 29).
16 Cf. Deleu (1970: 195–6).
17 Cf. Cort (1989: 459–60) and Ohira (1982: 55).
18 Cf. Dixit (1974: 5–7).
19 Cf. Bruhn (1987b).
20 Dixit (1974: 2).
21 Ibid.
22 Cf. Deleu (1970: 100). For intention, see Chapter 6.
23 See, for example, Bh 8.10 and Deleu (1970: 158). For Jain karma as a whole, see TS 8.5–14 and Jaini (1979: 131–3) and (1980).
24 Hemacandra (1931–62, volume three: 71).
25 Cf. Sangave (1980: 241–2).
26 See Prajnap, introduction: 303. See also Sth 461 where it is stated that the part of the body from which the *jiva* emerges at death is indicative of the next birth: if the feet, to hell; if the thighs, an animal birth; if through the chest, a human birth; if through the head, a god; and if through all of these, the *jiva* will attain spiritual deliverance.
27 Cf. Jaini (1980: 234–5). As John Cort has reminded me, the Shvetambaras perform a death ritual, the *Antaraya Karma Puja*, intended to diminish the effects of hindrance karma. The merit generated by this accrues to the dead relative. This partly counterbalances the Jain doctrine that the individual is solely responsible for his karma and the nature of his next birth.
28 Cf. Deleu (1970: 82–3).
29 For a discussion of the implications of this for Jain soteriology, see Jaini (1977a).
30 Cf. Jaini (1980: 223–9).
31 Cf. Deleu (1970: 165–6).
32 Compare KA 435 which states that even a god can be reborn as a tree.
33 Cf. Deleu (1970: 211).
34 Schubring (1977: 344–61). For the text of all the main works associated with Kundakunda, see KKBh. See also Faddegon (1935).
35 Cf. Bhatt (1974).
36 Ibid.
37 Cf. Sogani (1967: 35).
38 For late medieval Jain mystical poetry, see Jain, P. (1984).

5 HISTORY: FROM EARLY TIMES TO THE LATE MEDIEVAL PERIOD

1 Cf. Chatterjee (1978: 79–80).
2 JShLS, introduction: 8 and Shah and Bender (1989).
3 Handiqui (1949: 434).
4 Cf. Folkert (1989b). For Mathura as a cultural centre, see Srinivasan (1989).
5 Handiqui (1949: 433).
6 Cf. Ohira (1982: 120–3).
7 Ekambaranathan and Sivaprakasan (1987) and Ohira (1982: 116–17).
8 Cf. Chakravarti (1974).
9 Cf. Ryan (1985) and Vijayalakshmy (1981).
10 Hudson (1989: 373).

11 Zydenbos (1987).
12 Compare Haribhadra on AvNiry 153 who states that it is inappropriate for monks who come after the last fordmaker to take alms from kings. This also is true of the monks who came after the first fordmaker, although the primordial act of alms giving in this world era was King Shreyamsa's gift of sugarcane juice to Rishabha.
13 Singh, R.B.P. (1975: 6).
14 Jaini (1979: 279–82).
15 Singh, R.B.P. (1975: 113).
16 Cf. Deleu (1970: 142).
17 Dundas (1991: 175–6) and Stein (1980: 79–80).
18 Cf. Dundas (1991) and the translation of AP 34–6 by Ralph Strohl in Granoff (1990: 208–44). For Shravana Belgola as a Digambara holy place, see Chapter 7.
19 *Epigraphia Carnatica* (1973: no.360). Cf. also Hoernle (1891).
20 Shastri (1987: 16).
21 Guerinot (1908: no.548).
22 Settar (1986: 33).
23 Ekambaranathan and Sivaprakasan (1987: no.261) and Nawab (1986: 3 and 57).
24 Bharill (1973: 8–10).
25 Johrapurkar (1958: 11).
26 Carrithers (1988: 818). Cf. also Carrithers (1990: 150–1).
27 Premi (1956: 340–5).
28 Tod (1839: 388–9).
29 Ekambaranathan and Sivaprakasan (1987: nos.55–155).
30 Personal communication from Tony Good.
31 Clothey (1982).
32 Peterson (1989: 286–7).
33 See Hudson (1989: 392) for an illustration.
34 Champakalakshmi (1975).
35 Cf. Rao (1990: 200–13).
36 Saletore (1938: 288–92).
37 Kulke (1985: 132–3).
38 Zydenbos (1986).
39 Ibid: 184.
40 Cf. Granoff (1989b) and Upadhye (1971).
41 The *bhattarakas* were regarded as irreligious by some Digambaras for this reason.
42 Cf. Granoff (1989b: 351–62).
43 Cf. Brown (1933).
44 Cf. Granoff (1989a).
45 Williams (1963: 4–8) and (1965).
46 Merutunga (1899). See also Buhler (1936).
47 Hemacandra (1931–62, volume six: 308–12).
48 Handiqui (1949: 345).
49 Merutunga (1899: 130–3).
50 Chatterjee (1984: 27).
51 Jhaveri (1944: 178–9) and Jain, K.C. (1963: 88–91).
52 Dundas (1987–8: 182–3). Cf. also Premi (1956: 347–69).
53 See Sumati's account of the debate between Jineshvara and Sura reprinted at p.13 of the second introduction of KKP.
54 Dundas (1987–8: 190).
55 Sumati, reporting Sura's statement in debate with Jineshvara. See KKP, second

introduction: 15. For a discussion of Sura's 'Treatise on Giving', see Dundas (1987–8).

56 Cf. Dundas (1987–8: 189–90).

57 Shah, U.P. (1955a).

58 Cf. Dundas (forthcoming).

59 The term *gana* did not, however, completely disappear. Note that the term *gaccha* was also found among the Digambaras.

60 Cf. Jain, U.K. (1975: 72–3).

61 Cf. Klatt (1894: 181–2). This story is in fact traditional. It seems more likely that the name *Ancala* derives from *acala*, 'firm'.

62 For Jinapadma who was appointed *suri* at the age of eight, see KhGPS p.31.

63 For the *suris* Jinavallabha and Jinadatta, see KhGBG and KhGPS.

64 Dundas (1987–8: 191–3).

65 For contempt for ascetics being the last of ten astonishing things that take place in this world era, see Dundas (1987–8: 182).

66 Cf. Jain, K.C. (1963: 19) and Laidlaw (1985).

67 Cf. Klatt (1882: 254–5).

68 See Desai's introduction to BhGC: 21 and Ratnaprabhavijaya (1950: 143).

69 Cf. Dundas (forthcoming).

70 Desai's introduction to BhGC: 34–5 and 43.

71 Ratnaprabhavijaya (1950: 136ff). For male protector deities in Shvetambara Jainism, and especially the burgeoning contemporary cult of Ghantakarn Mahavir centred on the Gujarati town of Mahudi, see Cort (1989: 428–33). See also Humphrey (1991: 202 and 220) for the Rajasthani deity Nakora Bheruji, a form of Bhairava.

72 For a breakdown of the figures of *gaccha* affiliation in 1986 of the 1,330 monks and 4,360 nuns who define themselves as both Shvetambara and image-worshipping, see Cort (1989: 491–4).

73 Cf. Cort (1989: 78–9).

74 Cf. Misra, S.C. (1963: 68–9).

75 Cf. Desai's introduction to BhGC.

76 Findly (1987).

77 Commissariat (1957: 140–2) and Pearson (1976: 139).

78 For Jain castes, see Cottam-Ellis (1991) and Mahias (1985: 37–64). Of particular importance is Cort (forthcoming a).

79 Cf. Granoff (1989c).

80 Cf. Handa (1984: 10) who gives the traditional date for Ratnaprabha Suri as 165 CE.

81 Hoernle (1890a). Today the image-worshipping Oswals in Rajasthan tend to align themselves with the Kharatara Gaccha.

6 THE ASCETIC

1 For the list of *gunasthanas*, see Jaini (1979: 272–3).

2 Cf. Caillat (1975: 99) and Carrithers (1989).

3 Shanta (1985: 361), drawing on research by Bordiya. Clearly, a small number of the nuns questioned did not proffer replies.

4 Halbfass (1983: 104).

5 See the list of those not allowed to enter the Shvetambara order cited by Shakatayana at SNP 9. Cf. also Sen, M. (1975: 288) and Shanta (1985: 488).
6 Cf. Carrithers (1989: 222).
7 As recounted to me by a Digambara monk at Shravana Belgola, *caturmas*, 1986.
8 Barnett (1907: 71–7).
9 Shanta (1985: 361).
10 Cf. Agrawal (1972: 16), Cort (forthcoming c) and Holmstrom (1988: 21–8).
11 Carrithers (1990: 153–4), Deo (1956: 335) and Shanta (1985: 351–5).
12 Deo (1956: 216) and Prasad (1972: 72).
13 Cf. Carrithers (1989: 222–3).
14 Deo (1956: 209).
15 The alms bowls of image-worshipping Shvetambara *gacchas* are coloured in different ways.
16 Deleu (1970: 108).
17 For different perspectives on child initiation, see Moraes (1973: 29) and Sangave (1991: 236–7).
18 Thieme (1970: 770).
19 For the story of Rohini, see JnDhk 1.7 and Roth (1986: 117–27).
20 Dixit (1978: 7).
21 Dixit (1974: 3–4).
22 Translation in Jacobi (1884: 202–10).
23 Cf. Dixit (1974: 4).
24 Hemacandra (1931–62, volume five: 270–2) and Mahias (1985: 106–9). See also Williams (1963: 107–10).
25 There are statements in Hinduism to the effect that all religious duties are encompassed by non-violence. See Halbfass (1983: 19).
26 Mahaprajna (1988: 47).
27 The Shvetambara Terapanthi sect take a rather more radical view of the latter point.
28 Cf. Malvania (1986: 37–8).
29 Translation by Malvania (1986: 40, slightly emended).
30 Deo (1956: 426).
31 Cf. Singhi (1991: 156–8). For a discussion of lay attitude to non-violence, see Chapter 7.
32 As ascetics are not permitted to light lamps at night lest insects be burnt by them, nocturnal study centres around recitation, memorisation and discussion of the scriptures and other texts.
33 For Digambara monks, see Carrithers (1989). For Shvetambara image-worshipping monks, see Cort (forthcoming c). For Jain nuns in general, see Shanta (1985). Savitri Holmstrom's undergraduate dissertation is based on a period of time spent with a group of Terapanthi nuns. See Holmstrom (1988).
34 Ohira (1982: 109).
35 Barnett (1907: 115–18).
36 Cf. Caillat (1975: 90–1).
37 Cf. Bronkhorst (1986: 29–41), Ohira (1982: 89–98) and Tatia (1951: 281–93).
38 Cf. Jaini (1979: 254–6).
39 See Ohira's introduction to Dhs: 18 and 24, referring to Upadhye's citation of Abhinavagupta's *Tantraloka*. Note that 'Ocean of Knowledge' is also the name of a scriptural text of the Shaiva Kaula lineage. By using this title, Shubhachandra

may have been signalling that he was serving as a vector for the introduction of Hindu ideas into Jainism.

40 Shanta (1985: 372).

41 References to the *Avashyakas* occur at DVS 4 and UttS 29. These represent later prose interpolations.

42 Cf. Bruhn (1981: 18) and Leumann (1934). Now fundamental for any consideration of the *Avashyaka* literature is Dr Nalini Balbir's *thèse d'état*. See Balbir (1986).

43 Cf. Shanta (1985: 532–5).

44 Malvania (1986: 62) and Shanta (1985: 536).

45 Bruhn (1981: 24).

46 Translation by Williams (1963: 204).

47 Cf. Caillat (1975: 116–39) and Williams (1963: 203–7). Note the distinction between *samayika* as general cessation from negative activity and *pratikramana* as cessation from specific examples from it. See Aparajita on BhA 118.

48 Cf. Bruhn (1981: 31–2) and Shanta (1985: 532–5).

49 Cf. Deleu (1970: 130). See also Bh 7.5 and Deleu (1970: 148) for a layman performing *pratikramana* and *pratyakhyana*.

50 Williams (1963: 168).

51 Cf. Cort (1989: 246–52).

52 Sen, M. (1975: 218). Stays of up to a month in one place are, from the medieval period, regarded as perfectly acceptable.

53 Cf. von Glasenapp (1925: 331–2). Prominent Shvetambara laymen in the seventeenth century were able to legislate about who was eligible for preliminary initiation (Gokhale (1978: 137)), a practice which has occurred very occasionally in this century (personal communication from Kanubhai Sheth), and there were also occasions when lay influence was exerted upon the appointment of *acaryas*. Cf. Commissariat (1957: 143).

54 Cf. Mahias (1985: 241).

55 MA 812–28. Cf. Carrithers (1989: 227–8), Fischer and Jain (1978, part one), Mahias (1985: 246–51) and Williams (1963: 149–66). Note that the Shvetambara text, the *Kalpasutra*, differentiates between monks who eat out of their cupped hands and those who use alms bowls, signalling the existence side by side of two different styles of alms-taking in the ancient, pre-sectarian Jain ascetic community. See Jacobi (1884: 301–2).

56 Cf. Balbir (1982, introduction).

57 Cf. Williams (1963: 110–13).

58 See Dundas (1985: notes 45–7) for references.

59 Bollee (1977: 63) and Prasad (1972: 117–18).

60 Deo (1956: 172–3) and Sen, M. (1975: 139–40).

61 Cf. Caillat (1975), Sen, M. (1975) and Tatia and Kumar (1981). There is nothing truly comparable to the *chedasutras* among the Digambaras. The *Bhagavati Aradhana* (BhA) and the *Mulacara* (MA) are mainly concerned with the structure of the ascetic path in its broadest sense and seldom legislate for highly specific situations as do the Shvetambara texts.

62 Cf. Tripathi, C. (1983: 119–20).

63 NishithS, volume one (Hindi introduction): 12 and Shanta (1985: 315).

64 Cf. Caillat (1975: 81–6).

65 Cf. Malvania (1986: 31).

66 BhGC, introduction : 56.

67 Cf. Deleu (1970: 89–90). Note, however, that as recently as the nineteenth century, some Jain women in Rajasthan have engaged in the practice of *sati* ('suttee'), culturally prestigious among some Rajput groups, by immolating themselves on their husband's funeral pyre. See Somani (1982: 79–80).
68 Cf. Caillat (1977b).
69 Cf. Caillat (1977a).
70 Williams (1963: 166).
71 *Times of India*, September 19, 1989.
72 Caillat (1975: 51). Cf. also Cort (forthcoming c).
73 Deo (1956: 222).
74 *Acaryas* of the image-worshipping Shvetambara sects will also take a new name on installation. In the Tapa Gaccha all monks have either the words *Vijaya*, 'victory', or *Sagar*, 'ocean', as the second element of their post-initiation names. According to fairly recent custom, on becoming *acarya* a monk will reverse the order of the elements of his name. So Muni Vallabhavijaya subsequently became formally known as Vijayavallabha Suri (the latter word being an honorific title). Some prominent teachers continue to be known by their pre-*acarya* names. For example, only very rarely is the great Hiravijaya referred to as Vijayahira Suri.
75 Hoernle (1890a: 239).
76 Personal communication from Muni Jambuvijaya. Cf. also Cort (forthcoming c). Such authority as there was, was exercised by *ganins*.
77 Cf. Burgess (1884: 277–8) and Cort (forthcoming c). There is a very small number of *yatis* still in existence in west India today.
78 *Atmavallabh* (1989, first section: 63). For a list of *samudays* within the Tapa Gaccha, see Cort (1989: 491).
79 For Shantisagar's life, I have drawn on *Shri 108 Caritracakravarti Acarya Shantisagar... Smriti Granth*. See also Carrithers (1989 and (1990).

7 THE LAY PERSON

1 Cf. Deleu (1970: 181). See also Norman (1991).
2 Cf. Jaini (1979: 186).
3 The term *upasaka* seems to have remained longer in use among the Digambaras.
4 Ratnasenavijaya (1984: 4).
5 Cf. Jaini (1979: 169–87).
6 Cf. Cort (1989) and (forthcoming d). For the Jain understanding of auspiciousness, see Jaini (1985).
7 For prescriptions about lay behaviour in the medieval digests, see Williams (1963).
8 Cf. Cort (forthcoming d).
9 Muktiprabhavijaya (n.d.).
10 Ibid: 80.
11 Laidlaw (1985: 54).
12 Banarsidas (1981).
13 Ibid: 86.
14 Banarsidas (1981: 86–7).
15 Banarsidas (1981: 92).
16 Cf. Deleu (1970: 111).

17 For Shantidas and Virji, see Commissariat (1957), Gokhale (1978), Pearson (1976) and Tripathi, D. (1981).
18 Bayly (1983: 141).
19 Cf. Dobbin (1989: 128–9). Dobbin is specifically discussing the Marwaris, consisting of both Jains and Hindus, who migrated from Rajasthan to eastern India.
20 *India Today* (International edition), July 15, 1988. For north Indian business culture in the eighteenth and nineteenth centuries, see Bayly (1983). For *abru*, see Haynes (1987). For hospitals where sick and aged animals are given refuge, see Lodrick (1981).
21 Note the importance for the Hindu linkage of wealth, religious giving and piety of the story of Sudama which was in the medieval period very popular in Gujarat. The poor but pious brahman Sudama had vast wealth bestowed on him through his devotion to Krishna to whom he had been able to give in offering only a handful of rice. See Mallison (1979).
22 Bender (1986) and Bloomfield (1923).
23 Cf. Bayly (1983: 370–84) and Cort (forthcoming d).
24 If the bidding takes place in a temple, then the money raised becomes inalienable *devadravya*, 'property of the god', and should only be used for worship and the upkeep of the temple, although the matter in which such money is disbursed can in fact become a matter of controversy. For the bad karma which accrues from misuse of temple funds, see MSP pp.93–5.
25 Cf. Banks (1991a) for bidding amongst Jains in Britain.
26 Compare the *rohinitapas*, a fast undertaken on a particular astrological conjunction for a period of fourteen years and fourteen months, which was once observed by both men and women but is now followed by women only. See Johnson (1948: 168). For Jain fasting in general, see Cort (1989: Chapter 5), Mahias (1985: 111–25) and Williams (1963: 142–9).
27 For the connection between women and fasting, see Reynell (1985) and (1987). Singhi (1991: 144) states that fasting by women may sometimes be indicative of family problems.
28 Cf. Mahias (1985: 115).
29 Mahias (1985: 116).
30 Southern Digambaras do not seem to process in celebration of the completion of fasts. See Carrithers (1991: 278).
31 Bhadrankaravijaya (1980: 43).
32 Shah, U.P. (1987: 15 and 33).
33 Shah, U.P. (1987: Chapter 3).
34 Cf. Joshi (1989).
35 Ghosh, A. (1974: 479–81 and 487) and Shah, U.P. (1987: 37).
36 von Mitterwallner (1989: 370).
37 Ghosh, A. (1974: 38).
38 Cf. Shah, U.P. (1987: 23). See also Shah and Dhaky (1975). There is no standard architectural style for Jain temples and regional variations occur.
39 The medieval texts on lay behavior state that the ability to perform *puja* may be defined by the financial means of the worshipper and that a poor person should content himself with *bhavapuja*. See Williams (1963: 224).
40 Bhadrankaravijaya (1980: 8, 12, 25, 37–8 and 185).
41 Kalyanavijaya (1966: 7).
42 Williams (1963: 219–20).

43 Kalyanavijaya (1966: 70–3).
44 Cf. Kalyanavijaya (1966: 75–6) for the rejection of *arati* and other elements of the eightfold *puja* by the image-worshipping Shvetambara sect, the Ancala Gaccha. Spontaneous dancing by lay people in front of images does occur today.
45 Babb (1988), Humphrey (1985) and Mahias (1985: 253–7). The fullest account of Jain worship to date is Cort (1989: Chapter 7). For twentieth century Jain accounts, see Bhadrankaravijaya (1980) and Jain, C.R. (1926b).
46 Jains do, however, share the Hindu custom of the communal singing of devotional hymns (*bhajan*).
47 Very occasionally the four corners of the svastika are explained as representing the four components of the Jain community (monks, nuns, laymen and laywomen).
48 There is no total agreement about this among Babb (1988), Humphrey (1985) and Mahias (1985).
49 Bhadrankaravijaya (1980: 143–4).
50 Ibid.
51 Babb (1988: 83). Note, however, that the term *prasad* is often used informally by Jains to refer to the rather similar custom of *prabhavana*.
52 Cf. Cort (1987: 242–3).
53 Cf. Cort (1987: 242–3), Jaini (1991: 195) and Shah, U.P. (1987: 220).
54 Krause (1952: 12–13) and Shah, U.P. (1987: 213–14).
55 Shah, U.P. (1987: 278–9).
56 Singh, R.B.P. (1975: 55).
57 Cf. Cort (1987), Granoff (1990: 183–4) and Shah, U.P. (1987: 246–7).
58 Cort (1987: 236) and Ghosh, N. (1974: 78–98).
59 Bhuvanavijaya (1980: 81–91) and Pracandiya (1987: 209–10).
60 Misra, R. (1972: 21).
61 For the role of fairs in Rajasthan, see Humphrey (1991).
62 For a detailed account of the Shvetambara religious year, see Cort (1989: Chapter 4). For a list of Jain festivals, see Jain, J. P. (1975: 119–24).
63 Bhuvanavijaya (1980: 56) and Cort (1989: 223).
64 Cf. Cort (1989: 218–19). While Hastinapur is holy to both Shvetambaras and Digambaras, the continuous presence there of the prominent Digambara nun, Aryika Jnanmati, officially justified by her ill health, ensures Digambara pilgrimage to the site all year round. See Balbir (1990).
65 Cf. McCormick (forthcoming).
66 Cf. Hemacandra (1931–62, volume six: 352). But see also Shah, U.P. (1955b: 9).
67 Cf. Cort (1988).
68 See also VTK 8 translated by Cort in Granoff (1990: 258–60).
69 The others are Mount Girnar, Mount Abu, Mount Sammeta in Bihar, the site of the liberation of several fordmakers, and the legendary Mount Ashtapada, the scene of Rishabha's liberation, which Jains would identify with Mount Kailasa in the Himalayas. This system of five holy spots can be mapped onto smaller, regional pilgrimage networks. See Cort in Granoff (1990: 288).
70 PNN, pp.350–60.
71 Cf. Granoff (1988: 48).
72 For a translation of VTK 1 which describes Shatrunjaya, see Cort in Granoff (1990: 246–51).
73 Kanchansagarsuri (1982: 6).
74 Cf. *Atmavallabh* (1989) and Jain, J. (1980: 51).

75 Commissariat (1957: 245–6 and 253).
76 Tripathi, D. (1981: 50 and 199).
77 For Shravana Belgola, see Doshi (1981), *Epigraphia Carnatica* (1973), Kalghatgi (1981), Sangave (1985) and Settar (1986).

8 JAIN RELATIVISM AND RELATIONS WITH HINDUISM AND BUDDHISM

1 Sunavala (1922: 44). For the Hindi original of Vijayavallabha's statement, see *Atmavallabh* (1989: unpaginated section).
2 Todarmal (1987: 44).
3 For Hemacandra, see Merutunga (1899: 106).
4 *Lokatattvanirnaya* 38. Compare YB 525 and see also Halbfass (1988: 536).
5 Cf. Halbfass (1979: 196–8).
6 Sanghvi (1963).
7 Cf. Deleu (1970: 89) and Matilal (1981: 20–2).
8 Dixit (1971: 148). The *Tattvarthasutra* does not, like Mallavadin, define Jainism in terms of other contemporary religio-philosophical paths.
9 Cf. Matilal (1981: 41–6).
10 For references, see AJP, introduction: cxi–cxii.
11 Cf. Matilal (1981: 47–56).
12 Cf. Sinari (1969).
13 Cf. Jha (1978).
14 Cf. Kumar (n.d.).
15 Jaini (1977b).
16 Handiqui (1949: 332).
17 Jaini (1984).
18 But compare DhMV 25 where the Mahabharata war is described as having been brought about by Duryodhana, the leading Kaurava, having cursed a Jain monk.
19 Kansara (1976) and Shanta (1985: 454).
20 For the incorporation of the *vidyadharas* into Jain mythology, see Alsdorf (1974: 71–100).
21 Cf. Bollee (1977: 72ff).
22 Cf. Bollee (1974: 28). For parallels between early Jain and Buddhist literature, see Nakamura (1983).
23 Mahayana Buddhism is being travestied here.
24 Sen, M. (1975: 301). As noted in Chapter 6, there is evidence that early Jainism at times permitted the consumption of meat.
25 Cf. Bollee (1974: 34).
26 Cf. Granoff (1989b).
27 Jaini (1968) describes a Buddhist text which was employed for ritual purposes among the Shvetambaras of Gujarat, although it was most likely introduced by brahman temple-servants (*pujari*).

9 RECENT DEVELOPMENTS

1 Jnansundar (1936).
2 Malvania (1964).
3 See *Prashnavyakaranani* 1.6 quoted by Mahaprajna (1988: 36).

4 For the analogy of the well, see Kalyanavijaya (1966: 32–7). Cf. also Abhayadeva Suri on Sth 125 (quoting Haribhadra), KKP 16 and PP vol.2, p.71 and p.78. Yashovijaya wrote a treatise on the analogy of the well called *Kupadrishtantavishadikarana* (ed. Yashodevasurishvara, Bombay 1980).
5 Cf. Shah, U.P. (1987: 33–6).
6 Jnansundar (1936: 67–8).
7 Referred to by Malvania (1964: 378).
8 Jnansundar (1936: 63–5 and 109).
9 Malvania (1964: 378).
10 Cf. Jnansundar (1936: 271) and Malvania (1964: 371–2).
11 Jnansundar (1936: 110 and 273).
12 Jnansundar (1936: 5).
13 Commissariat (1957: 186).
14 There is uncertainty about the date. See Malvania (1964: 370–1).
15 Jnansundar (1936: 311) does not regard Lavaji as having had a guru while, according to Malvania (1964: 370), there is some evidence for him having taken initiation from a *yati* in either 1648 or 1652.
16 Jnansundar (1936: 123 and 126).
17 Bh 2.5 and see Shah, U.P. (1987: 20).
18 Cf. Williams (1977: 260).
19 Cort (1989: 140–1).
20 Rampuriya (1981).
21 Cf. Mahaprajna (1985: 34 and 38) and Rampuriya (1981: 213, 280, 353 and 357).
22 Mahprajna (1985: 6–8).
23 Jayacarya (1987: no.108).
24 Rampuriya (1981: 50).
25 Rampuriya (1981: 32–50).
26 Jayacarya (1981: vv.625–6).
27 Rampuriya (1981: 83–95).
28 Cf. Rampuriya (1981: 102–8, 129, 133 and 406). See also Mahaprajna (1985: 40 and 52).
29 Rampuriya (1981: 126).
30 Rampuriya (1981: 128, 289 and 502–3). See also Mahaprajna (1985: 42, 72 and 154).
31 Mahaprajna (1988: 135).
32 Mahaprajna (1985: 81–2, 92 and 98–9).
33 Mahaprajna (1985: 85).
34 Mahaprajna (1985: 75 and 111). See Jaini (1985).
35 Cf. Rampuriya (1981: 369).
36 Mahaprajna (1985: 118–19).
37 Rampuriya (1981: 60, 62 and 136).
38 Cf. Mahaprajna (1985: 505–19).
39 Jayacarya (1981: v.949).
40 Bhandari (1976).
41 According to Balbir (1983), in 1981 there were in the Terapanth 501 nuns and 218 monks. By 1987, out of a total Terapanthi population estimated at 50,000, there were 577 nuns and 150 monks. See Holmstrom (1988).
42 Bhatnagar (1985: 1).
43 Tulsi (1988: 8).
44 Mahaprajna (1987: 1).

45 Mehta (n.d.) and Mehta and Sheth (1971: 43).
46 Mehta and Sheth (1971: 111, altered) and *Shrimad Rajacandra* (1985: 172).
47 *Shrimad Rajacandra* (1985). This is a Hindi translation of the Gujarati original.
48 Mehta and Sheth (1971: 122, altered).
49 Rajacandra (1976: vv.35–44).
50 Rajacandra (1976: vv.115–16).
51 Gandhi (1949: 74–5).
52 *Shrimad Rajacandra* (1985: 533).
53 Bharill (1981: 11).
54 Bharill (1981: 44).
55 *Atmadharm Visheshank* (1989: 18).
56 Cf. *Atmadharm Visheshank* (1989: 96).
57 Bharill (1981: 93 and 100).
58 *Atmadharm Visheshank* (1989: 85).
59 Bharill (1981: 138–41).
60 *Atmadharm Visheshank* (1989: 22, 24 and 26).
61 Bharill (1981: 131–7).
62 Bharill (1981: 127).
63 Bharill (1981: 45). There also exist 'scripture-temples' among the image-worshipping Shvetambaras.
64 Cf. Deleu (1970: 256). Buddhism also has legends about disciples of the Buddha living in Mahavideha.
65 Cf. Krause (1952) and Shah, U.P. (1987: 100–1). The following references may be useful to future students of Simandhara.

The earliest reference to Simandhara (whose name is in origin probably some kind of regal epithet) is found in the *Vasudevahindi* (fourth century CE) where the possibility of journeying to Mahavideha to seek the fordmaker's advice is described (VH p.84), and similar accounts are found in the early Digambara Puranas (PadP 23.7–8 and HVP 43.79). In Shvetambara tradition, Simandhara is associated with learning and authority. On being questioned by the god Indra, he is able to identify a great teacher who can explain the difficult subject of the microscopic life-forms known as *nigoda* (Haribhadra on AvNiry 777). Other stories describe how portions of the *Acaranga* and the *Dashavaikalika* were retrieved from Simandhara. See Jambuvijaya, Sanskrit introduction to AS 25 and Ghatage (1935). Abhayadeva Suri was supposedly given Simandhara's exegetical assistance when composing his scriptural commentary (PC 19.110. Cf. also KhGPS p.45 for another connection between Simandhara and Abhayadeva). By the medieval period, Shvetambara and Digambara writings of dubious authenticity were being attributed to Simandhara and his influence, as were certain Shvetambara sectarian innovations. See SVT, introduction: 71–2, Sen, A.C. (1936: 478) and also Ratnaprabhavijaya (1950: 63–5) for a link between Simandhara and the founding of the Ancala Gaccha.

Some of the chroniclers of the Kharatara Gaccha, which seems to have been the first Shvetambara sect to engage in large-scale installation of images of Simandhara (but cf. PPS p.26 for a Simandhara temple consecrated by Devacarya at Dholka in Gujarat at the beginning of the twelfth century), claim that the *surimantra*, the magic and secret spell whose transmission validated the authority of the heads of that sect, was obtained from Simandhara (KhGPS p.20 and VP 1). Compare SMKS p.266 where the mantra is given by Simandhara to the goddess

Ambika who transmits it to the teacher Manadeva who in turn passes it on to Haribhadra. For Haribhadra's praise of Simandhara, see LV p.375.

Finally, a curious anecdote relating to Acarya Bhikshu, recorded in the nineteenth century by the fourth Terapanthi *acarya* Jaya, describes how a layman, plagued by doubts about Jain doctrine but living too far away from Bhikshu to get his assistance, committed suicide so that he might be reborn in the presence of Simandhara who would resolve his difficulties. See Jayacarya (1987: no.194).

66 *Atmadharm Visheshank* (1989: 98).

67 For Cambahen Mataji, see *Pujya Bahinshri Janmajayanti Visheshank* (1989).

68 Bharill (1981: 64–7, 81, 134–5 and 144). See also Malvania (1986: 24).

69 Carrithers (1991) and Sangave (1991).

70 Figures taken from Cort (1989: 342).

71 For Jains in East Africa, see Zarwan (1974) and (1975). See also Banks (1985).

72 Banks (1985), (1991a) and (1991b: 242–4).

73 Banks (1991b).

74 Krause (1930).

75 Cf. Hemacandra (1931–62, volume six: 340–4) and UR 54. For different Digambara names, cf. von Glasenapp (1925: 306).

Sources in Sanskrit and Prakrit

AJP: Haribhadra, *Anekantajayapataka*, ed. H.R. Kapadia, two volumes, Baroda 1940 and 1947.

AnDh: Ashadhara, *Anagaradharmamrita*, ed. Kailashcandra Shastri, New Delhi 1975.

AP: Jinasena, *Adipurana*, ed. Pannalal Jain, two volumes, Kashi 1964 and 1965.

AS: *Acarangasutra* with Shilanka's commentary, in Muni Jambuvijaya (ed.) *Acarangasutram and Sutrakritangasutram* (re-edition of Agamodaya Samiti edition), Delhi 1978.

Asht: Haribhadra, *Ashtakaprakarana*, Ahmedabad 1918.

Aup: *Uvavaiya Suttam*, ed. Ganesh Lalwani with English trans. by K.C. Lalwani, Jaipur 1988.

AvCu: Jinadasa, *Avashyakacurni*, two volumes, Ratlam 1928 and 1929.

AvNiry: Bhadrabahu, *Avashyakaniryukti* with Haribhadra's commentary (reprint of Agamodaya Samiti edition), volume one, Bombay 1981.

AvS: *Avashyakasutra* in *Dasaveyaliyasuttam, Uttarajjhayanaim and Avassayasuttam*, ed. Muni Punyavijaya and Amritlal Mohanlal Bhojak (Jaina Agama Series 15), Bombay 1977.

Bh: *Viyahapannatti (Bhagavai)*, in Pupphabhikkhu (ed.) *Suttagame* volume one, Gurgaon 1953.

BhA: Shivarya, *Bhagavati Aradhana* with Aparajita Suri's commentary, ed. Kailashcandra Siddhantashastri, Sholapur 1978.

BhGC: Siddhicandra, *Bhanucandraganicarita*, ed. Mohanlal Dalichand Desai, Ahmedabad/Calcutta, 1941.

BKK: Harishena, *Brihatkathakosha*, ed. A.N. Upadhye, Bombay 1943.

CMPC: Shilanka, *Cauppannamahapurisacariyam*, ed. Amritlal Mohanlal Bhojak, Varanasi 1961.

DhA: Haribhadra, *Dhurtakhyana*, ed. A.N. Upadhye, Bombay 1944.

DhAMK: Udayaprabha Suri, *Dharmabhyudayamahakavya*, ed. Caturavijaya and Punyavijaya, Bombay 1949.

DhMV: Jayasimha Suri, *Dharmopadeshamalavivarana*, ed. P.L.B. Gandhi, Bombay 1940.

DhS: Bhaskaranandin, *Dhyanastava*, ed. Suzuko Ohira, New Delhi 1973.

DKC: Dandin, *Dashakumaracarita*, ed. G. Buhler, Bombay 1887.

DS: Devasena, *Darshanasara*, ed. A.N. Upadhye, *Annals of the Bhandarkar Oriental Institute* 15 (1935): 198–206.

Dvatri: Siddhasena Divakara, *Dvatrimshika*, in A.N. Upadhye (1971).

DVS: *Dashavaikalikasutra*, ed. E. Leumann and trans. W. Schubring in Schubring (1977).

Gandhi, L.B., *Three Apabhramsa Works of Jinadattasuri*, Baroda 1967.

GSS: Jinadatta Suri, *Ganadharasardhashataka*, ed. Gandhi, *Three Apabhramsa Works*.

GV: *Ganadharavada*, ed. and trans. E.A. Solomon, Ahmedabad 1966.

HVP: Punnata Jinasena, *Harivamshapurana*, ed. Pannalal Jain, Kashi 1962.

IBh: *Isibhasiyaim*, ed. W. Schubring, Ahmedabad 1974.

JnA: Shubhacandra, *Jnanarnava*, ed. H.L. Jain, Kailash Chandra Siddhantacharya and A.N. Upadhye, Sholapur 1977.

JnDhK: *Jnatadharmakathah*, in Pupphabhikkhu (ed.) *Suttagame* volume one, Gurgaon 1953.

JnS: Yashovijaya, *Jnanasara*, ed. Girishkumar Parmanand Shah, Bombay 1986.

JShLS: *Jainashilalekhasamgraha* volume one, Bombay 1928.

KA: Svamikumara, *Karttikeyanupreksha*, ed. A.N. Upadhye, Agas 1978.

KhGBG: Jinapala, *Kharataragacchabrihadgurvavali*, ed. Jinavijaya, Bombay 1956.

KhGPS: *Kharataragacchapattavalisamgraha*, ed. Jinavijaya, Calcutta 1932.

KKBh: *Kundakunda-Bharati*, ed. Pannalal Sahityacarya, Phaltan 1970.

KKP: Jineshvara Suri, *Kathakoshaprakarana*, ed. Jinavijaya, Bombay 1949.

KP: Gunadhara, *Kasayapahuda* with Virasena's *Jayadhavala* commentary, volume one, ed. Phulcandra, Mahendrakumar and Kailashcandra, Mathura 1974.

KS: Bhadrabahu, *Kalpasutra*, ed. H. Jacobi, Leipzig 1879.

LV: Haribhadra, *Lalitavistara*, ed. Bhanuvijaya, Ahmedabad 1963.

MA: Vattakera, *Mulacara*, ed. Kailashcandra Shastri, Jaganmohanlal Shastri and Pannalal Jain, two volumes, New Delhi 1984 and 1986.

MSP: Pradyumna Suri, *Mulashuddhiprakarana* with Devacandra Suri's commentary, volume one, ed. Amritlal Mohanlal Bhojak, Ahmedabad 1971.

MV: *Maranavibhakti*, in PNN.

NBh: *Nishithabhashya*, in NishithS.

NishithS: *Nishithasutra* with *bhashya* and *curni*, ed. Amaramuni and Muni Kanhaiyalal, four volumes, Agra 1957–60.

NiyS: Kundakunda, *Niyamasara*, ed. and trans. Uggar Sain, Lucknow 1931.

NKC: Prabhacandra, *Nyayakumudacarita*, ed. Mahendra Kumar Jain, Bombay 1941.

NNJP: Kakka Suri, *Nabhinandanajirnoddharaprabandha*, ed. Bhagwandas Harakchand, Ahmedabad 1928.

NS: *Nandisuttam and Anogaddaraim* ed. Muni Punyavijaya, Dalsukh Malvania and Amritlal Mohanlal Bhojak (Jaina Agama Series 1), Bombay 1968.

NSH: Devavacaka, *Nandisutram* with Haribhadra's commentary, ed. Muni Punyavijaya, Varanasi/Ahmedabad 1966.

PadP: Ravishena, *Padmapurana*, ed. Pannalal Jain, three volumes, Kashi 1958–9.

PariP: Hemacandra, *Sthaviravalicarita or Parishishtaparvan*, ed. H. Jacobi, Calcutta 1883.

ParPr: Yogindudeva, *Paramatmaprakasha*, ed. A.N. Upadhye, Bombay 1937.

PC: Prabhacandra, *Prabhavakacarita*, ed. Jinavijaya, Ahmedabad/Calcutta 1940.

PNN: *Painnayasuttam: Part 1*, ed. Muni Punyavijaya and Amritlal Mohanlal Bhojak (Jaina Agama Series 17.1), Bombay 1984.

PP: Dharmasagara, *Pravacanapariksha*, Surat 1937.

PPS: *Puratanaprabandhasamgraha*, ed. Jinavijaya, Santiniketan 1936.

Prajnap: *Pannavanasuttam*, ed. Muni Punyavijaya, Dalsukh Malvania and Amritlal Mohanlal Bhojak (Jaina Agama Series 9.2), Bombay 1971.

PS: Kundakunda, *Pravacanasara* with Amritacandra's commentary, ed. A.N. Upadhye, Bombay 1935.

RP: *Rajaprashniyasutra* in Pupphabhikkhu (ed.) *Suttagame* volume two, Gurgaon 1954.

Samav: *Samavayangasutram*, in Muni Jambuvijaya (ed.) *Sthananga Sutram and Samavayanga Sutram* with Abhayadeva Suri's commentary (re-edition of Agamodaya Samiti Series edition), Delhi 1985.

SamK: Haribhadra, *Samaraiccakaha*, ed. H. Jacobi, Calcutta 1926.

ShP: *Shatprabhritadisamgraha*, ed. Pannalal Soni, Bombay 1920.

ShruAv: Indranandin, *Shrutavatara*, in Mohanlal Shastri (ed.) *Tattvanushasanadisamgrahah*, Bombay 1918.

SKhA: *Shatkhandagama* volumes two and three, ed. Hiralal Jain, A.N. Upadhye and Kailashcandra Siddhantashastri, Sholapur 1976 and 1980.

SKS: *Sutrakritangasutram*, in Muni Jambuvijaya (ed.) *Acarangasutram and Sutrakritangam* with Shilanka's commentary (re-edition of Agamodaya Samiti Series edition), Delhi 1978.

SMKS: *Surimantrakalpasamuccaya anekapurvacaryapranita*, part two, ed. Muni Jambuvijaya, Bombay 1977.

SNKBhP: Shakatayana, *Strinirvanakevalibhuktiprakarane*, ed. Muni Jambuvijaya, Bhavnagar 1974.

SNP: Shakatayana, *Strinirvanaprakarana*, in SNKBhP.

SP: Jinavallabha Suri, *Sanghapattaka*, in Gandhi, *Three Apabhramsa Works*.

SS: Kundakunda, *Samayasara*, text, trans. and comm. by A. Chakravarti, Banaras 1930.

SSh: Samayasundara, *Samacarishataka*, Surat 1939.

Sth: *Sthanangasutram*, in Muni Jambuvijaya (ed.) *Sthanangasutram and Samavayangasutram* with Abhayadeva Suri's commentary (re-edition of Agamodaya Samiti Series edition), Delhi 1985.

SVT: Anantavirya, *Siddhivinishcayatika*, ed. M.K. Jain, Varanasi 1959.

SVVD: Dharmasagara, *Sutravyakhyanavidhidipika*, ed. Muni Labhasagar, Kapadvanj 1961.

TS: Umasvati, *Tattvarthadhigamasutra*, in Sanghvi (1974).

TSRV: Akalanka, *Tattvarthavarttika (Rajavartikam)*, ed. Mahendrakumar, two volumes, Kashi 1953 and 1957.

UD: *Upasakadashah*, text and trans. in Hoernle (1890b).

UR: Jinadatta Suri, *Upadesharasayana*, in Gandhi, *Three Apabhramsa Works*.

UttS: *Uttaradhyayanasutra*, in Pupphabhikkhu (ed.) *Suttagame* volume two, Gurgaon 1954.

VH: Sanghadasa, *Vasudevahindi*, ed. Muni Caturavijaya and Muni Punyavijaya, Gandhinagar 1989.

ViAvBh: Jinabhadra, *Visheshavashyakabhashya*, ed. Dalsukh Malvania, three volumes, Ahmedabad 1966–8.

VijP: Hemavijaya, *Vijayaprashasti*, ed. Hargovinddas and Bechardas, Benares, 1911.

VMP: Jinaprabha Suri, *Vidhimargaprapa nama Suvihitasamacari*, ed. Jinavijaya, Bombay 1941.

VP: *Vriddhacaryaprabandhavali*, in KhGBG.

VPS: *Vipakashrutasutra*, in Pupphabhikkhu (ed.) *Suttagame* volume one, Gurgaon 1953.

VTK: Jinaprabha Suri, *Vividhatirthakalpa*, ed. Jinavijaya, Shantiniketan 1934.

VTP: Bhavasena, *Vishvatattvaprakasha*, ed. Vidyadhar Johrapurkar, Sholapur 1964.
YB: Haribhadra, *Yogabindu*, ed. and trans. K.K. Dixit, Ahmedabad 1968.
YDS: Haribhadra, *Yogadrstisamuccaya*, ed. and trans. K.K. Dixit, Ahmedabad 1970.
YS: Hemacandra, *Yogashastra*, ed. Muni Jambuvijaya, three volumes, Bombay 1977–86.

Bibliography of secondary sources

Works marked with an asterisk are written in Hindi. Fischer and Jain (1978) is an invaluable collection of photographs of much that is discussed in Chapters 6 and 7 of this book.

Agrawal, B.C. (1972) Diksha Ceremony in Jainism: an Analysis of its Socio-Political Ramifications, *Eastern Anthropologist* 31: 12–20.

Alsdorf, L. (1965) *Les Etudes Jaina*, Paris.

Alsdorf, L. (1974) *Kleine Schriften*, Wiesbaden.

Alsdorf, L. (1977) Jaina Exegetical Literature and the History of the Jaina Canon, in Upadhye *et al.*: 1–8.

Atmadharm Visheshank (1989) (*Pujya Gurudev Shri Kanji Svami Janmashatabdi*), Songadh.

Atmavallabh (1989) (Vijayavallabha Suri Commemoration volume: sections in Hindi, Gujarati and English), Delhi.

Babb, L.A. (1988) Giving and Giving Up: the Eightfold Worship among the Svetambar Murtipujak Jains, *Journal of Anthropological Research* 44: 67–86.

Balbir, N. (1982) *Danastakakatha: recueil Jaina de huit histoires sur le don*, Paris.

Balbir, N. (1983) Observations sur la secte Jaina des Terapanthin, *Bulletin d'Etudes Indiennes* 1: 33–9.

Balbir, N. (1986) *Etudes d'Exégèse Jaina: les Avasyaka*, University of Paris thesis.

Balbir, N. (1990) Recent Developments in a Jaina Tirtha: Hastinapur (U.P.), in H. Bakker (ed.) *The History of Sacred Places in India as reflected in Traditional Literature*, Leiden/New York/Kobenhavn/Köln.

Banarsidas (1981) *Ardhakathanaka: Half a Tale*, translated, introduced and annotated by Mukund Lath, Jaipur.

Banks, M. (1985) *On the Srawacs or Jains: Processes of Division and Cohesion among two Jain Communities in India and England*, University of Cambridge PhD dissertation.

Banks, M. (1986) Defining Division: an Historical Overview of Jain Social Organisation, *Modern Asian Studies* 20: 447–60.

Banks, M. (1991a) Competing to Give, Competing to Get: Gujarati Jains in Britain, in M. Anwar and P. Werbner (eds) *Black and Ethnic Leaderships in Action*, London: 226–50.

Banks, M. (1991b) Orthodoxy and Dissent: Varieties of Religious Belief Among Immigrant Gujarati Jains in Britain, in Carrithers and Humphrey: 241–59.

Barnett, L.D. (1907) *The Antagada-Dasao and Auttarovavaiya-Dasao*, London.

Basham, A.L. (1951) *History and Doctrine of the Ajivikas*, London.
Bayly, C.A. (1983) *Rulers, Townsmen and Bazaars: North Indian Society in the Age of British Expansion 1770–1870*, Cambridge.
Bechert, H. (1983) A Remark on the Problem of the Date of Mahavira, *Indologica Taurinensia* 11: 287–90.
Bender, E. (1976) An Early Nineteenth Century Study of the Jains, *Journal of the American Oriental Society* 96: 114–19.
Bender, E. (1986) The Dramatis Personae of an Old Gujarati Presentation, *Journal of the American Oriental Society* 106: 323–6.
*Bhadrankaravijaya, Muni (1980) *Pratima-Pujan*, Ajmer.
Bhandari, Sampat Mal (1976) *Shrimaj Jayacharya: a Spiritual Apostle*, Jodhpur.
*Bharill, Hukamchand (1973) *Pandit Todarmal: Vyaktitva aur Kartritva*, Jaipur.
*Bharill, Hukamchand (1981) *Yugpurush Shri Kanji Svami*, Jaipur.
Bhatnagar, R.P. (ed.) (1985) *Acharya Tulsi: Fifty Years of Selfless Dedication*, Ladnun.
Bhatt, Bansidhar (1974) Vyavahara and Niscayanaya in Kundakunda's Works, *Zeitschrift der Deutschen Morgenlandischen Gesellschaft* (*supplement*): 279–91.
*Bhuvanavijaya, Muni (1980) *Shri Parvakathadi Vividh Vishay Samgrah*, Bhinmal.
Bloomfield, M. (1919) *The Life and Stories of the Jaina Saviour Parsvanatha*, Baltimore.
Bloomfield, M. (1923) The Salibhadracarita: a Story of Conversion to Monkhood, *Journal of the American Oriental Society* 43: 257–316.
Bollee, W.B. (1974) Buddhists and Buddhism in the Earliest Literature of the Svetambara Jains, in Cousins *et al.*: 27–39.
Bollee, W.B. (1977) *Studien zum Suyagada: Teil 1*, Wiesbaden.
Bollee, W.B. (1981) The Indo-European Sodalities in Ancient India, *Zeitschrift der Deutschen Morgenlandischen Gesellschaft* 131: 172–91.
Bollee, W.B. (1983) Traditionell-indische Vorstellungen über die Fusse in Literatur und Kunst, *Beitrage zur Allgemeinen und Vergleichenden Archaeologie* 5: 227–81.
Bollee, W.B. (1988) *Studien zum Suyagada: Teil 2*, Stuttgart.
Bronkhorst, J. (1986) *The Two Traditions of Meditation in Ancient India*, Stuttgart.
Brown, W.N. (1933) *The Story of Kalaka*, Washington.
Brown, W.N. (1934) *A Descriptive and Illustrated Catalogue of Miniature Paintings of the Jaina Kalpasutra as executed in the Early Western Indian Style*, Washington.
Bruhn, K. (1981) Avasyaka studies 1, in Bruhn and Wezler: 11–49.
Bruhn, K. (1987a) Das Kanonproblem bei den Jainas, in Assmann, Aleida and Jan (eds) *Kanon und Zensur*, München: 100–12.
Bruhn, K. (1987b) Soteriology in Early Jainism, in H. Falk (ed.) *Hinduismus und Buddhismus: Festschrift für Ulrich Schneider*, Freiburg: 60–86.
Bruhn, K. and Wezler, A. (eds) (1981) *Studien zum Jainismus und Buddhismus: Gedenkschrift für Ludwig Alsdorf*, Wiesbaden.
Buhler, G. (1878) The Digambara Jains, *Indian Antiquary* 7: 28–9.
Buhler, G. (1936) *The Life of Hemacandracarya*, Santiniketan.
Burgess, J. (1884) Papers on Shatrunjaya and the Jainas 7, *Indian Antiquary* 13: 276–80.
Caillat, C. (1975) *Atonements in the Ancient Ritual of the Jaina Monks*, Ahmedabad.
Caillat, C. (1977a) Fasting unto Death according to Ayaranga-Sutta and to some Painnayas, in Upadhye *et al.*: 113–18.
Caillat, C. (1977b) Fasting unto Death according to Jaina Tradition, *Acta Orientalia* 38: 43–66.

Caillat, C. (1981–2) Notes sur les Variantes dans la Tradition du Dasaveyaliya-sutta, *Indologica Taurinensia* 8–9: 71–83.

Caillat, C. and Kumar, R. (1981) *The Jain Cosmology*, Basel/Paris/New Delhi.

Carrithers, M. (1988) Passions of Nation and Community in the Bahubali Affair, *Modern Asian Studies* 22: 815–44.

Carrithers, M. (1989) Naked Ascetics in Southern Digambar Jainism, *Man* (n.s.): 219–35.

Carrithers, M. (1990) Jainism and Buddhism as Enduring Historical Streams, *Journal of the Anthropological Society of Oxford* 21: 141–63.

Carrithers, M. (1991) The Foundations of Community among Southern Digambar Jains: an Essay on Rhetoric and Experience, in Carrithers and Humphrey: 261–86.

Carrithers, M. and Humphrey, C. (eds) (1991) *The Assembly of Listeners: Jains in Society*, Cambridge.

Chakravarti, A. (1974) *Jaina Literature in Tamil*, Delhi.

Champakalakshmi, K. (1975) Kurandi-Tirukkattampalli, an Ancient Jaina Monastery of Tamilnadu, *Studies In Indian Epigraphy* 2: 84–90.

Chatterjee, A.K. (1978) *A Comprehensive History of Jainism: Volume one*, Calcutta.

Chatterjee, A.K. (1984) *A Comprehensive History of Jainism: Volume two*, Calcutta.

Clothey, F.W. (1982) Sasta-Aiyanar-Aiyappan: the God as Prism of Social History, in F.W. Clothey (ed.) *Images of Man: Religion and Historical Process in South Asia*, Madras.

Collins, S. (1982) *Selfless Persons: Imagery and Thought in Theravada Buddhism*, Cambridge.

Collins, S. (1988) Monasticism, Utopias and Comparative Social Theory, *Religion* 18: 101–35.

Commissariat, M.S. (1957) *A History of Gujarat: Volume two*, Bombay/Calcutta/Madurai/New Delhi/Hyderabad.

Cort, J.E. (1987) Medieval Jaina Goddess Traditions, *Numen* 34: 235–55.

Cort, J.E. (1988) Pilgrimage to Shankheshvar Parshvanath, *Bulletin of the Center for the Study of World Religions, Harvard University* 14.1: 63–72.

Cort, J.E. (1989) *Liberation and Wellbeing: a Study of the Svetambar Murtipujak Jains of North Gujarat*, Harvard University PhD dissertation.

Cort, J.E. (1990) Models of and for the Study of the Jains, *Method and Theory in the Study of Religion* 2: 42–71.

Cort, J.E. (forthcoming a) Jains, Caste and Hierarchy in North Gujarat, in Arjun Appadurai (ed.) *Caste in Practice: Essays in Honor of Thomas Zwicker*, Philadelphia.

Cort, J.E. (forthcoming b) Svetambar Murtipujak Jain Scripture in a Performative Context, in J.R. Timm (ed.) *Texts in Context: Traditional Hermeneutics in South Asia*, Albany.

Cort, J.E. (forthcoming c) The Svetambar Murtipujak Jain Mendicant, *Man* (n.s.).

Cort, J.E. (forthcoming d) Two Ideals of the Svetambar Murtipujak Jain Layman, *Journal of Indian Philosophy*.

Cottam-Ellis, C. (1991) The Jain Merchant Castes of Rajasthan: Some Aspects of the Management of Social Identity in a Market Town, in Carrithers and Humphrey: 75–108.

Cousins, L. *et al.* (eds) (1974) *Buddhist Studies in Honour of I.B. Horner*, Dordrecht.

Deleu, J. (1970) *Viyahapanatti (Bhagavai): the Fifth Anga of the Jaina Canon*, Brugge.

Deleu, J. and Schubring, W. (1963) *Studien zum Mahanisiha*, Hamburg.

Deo, S.B. (1956) *History of Jaina Monachism*, Poona.
Derrett, J.D.M. (1976) Hemacarya's Arhanniti: an Original Jaina Juridicial Work of the Middle Ages, *Annals of the Bhandarkar Oriental Institute* 57: 1–21.
Dixit, K.K. (1971) *Jaina Ontology*, Ahmedabad.
Dixit, K.K. (1974) The Problems of Ethics and Karma Doctrine as treated in the Bhagavati Sutra, *Sambodhi* 2.
Dixit, K.K. (1978) *Early Jainism*, Ahmedabad.
Dobbin, C. (1989) From Middlemen Minorities to Industrial Entrepreneurs: the Chinese in Java and the Parsis in Western India 1619–1939, in J.C. Heesterman *et al., India and Indonesia: General Perspectives*, Leiden/New York/ Kobenhavn/ Köln: 109–32.
Doshi, Saryu (1981) *Homage to Shravana Belgola*, 1981.
Dundas, P. (1985) Food and Freedom: the Jaina Sectarian Debate on the Nature of the Kevalin, *Religion* 15: 161–98.
Dundas, P. (1987–8) The Tenth Wonder: Domestication and Reform in Medieval Svetambara Jainism, *Indologica Taurinensia* 14: 181–94.
Dundas, P. (1991) The Digambara Jain Warrior, in Carrithers and Humphrey: 169–86.
Dundas, P. (forthcoming) The Marginal Monk and the True Tirtha, *Festschrift for Jozef Deleu.*
Ekambaranathan, A. and Sivaprakasan, C. (1987) *Jaina Inscriptions in Tamilnadu*, Madras.
Eliade, M. (1987) *The Encyclopedia of Religion*, New York.
Epigraphia Carnatica (1973) Volume two: Shravana Belgola, University of Mysore.
Faddegon, B. (1935) *The Pravacanasara of Kunda-kunda Acarya, together with the commentary Tattvadipika by Amrtacandra Suri*, London.
Findly, E.B. (1987) Jahangir's Vow of Non-Violence, *Journal of the American Oriental Society* 107: 245–56.
Fischer, E. and Jain, J. (1978) *Jaina Iconography*, two volumes, Leiden.
Folkert, K.W. (1989a) Jain Religious Life at Ancient Mathura: The Heritage of Late Victorian Interpretation, in Srinivasan: 103–12.
Folkert, K.W. (1989b) The 'Canons' of 'Scripture', in M. Levering, *Rethinking Scripture: Essays from a Comparative Perspective*, Albany: 170–9.
Folkert, K.W. (1989–90) Notes on Paryusan in Sami and Ved (ed. J.E. Cort), *Center for the Study of World Religions, Harvard University* 16.2: 54–73.
Gandhi, Mahatma (1949) *An Autobiography*, London.
Ghatage, A.M. (1935) The Dasavaikalika Niryukti, *Indian Historical Quarterly* 11: 627–39.
Ghosh, A. (ed.) (1974) *Jaina Art and Architecture*, New Delhi.
Ghosh, Niranjan (1984) *Sri Sarasvati in Indian Art*, Delhi.
Glasenapp, H. von (1925) *Der Jainismus*, Berlin.
Gokhale, Balkrishna Govind (1978) *Surat in the Seventeenth Century*, London/Malmo.
Gombrich, R. (1988) *Theravada Buddhism*, London.
Graham, W.A. (1987) *Beyond the Written Word: Oral Aspects of Scripture in the History of Religion*, Cambridge.
Granoff, P. (1988) Jain Biographies of Nagarjuna: Notes on the Composing of a Biography in Medieval India, in P. Granoff and K. Shinohara (eds), *Monks and Magicians: Religious Biographies in Asia*, Oakville, Ontario.
Granoff, P. (1989a) The Biographies of Siddhasena: a Study of the Texture of Allusion and the Weaving of a Group Image, *Journal of Indian Philosophy* 17: 329–84.

Granoff, P. (1989b) The Jain Biographies of Haribhadra: an Enquiry into the Logic of the Legends, *Journal of Indian Philosophy* 17: 105–28.

Granoff, P. (1989c) Religious Biography and Clan History among the Svetambara Jains in North India, *East and West* 39: 195–215.

Granoff, P. (1990) *The Clever Adulteress and other Stories: a Treasury of Jain Literature*, Oakville, Ontario.

Guerinot, A. (1908) *Repertoire d'Epigraphie Jaina*, Paris.

Halbfass, W. (1979) Observations on Darsana, *Wiener Zeitschrift für die Kunde Sudasiens* 23: 195–203.

Halbfass, W. (1983) *Studies in Kumarila and Sankara*, Reinbek.

Halbfass, W. (1988) *India and Europe: an Essay in Understanding*, Albany.

Hanaki, Taiken (1970) *Anuogaddaraim*, Vaishali.

Handa, Devendra (1984) *Osian: History, Archaeology, Art and Architecture*, Delhi.

Handiqui, K.K. (1949) *Yasastilaka and Indian Culture*, Sholapur.

Haynes, D.E. (1987) From Tribute to Philanthropy: the Politics of Gift Giving in a Western Indian City, *Journal of Asian Studies* 46: 339–60.

Hemacandra (1931–62) *The Deeds of the Sixty-three Illustrious Persons*, trans. H.M. Johnson, Baroda.

von Hinuber, O. (1986) *Das Altere Mittelindisch im Uberblick*, Wien.

Hoernle, A.F.R. (1890a) The Pattavali or List of Pontiffs of the Upakesa-Gachchha, *Indian Antiquary* 19: 233–42.

Hoernle, A.F.R. (1890b) *The Uvasagadasao or the Religious Experience of an Uvasaga*, Calcutta.

Hoernle, A.F.R. (1891) Two Pattavalis of the Sarasvati Gachchha of the Digambara Jains, *Indian Antiquary* 20: 341–61.

Holmstrom, S. (1988) *Towards a Politics of Renunciation: Jain Women and Asceticism in Rajasthan*, University of Edinburgh MA dissertation (Department of Social Anthropology).

Hudson, D.D. (1989) Violent and Fanatical Devotion among the Nayanars: a Study in the Periya Puranam of Cekkilar, in A. Hiltebeitel (ed.) *Criminal Gods and Demon Devotees: Essays on the Guardians of Popular Hinduism*, Albany: 373–404.

Humphrey, C. (1985) Some Aspects of the Jain Puja: the Idea of 'God' and the Symbolism of Offerings, *Cambridge Anthropology* 9.3: 1–19.

Humphrey, C. (1991) Fairs and Miracles: at the boundaries of the Jain community in Rajasthan, in Carrithers and Humphrey: 201–25.

Jacobi, H. (1880) On Mahavira and his Predecessors, *Indian Antiquary* 9: 158–63.

Jacobi, H. (1884) *Jaina Sutras: Part One*, Oxford.

Jacobi, H. (1895) *Jaina Sutras: Part Two*, Oxford.

*Jain, Balbhadra (1978) *Bharat ke Digambara Jain Tirth*, volume four, Bombay.

Jain, C.R. (1926a) *The Jaina Law*, Madras.

Jain, C.R. (1926b) *The Jaina Puja*, Bijnor.

Jain, J. (1980) Spatial System and Ritual Use of Satrunjaya Hill, in *Art and Archaeology Research Papers* 17: 47–51.

Jain, J.P. (1975) *Religion and Culture of the Jains*, New Delhi.

Jain, K.C. (1963) *Jainism in Rajasthan*, Sholapur.

Jain, M.K. (1986) A Demographic Analysis on Jains in India, *Jain Journal* 21.2: 33–50.

*Jain, Nemicandra (1964) *Mangalmantra Namokar: Ek Anucintan*, Varanasi.

*Jain, Pushpalata (1984) *Madhyakalin Hindi Jain Kavya mem Rahasya-Bhavana*, Nagpur.

Jain, U.K. (1975) *Jaina Sects and Schools*, Delhi.

Jaini, Padmanabh S. (1968) *Vasudhara-Dharani*: a Buddhist Work in Use among the Jains of Gujarat, in Upadhye *et al.* (eds) *Shri Mahavira Jaina Vidyalaya Golden Jubilee Volume*, volume one, Bombay: 30–45.

Jaini, Padmanabh S. (1974) On the *Sarvajnatva* (Omniscience) of Mahavira and the Buddha, in Cousins *et al.* : 71–90.

Jaini, Padmanabh S. (1977a) *Bhavyatva* and *Abhavyatva*: a Jaina Doctrine of 'Predestination', in Upadhye *et al.*: 95–111.

Jaini, Padmanabh S. (1977b) Jina Rsabha as an *Avatara* of Visnu, *Bulletin of the School of Oriental and African Studies* 40: 321–37.

Jaini, Padmanabh S. (1979) *The Jaina Path of Purification*, Berkeley.

Jaini, Padmanabh S. (1980) Karma and the Problem of Rebirth in Jainism, in W.D. O'Flaherty (ed.) *Karma and Rebirth in Classical Traditions*, Berkeley: 217–38.

Jaini, Padmanabh S. (1984) *Mahabharata* Motifs in the Jaina *Pandava-Purana*, *Bulletin of the School of Oriental and African Studies* 47: 108–15.

Jaini, Padmanabh S. (1985) The Pure and the Auspicious in the Jaina Tradition, in J.B. Carman and F.A. Marglin (eds) *Purity and Auspiciousness in Indian Society*, Leiden.

Jaini, Padmanabh S. (1991) Is There a Popular Jainism?, in Carrithers and Humphrey: 187–99.

*Jayacarya (1981) *Jaya Anushasan*, Ladnun.

*Jayacarya (1987) *Bhikkshu Drishtamt*, Ladnun.

Jha, S. (1978) *Aspects of Brahmanical Influence on the Jaina Mythology*, Delhi.

Jhaveri, M.B. (1944) *A Comparative and Critical Study of Mantrasastra*, Ahmedabad.

Jhaveri, M.B. (1949) *Jain Views regarding Religious and Charitable Trusts*, Bombay.

*Jnansundar, Muni (1936) *Shriman Laumkashah*, Phalodi.

Johnson, H.M. (1948) Rohini-Asokacandrakatha, *Journal of the American Oriental Society* 68: 166–75.

*Johrapurkar, V.P. (1958) *Bhattarak Sampraday*, Sholapur.

Jones, J.H.M. (1991) Jain Shopkeepers and Moneylenders: Rural Informal Credit Networks in South Rajasthan, in Carrithers and Humphrey: 109–38.

Joshi, N.P. (1989) Early Jaina Icons from Mathura, in Srinivasan: 332–67.

Kalghatgi, T.G. (ed.) (1981) *Gommateshvara Commemoration Volume (A.D. 981–1981)*, Shravana Belgola.

*Kalyanavijaya, Muni (1966) *Shrijinapuja Vidhi-Samgrah*, Jalor.

Kanchansagarsuri, Acarya (1982) *Shri Shatrunjay Giriraj Darshan in Sculptures and Architecture*, Kapadwanj.

Kapadia, H.R.(1941) *A History of the Canonical Literature of the Jainas*, Surat.

Kansara, N.M. (1976) The Bhagavadgita Citations in Yasovijaya's Adhyatmasara, a Manual on Jaina Mysticism, *Annals of the Bhandarkar Oriental Institute* 57: 23–39.

Kapur, Rajiv A. (1986) *Sikh Separatism: the Politics of Faith*, London.

Kasliwal, Kastoor Chand (1967) *Jaina Grantha Bhandars in Rajasthan*, Jaipur.

Klatt, J. (1882) Extracts from the Historical Records of the Jainas, *Indian Antiquary* 11: 245–56.

Klatt, J. (1894) The Samachari-Satakam of Samayasundara and Pattavalis of the Anchala Gachchha and other Gachchhas, *Indian Antiquary* 23: 169–83.

Krause, C. (1930) The Social Atmosphere of Present Jainism, *Calcutta Review*: 275–86.

Krause, C. (1952) *Ancient Jaina Hymns*, Ujjain.

Kulke, H. (1985) Maharajas, Mahants and Historians: Reflections on the Historiography of Early Vijayanagara and Sringeri, in A.L. Dallapiccola (ed.) *Vijayanagara-City and Empire: New Currents of Research*, Stuttgart: 120–43.

Kumar, Lalit (n.d.) Saiva Traditions in the Jaina Iconography, *Puratan* (Bhopal) no.6: 116–19.

Laidlaw, J. (1985) Profit, Salvation and Profitable Saints, *Cambridge Anthropology* 9.3: 50–70.

Leumann, E. (1934) *Ubersicht über die Avasyaka-Literatur*, Hamburg.

Lieu, S.N.C. (1985) *Manichaeism in the Later Roman Empire and China*, Manchester.

Lodrick, D.O. (1981) *Sacred Cows, Sacred Places*, Berkeley.

McCormick, T. (forthcoming) The Jaina Ascetic as Pilgrim and Tirtha, in E.A. Morinis and R.H. Stoddard (eds) *Sacred Places, Sacred Spaces: the Geography of Pilgrimage*.

*Mahaprajna, Yuvacarya (1985) *Bhikshu Vicar Darshan*, Ladnun.

Mahaprajna, Yuvacarya (1987) *Preksha Dhyana: Theory and Practice*, Ladnun.

*Mahaprajna, Yuvacarya (1988) *Ahimsa Tattva Darshan*, Curu.

Mahias, M.-C. (1985) *Delivérance et Convivialité: le Système Culinaire des Jaina*, Paris.

Mallison, F. (1979) Saint Sudama of Gujarat: Should the Holy be Wealthy?, *Journal of the Oriental Institute Baroda* 29: 90–9.

*Malvania, Dalsukh (1964) Lokashah aur unki Vicar-Dhara, in Vijay Muni Shastri and Harishankar Sharma (eds) *Gurudev Shri Ratna Muni Smriti-Granth*, Agra.

Malvania, Dalsukh (1981) Beginnings of Jaina Philosophy in the Acaranga, in Bruhn and Wezler: 151–3.

Malvania, Dalsukh (1986) *Jainism: Some Essays*, Jaipur.

Matilal, Bimal Krishna (1981) *The Central Philosophy of Jainism (Anekanta-Vada)*, Ahmedabad.

Mehta, Digish (n.d.) *Shrimad Rajacandra: a Life*, Ahmedabad.

Mehta, Saryu R. and Seth, Bhogilal G. (1971) *Shrimad Rajacandra: a Great Seer*, Agas.

Merutunga (1899) *The Prabandhacintamani or Wishing-stone of Narratives*, trans. C.H. Tawney, Calcutta.

Misra, R. (1972) The Jains in an Urban Setting, *Bulletin of the Anthropological Survey of India* 21: 1–68.

Misra, S.C. (1963) *The Rise of Muslim Power in Gujarat*, Delhi.

von Mitterwallner, G. (1989) Yaksas of Ancient Mathura, in Srinivasan: 368–82.

Moraes, F. (1973) *Acharya Shree Vijaya Labdhisurishwarji Maharaj*, Bombay.

*Mukhtar, Jugalkishor (1956) *Jain Sahitya aur Itihas par Vishad Prakash*, Calcutta.

*Muktiprabhavijaya, Muni (n.d.) *Shravak Ko Kya Karna Cahiye?, Vadhvan Shahr*.

Nakamura, H. (1983) Common Elements in Early Jain and Buddhist Literature, *Indologica Taurinensia* 11: 303–30.

Nawab, Sarabhai M. (1986) *Jain Painting: Volume One*, Ahmedabad.

Norman, K.R. (1983) The Pratyeka-Buddha in Buddhism and Jainism, in P. Denwood and A. Piatigorsky (eds) *Buddhist Studies: Ancient and Modern*, London: 92–106.

Norman, K.R. (1991) The Role of the Layman according to the Jain Canon, in Carrithers and Humphrey: 31–9.

Ohira, Suzuko (1980) Problems of the Purva, *Jain Journal* 15: 41–55.

Ohira, Suzuko (1982) *A Study of Tattvarthasutra with Bhasya*, Ahmedabad.
Okuda, K. (1975) *Eine Digambara-Dogmatik: Das fünfte Kapitel von Vattakera's Mulacara*, Wiesbaden.
Pearson, M.N. (1976) *Merchants and Rulers in Gujarat: the Response to the Portuguese in the Sixteenth Century*, Berkeley/Los Angeles/London.
Peterson, I.V. (1989) *Poems to Siva: the Hymns of the Tamil Saints*, Princeton.
*Pracandiya, Kumvar Paritosh (1987) Jain Parv aur uski Samajik Upayogita, in Dinesh Muni, *Sadhviratna Pushpavatiji Abhinandan Granth*, Udaipur: 205–11.
Prasad, Nand Kishore (1972) *Studies in Buddhist and Jaina Monachism*, Vaishali.
*Premi, Nathuram (1956) *Jain Sahitya aur Itihas*, Bombay.
**Pujya Bahinshri Janmajayanti Visheshank* (1989), Songadh.
Rajacandra, Shrimad (1976) *Atma-Siddhi (Self-Realisation)* trans. D.C. Mehta, Bombay.
*Rampuriya, Shricand (1981) *Acarya Bhikshu: Jivan-Katha aur Vyaktitva*, Ladnun.
Rao, Velcheru Narayana (1990) *Siva's Warriors: the Basava Purana of Palkuriki Somanatha*, Princeton.
Ratnaprabhavijaya, Muni (1950) *Shramana Bhagavan Mahavira: Volume Five, Part Two*, Ahmedabad.
*Ratnasenavijaya, Muni (1984) *Shravak Pratikraman Sutra Vivecna*, Phalna.
Reynell, J. (1985) *Honour, Nurture and Festivity: Aspects of Female Religiosity amongst Jain Women in Jaipur*, University of Cambridge PhD dissertation.
Reynell, J. (1987) Prestige, Honour and the Family: Laywomen's Religiosity Amongst the Svetambar Murtipujak Jains in Jaipur, *Bulletin d'Etudes Indiennes* 5: 313–59.
Reynell, J. (1991) Women and the Reproduction of the Jain Community, in Carrithers and Humphrey: 41–65.
Roth, G. (1983) *Malli-Jnata: das Achte Kapitel des Nayadhammakahao im Sechsten Anga des Svetambara Jainakanons*, Wiesbaden.
Roth, G. (1986) *Studies in Indian Culture*, New Delhi.
Ryan, J. (1985) *The Civakacintamani in Historical Perspective*, University of California, Berkeley, PhD dissertation.
Saldanha, J. (1981) *Conversion and Indian Civil Law*, Bangalore.
Saletore, B.A. (1938) *Medieval Jainism*, Bombay.
Sandesara, B.J. (1959) *Progress of Prakrit and Jaina Studies: Presidential Address of the Prakrit and Jainism Section, Twentieth All India Oriental Conference*, Varanasi.
Sangave, V.A. (1980) *Jaina Community*, Bombay.
Sangave, V.A. (1985) *The Sacred Shravana Belgola: A Socio-Religious Study*, New Delhi.
Sangave, V.A. (1991) Reform Movements among Jains in Modern India, in Carrithers and Humphrey: 233–40.
*Sanghvi, Sukhlal (1963) *Samadarshi Acarya Haribhadra*, Jodhpur.
Sanghvi, Sukhlal (1974) *Pt. Sukhlalji's Commentary on Tattvarthasutra of Vacaka Umasvati*, trans. K.K. Dixit, Ahmedabad.
**Satyadarshan* (n.d.), Sirpur.
Schubring, W. (1910) *Acaranga-Sutra. Erster Srutaskandha*, Leipzig.
Schubring, W. (1926) *Wörte Mahaviras*, Gottingen/Leipzig.
Schubring, W. (1935) *Die Lehre der Jainas*, Berlin/Leipzig.
Schubring, W. (1977) *Kleine Schriften*, Wiesbaden.

Schubring, W. (1978) *Nayadhammakahao: das sechste Anga des Jaina-Siddhanta*, ed. J. Deleu, Wiesbaden.

Schubring, W. and Caillat, C. (1966) *Drei Chedasutras des Jaina-Kanons. Ayaradasao, Vavahara, Nisiha*, Hamburg.

Sen, A. (1941) The Angaculiya, a Sacred Text of the Jainas, *Indian Historical Quarterly* 17: 472–91.

Sen, A.C. (1936) *A Critical Introduction to the Panhavagaranaim, the tenth Anga of the Jaina Canon*, Wurzburg.

Sen, M. (1975) *A Cultural Study of the Nisitha Curni*, Amritsar.

Settar, B. (1986) *Inviting Death*, Dharwad.

Shah, A.P. (1989) Some Inscriptions and Images on Mount Satrunjaya, in *Atmavallabh*.

Shah, U.P. (1955a) A Forgotten Chapter in the History of Svetambara Jain Church, or, a Documentary Epigraph from Mount Satrunjaya, *Journal of the Asiatic Society of Bombay* (n.s.) 30: 100–13.

Shah, U.P. (1955b) *Studies in Jaina Art*, Banaras.

Shah, U.P. (1987) *Jaina-Rupa-Mandana: Volume One*, New Delhi.

Shah, U.P and Bender, E. (1989) Mathura and Jainism, in Srinivasan: 209–13.

Shah, U.P and Dhaky, M.A. (1975) *Aspects of Jaina Art and Architecture*, Ahmedabad.

Shanta, N. (1985) *La Voie Jaina*, Paris.

*Shastri, Balcandra (1987) *Shatkhandagam Parishilan*, New Delhi.

**Shri 108 Caritracakravarti Acarya Shantisagar Digambara Jain Jinavani Jirnoddharak Samstha ka Raupyamahotsav tatha P.Pu. 108 Acaryashri ka Janmashatabdi Mahotsav ka Upalaksh mem Smritigranth* (n.d.), Phaltan.

**Shrimad Rajacandra* (1985), Agas.

Sinari, R. (1969) A Pragmatist Critique of Jaina Relativism, *Philosophy East and West* 19: 59–64.

Singh, R.B.P. (1975) *Jainism in Early Medieval Karnataka*, Delhi.

Singh, R. (1974) *The Jaina Concept of Omniscience*, Ahmedabad.

Singhi, N.K. (1991) A Study of Jains in a Rajasthan Town, in Carrithers and Humphrey: 139–61.

Sogani, K.C. (1967) *Ethical Doctrines in Jainism*, Sholapur.

Somani, R.V. (1982) *Jain Inscriptions of Rajasthan*, Jaipur.

Srinivasan, D.M. (1989) *Mathura: The Cultural Heritage*, Delhi.

Stein, B. (1980) *Peasant State and Society in Medieval South India*, Delhi.

Stevenson, M.S. (1915) *The Heart of Jainism*, London.

Sunavala, A.J. (1922) *Vijaya Dharma Suri: his Life and Work*, Cambridge.

Tatia, Nathmal (1951) *Studies in Jaina Philosophy*, Banaras.

Tatia, Nathmal and Mahendra Kumar, Muni (1981) *Aspects of Jaina Monasticism*, New Delhi.

Thieme, P. (1970) *Kleine Schriften*, Wiesbaden.

Tieken, H. (1986) Textual Problems in an Early Canonical Jaina Text, *Wiener Zeitschrift für die Kunde Sudasiens* 30: 5–25.

Tod, J. (1839) *Travels in Western India*, London.

*Todarmal (1987) *Mokshamargaprakashaka*, Songadh.

Tripathi, C. (1975) *Catalogue of the Jaina Manuscripts at Strasbourg*, Leiden.

Tripathi, C. (1983) Narratives in the *Pancakalpabhasya* and Cognate Texts, *Indologica Taurinensia* 11: 119–28.

Tripathi, D. (1981) *The Dynamics of a Tradition: Kasturbhai Lalbhai and his Entrepreneurship*, New Delhi.
Tulsi, Acarya (1988) *Anuvrat: a Code of Conduct for Moral Development*, New Delhi.
Upadhye, A.N. (1971) *Siddhasena Divakara's Nyayavatara*, Bombay.
Upadhye, A.N. (1983) *Upadhye: Papers*, Mysore.
Upadhye, A.N. *et al.* (eds) (1977) *Mahavira and his Teachings*, Bombay.
Varni, G. (1967) *Meri Jivan Gatha*, Varanasi.
Varni, J. (1970–3) *Jainendra Siddhantakosha*, Delhi.
Vijayalakshmy, R. (1981) *A Study of Civakacintamani*, Ahmedabad.
*Vinayasagar, Mahopadhyaya (1987) *Gautam Ras: Parishilan*, Jaipur.
Weber, A. (1883–5) Uber die Heiligen Schriften der Jainas, *Indische Studien* 16–17: 1–90, 211–479.
Williams, R (1963) *Jaina Yoga: a Survey of the Medieval Shravakacaras*, 1963.
Williams, R. (1965) Haribhadra, *Bulletin of the School of Oriental and African Studies* 28: 101–11.
Williams, R. (1977) Accounts of the Jainas taken from Sixteenth and Seventeenth Century Authors, in Upadhye *et al.*: 259–69.
Wujastyk, D. (1984) The Spikes in the Ears of the Ascetic: an Illustrated Tale in Buddhism and Jainism, in *Oriental Art* (n.s.) 30.
Zarwan, J. (1974) The Social Evolution of the Jains in Kenya, *Hadith* 6 (History and Social Change in Africa ed. B.A. Ogot): 134–44.
Zarwan, J. (1975) The Social and Economic Network of an Indian Family Business in Kenya,1920–1970, *Kroniek van Afrika* 6: 219–36.
Zydenbos, R.J. (1986) Jainism Endangered: the View of the Medieval Kannada Poet Brahmasiva, in H. van Skyhawk (ed.) *Minorities on Themselves*, University of Heidelberg: 174–86.
Zydenbos, R.J. (1987) The Jaina Nun Kavunti, *Bulletin d'Etudes Indiennes* 5: 387–417.

Name index

Subject index